THE WORLD ALMANAC
OF THE
AMERICAN
REVOLUTION

THE WORLD ALMANAC®
OF THE
AMERICAN REVOLUTION

Edited by L. Edward Purcell
and David F. Burg

Introduction by John A. Garraty

WORLD ALMANAC
AN IMPRINT OF PHAROS BOOKS · A SCRIPPS HOWARD COMPANY
NEW YORK

Copyright © 1992 David F. Burg and L. Edward Purcell

Introduction © 1992 by John A. Garraty

Design by Janet Tingey

First published in 1992.

Library of Congress Cataloging-in-Publication Data

The World Almanac of the American Revolution / edited by L. Edward
Purcell and David F. Burg ; introduction by John A. Garraty.
                    p.   cm.
Includes bibliographical references and index.
ISBN 0-88687-574-9
1. United States—History—Revolution, 1775–1783.   I. Purcell, L.
Edward. II. Burg, David F.
E208.W85   1992
973.3—dc20   91-32057   CIP

Printed in the United States of America

World Almanac
An imprint of Pharos Books
A Scripps Howard Company
200 Park Avenue
New York, N.Y. 10166

10 9 8 7 6 5 4 3 2 1

Pharos Books are available at special discounts on bulk purchases
for sales promotions, premiums, fundraising or educational use.
For details, contact the Special Sales Department, Pharos Books,
200 Park Avenue, New York, NY 10166.

Cover illustration: John Trumbull, *Surrender of Lord Cornwallis
at Yorktown.* Copyright Yale University Art Gallery.

★ CONTENTS ★

★ PREFACE ★

At least five generations have added to the historical record since the first writings about the American Revolution appeared in print even before the war was over. We are deeply in debt to all of them. Some historians—Christopher Ward and Edmund Cody Burnett, for example—spent the best parts of their adult lives winnowing the sources and compiling detailed narratives of important aspects of the revolution. Mark Mayo Boatner III produced a reference work breathtaking in scope and accuracy. Others have pondered what the experience meant, both at the time of the rebellion and for the development of the nation since. The outpouring of print attending the celebration of the bicentennial of the Revolution added insightful new riches and revived long-forgotten treasures.

We have drawn freely on this work of previous historians and here gratefully acknowledge the care, devotion and skill they brought to the tasks of knowing and understanding the American Revolution.

Our access to these sources was made possible in large measure by the professional staff of the University of Kentucky's M. I. King Library, in particular the librarians of the Reference Department and Special Collections. Despite its difficult physical problems, the King Library houses a first-class research collection on the American Revolution.

We are also in the debt of Bill Cuffe of the Yale University Art Gallery and especially Peter Harrington of the Anne S. K. Brown Military Collection at the Brown University Library for their professional assistance with illustrations.

At the risk of echoing a time-worn formula, we give thanks to our families, without whose practical, emotional, and spiritual support none of our efforts would be possible.

L. Edward Purcell   David F. Burg
Maysville, Kentucky   Lexington, Kentucky

★ INTRODUCTION ★

by John A. Garraty

The American Revolution occurred in what seemed to most Europeans of the time a remote backwater on the edge of a vast wilderness, made by a relative handful of what those Europeans considered colonial bumpkins. It was in fact—and was soon widely recognized to be—an event of enduring and worldwide significance.

The Revolution—in particular the Declaration of Independence, with its bold democratic statements about "life, liberty, and the pursuit of happiness" and the right of a people to discard a tyrannical government and govern themselves (that is, establish a republic)—exerted a powerful impact on European liberal opinion. And opinion quickly led to action; as soon as fighting in America started, idealistic Europeans flocked there to help the revolutionaries. The best-known of these, the Marquis de Lafayette, was so impressed by the leader of the colonial Revolution and the cause for which he fought that he named his eldest son George Washington.

As important as the ideology of the Declaration of Independence in attracting liberals was the military success of the Americans—who, though greatly outnumbered, won a clear-cut victory over the most powerful nation in the Western world—which seemed to demonstrate that a popular government had a force and energy an autocratic government, no matter how strong, could not resist.

Besides the soul-stirring phrases of the Declaration, the practical experience of the thirteen colonies in drafting and ratifying state constitutions and establishing the institutions of state government provided the rest of the world with concrete proof that people could design and create the kind of governments they wanted even while fighting a war. That the Revolution was led not by firebrands and low-lifes but by eminently respectable men like the Virginia planters General Washington and Thomas Jefferson, the world-renowned scientist Benjamin Franklin, and the Massachusetts lawyer John Adams was a further reason for its appeal abroad.

For all these reasons prominent American revolutionaries such as Jefferson and Franklin were venerated when they served the new nation in Europe, and especially in France, where liberalism was popular even among the aristocracy. Jefferson was in Paris when the French Revolution broke out in 1789. His advice was eagerly sought by its leaders, who had been much influenced by the American example, as were the Latin American patriots who overthrew their Spanish masters during and after the Napoleonic wars, and the makers of just about every important revolution the world has seen since.

The passage of time only strengthened the appeal of the American Revolution to people of other lands. Before the Revolution conservatives had argued that democracy would surely lead to chaos because when a group of people disagreed with the majority they would draft their own declaration of independence, with the result that the country would swiftly splinter into smaller and smaller quarrelsome parts. Conservatives further argued that a republic, even if not based on a system where all people were considered equal, could never work in a large country like the United States. A relatively homogenous little country like Switzerland might succeed as a republic, the argument ran, but (as the case of the Roman republic in the time of Julius Caesar suggested) a large and diverse region would surely be dominated by demagogues or dictators. The history of the United States, according to this reasoning, would be short and probably bloody. (For a brief time, the Civil War threatened to prove conservative critics right. The war, as Abraham Lincoln put it in the Gettysburg Address, was testing whether "a nation conceived in liberty" could "long endure." But the North's victory in that conflict produced a still stronger—and more democratic—union; the United States was never thereafter in danger of breaking apart.) But as the decades passed and the nation grew and prospered; the appeal of its example to the rest of the world became steadily stronger.

The impact of the American Revolution on the people who fought it and on their descendants was equally profound and long-lasting. Whereas most later revolutions were caused by the rebels' desire to create a new nation and resulted if they succeeded in the achievement of independence, in America the thirteen colonies had joined together primarily for defense against the British: Franklin had warned that if they did not "hang together" they would surely "hang separately." Before the Revolution most colonists thought of themselves not as Americans but as Virginians or Pennsylvanians or New Yorkers. The land was vast and sparsely settled, communication difficult. There was no central government other than the royal authority in distant London. Few people knew very much about the residents of other districts. But service in the army and in the Continental Congress brought people from distant regions together. Strong national feeling was more a result of the Revolution than a cause. John Marshall of Virginia, later chief justice of the United States, fought in the Continental Army and endured the privations of the bitter winter of 1777–1778 at Valley Forge. Later he wrote:

> I found myself associated with brave men from different states who were risking life and everything valuable in a common cause. I was confirmed in the habit of considering America as my country.

The Revolution was also a force for democracy in the new country. In the colonial period circumstances had fostered democracy in practice even when most people did not believe that all people had a right to govern themselves. For example, in most colonies, by law no man could vote unless he owned a substantial amount of land or other valuable property. However, land was so cheap and widely available that most adult white males could qualify as voters. But when the British Parliament passed the Stamp Act, colonists raised the cry "Taxation without representation is tyranny," a statement of a democratic principle, and when they revolted, the theory of democracy was brilliantly expressed in Jefferson's Declaration of Independence. Thereafter it was only a matter of time before the *practice* of voting became the *right* to vote (at least for adult white men).

Breaking away from Great Britain fostered democracy in other ways. In many colonies the British church enjoyed a privileged position, being supported by taxation and possessed of other advantages. The new states put an end to this, though not at first to the idea of public support of religion. The Virginia Statute of Religious Liberty went further than most, stating flatly: "No man shall be compelled to frequent or support any religious worship, place, or ministry."

In the Northern states slavery was at least put on the road to extinction during and after the Revolution. Again, resistance to British policy after 1763 had much to do with this. To patriots, laws like the Stamp Act and the Tea Act, passed without their consent, seemed aimed at reducing them to a kind of political and economic dependence close to that endured by slaves. By complaining that the London government was "treating them like slaves" (and, of course, by eagerly embracing the "self-evident" truths in the Declaration), they were more likely to recognize the immorality of enslaving other human beings themselves. Even in the South, numbers of individual planters freed their slaves after the Revolution, a practice that had been severely restricted in the Southern colonies before 1776.

The Revolution also led to a less noticeable but ultimately more pervasive improvement of the position of women in the United States. Although the Declaration of Independence asserted only that "all *men* are created equal," it could be argued that Jefferson employed the word in its general, asexual sense. Certainly American women were as patriotic as their fathers, brothers, and husbands, and as eager to contribute to the winning of independence. Many of them began to believe in independence as a personal as well as a political right. At the practical level, countless women took on traditionally masculine tasks during the war, managing farms and shops and other businesses formerly run by men who had taken up arms. Their success in these occupations made them more aware of their capacities and more likely to think themselves entitled to the same rights and responsibilities as men.

Finally, the Americans of the late 1780s had not forgotten what it meant to be controlled by an outside power, even one euphemistically described as "the mother country." The Peace of Paris had given the new United States control of the enormous wilderness between the Appalachian Mountains and the Mississippi River. People were already flocking westward, eager to take up land and make new lives for themselves just as their European ancestors who came to America had been doing for generations. The states squabbled among themselves for a time over control of the western territory, but they soon realized that the West should belong to all and, more important, that as the population grew the territory should be divided into new states, these to be admitted to the Union on an equal footing with the original thirteen and governed by the people who settled them. The former colonies were not to create and rule over colonies of their own.

Ultimately there was a reaction of sorts against the heady stress on freedom resulting from the Revolution. Slavery did not disappear until the 1860s and women did not obtain the right to vote for a century and a half. Neither women, nor blacks, nor the members of other racial minorities have even today obtained easy access to many of the powers and privileges that most native-born American white males exercise as a matter of course. But the freedoms for which the Revolution was fought, especially the idea that people have the right to govern themselves, remain unchallenged.

PRELUDE TO REVOLUTION:
★ 1763-1774 ★

In 1763, Britain stood triumphant in North America after sweeping France from the continent with the help of the American colonists, and few would have predicted the end of the ties between crown and colonies. Yet by the last months of 1774, only the most indifferent observer could avoid the conclusion that Americans were headed toward open, armed rebellion.

The Americans did not rush to revolution. Before the final breach Great Britain and the colonies weathered a long series of conflicts that grew irreconcilable only toward the end, and during the twelve years of disagreements preceding the engagement of arms at Lexington and Concord, the clashes between mother country and colonies waxed and waned in intensity.

The thirteen American colonies, with something over two million inhabitants (including about 500,000 black African slaves), formed a diverse group of political entities grouped in a relatively narrow band of farms, cities, and plantations that stretched along the Atlantic coastline from Canada to Florida, with here and there significant fingers of settlement reaching westward toward the Appalachian mountain barrier. Most of the colonies had developed from seventeenth-century settlements that were attempts by the British crown or British entrepreneurs to set up strategic or profit-making outposts in the New World. By the latter half of the 1700s the colonies displayed distinctive regional and individual differences, based on topography, economics, and culture.

To the north lay the four colonies of New England: Massachusetts, Connecticut, New Hampshire, and Rhode Island. These colonies had been founded primarily by groups of religious dissenters—Massachusetts by Puritans who sought to establish a theocracy free from the trammels of what they saw as a decadent English church, the others by those who in turn could not live comfortably with the political and religious strictures of the Puritans. The New England colonies were characterized by farming, still to some degree organized around small villages, that produced foodstuffs and some salable surpluses. On the long coastline, fishing dominated economic life, along with shipping and smuggling. The thriving Massachusetts city of Boston, with 15,000 inhabitants, was the economic and cultural center of New England, and it proved to be as well the first center of revolt.

As with nearly all the American colonies, New England had passed through a long series of changes in form of government during the seventeenth century and the first decades of the eighteenth, but by the time of the French and Indian War (1754–1763), all four New England provinces—again, like other colonies—had established firm traditions of popular assemblies that served at least in some sense as counterpoints to royal governors and their administrations. Powerful local groups or individuals, such as the Wentworths of New Hampshire, often dominated local politics, but the voices of the freehold electors were not entirely still.

The four Middle Colonies—Pennsylvania, New York, New Jersey, and Delaware—had emerged from a long, muddled history of imperial rivalries and proprietary grants to form a prosperous, heterogeneous region by the eve of the Revolution. Philadelphia, a bustling seaport on the Delaware River, was the second largest city in the British overseas empire with 34,000 people. New York City numbered 22,000 and occupied a strategic point at the mouth of the Hudson River. The large reaches of woodland and farms in upper New York, Pennsylvania, New Jersey, and Delaware supported the soundest economies of any of the American colonies, and diverse immigration had peopled the lands with Germans, Scotch-Irish, and English settlers.

Politically, the Middle Colonies presented a confused picture of relatively weak local governments. In Pennsylvania, the Penn family was still the nominal proprietary power, but in order to deal with difficult land disputes and interests of Philadelphia merchants, the British crown was often the real authority. The organization of royal governments in New Jersey, Delaware, and New York changed often and in the latter case was influenced by powerful land-holding families such as the De Lanceys.

The Middle Colonies were destined to play crucial roles in the Revolution, especially during the first years, when most of the battles between Americans and British took place between the Canadian border and Delaware Bay.

Southward lay the great agrarian colonies of Virginia, Maryland,

North Carolina, South Carolina, and Georgia. Characterized by fertile coastal regions, piedmont, and western mountains, these colonies had grown from a variety of proprietary enterprises and had developed political and economic cultures based for the most part on staple crops. In the Carolinas, rice culture had grown rapidly after the introduction of black slave labor, with Charleston (a city of 12,000 by the mid-1770s) the chief port. In Virginia and Maryland, tobacco was king.

In Virginia, the House of Burgesses had long served as a focus for the political life of the colony. Similar assemblies in the Carolinas, Maryland, and Georgia were less developed, probably as the result of their longer histories as proprietorship colonies.

Despite important areas of small farms and ethnic enclaves, the South was a region dominated by powerful landowners who amassed plantations and slaves while they sought to emulate the culture of England. The Revolution was to draw heavily on the South for political and military leadership—particularly from Virginia—and the final years of the armed struggle focused on the South.

The disagreements between these American colonies and Great Britain began over money. The costs of the Seven Years' War, of which the French and Indian War in North American formed but a part, had left a huge national debt hanging over the government of Britain. The young King George, who came to the throne in 1760, was determined to establish his influence and to see the colonies take on what British ministers understood as merely the proper burden of defense. Consequently, as soon as the French had been banished from the North American continent, a series of British ministries began to reverse the easygoing economic policies of the previous decades. They sought to enact and vigorously enforce a series of taxes and trade laws that would result in tapping the colonial economies for the benefit of the royal budget.

Since they were long accustomed to a lighter hand, the colonists bristled at the new policies, particularly the Stamp Act (1765), and soon began to associate the crown's economic incursions with encroachments on colonial political rights. A full-blown conflict took shape by the mid-1760s. The immediate crisis passed, but the pattern of resistance was established.

(Not all colonists became revolutionaries, and very large numbers of Loyalists remained devoted to the crown. Whether held to Britain by ties of political belief, patriotic sentiment, or economic interests, many Loyalists were to suffer irreparable losses as a result of the Revolution. Most lost their property and standing in the colonies, and thousands were to depart for Canada or Britain during and after the war.)

Despite a general lessening of tensions by 1770, specific conflicts persisted, and with each new disagreement, the colonists came more and more to cloak their protests in political terms. Eventually, Boston became the turning point, with the other colonies somewhat surprisingly rallying to the cause of the northern city. When the British government shut down the port of Boston, moved in more troops, and appointed a major general as governor of Massachusetts, the impending clash seemed unavoidable.

★ 1763 ★

10 February 1763

PARIS.   The French and Indian War, the North American part of a global conflict known as the Seven Years' War, comes to a close with the Treaty of Paris. British and colonial American arms have triumphed, and France is swept entirely from the North American continent. The British assume control of Canada and all former French territories east of the Mississippi River except New Orleans. Complex diplomatic trading gives Spain, a French ally during the war, lands west of the Mississippi and New Orleans, but the British take over the Floridas. In a single stroke the British empire in North America is extended north, west, and south, with the traditional thirteen colonies at the heart.

7 October 1763

LONDON.   King George III signs the royal Proclamation of 1763, reorganizing the policy and administration of the North American colonies. Faced with vast new responsibilities and shuddering in the aftermath of Pontiac's costly Indian war the previous summer, British ministers seek to restrict white settlers to the Atlantic side of the Appalachians, in part as a way to bring order to the confused state of relations with the Indians. The proclamation decrees a line of demarcation along the crest of the mountains. All the lands to the west are to be the preserve of the native Indians, and no white settlers are to be allowed in. The American colonies' land claims west of the line are annulled and no new claims, settlement, or even travel will be allowed without royal permission. Canada, East and West Florida—the new territories gained from France—are made crown colonies, trade with the Indians comes under control of royal officials, and a small standing army is to be scattered along frontier posts to enforce the proclamation. The provisions of the royal proclamation dash the hopes of many Americans, who want to expand settlement westward into Indian lands.

★ 1764 ★

5 April 1764

LONDON. The Revenue Act of 1764, known in America as the Sugar Act, becomes law, marking an attempt by the new British ministry of George Grenville to deal with a 140,000,000-pound national debt from the French and Indian War and an estimated 200,000-pound yearly cost to maintain an armed defense of the western American frontier. To Grenville and other British officials the act is a reasonable and enlightened method of finance, but to American colonists it is an outrage. Although the act reduces the customs tax on imported foreign molasses from six pence a gallon to three pence, the tax will be enforced, seldom the case during the previous thirty years. An important segment of the colonial economy, especially in New England, is based on importing molasses from the West Indies and distilling it into rum, but Americans are accustomed to paying no more than a penny and a half per gallon in bribes to smuggle in Dutch and French Indies' molasses.

Moreover, the new customs tax is intended to raise revenue directly from the colonies, rather than simply regulate trade within the British empire—a distinction Americans seize on as a nefarious new economic intrusion and that James Otis of Massachusetts, the most vocal opponent of the Sugar Act, declares to be a denigration of the political rights of the colonies. As Otis says, "no parts of his majesty's dominions can be taxed without consent. . . every part has a right to be represented." The Boston Town Meeting contests the act, egged on by Otis and radical politician Samuel Adams, and the legislatures of New York and North Carolina pass formal protests.

British customs and naval officials have a hard time enforcing the new tax when hostile local officials refuse to cooperate and mobs aid smuggling merchants.

★ 1765 ★

March 1765

LONDON. Parliament passes a new revenue-raising act that requires American colonists to purchase stamped paper as a tax on all official documents, including legal papers, licenses, printed material, diplomas, even playing cards. What seems a reasonable measure to the Grenville ministry touches off a deep, sometimes violent, and widespread protest in the colonies. The Stamp Act outrages almost all colonists, from New England to Georgia, who object that it is a direct revenue tax levied without their consent. Moreover, despite the provision that colonists are to be named stamp masters, violations of the law are to be tried in juryless admiralty courts, putting trials outside the influence of local politics or mob pressure. The act touches nearly everyone in colonial society and therefore engenders much wider protest than did the previous Sugar Act. Lawyers, merchants, printers, and many others make a common cause.

Within weeks of the Stamp Act's passage, organized resistance, bordering on civil disorder, forms throughout the colonies. In Boston, the Sons of Liberty draw on all levels of society and wealth, taking their name from a speech in Parliament by radical Isaac Barré. The Sons intimidate royal officials and threaten violence to anyone foolish enough to sign on as a stamp master. Similar groups soon form in other colonies, using the same tactics to defeat the implementation of the Stamp Act. Royal governors discover that no one can be persuaded to fill the appointments as stamp officials, despite the attractive salary and opportunities for patronage. Colonial assemblies universally condemn the act, and courts shut down rather than agree to use of the hated stamps.

29–30 May 1765

WILLIAMSBURG, VA. In a stormy session of the House of Burgesses, political newcomer Patrick Henry introduces a set of five Resolves hitting at the Stamp Act and the idea of taxation without representation. He borders on treason in a speech supporting the resolutions. The House passes the resolves, but the following day (after Henry and other members have departed) rescinds the most inflammatory provision, which maintained that only the colonial assembly could tax Virginians. Nonetheless, the Newport (R.I.) *Mercury* publishes the full version of the resolves, and their message spreads across the colonies, giving heart to protesters.

June 1765

BOSTON. The General Court of Massachusetts issues a circular letter to other colonial assemblies, calling on them to elect delegates to a congress to protest the Stamp Act.

August 1765

BOSTON. Mob violence, organized

A Stamp Act official hanging in effigy.

by the Sons of Liberty, confronts Andrew Oliver, who has foolishly agreed to take the post of stamp master. Oliver is hung in effigy from the limbs of a large tree, which comes to be known as the Liberty Tree and serves thereafter as a symbol of Boston's antigovernment protests, and his home is attacked. (By the end of the year, he is made to renounce his appointment in a humiliating public apology.) Likewise, the mob attacks the homes of other officials, including the elegant house of Lt. Gov. Thomas Hutchinson. Royal governor Francis Bernard seeks refuge from the riots in the island fortress of Castle William in Boston Harbor.

1–25 October 1765

NEW YORK CITY. Twenty-seven colonial delegates meet in a Stamp Act Congress. The royal governors of Georgia, North Carolina, and Virginia prevent the selection of delegates, but all other colonies—save New Hampshire, which agrees in advance to support the actions of the Congress— send representatives. They debate the position of the colonies and pass a set of resolutions and petitions to the king and Parliament. The Stamp Act Congress recognizes the right of the crown and the British legislature to pass laws governing the colonies and regulating trade but asserts that no taxes can be imposed without the consent of the governed. Little is accomplished, but the congress sets a precedent for the future of collective colonial action. Elsewhere, colonial merchants agree to restrict imports from Great Britain for the duration of the stamp crisis.

★ 1766 ★

February 1766

LONDON.   Recognizing that the tax is unenforceable (only in Georgia are stamps ever issued) and pressured by British commercial interests, who have suffered from the American non-importation agreements, the new ministry of the Marquis of Rockingham abandons the struggle, and Parliament repeals the Stamp Act.

At the same time, it passes a little-noticed Declaratory Act, asserting the right of Parliament to legislate all matters for the American colonies, thus refuting the colonial argument against taxation without representation.

★ 1767 ★

June 1767

LONDON. George III gives royal assent to a series of import duties for the American colonies. The fees place taxes on popular English goods such as glass, lead, paint, paper, and tea. The new measures are the brainchild of Charles Townshend, a leading member of the cabinet who has taken control of government policy due to the illness of Lord Chatham (William Pitt). Townshend mistakenly believes that the colonial opposition to the Stamp Act was merely a statement against "internal" taxes, and that purely "external" import duties, which he justifies as regulating trade, will be accepted. In fact, Townshend is hard-pressed to find new sources of revenue, and he hopes the new duties will more than pay for the cost of keeping troops in the colonies. Moreover, even America's supporters among British politicians are beginning to weary of the cries about "representation," and a core of hard-liners is ready to put the colonials in their proper place: subservient to the crown and Parliament. Townshend also includes a provision in the new laws to pay royal officials from the revenue of the duties, thus removing the influence of local colonial assemblies, which have hitherto paid officials. And violations are to be tried in royal vice-admiralty courts, not by local judges and juries.

Colonial reaction to the Townshend Duties is more restrained than the violence that greeted the Stamp Act two years before, but it is no less adamant. The Americans are perfectly serious in their belief that taxation by Parliament without consent of colonial assemblies is somehow a violation of their fundamental rights and is "unconstitutional." They brush aside Townshend's distinction between internal and external taxes. The principal form of American opposition is a renewal of the nonimportation agreements that had proved so effective during the Stamp Act crisis. Beginning with a resolution by the Boston Town Meeting, colony after colony joins a pact—usually enforced by the Sons of Liberty—to eschew purchase or consumption of English goods. Resistance is bolstered by a series of *Letters from a Farmer in Pennsylvania*, written by moderate John Dickinson. Townshend himself dies within months of the passage of his measures, leaving others to reap the consequences.

★ 1768 ★

11 February 1768

BOSTON. A radical faction led by James Otis and Samuel Adams secures passage by the Massachusetts General Court of a circular letter to other colonial assemblies, urging united resistance to the Townshend Duties. Royal governor Francis Bernard has worked hard to prevent the action, but when rural members leave the session early, Otis and Adams have the votes to approve the measure.

March 1768

WILLIAMSBURG, VA. The Virginia House of Burgesses, which has been kept out of session by the royal governor for almost a year, drafts a strongly worded petition to the king and Parliament, protesting the Townshend Acts. The assembly also issues a harsh circular letter of its own in support of the Massachusetts letter.

April 1768

BOSTON. Royal customs commissioners file criminal charges against John Hancock, a foe of the government and one of Massachusetts' wealthiest merchants, after officials are prevented from inspecting the cargo of the *Lydia*, a ship owned by Hancock. The provincial attorney general drops the charges, but the affair signals a renewed struggle between royal administrators and the local business and political establishment.

10 June 1768

BOSTON. Customs officials attempt to seize another of Hancock's ships, the *Liberty*, which they suspect carries contraband. A Sons of Liberty mob, organized in part by Otis and Adams, prevents the seizure, which leads to riots in Boston. Over the following weeks, the situation deteriorates, and British officials in London— especially Lord Hillsborough, who is now in charge of colonial affairs—begin to take a hard stand against the factious Massachusetts protesters. On orders from London, Governor Bernard dissolves the General Court.

1 October 1768

BOSTON. Two regiments of British troops—the 14th West Yorks and the 29th Worcesters—land in Boston, put ashore from warships in the harbor. The government in London has decided that Governor Bernard can no longer deal with the dissident combination of radical politicians, merchants, and the Boston mob. The troops are intended to intimidate the colonists into submission.

★ 1770 ★

5 March 1770

BOSTON. After a year and a half of uneasy co-existence, Bostonians and British troops clash fatally. Tensions have been constant since the redcoats occupied the city in 1768, with almost daily clashes. Bands of disgruntled dockworkers, sailors, apprentices, and unemployed workers have roamed the streets for several days, spoiling for a fight and egged on by radical leaders. Headed by a free African-American named Crispus Attucks, a mob confronts a small detachment of British soldiers near the Customs House.

Paul Revere's engraving of the Boston Massacre, March 5, 1770.

Redcoats in Boston enduring the taunts of local boys.

Frightened by the taunts and threats of the civilians, many carrying stout firewood clubs, the soldiers' discipline fails and they open fire at point-blank range. Attucks and two others are killed instantly, two more are mortally wounded. Boston political leaders label the incident a massacre and demand the soldiers, including

Capt. Thomas Preston, be tried for murder. The resulting trial, at which John Adams defends Preston, frees the soldiers, but British troops are withdrawn to Castle William in Boston Harbor. There is no further violence, but the Boston Massacre has produced colonial martyrs and provides a rallying point for anti-British sentiments.

12 April 1770

LONDON. Parliament is caught on the horns of a dilemma over the failure of the Townshend Acts to produce revenue. The costs of maintaining troops in Boston far outstrip the taxes produced by the inflammatory import duties. Moreover, the colonial non-importation agreements—adhered to by all except the contrary merchants of Philadelphia and New Hampshire —have cut British exports to the American colonies by more than 30 percent. Since the acts were passed expressly to raise revenue, the effort is clearly a failure. However, revoking the Townshend Duties would give credence to the Americans' contentions about taxation without representation. Lord North, an intransigent opponent of colonial resistance, is now prime minister (and so he re-mains throughout the next decade), and he refuses to give in entirely. Consequently, Parliament repeals all the Townshend Duties except the tax on tea, hoping the actual effect will be to revive income but also hoping to maintain the principle that Parliament is supreme.

The response of all the colonies, except merchants in Boston, is to rescind the nonimportation agreements. A lull settles over British-American relations.

★ 1772 ★

9–10 June 1772

RHODE ISLAND. Commerce between Britain and the American colonies has revived with the repeal of the Townshend import duties, increasing in value more than four million pounds during 1771 alone; however, colonial merchants and shippers continue to evade customs tariffs whenever they can. Smuggling is not only commonplace but is the routine method of doing business for even the most respectable American merchants. The many inlets along the Narrangansett Bay coastline of Rhode Island offer a perfect setting for organized smuggling of goods. The royal navy, in support of the customs service, dispatches the schooner *Gaspee* with Lt. William Dudingston, an active young officer, in charge to halt the illicit trade. After several months of successful operations, the *Gaspee* runs aground while chasing a suspected smuggler. During the night, the ship is boarded by locals who shoot and wound Dudingston and burn the ship to the water. Dudingston is subsequently arrested by the local sheriff and freed only after his admiral pays the fine. Months later, a royal commission convenes to investigate but fails to identify the culprits. The commission's powers, however, include sending defendants to England for trial, a provision that alarms many in the colonies.

November 1772

BOSTON. Sam Adams, the indefatigable rebel, chafes at what he considers the complacency of the colonies after the repeal of the Townshend Acts. He seizes on the payment of royal officials' salaries by the government (rather than the colonial assembly) as an issue for agitation. He asks now-governor Thomas Hutchinson to convene the General Court to consider the issue. When Hutchinson refuses, Adams turns to the Boston Town Meeting, which authorizes a committee of correspondence to circulate protests. The committee draws up the so-called Boston Pamphlet, which categorically attacks the British government for taxation without representation; inflicting a standing army on Boston; using admiralty courts and commissions to deny trial by jury; and threatening to import Anglican bishops to subvert the people's religion. The pamphlet holds that the rights of all British subjects are absolute and cannot be abridged by government.

★ 1773 ★

March 1773

WILLIAMSBURG, VA. Influential members of the House of Burgesses, including Thomas Jefferson, Patrick Henry, and Richard Henry Lee, are alarmed after learning the *Gaspee* commission has the power to negate trial by jury in the colonies. They create a committee of correspondence to gather information on British actions and to communicate with other colonies; the Virginia assembly urges other colonies to do likewise. Within four months committees are established in Rhode Island, Connecticut, New Hampshire, Massachusetts, and South Carolina. By the following spring, all colonies except Pennsylvania have active communication through the committees, which serve as important agencies to keep colonial grievances alive.

10 May 1773

LONDON. Lord North's government attempts a clever move to rescue the financial fortunes of the British East India Company by passing a bill that allows the company to export surplus India tea directly to the American colonies. Regular export duties will be forgiven on the tea and only the token tea tax (remaining from the Townshend Duties) will be charged, making the company's tea cheaper for Americans than smuggled tea. Massachusetts governor Thomas Hutchinson estimates Americans consume 6.5 million pounds of tea a year. Loyal Tory merchants are to be given the privilege of selling the monopoly tea. The plan manages to offend nearly everyone in the colonies: Political radicals resist paying the tea tax on principle and wealthy colonial merchants see their smuggled tea profits threatened by monopoly. Royal consignees for the tea in New York, Philadelphia, and Charleston are forced to resign, but consignees in Boston stand firm against radical pressure. Ships laden with tea eventually sail for Boston, where a local meeting votes in November to boycott all East India Company monopoly tea.

16 December 1773

BOSTON. The tea crisis comes to a head as time runs out on either landing the tea from three merchant ships tied to the wharf or risking seizure of the vessels for nonpayment of duties. A huge mass meeting gathers at Old South Meeting Hall and eventually hears that Governor Hutchinson (a secret investor in the East India Company whose family stands to profit from the sale of the tea) refuses to release the cargoes. Donning thin disguises as Mohawk Indians, an organized gang heads for Griffin's Wharf, where the tea ships await. The men board the vessels, drag the tea chests from the holds, break the casks open, and dump the tea into the harbor: "making saltwater tea" they call it. Three hundred forty-two chests of valuable tea float with the tide the next

The Boston Tea Party.

morning as a result of the so-called Boston Tea Party. The act of defiance is the last straw for the government in London, which refuses to accept the insult to its sovereignty and the blow to its financial planning. Lord North prepares to take the sternest possible measures against Boston and the Massachusetts colony.

★ 1774 ★

January 1774

LONDON. The government begins its retaliation for the Boston Tea Party by calling Benjamin Franklin before the Privy Council on 29 January. Franklin, who is acting as the agent of Massachusetts in Great Britain, is forced to endure more than an hour of unrestrained invective from British solicitor general Alexander Wedderburn. The performance leaves no doubt about the British anger. The king is prepared to move against Massachusetts and Boston through royal executive action, but his ministers advise allowing Parliament to do the work. The government is frustrated by inability to prosecute the leaders of the Tea Party, so it turns to punitive legislation.

February–May 1774

LONDON. In a carefully planned series of actions, which unfold during the spring of the year, Parliament moves to quash Boston. The government's position is summed up by Lord North: ". . . we are not entering into a dispute between internal and external taxes, not between taxes laid for the purposes of revenues and taxes laid for the regulation of trade, not between representation and taxation, or legislation and taxation; but we are now to dispute whether we have, or have not any authority in the country."

Parliament's first salvo is the Boston Port Bill, which closes the port of Boston to all trade, commerce, and shipping except for the minimum needed to supply food and fuel to the city. The objective is to cut off the economic life of Boston and force the recalcitrant Bostonians into submission. The port is to remain closed until the East India Company is repaid for the lost tea. Parliamentary leaders also hope the Port Bill will isolate Boston from other colonies and cow the merchants in Philadelphia, New York, and Charleston with the threat of loss of trade. Much to the chagrin of royal officials, however, colonists everywhere rally to the support of Boston, sending foodstuffs and money to sustain the beleaguered city. Royal governors in several colonies are forced to dissolve assemblies to prevent passage of legislation supporting Boston.

The second parliamentary act brought forth during the spring, the Massachusetts Government Act, alters the Massachusetts charter and puts the administration of the colony entirely in the hands of royal officials. The Council, previously chosen by the elected assembly, is now to be appointed directly by the crown. The royal governor is empowered to appoint all colonial officials and town meetings are abolished.

A third bill requires that any royal official in Massachusetts who is accused of a capital crime must be sent home to England for trial. And, a new and stronger Quartering Act is passed,

A British cartoon of 1774 illustrating the Americans disregard for authority.

allowing military commanders to billet troops as they see fit in the city of Boston.

All of these acts, which come to be known as the Intolerable Acts, are seen in Massachusetts and the rest of the American colonies as raising the conflict to a new level. Adding to American fears and frustration is yet another new law, the Quebec Act, which extends the boundaries of British Canadian possessions to the Ohio and Mississippi Rivers, cutting off colonial land claims in the West, and which gives religious rights to Quebec Roman Catholics, a shuddering thought for the Protestants of the lower colonies.

Finally, the government declares, in effect, martial law in Massachusetts by naming Gen. Thomas Gage, the Army commander in the colonies, governor of Massachusetts with orders to establish as strong a military garrison as he sees fit in Boston. As the summer progresses, Gage begins to concentrate troops in the city.

June–August 1774
Several colonial bodies begin almost simultaneously to plan for a grand meeting of representatives from all the American colonies. The lower house in Connecticut moves through its committee of correspondence in June to choose delegates, followed within weeks by Rhode Island. Extralegal assemblies in Virginia, Maryland, New Hampshire, North Carolina, New Jersey, and Delaware select representatives. Local committees choose delegates in New York and South Carolina. Only Georgia, worried about an uprising among the Creek Indians, forgoes sending representatives to the meeting.

5 September–26 October 1774
PHILADELPHIA. The first Continental Congress meets. It is an extraordinary assemblage of political leaders, who gather for the first time to debate and plan a unified response to British policy and actions. While they may have been aware of each other, few of the delegates have met face to face before and never under these circumstances. They represent a wide spectrum of opinion, from radical to relatively conservative, but few fail to be impressed with the quality of the meeting. The delegates include Sam Adams and cousin John Adams from Massachusetts; George Washington, Peyton Randolph, and Richard Henry Lee from Virginia; Silas Deane from Connecticut; Caesar Rodney from Delaware; John Jay from New York; John Dickinson and Joseph Galloway from Pennsylvania; Christopher

Gadsden and Edward and John Rutledge from South Carolina among many. As John Adams writes: "The magnanimity and public spirit which I see here make me blush for the sordid, venal herd which I have seen in my own province."

Meeting in Carpenter's Hall, the Congress begins to debate the issues and what should be done. Much of the work takes place outside the hall, as members meet informally and talk late into the night. Deciding early to operate on a one-colony one-vote rule, the delegates take up a formal discussion of how to define American rights. The process is instructive and leads eventually to agreement that the co-

A MOVEABLE CONGRESS

Congress was the government of the United States throughout the Revolution—acting as both as a legislative body and as the nation's executive. Congress was not, however, anchored in one place. The delegates moved several times, usually in response to some danger that threatened their repose. The First Continental Congress convened in Philadelphia in September 1774 and sat for seven weeks before adjourning. The Second Continental Congress met again in Philadelphia in what was then known as the State House (later named Independence Hall) in May 1775, with a recess between August and September.

In the fall of 1776, the British defeated the Continental Army in New York and pushed Washington all the way out of New Jersey (which he, of course, soon reclaimed with the victories at Trenton and Princeton), so Philadelphia and Congress seemed at the mercy of the enemy. Congress moved in early December 1776 to Baltimore to avoid capture. In March of the following year, with Washington's army once again screening the British in New York, Congress moved back to Philadelphia. In Sep-

tember 1777, however, Gen. Howe invaded Pennsylvania from the Chesapeake, and Congress hastily scurried out of Philadelphia (which Howe seized and occupied) for the safety of York, Pa. With the British evacuation of Philadelphia the following spring, the Continental Congress again returned.

With the final ratification of the Articles of Confederation in March 1781, the Continental Congress became the Confederation Congress and continued to meet in Philadelphia. The victory at Yorktown removed all possibility of a new threat from the British, but in 1783, Congress again was forced to move. Disgruntled troops of the furloughed Continental Army surrounded the State House and threatened the delegates over back pay. When the authorities of Pennsylvania refused to protect them, the delegates adjourned and assembled again in Princeton, N.J. Failing to attract enough members to do business at Princeton, Congress adjourned again and reconvened in Annapolis, Md., where it presided over the official end of the Revolution.

lonial claims rest on three bases: natural rights, rights under the British constitution, and rights granted by the colonial charters. After much discussion, the Congress passes a "Declaration of Rights and Grievances" on 14 October.

Throughout the debates, a division emerges between the more conservative elements, lead by Galloway of Pennsylvania, and the radicals, lead by Gadsden of Carolina. Galloway desires a measured response to British policy and even submits a complex plan of union that would establish a colonial parliament under British rule. Gadsden, on the other hand, is prepared to launch an armed attack on the British garrison in Boston. The sense of the Congress is somewhere between the extremes.

The spirit of compromise shows itself in the decision to set up an economic boycott of British goods in the form of a Continental Association. The agreements are to be enforced by elected local committees, which will rely on peer pressure, and the measures are laid out in a series of steps over a year's time (allowing Virginia, for example, to sell the year's tobacco crop and South Carolina to ship its rice). Nonconsumption of British goods will begin immediately, nonimportation in December, and nonexportation in September 1775.

The congressional delegates draft petitions to the king and the people of America, Great Britain, and Quebec, and adjourn with an agreement to reconvene in May of the following year.

A variant of a cartoon first designed by Ben Franklin in 1754.

September 1774
BOSTON. Military governor Gage moves to fortify Boston Neck, the thin spit of land that connects the city to the mainland. With guards in place, the city is effectively cut off from the rest of Massachusetts. Boston is under siege.

October 1774
MASSACHUSETTS. Gage dissolves the Massachusetts General Court, but the members constitute themselves as an irregular but effective Provincial Congress. They set up a Committee of Safety with John Hancock at its head, and most significant, vote to recruit 12,000 men for a militia and call for the purchase of 5,000 muskets and

Carpenter's Hall, Philadelphia, site of the First Continental Congress.

bayonets, twenty field pieces, and four mortars. The Boston delegates receive strong support from surrounding towns, where militia have already begun to drill and where local arms stores are assembled, and from Western Massachusetts towns that have previously been under the thumb of royalists. In other colonies, similar extralegal bodies, often based on the elected local Continental Association committees, spring up and virtually take over the functions of government.

YEARS OF REVOLUTION:
★ 1775-1781 ★

★ 1775 ★

As the year begins, tensions between the British government and the thirteen American colonies continue their upward curve, with the focus of attention on Boston and Massachusetts. The large British force in Boston under the command of Gen. Thomas Gage is virtually a besieged garrison as militia in the surrounding countryside arm and train for the anticipated clash. Support is strong for Boston among the other colonies, as expressed in a fiery speech by Virginia's Patrick Henry.

The conflict simmers until mid-April, when Gage sends out an expedition in force to seize patriot arms caches in Concord and Worcester. The column meets resistance from patriot militia at Lexington and then at Concord. The British retreat under fire from gathering American minutemen, and eventually reach safety after suffering significant losses. The time of protest and debate has passed; the American Revolution has begun.

The British stay within Boston as a makeshift army of New England militia surrounds the city. Elsewhere, other colonies respond to the news of Lexington and Concord by organizing troops, and a small force seizes old Fort Ticonderoga on 9 May. The next day, the Second Continental Congress convenes in Philadelphia and begins to consider what to do. By June the Congress votes to assume control of the patriot army and appoints George Washington commander-in-chief. Before he can reach Boston, the British cross the Charles River and attack patriot field positions on Breed's Hill. The following battle inflicts shocking and severe casualties on the cream of the British army, although the patriots are finally swept from their positions. Following the battle, troops from other colonies arrive to join the New England militia to form the nucleus of the Continental Army.

In September, two American expeditions set out for Canada with the intent of taking Quebec. Although they occupy Montreal on 13 November, the ill-organized and ill-supplied force is repulsed at Quebec on the final day of the year.

18 January 1775

SAVANNAH, GA. Georgia's First Provincial Congress assembles in Savannah to organize an independent government as an expression of sympathy for opposition to British policies in Boston and in other colonies, but not because Georgians feel any serious grievance toward Great Britain. In fact, Loyalist sentiment is so strong that only five of the twelve parishes send representatives to this first congress. Consequently, Georgia's delegates to the Second Continental Congress do not claim seats in that national assembly nine months later. Revolutionary sympathies in Georgia center in St. John's Parish, which had been settled by New Englanders, principally from Dorchester, Massachusetts.

27 January 1775

BOSTON. Gen. Thomas Gage, commander of all British forces in North America who had been commissioned by George III as governor of Massachusetts in 1774, is now authorized to use force to maintain royal authority in the colony. By this time Gage has assembled in Boston a sizable force estimated at 4,000 troops comprised of nine regiments and parts of two regiments of British infantry. The full regiments are the 4th (King's Own), 5th, 10th, 23rd (Royal Welch Fusiliers), 38th, 43rd, 47th, 52nd, and 59th. Three companies represent the 18th Regiment (Royal Irish); six companies the 65th. There are also five companies of the Royal Artillery. And the 14th and 29th regiments have been stationed at Castle William since the Boston Massacre (5 March 1770). In addition, four ships—the *Scarborough*, the *Boyne*, the *Somer*

set, and the *Asia*, each equipped with at least sixty guns—are anchored in Boston Harbor along with many frigates and other vessels. From these Gage has secured 460 marines. In equipment, organization, training, and leadership these forces typify the British military. All that Gage lacks is cavalry. By the terms of the Quartering Act a British officer can demand lodging for these troops in any home, shop, or warehouse in Boston—a necessary arrangement to provide shelter for the troops, but an imposition to the city's residents. The city's population has also been swollen by the influx of hundreds of men put out of work by the crippling effects of the Boston Port Bill, one of the punitive Intolerable (or Coercive) Acts passed by Parliament.

1 February 1775

LONDON. William Pitt (First Earl of Chatham), who has in the past recommended conciliation with the Americans and championed their cause in Parliament but now suffers from debilities caused by age and illness, fails in a final effort to achieve a settlement. Pitt advocates repeal of the Intolerable Acts as a specific gesture of magnanimity. Pitt also proposes withdrawing British troops from Boston and passing legislation reaffirming the sovereignty of Parliament while stipulating that the colonies not be taxed without their consent. He praises correspondences from the Continental Congress for their "decency, firmness, and wisdom ... solidity of reasoning, force of sagacity, and wisdom of conclusion"; he characterizes the colonists' cause as "an alliance of God and nature" based on "immutable, eternal" principles guiding people who "will die in defence of their rights as men, as freemen."

Edmund Burke, also an eloquent and longstanding advocate of the colonists, joins Pitt in this effort toward amelioration, but to no avail. The government, headed by the able but uncompromising Lord Frederick North, who is adamantly loyal to the king and the king's insistence that the colonists be made to obey the royal government, has Parliament's overwhelming but shortsighted support.

BOSTON. The Second Massachusetts Provincial Congress convenes in nearby Cambridge. General Gage in 1774 had established the capital at Salem, where the General Assembly had met under protest. The assembly recommended the calling of the Continental Congress and elected five delegates to the congress. Called into session a second time in October 1774, members of the General Assembly had adjourned to Concord and organized themselves as the totally illegal Provincial Congress, operating as the government of Massachusetts beyond British-controlled Boston, with John Hancock as president. The Second Provincial Congress now meets to generate a policy in response to the royal government's augmenting of the Boston garrison and also in reaction to Parliament's passage of the Fishery Act, which prohibits all the New England colonies from trading with anyone but Great Britain, Ireland, and the West Indies and from fishing in the waters off Newfoundland. (The scope of this act is expanded in April to include all the colonies except North Carolina and New York, which have not yet joined

the Continental Association boycott of British goods.) Banning the colonies from the Newfoundland fisheries will prove devastating for Massachusetts, whose economic lifeblood derives from the taking of codfish and whales.

6 *February 1775*

BOSTON. John Adams' letter on "The Rule of Law and the Rule of Men" appears in the *Massachusetts Gazette* under the pen name Novanglus. It responds to letters by a Tory, Daniel Leonard, published under the pen name Massachusettensis in earlier issues of the same publication. Adams concedes that Parliament should have the right to control the regulation of commerce but "upon *compact* and *consent* of the colonies," not upon the basis of any law. He argues that the provincial legislatures are the "only supreme authorities in our colonies." Adams attacks the Tories for the argument that as subjects of the British empire the colonists should be obedient to the supreme power of the empire vested in Parliament. The British government is not an empire, he writes: "It is a limited monarchy." The British constitution, Adams argues, "is much more like a republic than an empire ... a *government of laws* and *not of men*." Adams discusses the question of colonial representation in Parliament and concludes: "That a representation in Parliament is impracticable, we all agree; but the consequence is that we must have a representation in our supreme legislatures here. This was the consequence that was drawn by kings, ministers, our ancestors, and the whole nation more than a century ago...." Adams is not yet ready to advocate independence for the colonists, still arguing their rights as Englishmen.

20 February 1775

CONCORD, MASS. The Massachusetts Provincial Congress adjourns temporarily in order to reassemble in Concord. The congress appoints John Thomas and William Heath as officers to serve with Hancock; provides for a commissary in which to store ordnance, arms, and other provisions; invites the Stockbridge Indians to enlist in the service of the colony; drafts rules for governing the army; elects delegates to visit other New England colonies and seek their support in providing militia to strengthen the Massachusetts force; and adopts still other measures that anticipate armed conflict with the British military—all actions that clearly evidence open rebellion.

27 February 1775

LONDON. Parliament approves Lord North's proposal, intended as conciliatory toward the colonies and grudgingly approved by George III, that the royal government would no longer tax any colony which passes legislation providing for internal taxes that will adequately support the British civil and judicial officials and military personnel within its boundaries. During the first week of February, however, Parliament has given its approval to a declaration addressed to the king declaring the colonies in a state of rebellion and mandating forceful actions to ensure that the colonists obey the laws of England and concede the mother country's sovereignty. In addition, Lord North's proposal indicates that his government will deal on an individual basis with each colony

and consequently avoid tacit recognition of the Continental Congress. The American congress is not impressed and will reject the North proposal on 31 July.

22 March 1775

LONDON. Edmund Burke presents a ringing address "On Conciliation with America" in the House of Commons. "The proposition," Burke declares, "is peace." He continues: "America, gentlemen say, is a noble object. It is an object well worth fighting for. . . . But I confess . . . my opinion is much more in favor of prudent management than of force; considering force not as an odious but a feeble instrument for preserving a people so numerous, so active, so growing, so spirited as this in a profitable and subordinate connection with us."

He points out the inefficacy of force and extols the Americans' love of freedom and liberty as a distinctly English heritage. "The colonies draw from you, as with their lifeblood," he observes, "these ideas and principles. Their love of liberty, as with you, fixed and attached on this specific point of taxing." Burke cites the popularity of the colonists' assemblies and the influence of their largely Protestant faith and interest in education (specifically in the law) on the quest for liberty. He advocates compliance with the American spirit as at least a necessary evil. Finally, he points out that the colonies have no representation in Parliament but have nevertheless been obliged to pay taxes and other subsidies to the royal government. Each colony, he adds, has its own legislative body, and these legislatures have freely voted large subsidies to the royal government in times past by their own choice—a method of payment he deems much more conducive to good relations.

And so he recommends leaving the question of subsidies to the discretion of the colonial assemblies: "Magnanimity in politics is not seldom the truest wisdom; and a great empire and little minds go ill together." The little minds prevail.

23 March 1775

RICHMOND, VA. Patrick Henry delivers a resounding speech before the convention meeting in Richmond after royal governor Lord Dunmore has suspended the Virginia Assembly. Henry, who has for ten years espoused the colonists' cause in the Virginia Assembly, now asserts that the expanded British military presence in America reveals, not a desire for reconciliation, but a presage of "war and subjugation" designed "to force us to submission." He declares that all the colonists' efforts at reconciliation through petitions, remonstrances, and supplications have been in vain.

"There is no longer any room for hope," he insists. "If we wish to be free . . . if we mean not basely to abandon the noble struggle in which we have been so long engaged . . . we must fight!" The ability to fight will not be enhanced by waiting; friends will be found to help the cause; and, in any event, there is now no other choice. Henry concludes with a forceful declaration: "It is vain, sir, to extenuate the matter. Gentlemen may cry peace, peace, but there is no peace. The war is actually begun! The next gale that sweeps from the north will bring to our ears the clash of resounding arms! Our brethren are already in the field! Why stand we here idle?

What is it that gentlemen wish? What would they have? Is life so dear or peace so sweet as to be purchased at the price of chains and slavery? Forbid it, Almighty God—I know not what course others may take; but as for me—give me liberty, or give me death!" As Henry sits down, William Wirt recounts: "The cry, 'To arms!' seems to quiver on every lip and gleam from every eye."

Patrick Henry, in a portrait by J.B. Longacre.

30 March 1775

LONDON. King George III gives his assent to the Parliamentary act (the Fisheries Act) restricting all of New England's commerce to trade with Great Britain, Ireland, and the West Indies—hardly what the colonials regard an extended olive branch.

BOSTON. Gen. Thomas Gage rouses himself from passivity in Boston and orders an entire brigade of his troops on a practice march that will wind through Cambridge and Watertown. The troops are commanded by Col. Hugh Percy, a former MP who disagrees with the royal government's policies but has nevertheless accepted duty with the royal forces in America, where he serves as Gage's second in command. (Lord Percy had arrived in the spring of 1774 in Boston and there became a popular dinner guest in the home of none other than John Hancock.) The Provincial Congress at Concord views the British brigades' march as a hostile act demonstrating Gage's intent to carry out his mandate and impose Parliament's seemingly vindictive policies by force. Forewarned by the congress, provincial militia station cannon at Watertown's bridge and remove planks from the bridge at Cambridge. The British troops return to Boston, but anxiety reportedly mounts among the Massachusetts patriots.

5 April 1775

CONCORD, MASS. The Massachusetts Provincial Congress adopts fifty-three articles of war, clearly provoking a challenge to Gen. Gage. The preamble to these articles spells out the congress' grievances. Beginning with a protestation of the innocence of the colonists, "unjustly and wickedly charged with licentiousness, sedition, treason, and rebellion," the preamble invokes the Pilgrims' legacy as justification for war preparations. It reads: "[B]eing deeply impressed with a sense of the almost incredible fatigues and hardships our progenitors encountered, who fled from oppression for the sake of civil and religious liberty for themselves and their offspring, and began a settlement here on

bare creation, at their own expense; and having seriously considered the duty we owe to God, to the memory of such invincible worthies, to the King, to Great Britain, our country, ourselves, our posterity, do think it our indispensable duty . . . to recover, maintain, defend, and preserve the free exercise of all those civil and religious rights and liberties for which many of our worthy forefathers fought, bled, and died."

King George III.

8 April 1775

NEWBERN, N.C. Josiah Martin, the royal governor of North Carolina since 12 August 1771, dissolves the provincial assembly, effectively ending royal rule of the colony. He had struggled with the assembly to reconcile issues of taxation and other royal policies without success, as the civic authority crumbled and the patriots organized. Martin remains among the British wishful thinkers who believe that the numbers of Loyalists are great enough to assure that royal rule will eventually prevail. But, as the patriots' militia gains support he sends his family to New York for safety and himself later (18 July) evacuates to Cape Fear and boards H.M.S. *Cruzier.*

14 April 1775

BOSTON. Gen. Gage receives instructions from Lord Dartmouth, secretary for the colonies, in a letter upbraiding the general for inaction and thus implicitly demanding he move against the patriots. Dartmouth instructs Gage to proceed secretively and to arrest the leaders of the Provincial Congress, even though doing so will probably provoke war. Gage has little choice, but he worries over being undermanned, his request for an additional 20,000 troops having been turned down.

15 April 1775

BOSTON. Gen. Gage orders the elite units of his grenadier and light infantry companies detached from their regiments as a separate force (some 700 men) to fulfill extra assignments. Rumor and speculation monopolize the conversations at the Green Dragon, the Bunch of Grapes, and other Boston taverns. Gage does not plan to arrest leaders of the Provincial Congress as recommended by Dartmouth, but to use the discretion Dartmouth's letter grants him. He decides to seize the provincial militia's stores of arms and ammunition at Concord and Worcester. In Concord the Provincial Congress adjourns, its members disbanding to go their separate ways.

16 April 1775

BOSTON. Patriot Dr. Joseph Warren sends Paul Revere to Lexington to warn John Hancock and Samuel Adams that Gen. Gage might send troops to arrest them. They in turn send word to Concord, and alarmed residents there hastily pack up the store of arms and ammunition and ship them to Worcester. On his return to Boston Revere makes arrangements with "a Col. Conant and some other gentlemen" in Charlestown that a signal will be shown from the steeple of Old North Church: two lanterns if the British force sets out by water, one lantern if by land across Boston Neck. The signal is actually intended for the Charlestown "gentlemen," so they might warn Concord, rather than for Revere, who expects he will not be able to get out of Boston.

Paul Revere's famous ride, April 18, 1775.

18 April 1775

BOSTON. Gen. Gage makes every effort to keep secret his plan for a surprise march on Concord to begin well after dark, but secrecy proves impossible. Dr. Warren receives the news before the troops have left their barracks, and he summons Revere and William Dawes. The latter arrives first and immediately rides out over Boston Neck for Lexington to warn

Hancock and Samuel Adams. Revere, close on Dawes' heels, gathers his boots and overcoat; sends Capt. John Pulling to shine two lanterns in Old North's steeple; and embarks by boat across the Charles River, rowed by two men and headed for Charlestown. Conant and other "gentlemen" meet him at wharfside with a horse. He sets off on a harrowing and furious ride at about eleven o'clock, half an hour after Gage's special force has mustered on Boston Common. Revere's fellow courier Dawes encounters no obstacles on his race to Lexington, but Revere is not so lucky. Accosted by British officers, he has to flee and pursues a different course toward his goal. He shouts his warning at Medford, arouses the leader of the town's militia, and speeds on to sound the alarm in Menotomy.

Revere gallops into Lexington ahead of Dawes at about midnight. He heads straight to Parson Jonas Clark's house to warn Hancock and Adams, who prepare to flee. Revere waits at the house for Dawes. The two couriers set off together for Concord, joined en route by Dr. Samuel Prescott. Stopped by four British officers with drawn pistols, the three messengers try to escape. Dawes reins about and flies back to Lexington. Prescott and Revere race off in different directions; the doctor making good his escape by spurring his horse over a stone wall. But Revere, heading into the safety of the woods, is unexpectedly trapped by six British officers hidden there. His ride has ended. When questioned, Revere says 500 militia are assembling at Lexington. The officers, deeply concerned, deposit Revere horseless in Lexington and ride off. At Parson Clark's house Revere finds Hancock

and Adams ready to leave and escapes with them to Burlington in a chaise.

A Minuteman behind his plow and *ready for battle.*

19 April 1775

LEXINGTON, MASS.   In the early morning hours Gage's troops. commanded by Lt. Col. Francis Smith with Maj. John Pitcairn, march toward Lexington—Pitcairn's command of light infantry well in advance by Smith's order. Their march has awakened local patriots, who ride to spread the alarm and swell the assembling militia ranks. In Lexington 130 minutemen—members of elite militia units designated to respond to alarm at a minute's notice—join Capt. John Parker on the

A Minuteman giving the call to arms to a fellow patriot.

village green and wait. At 4:30 courier Thaddeus Bowman brings the news that the British are half an hour away. Only seventy of the assembled minutemen bear arms; they form into two lines. The British march into sight about 100 yards away on the road to Concord as daylight breaks. To oppose the British troops is foolish, perhaps even suicidal, since their objective is known to be Concord and since they outnumber the minutemen ten to one; but Parker declares he will shoot any man who runs. So, for the moment, they stand their ground. Pitcairn rides forward and orders the remaining rebels to disperse. Realizing the futility of their position, the patriots begin to do so but refuse to surrender their arms.

his musket, he meets his fate—a bayonet thrust. With great difficulty the British officers regain control over their "wild" troops. One British private has received a minor leg wound. Eight dead patriots lie on Lexington Green; ten wounded have escaped. The Battle of Lexington is over.

A closer look at the action at Lexington.

CONCORD, MASS. Rejoined now by Smith's detachment, the British force proceeds to Concord as the news of their march is spread through eastern Massachusetts by a prearranged system of couriers, church bells, and drums. Dr. Prescott has reached Concord after 11:00 A.M. and the alarm bell has summoned the minutemen there. While some remove the armaments still remaining in Col. James Barrett's house—the British objective— volunteer Reuben Brown rides to Lexington and returns with news of the skirmish there: He heard shooting and saw smoke as he neared Lexington Green. The minutemen, now numbered about 150, tramp forth to meet the British force but on sighting it turn about and march back to Concord as drum-and-fife music swells from both their own and the British ranks.

The Battle of Lexington, April 19, 1775.

One shot rings out; who has fired it will never be known. A British officer —not Pitcairn—orders his troops to fire. Their volley sings over the minutemen's heads. Pitcairn vainly shouts an order to cease fire. His frenzied troops let loose another volley and charge the fleeing minutemen. The aged Jonas Parker, John's cousin, sprawls wounded; struggling to reload

The British approach Concord, dispersing the minutemen, now stationed on a ridge above the roadway. The patriots fall back to a second ridge, and Barrett orders them to reassemble on Punkatasset Hill, a 200-foot elevation north of the Concord River fronting his home. There they await reinforcements as the British enter Concord. Sending a detachment to Barrett's house and stationing troops under Capt. Walter Laurie to guard the North Bridge, British officers take refreshment in the local taverns while their men search the town's houses, finding inconsequential stores of arms. Meanwhile, the minutemen descend from Punkatasset Hill to a ridge nearer the North Bridge as reinforcements arrive from nearby villages, bolstering their strength. Seeing that the British have set fire to the courthouse and a blacksmith shop (though they soon extinguish the flames themselves), Barrett's adjutant Joseph Hosmer questions whether the patriots intend to let the town be burned down. They decide to come to the town's defense, and Barrett gives the order to advance but to hold fire unless fired upon.

Led by Barrett, Maj. John Buttrick, and Lt. Col. John Robinson from Westford, the minutemen advance while two fifers play "The White Cockade." Capt. Laurie sends to Col. Smith for reinforcements, but the fat, middle- aged colonel responds slowly. Laurie withdraws his men to the east end of the bridge as the minutemen crowd the west end. The British fire first. An American is wounded. Then a British volley kills two patriots and wounds two others. Buttrick orders his minutemen to fire; three British soldiers fall dead, while several offi-

The scene at Concord's North Bridge where colonial militia met the red coats.

cers and men suffer wounds. The British fall back in disarray, meet Smith's reinforcements, re-form, and halt in Concord. The minutemen follow hard after, but lack of discipline aborts their advance; they even allow the British troops returning from Barrett's house to recross the bridge and regroup with their force without firing a shot. The Battle of Concord fizzles out.

At noon, the British force begins the return march to Boston. For an hour all is quiet. But the minutemen, continuously augmented by hundreds of arrivals from throughout the region, run before and after the British column to crouch behind walls and trees as the troops pass. The battle resumes. As the British approach Meriam's Corner a mile east of Concord, their flanking troops fire a warning volley at the Meriam house. Unexpectedly, minutemen fire back and two British soldiers collapse in death; others are wounded. The British crowd onto a bridge at a stream lined by dense woods from which the Americans let loose a withering fire that kills many of their enemy. For sixteen miles the minutemen race ahead and hide behind rocks, houses, barns, and trees to rake the British soldiers with repeated musket barrages. Some patriots are killed by the flanking troops; others abandon the fight, but new arrivals replace them.

Dismayed by the sniper warfare, the British troops retreat in panic toward Lexington. More shots explode from the ranks of hidden minutemen. Smith is wounded. Pitcairn's horse throws him and bolts toward the minutemen, carrying the major's brace of pistols—battle trophies for the rebels. The British troops stagger dead-tired onto Lexington Green, fearing a final debacle. But Lord Percy comes to their rescue with reinforcements from Boston that nearly triple the British number, and the retreat resumes. The American militiamen continue their harrying tactics. Enraged by the sniping, British soldiers attack houses, killing all the males inside, looting, and burning. The British struggle back through Cambridge, finally arriving at the hills outside Charlestown known as Bunker and Breed's. They collapse with fatigue, but they are safe here, protected by the guns of his majesty's ships lying at anchor in the Charles River.

The Americans have suffered a total of ninety-five casualties, with forty-nine killed. The British casualties have been surprisingly light—a total of 273, with only seventy-two dead, out of 2,000 troops—and their ordeal is over. But the meaning of this day's tragic drama will reverberate throughout the colonies, all the way to Whitehall: The War of the Revolution has begun. The minutemen who have pursued the British to Boston following the battles of Lexington and Concord begin to encircle the city and lay siege to the British garrison.

British soldiers wait for action during the seige of Boston.

23 April 1775

CONCORD, MASS. The Massachusetts Provincial Congress reconvenes; votes to call up 30,000 militia, with 13,600 of the men to be recruited immediately in Massachusetts alone; and names Artemus Ward commander of the Massachusetts troops. The congress sends committees to the other New England colonies requesting their help in raising the full quota of 30,000. Massachusetts troops, joined by others from Rhode Island commanded by Nathanael Greene, from New Hampshire commanded by Nathaniel Folsom but led by Col. John Stark, and from Connecticut commanded by David Wooster, swell the ranks of the patriot force surrounding Boston. Gen. Artemas Ward is their commander-in-chief. Gen. Gage anticipates a massive attack.

3 May 1775

CAMBRIDGE, MASS. Benedict Arnold, a merchant and militia officer of Connecticut, persuades the Committee of Safety that Fort Ticonderoga must be taken. He says it is deteriorated, inadequately defended by only fifty men, and affords a chance to capture eighty cannon, twenty brass pieces, and a store of small arms. The committee commissions him a colonel and authorizes him to raise a force of 400 men.

PHILADELPHIA. Benjamin Franklin, now nearly seventy years old, arrives home. He has resided in London since 1757, serving there as an agent for Pennsylvania, Georgia, and Massachusetts. He has been America's chief spokesman in England and an advocate of reconciliation. But since being severely denounced before the Privy Council in 1774, Franklin has gravitated toward an alliance with the Adamses.

6 May 1775

PHILADELPHIA. One day after his return from England, Benjamin Franklin is chosen a member of the Second Continental Congress.

NEW YORK. John Hancock, Samuel Adams, and other New England delegates arrive in New York en route to Philadelphia, where delegates from Pennsylvania and the colonies to the south eagerly await their arrival.

8 May 1775

CHARLESTON, S.C. The brigantine *Industry* arrives in Charleston with news of the conflict at Lexington and Concord. In response the South Carolina Assembly votes to raise two 750-man infantry regiments and a 450-man squadron of rangers and appropriates one million pounds in support.

BENNINGTON, VT. (NEW HAMPSHIRE) A small force under Col. Samuel H. Parsons of Connecticut, who has been persuaded by Benedict Arnold that capturing Fort Ticonderoga will pro-

vide cannon for Artemas Ward's troops at Boston, meets with Ethan Allen and about 100 of his Green Mountain Boys, an irregular militia force from the Hampshire Grants section of New Hampshire (eventually to become Vermont). They send men to Skenesboro and Panton to capture boats to transport their men across Lake Champlain for the assault on the fort.

Arnold, having got word of the rival Parsons–Allen expedition, arrives on his own and claims command of the attacking force, but Allen's Boys object. Allen has already left for Shoreham (Hand's Cove), two miles below the fort, where the body of about 200 men has planned to assemble. Arnold finds him there, and the two men agree—grudgingly—to work together.

The capture of Fort Ticonderoga.

10 May 1775

FORT TICONDEROGA, N.Y. Although their raiders have not yet brought the boats from Skenesboro, two barges are available; and to preserve the element of surprise, Allen and Arnold with eighty-three men cram into the barges and push off into Lake Champlain. They land at daybreak half a mile from the fort. Allen and Arnold lead the attack. The men quickly scramble over the ruins of the fort's south wall and come upon a lone sentry, whose musket misfires. The sentry flees, with whooping Green Mountain Boys hot behind. Meeting a second sentry, who inflicts a bayonet wound on Allen's second in command, Allen crashes the flat of his sword on the British soldier's head. The sentry is persuaded to guide Allen and Arnold to the officers' quarters.

Hearing the commotion, Lt. Jocelyn Feltham, who had arrived only twelve days earlier with twenty soldiers, awakens the fort's commander, Capt. William De la Place, and attempts to dress. Allen and Arnold find the lieutenant still holding his breeches. He asks them by what authority they are there. Allen later says he answered: "In the name of the Great Jehovah and the Continental Congress" (others report Allen stood at the door and said: "Come out of there you sons of British whores, or I'll smoke you out"). Allen demands surrender of the fort, threatening to kill every inhabitant if the demand is not met. De la Place enters from another room and accedes to the surrender.

The Americans have captured fifty prisoners, including the two officers, about 100 cannon, and other stores. Many of the prisoners are invalids. In addition, there are twenty-four women and children. Once their comrades arrive from Hand's Cove the victors set to plundering and destroying, much to Arnold's disgust. Fort Ticonderoga is secure for the moment, except perhaps from the victors.

PHILADELPHIA. The Second Continental Congress convenes. Among the delegates are many who attended the First Continental Congress in the previous year. New to this Congress are John Hancock of Massachusetts, Benjamin Franklin and James Wilson of Pennsylvania, and several delegates from New York: George Clinton, Francis Lewis, Robert R. Livingston, Lewis Morris, and Philip Schuyler. Everyone is pleased that Georgia has sent a delegate, Lyman Hall, because the colony had no representation in the first congress. All the colonies are now represented.

12 May 1775

CROWN POINT, N.Y. Lt. Col. Seth Warner with a party of Allen's men captures Crown Point on Lake Champlain without resistance and takes nine prisoners.

17 May 1775

ST JOHN'S (ST. JEAN-IBERVILLE), QUEBEC. Having acquired a schooner captured at Skenesboro on 14 May, Arnold sets out for St. John's with about fifty men; Allen follows later with about sixty men. Arnold's force surprises the garrison of fifteen British soldiers at the fort on the Richelieu River, captures the sloop *George III*, destroys five boats, takes some boats and stores, and heads back to Ticonderoga. He meets Allen, who intends to occupy the fort at St. John's against Arnold's advice. At St. John's, Allen is repulsed by a British relief force arrived from Chambly, and he withdraws, with three of his men captured.

18 May 1775

PHILADELPHIA. Delegates to the Continental Congress choose Peyton Randolph of Virginia as president and Charles Thomson of Philadelphia secretary—the same positions they held in the first congress. Randolph informs the delegates of the capture of Ticonderoga, uplifting news brought the night before. American control of Lake Champlain might facilitate joining forces with Canada, believed to be largely in sympathy with the Americans.

24 May 1775

PHILADELPHIA. Peyton Randolph, speaker of the Virginia House of Burgesses, leaves the Continental Congress in order to attend a session of the Virginia assembly. Because Henry Middleton of South Carolina (the delegates' first choice to succeed Randolph) declines to serve because of his health, the congress elects John Hancock president.

25 May 1775

BOSTON. Major generals William Howe, John Burgoyne, and Henry Clinton arrive from England aboard the *Cerebus*. They bring to Gage instructions from the British Cabinet directing him to raid the military depot at Concord and to issue a pardon to any rebellious Massachusetts leaders who might be apprehended. The instructions, of course, have been precluded by the events of 19 April.

27 May 1775

BOSTON. Artemas Ward sends an expedition against Hog and Noodle islands in Boston Harbor, intending to drive off the livestock. The force succeeds on Hog Island. But Adm. Samuel Graves, who has sizable stores on Noodle Island, dispatches the *Diane* and some marines. The Americans make off with hundreds of animals, kill others, and burn the hay before

being attacked by the British. While the opposed troops skirmish and darkness approaches, the *Diana* founders in unfavorable winds and runs aground. Her crew is taken aboard the *Britannia*. Gen. Israel Putnam's troops board the *Diana*, loot the ship's stores, and put it to the torch.

29 May 1775

PHILADELPHIA. The Continental Congress sends a public appeal, drafted by John Jay, inviting support from the Canadians. The hope is to enlist Canada as the "fourteenth colony." The appeal states: "The taking of the fort and military stores at Ticonderoga and Crown Point . . . was dictated by the great law of self-preservation . . . you may rely on our assurances that these colonies will pursue no measures whatsoever but such as friendship and a regard for our mutual safety may suggest." It concludes: "We yet entertain hopes of your uniting with us in the defense of our common liberty. . . ."

31 May 1775

CHARLOTTE, N.C. (MECKLENBURG COUNTY) A committee drafts twenty resolutions for the delegates from North Carolina to present to the Continental Congress. The resolutions declare all royal or Parliamentary laws and commissions suspended and assert that all future executive and legislative authority should reside in the colonies' assemblies under the Continental Congress. This so-called Mecklenburg Declaration of Independence, though approved, is never presented to the Congress.

2 June 1775

PHILADELPHIA. The Continental Congress begins to confront two issues addressed to it by the Massachusetts Provincial Congress: Should the colony assume control of its civil government and should the Continental Congress assume control of the militia besieging Boston? Although not yet controlling the army, the Congress creates an Army Pay Department.

6 June 1775

NEW YORK CITY. Members of the Sons of Liberty led by Lt. Col. Marinus Willett capture five wagonloads of arms that a group of British soldiers tries to sneak out of the city. Willett had participated in an attack on 23 April on the city arsenal.

8 June 1775

YORKTOWN, VA. Lord Dunmore takes refuge on HMS *Fowey*, signaling the beginning of open conflict between the patriots and the Tories in Virginia.

10 June 1775

PHILADELPHIA. Hancock sends a letter to the Massachusetts Provincial Congress stating that the Continental Congress is deliberating the questions that body raised on 2 June. The Continental Congress establishes committees to solicit loans and to determine how much money must be raised and also urges the colonies to secure powder for the coming conflict.

11–12 June 1775

MACHIAS, ME. Ichabod Jones, a Boston Loyalist, arrives aboard the armed schooner *Margaretta*, accompanied by two transport sloops, to negotiate a supply of lumber. Offended by his manner, the townspeople seize him. Jones' midshipman, however, returns

safely to the *Margaretta* and threatens to bombard the town unless Jones is surrendered. The townspeople refuse to comply, instead demanding the schooner's surrender. Meanwhile, the Sons of Liberty capture the two sloops; the *Margaretta* runs aground, and the Americans fire on it. The next morning, the midshipman, having freed and anchored the schooner the previous day, attempts to escape. Patriots led by Jeremiah O'Brien and Benjamin Foster pursue the schooner in one of the captured sloops, fire on her, and board her, fatally wounding the midshipman—the only casualty of the Revolution's first naval engagement. British commanders are livid over the *Margaretta*'s loss.

12 June 1775

BOSTON. Gen. Gage, under instructions from the royal Cabinet, declares martial law in Massachusetts. He hopes the proclamation will preclude further conflict, especially since it is introduced by an offer of amnesty to all rebels who lay down their arms and revert to allegiance to the crown—except for Samuel Adams and John Hancock, whose offenses are pronounced so egregious as to demand trial and punishment. The proclamation's inflated wording, composed by Gen. John Burgoyne, instead of placating the patriots, arouses their contempt and ridicule.

14 June 1775

PHILADELPHIA. The Continental Congress passes a resolution to raise six companies of back-country riflemen (known for their marksmanship) from Pennsylvania, Maryland, and Virginia—two companies from each colony. A committee is appointed to draw up rules for administering the Continental Army, which includes militia forces in Massachusetts and New York. Massachusetts' second question of 2 June is answered. Subsequently the Congress raises Pennsylvania's quota to six companies.

15 June 1775

PHILADELPHIA. The Continental Congress resolves to appoint a general "to command all the continental forces, raised or to be raised, for the defense of American liberty." George Washington of Virginia, nominated by Thomas Johnson of Maryland with the adept support of John Adams, is the unanimous choice to be commander-in-chief.

CAMBRIDGE, MASS. Responding to intelligence that Gen. Gage intends to occupy Dorchester Heights (heretofore curiously ignored by both sides despite its obvious strategic value as an overlook of Boston Harbor), the Committee of Safety orders Gen. Ward to occupy Bunker Hill on the Charlestown peninsula immediately and to take Dorchester Heights afterward.

16 June 1775

PHILADELPHIA. Washington assumes command of the Continental Army. A general plan for the organization of the army is drafted, calling for appointment of two major generals, five brigadier generals, one adjutant general, one commissary general, one quartermaster general, one paymaster general, and a variety of engineers, aides, assistants, and others. As with the choice of Washington, political considerations—specifically the need to enlist Southern support and to pro-

mote a sense of unity between the Southern and New England colonies —influence the geographic distribution of the men chosen. And so congress chooses Artemas Ward of Massachusetts and Charles Lee of Virginia as the two major generals. But in choosing the brigadier generals congress fails the test of geography. Its remedy is to increase the numbers: major generals to four, brigadiers to eight. Members select Philip Schuyler of New York and Israel Putnam of Connecticut as the two additional major generals.

General George Washington takes command, June 16, 1775.

CAMBRIDGE, MASS. Col. William Prescott, under orders of Gen. Ward, leads a force of about 1,000 men—two Massachusetts militia regiments with elements from the Connecticut regiment—to Bunker Hill after 9:00 P.M. Their assignment is to fortify the hill. Gen. Putnam meets them at the neck of the Charlestown peninsula with wagonloads of dirt and brushwood to be used in preparing the fortifications. Arrived at the hill, Prescott, Putnam, and chief engineer Col. Richard Gridley decide to leave a detachment at Bunker Hill and, despite Ward's orders, to fortify Breed's Hill, closer to Boston Harbor. The troops work rapidly between midnight and dawn, digging trenches and raising six-foot perimeter walls.

17 June 1775
BREED'S HILL AND BUNKER HILL. With the sunrise, observers aboard British ships in Boston Harbor detect the fortification work in progress on Breed's Hill. The *Lively* opens fire. Other ships and the battery on Copp's Hill join in, but with little effect: the fortification work continues. Patriot reinforcements—New Hampshire regiments under John Stark and James Reed—arrive, but Prescott's force is weakened when, at Putnam's urging, he sends men with tools to fortify Bunker Hill. The American position is relatively strong along the rise of Breed's Hill with stout earthworks to shield the defenders, including Dr. Joseph Warren, president of the Massachusetts Provincial Congress, but the fortifications weaken to the left as they approach the beach of the Mystic River. Stark's New Hampshire troops, holding the left line, crouch behind little more than rail fences stuffed with mown grass.

The Americans open fire on Breed's Hill.

The British assault force of several regiments of regulars (minus their light infantry and grenadier companies which have been detached) crosses the Charles River on barges at midday under covering fire from the British warships and batteries. They land unopposed and are joined by another regiment, several light infantry and grenadier companies, and a battalion of Royal Marines. Gen. William Howe personally leads the British force. He intends to drive his superbly trained troops straight at the patriots, assuming that a bayonet attack pressed home in the approved European fashion will scatter the untried rebel militia. The ranks form up and move toward the fortifications.

The Battle of Breed's Hill.

As the Royal Welch Fusiliers approach his position Stark orders his men to hold fire, supposedly until they "see the whites of their eyes." When the fusiliers are within yards, Stark gives the order to fire, and a sheet of musket balls cuts down the

British ranks. Decimated and facing slaughter, the fusiliers retreat. The other British formations experience the same fate as they march resolutely up to the fortifications and are hurled back by surprisingly disciplined and accurate volleys from the patriots, who stand fast behind their manmade wall. The British officers suffer most particularly from the fire. Howe and his commanders rally the troops and prepare to launch another frontal assault despite heavy losses. As the third attack reaches the patriot position, Prescott's men run out of ammunition and the British troops pour over the wall and bring their bayonet attack home. The Americans must abandon the fight, and many are run through or shot at close range, Dr. Warren among them. Stark's men provide covering fire, but the American survivors suffer heavy losses as they fall back to Bunker Hill, where Put-

INFANTRY FIREPOWER

Armies of the Revolutionary War when fighting in traditional, stand-up battles relied on massed firepower from foot soldiers armed with smoothbore muskets. These weapons threw a heavy projectile—seven-tenths of an inch in diameter and weighing almost an ounce—that could mow down opposing formations when fired in disciplined fashion. The trick was to train foot soldiers to load and fire as rapidly as possible under combat conditions.

The loading of a smoothbore involved a relatively complex series of steps, which then were reduced to precise drill stages. The main point of training was to teach soldiers how to carry out the twelve stages of loading and firing in coordination with their fellows. Well-trained infantry could get off as many as four volleys per minute under the best conditions, a rate of fire that could destroy opposing troops if they were in the open.

Although the smoothbore muskets of the day were reasonably accurate up to 100 yards or more, tactics called for delivering a heavy volley rather than aimed shots. Infantry advanced toward each other in lines and delivered volleys on command, hoping to catch their opponents with a demoralizing blast before charging on with the bayonet. If a line of infantry could deliver two or three volleys at close range while withstanding its own losses, victory was likely. Once the opposing line broke up or turned and ran, it was usually all over.

Thus, while the Continental Army appeared on the surface to be a potent force during the first years of the Revolutionary War, it was almost always at a distinct disadvantage on the battlefield. The British regulars were highly trained and disciplined to perform the precise musketry drill under the stress of combat. Until late in the war, few units in the American army could match them volley for volley, and the large numbers of militia usually found on the American side were hopelessly outclassed unless protected by bulletproof barricades.

nam's troops join them in an orderly retreat, abandoning the peninsula. Gen. Clinton, who has arrived in time for the final British assault, cannot regroup his men in time to give pursuit.

Nevertheless, the British have won and now control Charlestown peninsula. But, they have suffered shocking losses—226 dead and 828 wounded: nearly 48 percent of their attacking force. The Americans have lost 140 dead and 271 wounded. Those British officers who have survived are demoralized, while the Americans have discovered that the vaunted British infantry is vulnerable, even in a stand-up battle. The Battle of Breed's Hill and Bunker Hill emerges as a costly victory for the British, one that will sow doubt and caution among their

MUSKETS

The smoothbore flintlock musket was the basic firearm of the Revolution, used by virtually all the troops on both sides. It was a weapon of considerable power and even flexibility when employed by trained soldiers. Other than refinements and minor variations, the flintlock muskets of the 1770s differed little from those introduced to European armies several generations before, so combatants took the field with weapons they understood well from both accumulated military wisdom and personal experience.

The British "Brown Bess" musket was the most numerous on any Revolutionary battlefield, since it was not only the standard weapon of the British Army but also used in large numbers by the Americans, who had little capability to produce muskets on their own. Introduced during the reign of Queen Anne in the first decade of the century, the weapon was .753-inch caliber, with a forty-six-inch barrel on most models. It weighed a hefty eleven and a quarter pounds. The Bess was considered by military manuals to be effective up to 100 or 150 yards, although accounts of actual combat tend to discount this standard considerably. Because it was a smoothbore and because the actual bullet was nearly 7 percent smaller in diameter than the barrel, thereby allowing the projectile to bounce back and forth off the sides of the tube during firing, the Bess was not very accurate. However, it was a sturdy weapon and could take a great deal of pounding in the field without serious malfunction or disrepair. The large bullet propelled at relatively low muzzle velocity could produce massive wounds.

The American army eventually came to have large numbers of French muskets. The French ally supplied quantities of the "Charleville" musket, which also dated in design from the early eighteenth century. The French version of the standard infantry arm was lighter than the British Bess, with a .69-caliber barrel of thinner construction and a lighter wooden stock. The smaller caliber (and thus smaller projectile) gave some advantage to use by Americans, since lead was scarce.

Samuel Adams, an early spokesman for the people of Boston.

John Adams, from a portrait by Gilbert Stuart.

field commanders for months to come.

20 June 1775

PHILADELPHIA. Washington receives his orders from the Continental Congress, interpreting them to mean that he should not only solicit the counsel of his staff of generals, but also have their approval before pursuing a course of action—a self-effacing attitude that will unfortunately impede making incisive decisions. For his first military ceremony since his appointment, Washington reviews the Philadelphia militia. Thomas Jefferson arrives in the city to replace Peyton Randolph as a Virginia delegate to the Continental Congress.

22 June 1775

SAVANNAH, GA. Although Georgia had lagged behind its fellow colonies in joining the Continental Congress (it had no delegates at the first Continental Congress in 1774), its citizens now form Committees of Safety and begin to plant themselves firmly in the rebel ranks.

PHILADELPHIA. The Continental Congress authorizes "a sum not exceeding two million of Spanish milled dollars ... for the defense of America" and pledges "the twelve confederated colonies" (Georgia not yet among their number) to redeem all present and future bills of credit, thus committing itself to funding the war effort with paper money.

23 June 1775

PHILADELPHIA. Ceremoniously escorted by a cavalcade of congressional delegates and accompanied by Philip Schuyler, Charles Lee, and Thomas Mifflin (his aide-de-camp), Washington leaves Philadelphia for New York en route to Boston to assume command of the army.

25 June 1775

PHILADELPHIA. The Continental Congress appoints Gen. Philip Schuyler commander of the Northern Department—the army of New York.

NEW YORK CITY. Washington arrives on his journey to Boston. Ironically,

THE BAYONET

Bayonet tactics gave the British army a distinct advantage early in the war. The redcoat infantry—regiments of foot, as they were known—were equipped with a seventeen-inch bayonet for their muskets. A socket at the base of the heavy, triangular blade fit over the muzzle of the firearm and a slot for the foresight locked the bayonet in place. The result was a heavy and somewhat unwieldy weapon that combined firepower and the age-old infantry pike. When well trained in how to use the bayonet, soldiers could advance with cold steel on foes discombobulated by musket volleys.

This is exactly what the British did in many of the opening engagements of the war. The tactic was to march resolutely toward the enemy, even if they were well situated, and after getting close enough to fire several massed volleys, to then advance on with the bayonet attack to finally destroy or scatter the opposition. The early American armies neither had bayonets nor were they trained in their use. American troops could only do damage with musket fire before the British got close enough for the final bayonet rush. Seldom could even the steadiest American troops stand up to the bristling, inexorable advance.

During the latter years of the war, however, most regiments of the Continental Line had bayonets of their own, usually French imports or homemade, and they had learned how to use them. When the opportunity presented itself, American regulars could—after about 1777 or 1778—use the same tactics as the British.

The result was a particularly brutal form of killing at close range.

---

on the same day, the royal governor, William Tryon, returns from a visit to England. Residents and officials of the colony of New York must choose concretely between siding with the rebels or the crown. Washington sends Schuyler to assume command of the rebel forces in the colony and to occupy posts on Lake Champlain and Lake George.

26 *June 1775*

PHILADELPHIA. A congressional committee appointed on 23 June to draft a "Declaration on Taking up Arms" to be published by Washington when he reaches Boston makes its report to the congress. Dissatisfied, congress increases the original committee of five members (John Rutledge, William Livingston, Benjamin Franklin, John Jay, and Thomas Johnson) with the addition of Thomas Jefferson and John Dickinson. The committee assigns Jefferson to draft a new declaration, which is perceived as too harsh. Jefferson asks Dickinson to revise it.

27 *June 1775*

PHILADELPHIA. Having, as recently as 1 June, prohibited any invasion of Canada, the Continental Congress

General Israel Putnam; he served at Bunker Hill and Long Island.

now reverses itself and authorizes Schuyler to invade and to secure any captured territory when and if such action becomes practicable.

30 June 1775

PHILADELPHIA. The Continental Congress approves sixty-nine articles of war, a statement of regulations for the Continental Army. Ironically, they are based on the British Articles of War, but they do attempt to enforce moral strictures to ensure that the American citizens' army behave as if in civil society. Church attendance, for example, is "earnestly recommended." Death is the sentence for some major crimes, but courts-martial are forbidden to order more than thirty-nine lashes for any whipping, a fine exceeding two months' pay, or imprisonment of more than a month.

2 July 1775

CAMBRIDGE, MASS. Washington arrives and assumes command of the Continental Army, supposed to total 16,600 men, but only about 14,000 of them have reported for duty, and the commander believes he will need 20,000 to attack the British. Learning that Ward has completed an arc of fortifications extending from the Mystic River south to Dorchester, Washington decides to expand the fortifications to other areas in order to contain the British in Boston while the Continental Army is trained and provisioned.

3 July 1775

CAMBRIDGE, MASS. Washington, already perceiving that he faces a formidable task, begins issuing general orders. He has to impose discipline where disorderliness has prevailed—an army of independent-minded volunteers who leave their posts before being replaced, wander off without leave, chat openly with British sentries, disregard orders, and even casually desert. Consequently, his orders will address every aspect of army life, mandating food inspections, weekly replacement of latrines, intolerance of drunkenness and swearing, attendance at worship service, punishment of offenses (thirty-nine whip lashes for desertion, for example). And the disciplining and training effort confronts a deadline, as the men's enlistments expire at the end of the year. Only 10,000 of them will be persuaded to re-enlist.

5 July 1775

PHILADELPHIA. The Continental Congress approves the so-called Olive Branch Petition, strongly favored by John Dickinson but disdained by John Adams. The petition, addressed to George III, restates the colonists' grievances but seeks reconciliation and negotiations and solicits the king to prevent hostilities while negotiations proceed. Richard Penn, a Loyalist and descendant of William Penn, is dispatched to London with the petition, arriving on 14 August.

6 July 1775

PHILADELPHIA. Congress adopts the "Declaration of Causes of Taking up Arms." The revised declaration explains the colonies' reasons for resorting to arms, denies any intention of seeking independence, and advocates reconciliation. It also, however, clearly brands England the aggressor. It asserts "We exhibit to mankind the remarkable spectacle of a people attacked by unprovoked enemies, without any imputation or suspicion of offence. They boast of their privileges and civilization, and yet proffer no milder conditions than servitude or death." The declaration also avows that the colonists' cause is just and their union perfect, and it contains the not-so-veiled threat that "foreign assistance is undoubtedly attainable." Some readers might have questioned whether the "harshness" of the original declaration was not still intact.

8 July 1775

BOSTON. Continental Army volunteers led by Maj. Benjamin Tupper and Capt. John Crane attack a British outpost on Boston Neck, rout the guard, and burn the guardhouse. Similar small probes continue through July.

10 July 1775

CAMBRIDGE, MASS. Horatio Gates, chosen adjutant general by the Continental Congress on 17 June with the rank of brigadier general, issues instructions to recruiters for the Continental Army. They are not to enlist British deserters, blacks, vagabonds, or anyone under the age of eighteen.

Those recruited must be either American-born or, if foreign-born, settled with a wife and family. Rather ironically, Gates himself is English-born and a former officer of the British army.

13 July 1775

PHILADELPHIA. Eager to preclude entry of the Indians into hostilities on the side of the British, the Congress begins appointing commissioners to hold councils with the Indians, and through diplomacy, to try to secure their peaceableness in treaty agreements.

18 July 1775

TICONDEROGA, N.Y. Gen. Schuyler and his entourage arrive from New York. The general discovers unpromising conditions: a defenseless garrison; insufficient food, ammunition, and other supplies; no lumber or other materials for building boats; a motley group of men, many of them insubordinate, from New York, Connecticut,

John Hancock; he was the richest man in Boston before the Revolution.

and Massachusetts—and a few Green Mountain Boys from the Vermont region.

20 July 1775

NEW YORK CITY. Patriots raid a British storehouse at Turtle Bay, seize the stores, and ship them to Boston and Lake Champlain.

21 July 1775

BOSTON. A party of American soldiers led by Maj. Joseph Vose sets out in whaleboats for Nantasket Point and there drives off the British guard and destroys the lighthouse on Great Brewster Island.

PHILADELPHIA. As the subject of a permanent union among the colonies hovers in the background, Benjamin Franklin draws up a tenative "Articles of Confederation and Perpetual Union," approved by Jefferson, which Franklin presents to the Continental Congress. Many members do not wish to confront this issue yet, so Franklin's articles are not entered in the official journal. The issue, for the time being, is shelved. Also shelved is the issue of opening up ports to trade, contrary to the Continental Association's nonexportation agreement, as discussion of a committee report and recommendations is postponed.

24 July 1775

TICONDEROGA, N.Y. Gen. Schuyler sends Maj. John Brown north, accompanied by three soldiers and a Canadian, to seek information about St. John's and Montreal and about the attitudes of the Indians and Canadians.

25 July 1775

CAMBRIDGE, MASS. Dr. Benjamin Church is made the first surgeon general of the Continental Army. He has the confidence of high officials, even though Paul Revere and others suspect him of being a British informer.

PHILADELPHIA. Finally responding to a petition of 16 May from the Massachusetts Provincial Congress (hand-delivered by Dr. Church), the Continental Congress officially "adopts" the Continental Army, assuming the authority of regulating and directing the army.

26 July 1775

PHILADELPHIA. Considering the report of a committee (chaired by Franklin) appointed to create some means of providing rapid transmission of information throughout the colonies, congress establishes a post office department and appoints Franklin postmaster general—a position he had held previously for many years on behalf of the royal government.

27 July 1775

DORSET, N.H. Schuyler has been expecting an addition to his force of 500 Green Mountain Boys. But the Boys, disgruntled with Ethan Allen, meet at Cephas Kent's tavern and elect Seth Warner as their lieutenant colonel, leaving Allen's former post of colonel unfilled. Allen will show up alone as a volunteer at Ticonderoga.

29 July 1775

PHILADELPHIA. With the two million Spanish dollars worth of bills of credit it had authorized now issuing from the presses, plus another million authorized on 25 July, congress decides on a plan for the currency's redemption. Each colony must assume responsibility for its portion of the debt (based on population) and devise means of redemption. Four equal installments are set for the redemption—payable on the last day of November in 1779, 1780, 1781, and 1782.

31 July 1775

PHILADELPHIA. The Continental Congress rejects Lord North's proposals for reconciliation (27 February). The delegates' statement asserts the colonies' right of raising appropriations and having a say in how they are dispersed. Citing the "great armaments" and "cruelty" with which the British ministry has "prosecuted hostilities," the statement concludes "can the world be deceived into an opinion that we are unreasonable, or can it hesitate to believe with us that nothing but our own exertions may defeat the ministerial sentence of death or abject submission?"

2 August 1775

CAMBRIDGE, MASS. Daniel Morgan and his contingent of Virginia riflemen arrive—the second of the rifle units authorized by congress to report to the Continental Army. Michael Cresap and his First Maryland Rifles had already arrived. The total of twelve rifle companies from these two colonies and Pennsylvania contains expert marksmen, but they are an unruly lot, rejecting regulations and work assignments, and compounding Washington's problems in imposing discipline on his troops.

9–10 August 1775

GLOUCESTER, MASS. HMS *Falcon*, commanded by Capt. John Linzee, gives chase to two American schoon-

ers returning to Salem from the West Indies. Linzee captures one of the schooners and pursues the other into Gloucester harbor. There troops on shore fire on the *Falcon*, which fires back but is forced to withdraw after losing both schooners, two barges, and thirty-five men.

14 August 1775

TICONDEROGA, N.Y. Maj. Brown reports to Gen. Schuyler that the French in Quebec will not fight the Americans, the Indians will remain neutral, and St. John's is being fortified but is manned by only 300 troops (there are only fifty at Quebec). Brown urges that the time is ripe for the invasion.

23 August 1775

LONDON. George III proclaims the colonies in a state of "open and avowed rebellion."

24 August 1775

NEW YORK CITY. Capt. John Lamb with about sixty men, under orders from the New York Provincial Congress, at about midnight begin dismantling the cannons in Battery Park to remove them to a safe site. Capt. George Vandeput of HMS *Asia* sends a bargeload of men to investigate; they fire a shot to warn the captain what is afoot. Lamb's men fire on the barge, killing one man. The *Asia* opens fire on the Battery, and alarms sound on shore. Expecting their city to be attacked and pillaged, many residents flee—the beginning of a general exodus to New Jersey and Long Island.

26–28 August 1775

CAMBRIDGE, MASS. Washington sends Gen. John Sullivan with a fatigue unit of 1,200 accompanied by a guard of

RIFLES AND RIFLEMEN

The rifle was the distinctive American weapon of the Revolutionary War. The notion of grooving the barrel of a long weapon in order to give the ball a stabilizing spin went back to the late fifteenth century and rifled hunting and military arms were common in Europe by the mid-1700s; however, the rifle reached refinement in America. Imported by German and Swiss gunmakers, the concept of the rifle was further developed by frontier gunsmiths. They reduced the caliber to about .45 inches, thus making the weapon more economical and probably more accurate. The stock became more slender and graceful. The result was a lightweight, highly accurate hunting gun, popular throughout the Western regions and the Southern colonies (few New Englanders made or used rifles).

Riflemen wrapped their carefully molded bullets in leather or cloth patches and rammed the projectile tightly down the barrel. The fit was close, and the series of long spiral grooves (the "rifles") spun the bullet on its way out. While the spin gave the bullet a drift, it was still vastly more accurate then any musket could be. The tight fit also produced a more efficient propulsion of the projectile and thus a higher muzzle velocity.

If allowed to stand off and fire at leisure against officers or troops in the open, riflemen were deadly. However, their loading procedure was precise and slow, which put riflemen at risk of a brisk charge by light infantry. And a bayonet could not be affixed to a rifle. A considerable difference of opinion existed about the overall military effectiveness of riflemen, many professionals dismissing them as seldom useful. The British did recruit companies of German mercenary riflemen (jaegers), however, and Maj. Patrick Ferguson organized a rifle unit using a rapid-fire breech-loading rifle of his own invention (ironically, Ferguson died at the hands of American frontier riflemen at King's Mountain).

The first riflemen attached to the Continental Army were recruited in response to a plea from Congress to Pennsylvania, Virginia, and Maryland to raise two rifle companies each. Armed with their accurate weapons and dressed in hunting shirts, the rifle companies under such famous leaders as Daniel Morgan figured prominently in several campaigns during the first years of the war, although they usually had to be supported by regulars. The greatest triumph of the rifle was at King's Mountain in 1780, when Western American riflemen destroyed Loyalist militia in a fight over rugged, heavily wooded terrain that was ideally suited for their slow but accurate weapons.

2,400 (including 400 Pennsylvania riflemen) to fortify Ploughed Hill, which will provide a position commanding the Mystic River and a clear shot at the British force on Bunker Hill. At daylight on the twenty-seventh, two floating batteries and one on Bunker Hill begin a daylong shelling of the Americans. Sullivan has only one cannon, but it sinks one of the floating batteries and incapacitates the other. No battle ensues; the Americans lose four men.

28 August 1775

TICONDEROGA, N.Y. The advance into Canada finally begins. Gen. Richard Montgomery, Schuyler's second in command, responding to the urgency of a second scouting report from John Brown, decides to move without orders from Schuyler. He sends his commander notification of his decision to start the advance and embarks on Lake Champlain with a force of about 1,200 men—headed for Ile aux Noix on the Richelieu River, just south of Fort St. John.

30 August 1775

TICONDEROGA, N.Y. Schuyler, who has been in Albany at a council fire with Indians of the Six Nations and there received Montgomery's notification (of which he approves), returns to the fort. Although ill, he sets out the next day with about 500 men to join Montgomery.

1 September 1775

CAMBRIDGE, MASS. Washington has eight coastal vessels armed and manned by New England seamen—some from Col. John Glover's Essex County (Mass.) regiment—and com-

missions them to interdict British merchant ships resupplying the troops in Boston. First of the ships to be commissioned is the schooner *Hanna*. During the fall, these privateers will capture twenty-three ships, not bothering to discern whether they all carry military supplies, and relieve them of their cargoes, including large quantities of muskets and ammunition.

5 September 1775

ILE AUX NOIX, QUEBEC. Having joined Montgomery, Schuyler orders his force to continue its advance. Leaving behind supplies in order to facilitate their march, the men embark again on the Richelieu River. Going ashore a mile and a half from the fort at St. John's, they attempt a flanking movement and are ambushed by a hundred Indians led by Capt. Tice, a New York Tory. The Americans drive off the Indians but suffer eight dead. During the night, warned by an informant that he cannot take the fort, Schuyler falls back to his encampment at Ile aux Noix.

10 September 1775

ILE AUX NOIX, QUEBEC. Having fortified this island encampment and welcomed 700 reinforcements (he now has a force of 1,700), Schuyler launches a second effort to attack St. John's—this time with 800 men. But his troops, fearful of another ambush, break and run when threatened. Schuyler's second effort fails; once again he retreats to Ile aux Noix.

12 September 1775

CAMBRIDGE, MASS. While Schuyler struggles to take St. John's, Washington—without authorization from Congress—sends Benedict Arnold forth with an expeditionary force of 1,050 men (including Capt. Daniel Morgan's riflemen) that is to make its way by rivers and portages through Maine to the St. Lawrence River and attack Quebec City. The expedition is poorly prepared and sets out with inadequate supplies and only an approximate idea of the route it must follow through a rugged wilderness.

13 September 1775

PHILADELPHIA. Its membership slow to assemble, the Continental Congress convenes with at least a quorum and its president John Hancock present. Georgia is now represented by a full delegation from the entire colony.

16 September 1775

ILE AUX NOIS, QUEBEC. Too ill to continue, Schuyler embarks for Ticonderoga, leaving Montgomery in command. Expected reinforcements begin to arrive, including Seth Warner and 170 Green Mountain Boys, increasing the force to about 2,000.

18 September 1775

ST. JOHN'S, QUEBEC. Having posted 350 men in boats on the Richelieu River to prevent the British ship *Royal Savage* from moving south into Lake Champlain, Gen. Montgomery lands with the remainder of his force at St. John's and begins the siege of the fort.

PHILADELPHIA. Congress sets up the Secret Committee to seek sources of ammunition and powder and to contract for their delivery.

25 September 1775

MONTREAL, QUEBEC. Ethan Allen,

sent by Montgomery to Chambly to organize a group of English Canadian volunteers, becomes overzealous and wants to seize the opportunity to capture Montreal. He meets Maj. Brown, returning with a force of Canadians organized at La Prairie, and they agree to attack Montreal from two directions—Brown to give a signal when he is ready to move. Unfortunately for Allen the signal never comes. Learning of Allen's presence, Sir Guy Carleton, royal governor of the province, sends forth from Montreal a group of soldiers, volunteers, and Indians to the attack. Allen, deserted by many of his English Canadians and now surrounded, has no choice but to surrender. He will narrowly avert execution by the British as a traitor and will be shipped in irons to England for imprisonment. Given the harm his precipitous action inflicts on American strategy, Montgomery may wish Allen's capture had occurred earlier.

30 September 1775

WILLIAMSBURG, VA. The *Constitutional Gazette* reports that the British ministry plans to hire 10,000 mercenary troops from Hanover to be quartered in New England, New York, Pennsylvania, and Virginia. They are to be provided with barracks and all other necessities, plus a fleet of twenty-five ships to back them up. The expenses are to be paid by the colonies. Worse still, perhaps, as the article concludes, since "the Germans are known to be a very prolific people, it is supposed that by the beginning of the year 1800, there will be no less than a million of that nation, including their offspring, within the four New England Provinces alone."

4 October 1775

PHILADELPHIA. The three-man committee—Franklin, Thomas Lynch of South Carolina, and Benjamin Harrison of Virginia—chosen by Congress on 30 September to visit Gen. Washington and inquire into the status of the army and its operations, leaves for Cambridge. They carry Congress' counsel that, if it appears the British can be driven from Boston by the end of December, an attack should be made.

7 October 1775

BRISTOL, R.I. Frustrated over his inability to stop American privateering and by carping from Burgoyne and others about his failure to support the Boston garrison, Vice-Adm. Samuel Graves has conceived a series of punitive raids. The first one strikes at Bristol. Capt. James Wallace, with a small British fleet operating out of Newport Harbor, sends an officer ashore to order that a delegation of residents be sent to his ship to hear his demands or he will fire on the town. Spokesman William Bradford replies that Wallace should himself come ashore. The British ships unleash an hour-and-a-half bombardment. The town then accedes to Wallace's demands and hands over forty sheep as a tribute.

10 October 1775

BOSTON. Gen. William Howe replaces Gen. Thomas Gage as commander of his majesty's forces in Boston. Gage is ostensibly ordered back to London for consultation, although he is actually being sacked; but as no transport is available, he is compelled to remain in despised Boston, an added humiliation.

13 October 1775

PHILADEPHIA. The Continental Congress authorizes the outfitting of two swift ships: an incipient navy.

18 October 1775

FALMOUTH (PORTLAND), ME. In another of Adm. Graves' punitive raids, Capt. Henry Mowat fruitlessly attempts to intimidate the residents of Falmouth and then opens fire. His warships *Canceau* and *Halifax* shell the town for nine hours. Since most of the residents, having taken Mowat's warning at face value, have already fled, no lives are lost. Mowat sends landing parties ashore to torch the town. They meet only sporadic resistance. Most of Falmouth is destroyed: 139 houses and 278 other structures including the church, the courthouse, the town meetinghouse, the library, the wharves, and the warehouses. Americans are outraged by the town's pointless destruction, and Washington sends a detachment of riflemen to help defend Portsmouth, N.H., expected to be the next target. But Graves is content; the raids cease.

British soldiers destroying livestock.

CHAMBLY, QUEBEC. With cannon having been shipped to the site during the night, fifty Americans under Maj. Brown and Col. Timothy Bedel join with 300 Canadians under Col. James Livingston to attack the fort. Their cannonade alone proves adequately persuasive. Maj. Stopford, commander of the fort, surrenders his garrison of ten officers and seventy-eight privates of the Royal Fusiliers. The fort also houses eighty-one women and children. The attackers confiscate sizable stores of arms, powder, and ammunition and 138 barrels of edibles.

19 October 1775

NEW YORK CITY. Receiving word that the Continental Congress has recommended to the various provincial congresses that they arrest "all persons who might endanger the liberties of Americans" and that plans to arrest him are in process, Gov. William Tryon discreetly takes refuge aboard HMS *Duchess of Gordon* in New York harbor. He will make the warship his headquarters for nearly a year.

24–25 October 1775

HAMPTON, VA. Gov. Dunmore heats up the conflict with the rebels by sending a naval unit to destroy Norfolk. Six tenders commanded by Capt. Squire sail into Hampton Creek on the twenty-fourth, begin bombarding the town, and embark landing parties to torch the place. Riflemen drive them off. One hundred rebel militia under Col. William Woodford move into the town at dawn on the twenty-fifth to defend against a second attack. These marksmen pick off Squire's sailors on deck and in the riggings, forcing a disorderly withdrawal. Two sloops run aground and are captured. The British force suffers several deaths; the rebels not a single casualty.

26 October 1775

ST. JOHN'S, QUEBEC. A regiment of 335 Connecticut troops (the command of Gen. David Wooster) and 225 4th New York troops under Maj. Barnabas Tuthill arrive to reinforce the American siege.

27 October 1775

CAMBRIDGE, MASS. Having discovered Surgeon General Benjamin Church's treason in September—he had actually sold out to Gen. Gage many years before—the army now puts him on trial. His treachery has been exposed when Nathanael Greene intercepts an encoded letter (entrusted to a whore for delivery) and brings it to the attention of Washington. The prostitute reveals the letter's source; when confronted by Washington, Church contends he sent it to his brother in Boston. However, when deciphered by two cryptologists, the letter is clearly an intelligence report. Since the Articles of War call for a punishment of cashiering only, Church gets off lightly. He is expelled from Massachusetts and imprisoned. Eventually he is allowed to sail for the West Indies, but the ship disappears en route.

30 October 1775

PHILADELPHIA. Congress appoints a committee of seven members—cumbersomely designated "the committee for fitting out armed vessels" but soon to be the Naval Committee—and authorizes its members to procure and outfit two more ships. The American navy doubles in size.

MONTREAL. Gen. Carleton, hoping to rescue St. John's with a force of about 800—comprised of elements of Lt. Col. Allan McLean's Royal Highland Emigrants, some Caughnawaga Indians, and Royal Fusiliers—attempts to cross the St. Lawrence to Longeuil. But Green Mountain Boys and troops from the 2nd New York under Seth Warner occupy the opposite bank, and their fusilade forces Carleton's boats to turn back. The siege of St. John's continues.

2 November 1775

ST. JOHN'S, QUEBEC. Maj. Charles Preston, who has steadfastly resisted the American siege, concedes that no help will come from Gen. Carleton and his position is untenable, especially since Montgomery has in place overlooking the fort a battery whose shelling wreaks devastation. In addition, Montgomery's troops have finally managed to destroy the *Royal Savage,* so St. John's has no protection from the water. The major capitulates. He has held off the Americans for fifty-five days, however, and thus has bought valuable time for the defense of Canada, forestalling the Americans' thrust toward Montreal into the winter months. Among Montgomery's prisoners is a young officer of the 7th Royal Fusiliers, Maj. John André. Montgomery magnanimously permits the Canadians to return to their homes and the British regulars to head for ports of embarkation.

5 November 1775

ST. JOHN'S, QUEBEC. Montgomery and his troops begin the march to Montreal, slogging through mud under a cold rain.

PHILADELPHIA. Congress appoints Esek Hopkins commander-in-chief of the newly created navy assembling at Philadelphia. A Rhode Islander, Hop-

kins has been a merchant captain and also a privateer in the French and Indian War. Brother of Stephen Hopkins, chairman of the original Naval Committee, he also has good connections. His son John is given command of the brig *Cabot,* while Dudley Saltonstall is assigned the *Alfred.* The two other ships in the new fleet are *Columbus* and *Andrea Doria.* (By the end of the year the navy will have eight ships.) Among Hopkins' lieutenants is John Paul Jones.

7 November 1775

NORFOLK, VA. Lord Dunmore proclaims martial law in Virginia. He appeals to all loyal subjects to support the royal government "or be looked upon as traitors," and he offers freedom to indentured servants and to slaves on plantations owned by rebels if the slaves will join British forces and enter the fight against their masters. The latter tactic boomerangs, as the threat of freed and armed black slaves triggers universal fear among whites and promotes their solid opposition to the governor. The anxiety of whites will increase as many slaves accept Dunmore's offer.

PROVIDENCE, R.I. The General Assembly of Rhode Island deposes Gov. Joseph Wanton.

9 November 1775

QUEBEC. Having sailed out of Newburyport, Mass., on 19 September for the mouth of the Kennebec River in Maine and from there proceeded by river and overland portages, Benedict Arnold and the remnant of his force finally reach the St. Lawrence River. Arnold had estimated their trek would require twenty days; it takes forty-five. His men have traversed 350 miles, nearly twice the distance he anticipated. The expedition has been an enormous ordeal. The men have transported thousands of pounds of ammunition, food, boats, and other necessities; slept in rain-soaked, frozen clothes; floundered through menacing bogs; scaled mountains and precipices; suffered dysentery and other maladies; endured tempestuous storms; battled raging waters; and survived near-starvation. They emerge from the Maine forest onto the shore of the river in tattered clothes, their bodies battered and emaciated, exhausted. Only 675 of is original force of more than 1,000 remain; the others had turned back or succumbed to illness or death.

BOSTON. About 500 British regulars cross from Charlestown Point to Lechmere's Point, intending to confiscate sheep and cattle from the Phipps farm. They seize a drunken sentry, but other sentries fire on them and spread the alarm. Washington orders Pennsylvania riflemen commanded by Col. William Thompson to the attack. The British withdraw with a prize capture of ten cows. The Americans suffer two wounded.

PHILADELPHIA. Congress receives word that George III has rejected the Olive Branch Petition and has also declared the colonies in a state of rebellion. Members authorize the creation of two battalions of Marines.

11–12 November 1775

CHARLESTON, S.C. In Charleston Harbor, Capt. Simon Tuft's ship *Defence*, attempting to blockade Hog Island Creek, accosts two British ships, HMS *Tamer* and HMS *Cherokee*. Tufts succeeds in sinking four hulks towed to the site to effect the blockade. No casualties result from the confrontation.

13 November 1775

MONTREAL. Perceiving himself in an indefensible position with only 150 regulars and some militia, Gen. Carleton has abandoned the defense of Montreal two days earlier, sailing off with his troops and many of his supplies under American fire. Montgomery now sends a deputation to the residents of Montreal, and they surrender. Montgomery occupies the city while he awaits news from Arnold, promising to respect the residents' religion and to pay fair prices for whatever supplies his troops need. Upriver at Sorel the Americans attack Carleton's flotilla, causing the surrender of two armed vessels and the *Gaspee* and capturing the troops who had garrisoned Montreal. Carleton himself manages to escape by rowboat to make his way to Quebec.

QUEBEC. Having procured over twenty birch-bark canoes and a dozen dugouts to transport his troops across the mile-wide St. Lawrence, Arnold crosses the river under cover of intense darkness and lands near Quebec without threat from the many British patrol boats or the eight armed vessels at anchor in the city's harbor.

14 November 1775

KEMP'S LANDING, VA. Learning that about 150 militiamen are marching to join forces with other militia under Col. William Woodford, Lord Dunmore leads some 350 men— regulars, Loyalists, sailors, and runaway slaves—from Norfolk to head them off. Dunmore's larger force succeeds in dispersing the Americans, who suffer a few dead and wounded. An account in the *New York Gazette and Weekly Mercury* declares the public will be incensed "on finding Lord Dunmore has taken into his service the very scum of the country, to assist him in his diabolical schemes."

15 November 1775

QUEBEC. Arnold's force occupies the Plains of Abraham, site of the victory in 1759 that secured Canada for the British and cost the lives of generals Wolfe and Montcalm. Arnold tries unsuccessfully to bluff the garrison into surrender by parading his troops. The defenders, numbering about 1,200 British and French-Canadian militia with some marines and sailors from the ships in the harbor, shout jeers from the city's walls. Arnold believes that cannons, which he lacks, and 2,000 men will be needed for the assault to succeed.

19 November 1775

QUEBEC. Arnold learns that Lt. Col. Allan McLean, who had arrived in Quebec on the thirteenth with eighty of his Royal Highland Emigrants, plans to assault the Americans with a force of 800 men. Arnold orders a quick march during the night to Point aux Trembles, twenty miles west of the city. Here he will wait and recuperate for two weeks, allowing McLean time to continue preparing a defense. Meanwhile, Carleton arrives from Montreal to assume command of the British.

NINETY-SIX, S.C. The scene during the previous September of a confrontation between patriot and Loyalist

forces, Ninety-Six becomes the site of a new skirmish. About 1,800 Loyalists attack the fort manned by about 600 patriots under Maj. Andrew Williamson. After two days of shooting and modest bloodshed they call a truce.

25 November 1775

PHILADELPHIA. The Continental Congress declares British ships subject to capture and establishes admiralty courts to assign prizes and prize money for their captors.

28 November 1775

PHILADELPHIA. Congress adopts "Rules for the Regulation of the Navy of the United Colonies," prepared by the Naval Committee and largely the work of John Adams.

29 November 1775

PHILADELPHIA. Congress sets up a five-man committee "for the sole purpose of corresponding with our friends in Great Britain, Ireland, and other parts of the world," giving the members leeway to use their own initiative but to reveal their correspondence to Congress when so directed. Congress also votes to pay for any agents the committee might see fit to hire. The members are Benjamin Harrison, Franklin, John Jay, Thomas Johnson, and John Dickinson. They will dub themselves the Committee of Secret Correspondence and will function as a kind of elementary foreign service.

BOSTON. In Boston Harbor the American schooner *Lee*, commanded by Capt. John Manley, chases and captures the *Nancy*, a 250-ton British ordnance brig. Washington is greatly pleased because the booty seized by Manley includes 2,000 muskets with bayonets, scabbards, ramrods, thirty-one tons of musket shot, a 2,700-pound mortar, and other valuable military supplies.

2 December 1775

POINTE AUX TREMBLES, QUEBEC. Montgomery, having learned two weeks earlier of Arnold's arrival at Quebec, has floated down the St. Lawrence to join him. He brings fresh clothes (captured at Montreal) for Arnold's men, artillery, ammunition, provisions, and 300 troops for the assault force, now to be under his command. Arnold's troops occupy a position to the north of Quebec City; Montgomery's force is to the west on the Plains of Abraham. The two commanders face a tough decision: the winter conditions are bitter; their troops' enlistments expire at year's end; and the coming of spring weather will free the St. Lawrence for British ships to bring reinforcements—can they really afford to lay siege to Quebec or must they attack?

6 December 1775

PHILADELPHIA. The Continental Congress adopts an official reply to George III's Proclamation of Rebellion issued on 23 August. The reply denies the colonies are in a state of rebellion, stresses that their conduct has evidenced allegiance to the crown, but declares opposition to royal or parliamentary "exercise of unconstitutional powers." It makes no threat of independence.

QUIBBLETOWN, N.J. A local cooper, Thomas Randolph, who has publicly opposed rebellion and the proceedings of the Continental Congress and the provincial congress, is "stripped naked, well coated with tar and feathers, and carried in a wagon publicly around town." He quickly repents his offense and is released within a half-hour to return home. "The whole," reports the *New York Journal*, "was conducted with that regularity and decorum that ought to be observed in all public punishments."

NEW YORK CITY. Gov. Tryon has the public records seized and taken aboard HMS *Duchess of Gordon* for safe-keeping.

8 December 1775

QUEBEC. Montgomery and Arnold begin the siege of Quebec. Montgomery realizes that a siege will not succeed, given his difficulties with weather, expiring enlistments, and obtaining supplies; but Carleton obdurately rejects his calls for surrender.

9 December 1775

GREAT BRIDGE, VA. The Virginia Council of Safety hopes to end Gov. Dunmore's raid on coastal towns and plantations by driving him from Norfolk. The Council orders Col. William Woodford to station 1,000 militiamen at the southern end of the Great Bridge, a causeway spanning a swampy part of the Elizabeth River about ten miles from Norfolk. Dunmore with his motley troops—about 200 regulars, some Loyalists and marines, and the "Loyal Ethiopians," as he calls his recruited runaway black slaves—occupies the other end. Dunmore's regulars attack but, bottlenecked on the causeway, they present easy targets. The patriots inflict sixty casualties in half an hour, effectively neutralizing Dunmore's "army" while receiving only a single hand wound among their own ranks. With the militiamen in pursuit, Dunmore retreats to Norfolk, where he evacuates as many Tories as possible to ships in the harbor before abandoning the town to the rebels.

14 December 1775

PHILADELPHIA. The Continental Congress establishes the Marine Committee, with one member from each of the colonies, as a successor to the Naval Committee with the responsibility to fulfill the outfitting and organizing of the navy and direct its operations.

22 December 1775

LONDON. Parliament approves the American Prohibitory Act, ordering cessation of all trade with the colonies. Any ships involved in commerce with the colonies are subject to impoundment by the Royal Navy.

PHILADELPHIA. The Naval Committee submits to Congress for approval the names of the officers for the four ships constituting the navy, with Esek Hopkins as commander-in-chief.

CANE BREAK (REEDY RIVER), S.C. Following the truce that resulted from the skirmish at Ninety-Six, about 4,000 rebel militia and regulars—commanded by colonels Richard Richardson, William Thompson, Thomas Polk, and Alex Martin—have been successful in dispersing Loyalist opposition. They finish the job during a skirmish that routs the last of the resisters, commanded by William Cunningham.

28 December 1775

PHILADELPHIA. A French agent, Ar-chard de Bonvouloir, appears as a traveler in the city. Although disclaiming any official capacity with the French government, he assures the Committee of Secret Correspondence that his government sympathizes with the colonies and will discreetly overlook their efforts to obtain supplies in France.

31 December 1775

QUEBEC. After a false start on 29 December, Montgomery launches the attack on the city in a raging blizzard. Since his men's enlistments expire the following day he has little choice left. He has targeted the Lower Town, approaching it from the south along the river. Rockets signal the advance at 4:00 A.M. but also alert Carleton, giving him time to rouse his garrison for battle. Montgomery's troops flounder through snowdrifts and ice mounds thrown ashore by the river. Arnold's force attacks from the north, blinded by the snow, and enter the city by the Palace Gate.

Having lost one cannon and discovering his second to be unusable, Arnold lacks any possibility of a softening-up salvo and so orders his men to storm the British barricades. A ricocheting bullet severely wounds Arnold in the leg, and two men carry him rearward for care. Daniel Morgan assumes command. He leads an abortive assault, taking bullets through his cap and beard. Morgan's second assault succeeds, opening the way into the Lower Town. His men reassemble and attempt to overwhelm yet another barricade but are driven back. They hesitate, hoping for Montgomery's force to join them.

But Carleton has thwarted Montgomery's advance, using the Bunker

Hill tactic of delayed fire, and Montgomery himself lies dead with a bullet in his brain. His surviving troops retreat, some of them reaching safety across the frozen St. Lawrence but many being forced to surrender. Carleton sends forth a sortie that captures Arnold's redoubt at St. Roche. Overall, Carleton captures 426 men from the American force, reducing Arnold's surviving command to only 600. The Americans have sixty dead and wounded, the British five dead and thirteen wounded. The Battle of Quebec goes to the British.

⋆ 1776 ⋆

The war spreads and intensifies during this momentous year. The fledgling Continental Army surrounding British-held Boston is strengthened in February by the guns captured at Fort Ticonderoga, which have been brought overland by Henry Knox. In early March the Americans seize the heights overlooking the city, mount the guns, and make the British position intolerable. The British force evacuates by sea.

Meanwhile, to the south a Loyalist force is soundly defeated at Moore's Creek, North Carolina, and the North Carolina convention gives its delegates the power to vote for independence.

In April Washington moves the American army to New York, hoping to forestall and defeat the British there. Arnold begins his retreat from Canada to Lake Champlain, where he fights a running series of battles. On the international scene, the French government begins secret shipments of munitions to the revolutionary colonists. American naval squadrons raid the British Bahamas, but the British position a fleet and expeditionary force off Charleston, South Carolina.

The movement in Congress for independence gathers force during the spring and early summer. In May Congress advises the "states" to set up new governments. On 7 June Richard Lee of Virginia introduces a resolution for independence to Congress, which appoints a committee to draft a Declaration of Independence a few days later. Thomas Jefferson presents a draft declaration to Congress on 28 June, the same day the British fleet sails into New York Harbor and the British southern forces are repulsed at Sullivan's Island off Charleston.

The Continental Congress gives preliminary approval to the Declaration of Independence on 2 July and accepts the final draft on 4 July, when it is signed by presiding officer John Hancock. A week later, draft Articles of Confederation are presented to Congress.

A strongly reinforced British army attacks in New York and defeats Washington at Long Island in late August, forcing him to withdraw. Ensuing defeats, including White Plains, during September and October push the Americans out of New York and into a retreat through New Jersey. The war on the battlefield goes badly for the American cause by the last months of the year, with the British in control of New York and most of New Jersey. Washington's defeated army seems to be licking its wounds in Pennsylvania.

At Christmas, however, Washington in a daring move ferries his men across the Delaware River at night and attacks the Hessian forces holding Trenton, New Jersey. His victory is complete and the year ends on a high note.

---

1 January 1776
CAMBRIDGE. Washington issues General Orders opening with the words "This day giving commencement to the new army, which, in every point of View, is Continental, The General flatters himself, that a laudable Spirit of emulation will now take place and pervade the whole of it." Then for the first time is "hoisted the union flag in compliment to the United Colonies." Its field contains thirteen alternating red and white stripes.

NORFOLK. His fleet anchored offshore, Lord Dunmore demands provisions from the town, but the Norfolk rebels refuse. Dunmore orders a cannonade of the town lasting into the night and sends men ashore to torch houses and warehouses along the shore. Rebels retaliate by setting fire to homes of prominent local Tories.

MONTREAL. Following the death of Gen. Montgomery, Maj. Gen. David Wooster assumes command of the Continental Army in Canada.

2 January 1776
NORFOLK. Flames sweep the town in a fifty-hour conflagration. Three non-combatants die; seven are wounded. A writer editorializes in the *Virginia Gazette*, "They have destroyed one of the first towns in America, and the only one (except two or three) in Virginia, which carried on anything like a trade.... They have done their worst, and ... to no other purpose than to give the world specimens of British cruelty and American fortitude, unless it be to force us to lay aside that childish fondness for Britain, and that foolish, tame dependence on her. We had borne so long with the oppressions of an ungenerous restriction of our trade ... that our patience and moderation served but to encourage them to proceed to greater lengths. To greater lengths they have proceeded, as far as the proudest tyrant's lust of despotism, stimulated by cruelty, a rancorous malice, and an infernal spirit of revenge, could hurry them. How sunk is Britain!" The Council of Safety orders the town razed to render it useless to both Dunmore and the patriots.

5 January 1776
PORTSMOUTH. New Hampshire becomes the first colony to establish an independent government, adopting a constitution that designates governance by a president and a General Court comprised of a Senate and a House of Representatives.

6 January 1776
NEW YORK. Alexander Hamilton

founds the Provincial Company of Artillery of the Colony of New York. A native of St. Croix, Hamilton had entered King's College in New York City in 1773 but gave up his studies to join the revolutionary cause.

BOSTON. Gen. William Howe, whose relations with Lt. Gen. Sir Henry Clinton are rather strained, orders Clinton to sail for Cape Fear, N.C., where he is to command naval and military forces in an attack on Charleston. Clinton is to rendezvous at Cape Fear with a fleet under the command of Commodore Sir Peter Parker that sails from Cork, Ireland, carrying regiments under Charles, Lord Cornwallis. Howe's orders to Clinton are to secure British authority in Virginia, Georgia, and the Carolinas; place Loyalists in charge of these colonies; and return as soon as possible to Boston.

8 January 1776

CHARLESTOWN. A performance of Gen. John Burgoyne's farce *The Blockade of Boston* is ironically interrupted by the announcement that rebel troops are conducting a raid. The audience mistakenly thinks the announcement, made by an actor dressed in the uniform of a rebel sergeant, marks the opening of the play. The raid, led by Maj. Thomas Knowlton, a veteran of Bunker Hill, succeeds in capturing five prisoners and burning eight houses. Knowlton's force suffers no casualties.

9 January 1776

PHILADELPHIA. Thomas Paine's *Common Sense* is published. A child of poverty, Paine is self-educated: he met Benjamin Franklin in London and arrived in Philadelphia at the end of 1774 with letters of introduction from Franklin. Of the conflict between Britain and America, Paine asserts simply: "Arms, as the last resource, must decide the contest; the appeal was the choice of the king, and the continent has accepted the challenge." Reconciliation, Paine contends, has become "a fallacious dream," a chimera for the deluded, as the king's tyranny mandates rebellion; the struggle now is for independence. And Paine defines the significance of this necessary struggle: "The sun never shone on a cause of greater worth. 'Tis not the affair of a city, a county, a province, or a kingdom but of a continent—of at least one-eighth part of the habitable globe. 'Tis not the concern of a day, a year, or an age; posterity are virtually involved in the contest and will be more or less affected even to the end of time by the proceedings now." Paine advocates an independent, continental republic under a constitution that provides for a president and a Congress, arguing "A government of our own is our natural right." And his closing appeal evokes the international cause of freedom:

Thomas Paine, author of the famous pamphlet, Common Sense.

"O! ye that love mankind! Ye that dare oppose, not only tyranny but the tyrant, stand forth! Every spot of the Old World is overrun with oppression. Freedom has been haunted round the globe. . . . O! receive the fugitive, and prepare in time an asylum for mankind."

10 January 1776

CAPE FEAR, N.C. Royal Governor Josiah Martin, still confident of widespread support in North Carolina yet still cautiously stationed aboard an offshore sloop—now HMS *Scorpion*—issues an appeal to all Loyalists to help him quash the rebellion in the colony instigated by "the base and insidious artifice of certain traitorous, wicked and designing men," whose lives and property he promises will be forfeit. Martin confidently expects, as he had earlier informed Gen. Gage and the government in London, that 20,000 Loyalists will take up arms, with strong support coming especially from Scottish Highlanders. He urges these potential enlistees to congregate by 15 February near Brunswick, where they can be ready to join in a British offensive in the South.

11 January 1776

ANNAPOLIS. The Maryland Convention joins the assemblies of Pennsylvania, New Jersey, and Delaware in advocating moderation and lack of support for independence, instructing the colony's delegates to the Continental Congress to support efforts at reconciliation with England. The delegates are to respond favorably to any proposals from crown or Parliament that may foster reconciliation, "taking care to secure the Colonies against the exercise of the right assumed by Parliament, to tax them, and to alter and change their Charters, Constitutions, and internal polity, without their consent."

12 January 1776

RHODE ISLAND. British forces, having taken possession of the colony in early December without opposition, raid Prudence Island.

17 January 1776

JOHNSTOWN, N.Y. Sir John Johnson, noted Loyalist and son of the deceased former Superintendent of Indian Affairs Sir William Johnson, is forced to make terms with Gen. Philip Schuyler. Johnson has accumulated munitions at his estate, Johnson Hall, and has mustered 200 Loyalist Highlanders and a force of Mohawk Indians there, lending credence to reports that he represents a danger to the patriots in the area. Dispatching a force of 3,000 militia to the environs of Johnson Hall, Schuyler obliges Johnson to disarm his followers, surrender the armaments, and submit to imprisonment leading to parole under the orders of Congress. Thus Tory resistance in the Albany area is effectively terminated.

19 January 1776

DELAWARE. Organized under Col. John Haslet, a native of Ireland, the Delaware Continentals now form this colony's single regiment for the Revolution. Being equipped with recently imported English muskets, they are among the few American troops to have bayonets.

PHILADELPHIA. Congress, responding to a letter from Gen. Schuyler carried by Edward Antil, votes to

LOYALISTS

No one knows the actual number of Americans who remained loyal to the crown during the Revolution, but it must have been high—the traditional estimate, from the lips of John Adams, was that roughly one-third of the population were loyal in some degree, only one-third were active patriots, and one-third just wanted to be left alone. Unquestionably, however, many Loyalists emigrated during and after the war to avoid living in an independent United States. Thousands of Loyalists sat out the war in British-held territories, and when the time came for the British to leave in 1783, the Loyalists went too. For example, at least 7,000 evacuated from New York City when the British withdrew. Some historians estimate that as many as 100,000 left in 1783 alone.

During the earliest days of the Revolution, Loyalists were slow to organize, and many must have hoped their rebellious neighbors would come to their senses. With the beginning of the war, however, and especially after the Declaration of Independence, the issue could not long be avoided. With the passing of time and more and more fighting, conflict, and bitterness, Loyalists found it impossible to remain on the sidelines. Many patriot state governments eventually passed laws barring Loyalists from public life and confiscating their property. Tens of thousands of Loyalists fought for the British as either militia or in orga-

nized "loyal American" units—many of them hard, effective fighters. Historians have noted that New York state probably supplied more troops to the British side than it did recruits for George Washington. In the South, Loyalists presented a military threat until the last days of the war.

Many motives prompted Loyalism. The most prominent Loyalists —New Jersey governor William Franklin, for example (Benjamin Franklin's illegitimate son)—stood to lose office, power, and influence with a revolution. Others simply did not agree that the colonies had the right to separate from the mother country and the throne over such flimsy issues as rights and taxation. And many Loyalists were reacting to personal feuds and local antagonisms—if your family's enemies were patriots, you might be a Loyalist.

After the war, the British government set up a claims commission to award compensation to Loyalists who suffered for the royal cause. More than 5,000 claims were submitted, and more than three million pounds were paid in compensation.

During recent years there has been a strong upsurge of interest in tracing the history of Loyalists and a more sympathetic view—especially toward Loyalists of principle, who resisted the Revolution out of conviction. For most of the more than 200 years since the Revolution, however, Americans have regarded Loyalists as Tory scum.

reinforce the army in Canada. Antil, who was sent from Quebec by Gen. Arnold, has unsuccessfully sought reinforcements from Montreal (held by Maj. Gen. David Wooster), Chambly, St. John's, and finally Albany, where Schuyler is in command. Congress requests New Hampshire, Connecticut, New York, Pennsylvania, and New Jersey to send troops to reinforce Arnold's forces as soon as possible. Congress also authorizes Washington to send one of his battalions at Cambridge and Moses Hazen to raise a regiment in Canada, with Antil to serve as lieutenant colonel.

20 January 1776

BOSTON. Gen. Clinton sails with two companies of light infantry for the rendezvous at Cape Fear, N.C., with the Loyalists enlisted by Gov. Martin and the naval squadron under Commodore Parker including the contingent of troops commanded by Lord Cornwallis. They plan an initial swift incursion into the Carolinas and expect to solidify the presumed Tory support there, thus improving the British position through minimal effort while also securing a base for reconquering the South.

22–23 January 1776

SANDY HOOK, N.Y. The Committee of Safety of Elizabethtown, N.J., receives word that a British supply ship is off the coast and authorizes an effort to capture it. Volunteers in four small craft sight HMS *Blue Mountain Valley* about forty miles out from Sandy Hook. Mistaken as fishermen, the patriots are allowed alongside the ship, capturing it in a surprise attack.

24 January 1776

CAMBRIDGE, MASS. Col. Henry Knox, Washington's expert on artillery, arrives with the guns captured at Fort Ticonderoga. Gen. Washington sent him in November to transport the artillery so that the weapons could be used in the siege of Boston. Having the benefit of neither wagons nor roads, Knox and his men have transported forty-four cannon, fourteen mortars, and one howitzer about 300 miles— first on flat-bottomed scows across Lake George; then by specially constructed sleds across snow and ice, hills, and frozen lakes; and finally in trains pulled by horses and oxen.

Colonel General Henry Knox, one of Washington's commanders. He was later promoted to general.

PHILADELPHIA. Responding to the king's charges that the colonies are seeking independence and also to a like charge by royal governor William Franklin of New Jersey, Congress appoints a committee headed by James Wilson of Pennsylvania to draft a statement that will help prepare the

American public for the prospect of independence from Britain. (Other members of the committee are Robert Alexander of Maryland, James Duane of New York, William Hooper of North Carolina, and John Dickinson of Pennsylvania.) At the same time Congress, having received news of the Canadian expedition's failure the week before, begins seriously considering establishment of a war office.

31 January 1776

CAMBRIDGE, MASS. Washington writes to Joseph Reed, his erstwhile military secretary now seated in Congress, praising "the sound doctrine and unanswerable reasoning" of Paine's *Common Sense*.

4 February 1776

NEW YORK. Maj. Gen. Charles Lee, having been withdrawn from the siege of Boston and sent into Connecticut to enlist volunteers for the defense of New York City, arrives in the city; he has been delayed by an attack of gout.

SANDY HOOK, N.Y. Lt. Gen. Sir Henry Clinton, under Gen. Howe's orders to command the Charleston expedition, arrives off Sandy Hook en route from Boston to Cape Fear, N.C. Uncertain of Clinton's intentions and objective, New Yorkers react with some panic.

6 February 1776

NORFOLK. The militia forces, commanded by Col. Robert Howe of North Carolina, that resisted Gov. Dunmore now abandon the town. They have removed the inhabitants to safety; have destroyed the entrenchments Dunmore's forces built before returning to their ships; and have burned all the remaining houses. Formerly a thriving commercial center of 6,000 inhabitants, Norfolk is now totally desolate.

7 February 1776

NEW YORK. Col. William Alexander, who prefers being known as Lord Stirling, arrives in the city with 1,000 troops from New Jersey.

13 February 1776

PHILADELPHIA. James Wilson's laborious, 6,000-word address designed to prepare the American public for independence is finished. Its contents straddle the issue of independence, but its final words are strongly suggestive: "That the colonies may continue connected, as they have been, with Britain is our second wish. Our first is—*That America may be free.*" Wilson shows the address to some colleagues in the Congress besides his fellow committee members who have helped draft it; but by this time the public reception of Tom Paine's *Common Sense* has obviated the need for such a statement, and so Wilson's address is tabled and not published.

16 February 1776

CAMBRIDGE, MASS. Washington, restive from weeks of idleness and inspired to bold action by the coming of exceptionally cold temperatures, holds a council of war and proposes taking advantage of the ice formed on Back Bay to send troops across the bay for a surprise attack against the British in Boston. He estimates the British force at 5,000 and believes his assembled 16,000 militia and Continentals have a great chance of success, especially since Knox has hauled into camp some fifty pieces of the artillery from Fort Ticonderoga. The general even believes that an attack now, before the British receive reinforcements, "might put a final end to the war." Washington's officers oppose the proposal, arguing that their commander is underestimating the British strength while overestimating his own troops' capability and that there is insufficient powder for an artillery barrage by the guns Knox is assembling. They propose instead that, while more powder is being acquired, the army seize a site that affords the advantages of being readily fortified and drawing the British out of the city for an attack. Disappointed, Washington nevertheless pursues his officers' proposal. He will decide to have Knox's artillery emplaced on the heretofore unoccupied Dorchester Heights (for some reason the British have left the site unfortified and themselves therefore vulnerable) and have entrenchments built for defending this position, from which the artillery can bombard both Boston and the harbor.

17 February 1776

PHILADELPHIA. Esek Hopkins of Rhode Island, brother of congressional delegate Stephen Hopkins (member of the first naval committee) and commander of the infant Continental navy, embarks the American fleet headed for open waters through the Delaware Bay. His squadron includes the *Alfred*, the *Columbus*, the *Andrea Doria*, the *Cabot*, the *Providence*, the *Hornet*, and the *Wasp*. Hopkins' orders from Congress are to drive Dunmore's fleet from the Cheasapeake and other British ships from the coast of the Carolinas and to chase the Royal Navy from the waters of Rhode Island—a formidable task, considering that his total of eight ships mount only 110 guns against 2,000 guns mounted in seventy-eight British ships. Taking advantage of a clause in

his orders that gives him discretion to use his own judgment about the best course of action, Hopkins sets sail for Nassau.

Congress orders Maj. Gen. Charles Lee to replace Gen. Schuyler as commander of the Northern Department. Lee is in New York City, making preparations for its defense.

27 February 1776

MOORE'S CREEK BRIDGE, N.C. Fifteen hundred Highlanders and others loyal to the crown have responded to Gov. Martin's call and, led by Col. Donald McLeod, are moving toward the coast for the designated rendezvous at Brunswick with Clinton and Parker. North Carolina militia under Col. James Moore, assisted by colonels Alexander Lillington, John Ashe, and Richard Caswell, meanwhile entrench themselves at Moore's Creek Bridge, which the Highlanders must cross on their way to the coast. As at the Great Bridge battle, the patriots have removed planks from the bridge floor and have massed on the east bank of the stream a thousand strong. To the sound of bagpipes and drums McLeod leads his force—in the vanguard eighty Scots armed with rifles, broadswords, and dirks—onto the bridge, where they are shot up in a fusillade from the patriots. Fifty Loyalists, McLeod reportedly among them, fall dead or wounded. The others flee, but half are taken prisoner. The patriots suffer only one man dead and one wounded. This patriot victory shatters the strength of the Tories in North Carolina.

29 February 1776

PHILADELPHIA. For the third time this month, while discussing the issue of commercial trading congressional delegates launch into debate on whether it is feasible or proper to enter into trade alliances with other nations, principally Spain and France. The debate again provokes the issue of independence. Nothing is resolved.

1 March 1776

PHILADELPHIA. Giving in to pressure exerted by New York delegates in favor of Gen. Philip Schuyler, Congress countermands its order of 17 February and restores Schuyler to command of the Northern Department, awarding Maj. Gen. Charles Lee command of the Southern Department instead.

2 March 1776

CAMBRIDGE, MASS. In order to distract the attention of the British forces in Boston so that they will not anticipate the occupation of Dorchester Heights, American artillery carry out a heavy nighttime bombardment from Lechmere Point, Cobble Hill, and Roxbury.

3 March 1776

PHILADELPHIA. The secret correspondence committee of the Continental Congress decides to send an agent to France for the dual purposes of trying to procure supplies for the war effort and feeling out the attitudes of Charles, comte de Vergennes, the French foreign minister, toward the American cause. For this task they commission Silas Deane, former delegate to the Congress from Connecticut.

3–4 March 1776

NASSAU, THE BAHAMAS. The American navy's first planned operation results in the capture of New Providence and substantial supplies of munitions as plunder. Esek Hopkins' fleet of eight ships sails into this port town of Nassau Island, where 200 members of the new marine corps under Samuel Nicholas comprise the major part of the landing party that occupies the town and its two forts—Fort Nassau being the principal fort on the island. This is the marines' first taste of "combat," although they actually encounter no resistance. They confiscate seventy-one cannons and twenty-four casks of powder.

4 March 1776

DORCHESTER HEIGHTS, MASS. Under cover of a third night of artillery bombardments Gen. John Thomas secretly occupies Dorchester Heights with a force of 2,000 men and digs in. The *Pennsylvania Journal* reports that the American artillery "played incessantly. The shot and shells were heard to make a great crashing in the town. . . . The Regulars returned the fire from their batteries at West Boston, and from their lines on the Neck, very vigorously. . . . The grand object of the Americans was to draw off the attention of the British from Dorchester Heights, until they could take possession of that position. . . . This was accomplished. . . ." Three hundred sixty oxcarts haul the materials for building the entrenchments; they and the troops are concealed during their traverses by fog and by hay bales scattered along Dorchester Neck. Surmounting the heights are Nook's Hill and Castle William. Under bright moonlight the men work throughout the night—supplanted by a relief party at 3:00 A.M.—digging trenches, strengthening breastworks, erecting barricades at these two sites. Five companies of riflemen and companies of other troops march over to man these defensive positions, and by daybreak the fortification and occupation are complete. After seeing the fortifications, Archibald Robertson, a British engineer, describes them in his diary as "A most astonishing night's work [that] must have employ'd from 15 to 20,000 men."

CAMBRIDGE, MASS. Gen. Washington expects a British attack on Dorchester Heights since 5 March is the anniversary of the Boston Massacre, and he plans to send troops to Boston for a counterattack. In Boston Gen. Howe, in fact, begins to plan the attack immediately, although the British reportedly fear a re-enactment of the horror they experienced at the Battle of Bunker Hill. Howe responds to the urgency of the situation pressed by Rear Adm. Molyneux Shuldham, now in charge of the fleet in Boston Harbor, who argues that both his ships and the British troops in the city are imperiled by the guns on Dorchester Heights. The alternatives, Shuldham says, are immediate attack or rapid evacuation of the harbor and the city. Howe orders 2,200 men to disembark from the Long Wharf for a night attack on Castle William from the extremity of the Dorchester peninsula while two other regiments, grenadiers, and light infantry, ferried across on flatboats, attack from the north. They are ordered to use bayonets only. If they succeed, they are to attack the Americans at Roxbury. Before the plan can be carried out a violent storm with high winds and heavy squalls intervenes, preventing launching of the boats; in addition, unknown to his men, Gen. Howe changes his mind

and opts for evacuation at the recommendation of a council of war.

5 March 1776

BOSTON. Archibald Robertson tries to see Gen. Howe to advise him that the Dorchester Heights defenses are impregnable and an attack would result in disaster; an officer informs him that Howe has decided on evacuation. Preparations will begin immediately.

7 March 1776

SAVANNAH, GA. Georgia patriots take control of Hutchinson's Island, located opposite the town across the Savannah River. From here they threaten the jurisdiction of Gov. Sir James Wright.

9 March 1776

BOSTON. While the British prepare to leave, the Americans continue to bolster their fortification of Dorchester Heights, stationing troops on Nook's Hill. When the British artillery bombards this position the Americans respond in kind. Five Americans are killed, and the Continentals withdraw from the hill.

CHARITON CREEK, VA. The Maryland ship *Defence* and Maryland militiamen attack and drive off HMS *Otter*, one of the ships in Dunmore's "navy," in Chesapeake Bay.

12 March 1776

CAPE FEAR, N.C. Gen. Sir Henry Clinton's small fleet arrives off the coast. The general is discouraged by news that the Loyalists have been defeated at Moore's Creek Bridge and that in South Carolina the Loyalist leaders are captives of the rebels and their up-

ARTILLERY

Even though artillery was indispensable in conducting sieges, its role on the open battlefield was relatively restricted during the war of the American Revolution. The problem was immobility. No one had yet invented efficient ways to move heavy cannon rapidly about the battlefield, so commanders usually placed their guns before the battle where they hoped to do some good and were stuck with these dispositions throughout the ensuing engagement.

The basic artillery weapons of the war were bronze or iron cannon, mounted on heavy, cumbersome gun carriages drawn by horses. It was a slow process to site or move guns. Moreover, transportation was in the hands of hired civilian contractors who tended their draft animals free of military discipline. The civilians were loath to stay on the battlefield after depositing their cargo, so artillerymen were immobile. Very little ammunition was carried with the guns, and after a few salvoes, the gunners had to rely on ammunition wagons that may or may not have arrived on schedule.

The British army was equipped with guns that ranged from the small three-pounder Grasshopper (so named for the way it jumped when fired) that was relatively mobile but delivered a small charge to massive forty-two pound siege guns that were usually transported by water.

Eighteen- and twenty-four-pounder guns were the most common on the battlefield. These weapons fired in a low, flat trajectory and could do terrible damage when given the opportunity, but they were easily masked by the movements of the artillerymen's own troops or by even gently rolling terrain.

The American artillery arm was one of the best trained and organized parts of the Continental Army. Washington made a wise decision at the beginning of the war when he assigned Henry Knox as chief of artillery: Knox was a good manager and learned his craft well. The Americans inherited many artillery pieces from colonial militia and used many of the same pattern guns as the British. The French army was in the midst of a major change in the manufacture and classification of artillery and donated to the Americans relatively large numbers of weapons it now found obsolete.

Artillery was, of course, crucial to the success of siege warfare. Given proper time and transport, both sides proved effective in using siege guns to batter the defenses of fortifications. The British siege of Charleston in 1780 was successful due to the siege train brought to the scene by the Royal Navy, and the allies were assured of victory at the siege of Yorktown when the French navy delivered siege guns to supplement Knox's batteries.

rising is dispelled. He takes his two companies of foot soldiers ashore, sightsees along the coastline, replenishes his supplies, and awaits the coming of Adm. Parker and Gen. Cornwallis.

17 March 1776

BOSTON. Since both Tories and patriots had pleaded with Howe not to burn Boston upon the British departure, he had arranged a tacit agreement with Gen. Washington not to do so if the British are left unmolested by Washington's forces. Consequently, after nearly two weeks, he now has completed preparations for departure, with the last of his troops and supplies loaded aboard ship on this day. A fleet of 125 vessels lingers in Boston Harbor, awaiting orders to set sail. On board the ships are 9,000 troops and officers, over 1,100 Loyalists, nearly 1,000 women and children connected with the soldiers, and tons of supplies and arms. While leaving Boston intact, Howe's men have fulfilled his orders to confiscate all supplies in the city that might be useful to Washington and to destroy those supplies that cannot be accommodated on the ships. They also, despite Howe's orders, have plundered many of the homes, generating increased enmity among Boston's residents. The *Pennsylvania Evening Post* reports: "The command of the whole being then given to General Putnam, he . . . became possessed, in the name of the Thirteen United Colonies of North America, of all the fortresses in that large and once populous and flourishing metropolis, which the flower of the British army, headed by an experienced general, and supported by a formidable fleet of men-of-war, had, but an hour before, evacuated in the most precipitate and cowardly manner. God grant that the late worthy inhabitants . . . may speedily reoccupy their respective dwellings, and never more be disturbed by the cruel hand of tyranny; and may the air of that capital be never again contaminated by the foul breath of Toryism." While warily watching his enemy's preparations for the evacuation, Washington, assuming that Howe will sail for New York City, the midpoint between the northern and southern colonies, has been sending units of his army southward to prepare for battle there.

19 March 1776

PHILADELPHIA. Having tabled a 13 February motion by Samuel Chase that Adm. Hopkins be authorized to seize British merchant ships and the colonies be encouraged to oufit privateers—in response to Parliament's passage of the Prohibitory Act—the Continental Congress now resolves the issue, responding to public petitions. The members decide "That the inhabitants of these colonies be permitted to fit out armed vessels to cruize on the enemies of these United Colonies."

20 March 1776

BOSTON. American troops take full possession of the city. But the British fleet has anchored at Nantasket Roads, five miles below Boston, creating concern among Washington and his officers about their true intentions. The British, it turns out, are simply shifting cargoes and taking fresh water on board.

PHILADELPHIA. Congress adopts the instructions for its mission to Canada. The commissioners (Benjamin Franklin, Samuel Chase, Charles Carroll, and the Rev. John Carroll) are to inform the Canadians that American troops invaded Canada only in an effort to frustrate British plans, that the Americans will assist Canada in any way possible toward independence, that "their interests and ours are inseparably united," that Congress wishes to adopt them into the union, and that "we hold sacred the rights of conscience, and . . . the free and undisturbed excercise of their religion."

25 March 1776

PHILADELPHIA. Congress receives a letter from Gen. Washington imparting the news that the British have evacuated Boston. In token of their thanks the members direct that Washington's achievement be commemorated with a gold medal. Members of the Congress' commission to Canada embark on their mission.

26 March 1776

CHARLESTON, S.C. South Carolina declares a temporary constitution, in effect establishing its independence.

27 March 1776

BOSTON. Gen. Howe's fleet at last sets sail—not for New York, as Washington has assumed, but rather for Halifax, Nova Scotia, there to disembark the Loyalists, refit the ships, and acquire fresh supplies.

2 April 1776

QUEBEC. Maj. Gen. David Wooster arrives from Montreal with reinforcements to help continue the siege of

the city. Wooster assumes command from Arnold. Awarded a brigadier-generalcy by Congress for his efforts in the Canada campaign, Arnold, still recovering from his injuries and a fall from his horse, leaves for Montreal.

4 April 1776

NEW YORK. Heading for home after his success in Nassau, Commodore Hopkins and his fleet have already captured half a dozen British ships. Today the *Columbus* handily captures the small British schooner HMS *Hawk*.

5 April 1776

NEW YORK. Continuing his successes, Hopkins' command ship *Alfred* captures the British brigantine HMS *Bolton*.

6 April 1776

BLOCK ISLAND, R.I. Hopkins' fleet experiences a final encounter when HMS *Glasgow* sails into their midst after midnight. The ensuing pitched battle lasts three hours, with British Capt. Tryingham Howe displaying superior seamanship in a series of bold moves. Though greatly outnumbered, the *Glasgow* inflicts twenty-four casualties while suffering only four, and its guns knock out the *Alfred's* wheel block and rake that ship's deck with shot. During the battle Tryingham Howe throws overboard dispatches he is carrying from Gen. Howe in Halifax to Gen. Clinton. Although badly damaged, the *Glasgow* escapes. Hopkins rather lamely explains: "I had upwards of 30 of our best Seamen on board the Prizes, and some that were on board had got too much Liqour out of the Prizes to be fit for Duty."

PHILADELPHIA. After many months of debate on whether to open American ports to trade, Congress finally makes a decision—responding to the Prohibitory Act of Parliament that has technically ended foreign commerce with the colonies and set up a naval blockade against commercial shipping. American ports are to be open to trade from all nations except Great Britain and her dominions. Some hesitant members still express concern that the decision will help propel the colonies toward independence. Others, such as John Adams, hope that will indeed be the effect.

12 April 1776

HALIFAX, N.C. In the aftermath of the victory at Moore's Creek Bridge, the Fourth Provincial Congress of North Carolina adopts the so-called Halifax Resolves, becoming the first colony to officially endorse independence. The resolves authorize the colony's delegates to the Continental Congress to "concur with the delegates of the other colonies in declaring independency, and forming foreign alliances, reserving to this Colony the sole and exclusive right of forming a Constitution and laws for this Colony."

13 April 1776

NEW YORK CITY. After over a year of immobility during the siege of Boston, the main army commanded by Gen. Washington is on the march, heading for New York. Hurrying ahead of his troops after overseeing the beginning of their march, Washington arrives in the city convinced of the absolute need to defend it against an anticipated attack by Gen. Howe. He knows that Howe's forces in Halifax, Nova Scotia, are to be reinforced and that

another expedition is en route from England. Washington fears that if the British gain control of the city and the North River, they will be able to totally disrupt commerce and communication between the northern and southern colonies.

15 April 1776

PROVIDENCE, R.I. Two new American warships, the *Warren* and the *Providence*, are launched.

17 April 1776

VIRGINIA COAST. Capt. John Barry in command of the *Lexington* does battle with the British sloop HMS *Edward.* Although Barry's ship has more guns than the *Edward*, British experience again tells. The *Lexington* endures heavy battering and four casualties but inflicts severe damages to the *Edward*'s sails and rigging. The *Edward* finally strikes its colors, and Barry thus becomes the first American naval captain to capture a British ship in actual battle. A wealthy Philadelphia shipowner, Barry had before hostilities been master of the *Alfred*, now under Hopkins's command.

18 April 1776

CAPE FEAR, N.C. The first ship of Commodore Sir Peter Parker's fleet finally arrives, but the commodore himself is many days behind.

1 May 1776

QUEBEC. Although during April the inept Maj. Gen. Wooster has placed batteries on the Heights of Abraham and on Pointe Levis and from these vantage points has bombarded the city, his tactics have failed miserably, with Sir Guy Carleton's artillery returning still heavier fire against the

Americans. Wooster's plan to burn the British vessels in the harbor has also failed. Consequently, on this day he is relieved of command and replaced by Gen. John Thomas. The new commander discovers that the American force has been reduced to 1,900, of whom only 1,000 are fit for duty, and only 500 of these are reliable. This small force has been laying siege to a city whose inhabitants outnumber their besiegers ten to one; yet for some reason Carleton's force has remained within the city walls, never once attempting to attack their foe.

2 May 1776

PARIS, FRANCE. Having secured assurances in March from Marquis Grimaldi that the Spanish government will support French clandestine aid (both arms and money) to the Americans, comte de Vergennes has also secured approval of his efforts from the reluctant Louis XVI and Baron Turgot, who has been vehemently opposed but is outvoted by the king's other ministers. Today the king directs that one million livres be provided to Pierre-Augustin Caron de Beaumarchais to set up a dummy company, Roderigue Hortalez et Cie. Beaumarcahis is to pose as a merchant for the purpose of purchasing arms and munitions to send to the Americans.

QUEBEC. Gen. John Thomas learns that a fleet of fifteen British ships has arrived in the St. Lawrence River. The fleet is carrying Gen. John Burgoyne, seven Irish regiments, one English regiment, and 4,300 German mercenaries under Gen. Baron Friedrich von Riedesel to reinforce the British garrison in the city. The American siege collapses.

3 May 1776

LONDON. Following Lord North's urgings, George III appoints a Peace Commission to negotiate separately with each of the colonies. The two commissioners are Gen. Sir William Howe and his brother Adm. Lord Richard Howe, who also is to assume command of British naval operations in America. Although filling apparently conflicting roles, Lord Howe is a sound choice for peace commissioner, as he had offered himself for such service in 1774 and has an affectionate regard for the colonies, especially New England. Through Lord George Germain's efforts, however, the commissioners are locked in to at least one nonnegotiable stipulation: "that no colony should be restored to the King's peace till it had acknowledged the supremacy of Parliament." In addition, the king directs that military operations must proceed. And by this time, in response to British actions following Bunker Hill, including the policy of hiring foreign mercenary troops, and sentiments aroused by Paine's *Common Sense*, opinion in the colonies is increasingly in favor of independence.

CAPE FEAR, N.C. Commodore Parker and Lord Cornwallis arrive off the coast, but many ships in their convoy still trail behind.

PROVIDENCE, R.I. The General Assembly approves an act declaring the colony's independence and designation as the State of Rhode Island and Providence Plantations.

6 May 1776

QUEBEC. The British fleet arrives. Gen. Carleton, having received a report that the Americans are preparing to retreat from the Plains of Abraham, forms a reconnaisance mission. With four guns and 900 men, including the first 200 to disembark from the ships, he approaches the American encampment. Gen. Thomas can muster only 250 troops in opposition, and the Americans flee westward in panic, abandoning 200 sick comrades and muskets and artillery. Carleton decides not to pursue them but to await the full complement of reinforcements under Burgoyne, swelling the British force at Quebec to 13,000.

PHILADELPHIA. The Continental Congress belatedly responds to a query sent by Gen. Washington on 24 March, shortly after the American army occupied Boston, concerning what course he should follow if a British peace commission lands in Boston. The Congress directs that the general be informed that when a commission intends to arrive Great Britain will request passports of safe conduct, and when the applications are made Congress will then decide what is the proper course. In short, wait and see.

8–9 May 1776

WILMINGTON, DEL. Near the mouth of Christiana Creek thirteen Pennsylvania galleys attack two British ships, which they force to withdraw downriver.

10 May 1776

PHILADELPHIA. John Paul Jones is given command of the recently launched sloop *Providence*.

The Continental Congress adopts a resolution encouraging the individual colonies to establish independent governments: "That it be recommended to the respective assemblies and conventions of the United Colonies, where no government sufficient to the exigencies of their affairs have been hitherto established, to adopt such government as shall, in the opinion of the representatives of the people, best conduce to the happiness and safety of their constituents in particular, and America in general." Following approval, Congress appoints a committee (John Adams, Edward Rutledge, and Richard Henry Lee) to prepare a preamble before the statement is made public.

14 May 1776

PHILADELPHIA. After an absence of four and a half months, Thomas Jefferson returns to Congress as a delegate from Virginia.

15 May 1776

PHILADELPHIA. Congress adopts the preamble to its resolution encouraging independent governments for the colonies. The debate over the preamble generates more opposition than the resolution itself—it is, in fact, a more pointed call for independence. Written by John Adams, according to his own assertion, the preamble is freighted with his bias for immediate independence. It opens with a recounting of the transgressions committed by the king and Parliament against the colonies; then it asserts that "it appears absolutely irreconcilable to reason and good conscience" for the colonists to take oaths of support for the British government and that it is "necessary" that all authority of the crown "should be totally suppressed. . . ." The preamble then concludes that it is necessary that all governmental powers should be "exerted, under the authority of the people of the colonies, for the preservation of internal peace, virtue, and good order, as well as for the defence of their lives, liberties, and properties, against the hostile invasions and cruel depredations of their enemies; therefore, resolved, etc." Adoption of the entire statement clearly establishes the Continental Congress as in favor of independence. Adams writes to his good friend James Warren: "This Day the Congress has passed the most important Resolution that ever was taken in America."

The momentum toward independence accelerates.

WILLIAMSBURG, VA. Reacting to a deluge of petitions (some containing wrathful denunciations of Great Britain) from many Virginia counties requesting that the colony's delegates to the Continental Congress be instructed to support independence, the Virginia Convention evidences its total agreement with this popular sentiment by adopting a resolution that instructs the delegates to propose to the Congress "to declare the United Colonies free and independent States, absolved from all allegiance to, or dependence upon, the Crown or Parliament of Great Britain; and that they give the assent of this Colony to such decleration, and to whatever measures may be thought necessary by the Congress for forming foreign alliances, and a Confederation of the Colonies...," reserving to each colony the power to form a government and regulate its internal affairs.

16 May 1776

PHILADELPHIA. The local Committee of Safety, having previously requested that families turn in objects made of lead "to be employed in the defence of this country," announces that in order to expedite procurement of the lead a team of four men will go from house to house, paying six pence per pound for items received. The *Pennsylvania Evening Post* reports the committee's opinion: "It is expected that every virtuous citizen will immediately and cheerfully comply with this requisition, but if any persons should be so lost to all sense of the public good as to refuse, a list of their names is directed to be returned to the committee."

The Continental Congress, apparently now convinced that the time for equivocation is past and the War of the Revolution must proceed, sends a request to Gen. Washington to come to Philadelphia "in order to consult with Congress upon such measures as may be necessary for the carrying on the ensuing campaign."

THE CEDARS, CANADA. Col. Moses Hazen, temporarily in charge at Montreal since Arnold is away with John Thomas' men, has ordered Col. Timothy Bedel and a force of 400 men to defend this small post about thirty miles west of Montreal. Having learned on 15 May that a British force of 650 men under Capt. Forster is approaching, Hazen has left Maj. Isaac Butterfield in charge and gone to Montreal for reinforcements. While Maj. Henry Sherburne sets out with a relief column from Montreal, Butterfield surrenders his garrison without resistance after receiving assurances from Forster that the Americans will be protected from the Indians accompanying him.

17 May 1776

SOREL, CANADA. At the mouth of the

Richelieu River Thomas' men and others encountered on their way to Quebec, some from Trois Rivières, and a regiment fleeing from Pointe Levis, assemble in a disorganized mob. Thomas, ravaged by smallpox, and his council of war recognize that their only recourse is to continue the retreat. They begin to march up the Richelieu to Chambly.

NANTASKET ROADS, MASS. One of the ships in "Washington's navy," the *Franklin*, commanded by Capt. James Mugford, captures HMS *Hope*, a supply ship transporting entrenching tools and 1,500 barrels of powder to Boston. Reacting furiously, the British command in Boston Harbor sends out thirteen boats with more than 200 men to board the *Franklin* during the night. Armed with muskets and spears, Mugford's sailors drive off the British, but Mugford himself dies in the struggle.

20 May 1776

THE CEDARS, CANADA. About four miles out from the garrison Sherburne's relief column of 100 men is ambushed and forced to surrender. Two of the prisoners are executed.

24–25 May 1776

PHILADELPHIA. Gen. Washington confers with members of the Congress about the conduct of the war. The Congress appoints a committee of fourteen members, two from Virginia and one from each of the other twelve colonies, to devise a plan "for the carrying on the ensuing campaign." At the same time Congress passes a resolution supporting the recruitment of Indians for the Continental Army.

26 May 1776

QUINZE CHIENS, CANADA. The British force of 150 English and Canadian troops and 500 Indians with the American prisoners from The Cedars, learns that Arnold is approaching with a relief force. So Capt. Forster sends Maj. Sherburne to tell Arnold that Forster will hand his prisoners over to the Indians if Arnold attacks. Arnold and Forster negotiate. Arnold agrees to accept the American prisoners, who can be exchanged later, and return to Montreal.

31 May 1776

CAPE FEAR, N.C. The last of Parker's fleet arrives off the coast. The fleet sets sail immediately, heading down the coast for Charleston.

1 June 1776

WILMINGTON, N.C. Maj. Gen. Charles Lee, commanded by Congress in March to take command of the Southern Department and recently arrived here from Williamsburg, sends word that Parker's fleet has sailed, presumably for Charleston, and that he himself will leave for that destination the next day.

ST. JOHN'S, CANADA. Gen. John Sullivan arrives with a brigade of 3,300 men from New York. His orders are to assume command from Maj. Gen. John Thomas. At St. John's he joins forces with Brig. Gen. William Thompson, who has brought a brigade of four regiments sent by Gen. Washington. With full supplies of food, ammunition, and arms, Sullivan and his troops anticipate a second attack on Quebec.

2 June 1776

CHAMBLY, CANADA. During the retreat march up the Richelieu River Gen. Thomas dies of smallpox.

4 June 1776

CHARLESTON, S.C. Gen. Charles Lee arrives. He is enthusiastically welcomed by Col. William Moultrie of the Second South Carolina Colonial Regiment, who has been overseeing the construction of the fort on Sullivan's Island at the entrance to the harbor.

6 June 1776

ST. JOHN'S, CANADA. Under Gen. Sullivan's orders 2,000 troops commanded by Gen. Thompson set out in bateaux for an attack on the stronghold at Trois Rivières, strategically located about halfway between Montreal and Quebec. Thompson's regimental commanders are Anthony Wayne, William Irvine, Arthur St. Clair, and William Maxwell.

7 June 1776

CHARLESTON, S.C. Having been delayed by inclement weather, Parker's fleet enters the outer harbor and drops anchor. Gen. Clinton begins conducting a reconnaisance of the various waterways surrounding the city. In the meantime Lee has issued a flurry of instructions on speeding up defensive measures for the city.

NEWBURYPORT, MASS. The American privateer *Yankee Hero*, en route to Boston, is attacked by the British frigate *Melford* commanded by Capt. John Burr. Outnumbered four to one, the *Yankee Hero*'s crew battles gallantly for two hours before surrendering.

Independence Hall, Philadelphia.

PHILADELPHIA. Richard Henry Lee, acting on the mandate from the Virginia Convention and on his own sense of outrage over British treaties with German states to provide mercenaries (a sense of outrage shared by his fellow delegates), introduces a resolution to the Continental Congress calling for independence. It contains three propositions:

> That these United Colonies are, and of right ought to be free and independent States, that they are absolved from all allegiance to the British Crown, and that all political connection between them and the

State of Great Britain is, and ought to be, totally dissolved.

That it is expedient forthwith to take the most effectual measures for forming foreign Alliances.

That a plan of confederation be prepared and transmitted to the respective Colonies for their consideration and approbation.

Congress decides to postpone consideration of the resolution for one day.

8 June 1776

PHILADELPHIA. Congress forms itself into a committee of the whole to discuss Lee's resolution, but ends the discussion with the decision to continue consideration of the resolution on the following Monday, 10 June.

TROIS RIVIÈRES, CANADA. A series of mishaps thwarts the American attack. Leaving behind 250 men to guard the boats, the main force sets out at 3:00 A.M. intent on a surprise attack. Misled by their local guide, they try to find the right road by going across country and become mired down in a swamp. Finally reaching the shore near daybreak, they are fired upon from enemy vessels and seek safety in the woods only to fall into another swamp and become separated. With 200 men Wayne reaches firm ground after eight o'clock and drives off a group of British regulars. Thompson, with the main force, emerges to see Trois Rivières but with a line of entrenchments intervening: Many of Gen. Burgoyne's 8,000 troops have already arrived on their way up the St. Lawrence. The Americans attack but fall back under heavy fire.

Their retreat is cut off by enemy forces and they scatter into the woods in hope of fleeing toward Sorel. Hounded by Indians and Canadian irregulars, they flounder northward for two days. Carleton, not wanting them as prisoners, allows them to cross the bridge at Rivière du Loup, and their remnants straggle into Sorel. Some 236 have surrendered to Carleton despite his wishes; another 400 are dead, lost, or captured. British casualties number about a dozen. The American hope of annexing Canada evaporates.

9 June 1776

MONTREAL. Conceding that their position is hopeless, Gen. Arnold and the 300 men holding Montreal evacuate the city, cross the river to Longueuil, and head for St. John's—only one step ahead of their British pursuers.

10 June 1776

PARIS, FRANCE. Beaumarchais' dummy company, Hortalez et Cie., receives a million livres in gold coin from the French treasury, under an order of 5 June from Vergennes, to be used for secret aid to the Americans. As previously agreed with the French government, the Spanish government, with the consent of King Charles III, approves providing Beaumarchais another million livres.

PHILADELPHIA. Conservatives in the Congress succeed in getting consideration of independence postponed until July, but the necessary preliminary preparations will continue.

11 June 1776

PHILADELPHIA. Congress appoints a

committee to prepare a draft proposal of a declaration of independence. The committee members are Thomas Jefferson, John Adams, Benjamin Franklin, Roger Sherman, and Robert R. Livingston. Congress also passes a resolution to appoint two other committees, one to draft a proposal on confederation and the other "to prepare a plan of treaties to be proposed to foreign powers."

12 June 1776

PHILADELPHIA. Congress appoints the two committees authorized on 11 June. The committee to deal with the question of confederation consists of one member from each colony and is chaired by John Dickinson. The committee for planning foreign treaties includes John Dickinson, John Adams, Franklin, Benjamin Harrison, and Robert Morris. Congress also resolves to set up a war office to be supervised by a congressional committee of five members known as the Board of War and Ordnance.

WILLIAMSBURG, VA. The Virginia Convention adopts a Declaration of Rights, largely the work of George Mason. Its first article reads: "That all men are by nature equally free and independent, and have certain inherent rights, of which, when they enter into a state of society, they cannot by any compact deprive or divest their posterity; namely, the enjoyment of life and liberty, with the means of acquiring and possessing property, and pursuing and obtaining happiness and safety." The subsequent fifteen articles affirm the sovereignty of the people, the people's right to alter or abolish a government that does not

serve them, the need for periodic elections, the principle of due process, trial by jury, a free press, and "the free exercise of religion."

14 June 1776

SOREL, CANADA. Gen. Sullivan orders a retreat to Lake Champlain. He loads his 2,500-man force aboard bateaux and evacuates Sorel. The British fleet arrives within an hour of the Americans' departure.

15 June 1776

NEW YORK CITY. Thomas Hickey, a member of Gen. Washington's Life Guard, and Michael Lynch, a Continental soldier, are brought before the provincial assembly charged with passing counterfeit bills.

16 June 1776

CHAMBLY, CANADA. Arnold's men fight a rear-guard action against the pursuing British and continue their retreat.

CHARLESTON, S.C. With his reconnaissance completed, Gen. Clinton sends 2,000 regulars and 500 seamen to Long Island in Charleston harbor. He is confident that they can wade from here for an attack on Sullivan's Island during low tide while Parker's ships bombard the fort. To Clinton's dismay his men discover that the breach between the islands is filled with such deep potholes that passage is impossible.

17 June 1776

PHILADELPHIA. The Continental Congress receives news of the disastrous defeat at Trois Rivières and instructs Gen. Washington to place Gen. Horatio Gates in charge of the American troops in Canada. Of course, by this time all the American troops in Canada are rapidly fleeing homeward.

21 June 1776

NEW YORK CITY. An ostensible plot to abduct or assassinate Gen. Washington is discovered when Thomas Hickey and Michael Lynch brag about their involvement. The plot is apparently masterminded by Gov. Tryon, stationed aboard his warship in the harbor and working through paid agents in the city.

PHILADELPHIA. New Jersey's Provincial Congress, having deposed and arrested royal governor William Franklin (Benjamin Franklin's illegitimate son), sends a new delegation to Congress with instructions to support resolutions for declaring American independence, creating a confederation, and making treaties with foreign nations at their own discretion. The delegates are Richard Stockton, Abraham Clark, John Hart, Francis Hopkins, and Dr. John Witherspoon.

24 June 1776

ILE AUX NOIS, CANADA. The retreating Americans, Arnold's and Sullivan's troops now combined, have paused here. Although numbering 8,000, the majority of them are suffering from smallpox, dysentery, or malaria; all are suffering from exhaustion, hunger, hardship, and the demoralization of defeat. Thus they are barely able to repulse a modest British probe by an advance guard. Sullivan orders the retreat to continue, accepting the failure of the Canada expedition.

26 June 1776

NEW YORK CITY. Thomas Hickey is tried by court-martial, found guilty of mutiny and sedition, and sentenced to be hanged.

28 June 1776

NEW YORK CITY. Just before noon Thomas Hickey is hanged in a field near Bowery Lane—a public execution witnessed by 20,000 spectators, including by Washington's order all the Continentals in the city who are not on duty.

CHARLESTON, S.C. Parker's fleet of nine ships, including two mounted with fifty guns, sails up the channel of Charleston Harbor. Three of his frigates are assigned to sail by Sullivan's Island and bombard the fort on the island from the southwest, the side of the fort that is incomplete, while the other ships attack from the southeast. The frigates run aground, aborting their mission—a decisive mishap for the outcome of the battle —and forcing Parker into a frontal bombardment. One hundred guns rain shells upon the fort, where only twenty-one guns are available to return fire. But Col. William Moultrie's fortifications hold, their construction of spongy palmetto logs and sand absorbing the cannon balls; his guns inflict severe damage on the British ships, especially the grounded frigates. Though low on powder by early afternoon, Moultrie is resupplied by Lee and continues firing. The shelling keeps the British at bay until nightfall, when Parker withdraws his ships, abandoning one of the frigates to the shoals of Charleston Harbor. His fleet is now unfit for further combat: He has reportedly lost 64 men and has 131 wounded. The patriots' losses number seventeen, with twenty wounded. Fort Sullivan's improvised flag, with a blue field bearing a white crescent and the word *Liberty*, continues to fly. For the present the British southern strategy is undone.

ANNAPOLIS, MD. The Maryland Convention votes unanimously to instruct the colony's congressional delegates to support a resolution for independence.

PHILADELPHIA. The committee assigned to draft a declaration of independence brings its proposed statement before the Continental Congress for consideration. Thomas Jefferson composed the original, amended slightly in response to recommendations from Adams and Franklin.

29 June 1776

NEW YORK CITY. A British fleet is sighted off Sandy Hook. The ships have carried Gen. Howe and his 10,000 troops from Halifax, Nova Scotia. An American sentinel says the flotilla resembles "a fleet of pine trees trimmed . . . I could not believe my eyes." Nearly 100 ships are anchored in the Hook by afternoon. Howe waits for the remainder of his fleet and an additional fleet sailing from England commanded by his brother to arrive.

WILLIAMSBURG, VA. The House of Burgesses adopts a constitution, making Virginia an independent state. The document begins with a statement of grievances against George III and then defines a government of three departments: executive, legislative, and judiciary. The legislature is to be bicameral, with a House of Delegates and a Senate. Two members elected by freeholders will represent each county in the House. The Senate will have twenty-four members indirectly elected by county delegates. The governor, chosen by vote of the legislature, will serve a maximum of three one-year terms. The document also specifies a variety of other offices, including congressional delegates, their methods of selection and duties.

30 June 1776

NEW YORK CITY. The last of Howe's ships from Halifax sail in. Now 127 ships are assembled in the Hook.

1 July 1776

PHILADELPHIA. Following a debate on the question of independence in which John Dickinson spoke against and John Adams for, the New Jersey delegation arrives with its new instructions and request that the arguments in favor of independence be summarized. Prodded by South Carolina's Edward Rutledge, an opponent, and New Jersey's John Witherspoon, Adams complies. Afterward a canvass of the delegates indicates only nine colonies in firm support of independence. An afternoon and night of bargaining, maneuvering, and cajoling ensues in preparation for the crucial vote on the morrow. Richard Henry Lee persuades Rutledge to agree that he and the other South Carolina delegates will vote in favor if Pennsylvania and Delaware do.

2 July 1776

PHILADELPHIA. With heavy rains

falling the Congress assembles and spends the morning doing routine business while awaiting the arrival of Caesar Rodney, a delegate from Delaware who has been home ministering to his sick wife and is known to be en route to the meeting. Rodney, who favors independence, arrives splattered with mud after a furious ride. Delaware votes for independence, followed by South Carolina and Pennsylvania. New York abstains. Lee's resolution carries by a vote of twelve for, none against. Congress forms itself into a committee of the whole to resume discussing the proposed declaration.

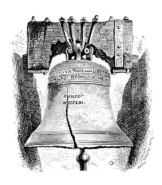

The Liberty Bell.

3 July 1776

PHILADELPHIA. John Adams writes to his beloved wife, Abigail: "Yesterday the greatest question was decided which ever was decided in America, and a greater, perhaps, never was nor will be decided among men." He expresses amazement over "the suddenness as well as the greatness of this Revolution!" So moved is he by this momentous event that he writes Abigail a second letter during the night, declaring: "The second day of July,

1776, will be the most memorable epoch in the history of America.... It ought to be solemnized with pomp and parade, with shows, games, sports, guns, bells, bonfires, and illuminations, from one end of the continent to the other, from this time forward, forevermore." He anticipates a heavy cost in blood, toil, and treasure to secure the independence: "Yet through all the gloom I can see the rays of ravishing light and glory. I can see that the end is more than worth all the means; and that posterity will triumph in that day's transactions."

NEW YORK CITY. Gen. Howe lands 9,300 British troops on Staten Island.

4 July 1776

PHILADELPHIA. After nearly two days of discussion the Continental Congress accepts a final draft of the Declaration of Independence. The discussions have resulted in various revisions of phrasing and the deletion of two passages, one that censured the people of Great Britain rather than the government and a second that condemned the slave trade. But the approved declaration preserves intact most of Thomas Jefferson's original wording. Its eloquent second paragraph declares:

We hold these truths to be self-evident, that all men are created equal, that they are endowed by their Creator with certain unalienable rights, that among these are life, liberty, and the pursuit of happiness. That, to secure these rights, governments are instituted among men, deriving their just powers from the consent of the governed. That, whenever any form of govern-

Thomas Jefferson.

ment becomes destructive of these ends, it is the right of the people to alter or to abolish it, and to institute new government, laying its foundation on such principles, and organizing its powers in such form, as to them shall seem most likely to effect their safety and happiness.

There follows an outline of the abuses ascribed to George III, a remonstrance addressed to the people of Great Britain, and a declaration of independence incorporating the wording of Lee's resolution. The document concludes with a solemn affirmation: "And for the support of this declaration, with a firm reliance on the protection of Divine Providence, we mutually pledge to each other our lives, our fortunes, and our sacred honor."

As with the Lee resolution, the vote on the declaration is twelve to nothing, with New York again abstaining. Upon its passage John Hancock signs the declaration as presiding officer of the Continental Congress, which then directs that it be authenticated and printed, with copies to "be sent to the several assemblies, conventions and committees, or councils of safety, and to the several commanding officers of the continental troops; that it be proclaimed in each of the United States, and at the head of the army."

5 July 1776

PHILADELPHIA. Complying with Congress' directive, President Hancock begins transmitting copies of the Declaration of Independence, authenticated by his signature and that of the secretary of Congress, Charles Thomson. He includes the request that the declaration be proclaimed universally.

WILLIAMSBURG, VA. Patrick Henry is sworn in as governor of Virginia. He had been elected to the post on 29 June.

CROWN POINT, N.Y. Generals Gates and Schuyler arrive.

7 July 1776

CROWN POINT, N.Y. The last remnants of Sullivan's and Arnold's force find refuge after rowing the length of Lake Champlain. They have reached the fort from which, ten months earlier, Gen. Richard Montgomery set forth to attain the conquest of Canada. The 8,000 survivors of that invasion have left behind in Canada approximately 5,000 casualties; of their own number 3,000 require hospitalization. Gen. Schuyler has the entire northern army withdraw to Fort Ticonderoga, ten miles farther south.

PARIS, FRANCE. Silas Deane arrives on his diplomatic mission as representative of Congress' Committee of Secret Correspondence.

8 July 1776
PHILADELPHIA. The Declaration of Independence is proclaimed in public for the first time. The *Constitutional Gazette* reports:

> At twelve o'clock to-day, the Committee of Safety and Inspection of Phildelphia, went in procession to the State House, where the Declaration of the Independency of the United States of America was read to a very large number of the inhabitants of the city and county, and was received with general applause and heartful satisfaction. And, in the evening, our late King's coat-of-arms was brought from the hall in the State House ... and burned amidst the acclamations of a crowd of spectators.

9 July 1776
NEW YORK CITY. By order of Gen. Washington the Declaration of Independence is read to the assembled troops. The general's order states that he "hopes this important Event will serve as a fresh incentive to every officer and soldier ... knowing that now the peace and safety of his Country depends (under God) solely on the success of our arms."

10 July 1776
NEW YORK CITY. The Declaration of Independence is publicly proclaimed. The *Pennsylvania Journal* reports that the declaration has been "received everywhere with loud huzzas, and the utmost demonstrations of joy; and to- night the equestrian statue of George III, which Tory pride and folly raised in the year 1770, has, by the

King George's statue is torn down after the reading of the Declaration of Independence.

Sons of Freedom, been laid prostrate in the dirt—the just desert of an ungrateful tyrant! The lead wherewith the monument was made is to be run into bullets, to assimilate with the brains of our infatuated adversaries, who, to gain a pepper-corn, have lost an empire."

GWYNN ISLAND, VA. Following the destruction of Norfolk, Lord Dunmore has established a base here on the Chesapeake Bay, where he hopes to maintain a foothold in Virginia with his small fleet and about 500 Tory troops, including runaway slaves. But he is attacked on 9. July by a brigade of Virginia troops under Gen. Andrew Lewis that bomdards Dunmore's fleet, wounding the former governor. Some of the British vessels run aground in their efforts to flee, but Dunmore and the remaining ships escape. The victorious patriots find numerous graves and dead and dying victims of smallpox when they cross to the island.

12 July 1776
NEW YORK CITY. Admiral Richard

Howe arrives with a fleet of 150 ships carrying 11,000 fresh troops to join his brother. Two British frigates, the *Phoenix* and the *Rose*, sail up the Hudson River to Tappan Sea barely threatened by American artillery supposed to prevent such an outflanking movement.

PHILADELPHIA. The committee designated to prepare a proposal on confederation presents to the Congress "Articles of Confederation and Perpetual Union," largely the work of John Dickinson. There are thirteen articles in the proposal.

15 July 1776

PHILADELPHIA. As the New York Convention has adopted a resolution on 9 July giving approval to the Declaration of Independence, the New York delegates now present this resolution in Congress, making support of the declaration unanimous.

16 July 1776

POTOMAC RIVER. Lord Dunmore and his remnant force begin a raid up the river, apparently intending to reach Mount Vernon and there to attempt the capture of Martha Washington.

21 July 1776

CHARLESTON, S.C. After lingering for three weeks Parker and Clinton abandon hope of success and set sail for New York.

29 July 1776

NORTH CAROLINA. Gen. Griffith Rutherford, with a force of 2,400 men, launches an invasion of the Cherokee Nation's territory in an effort to derail the Indians' alliance with the British and their attacks on American frontier settlements. Complementing his effort are South Carolina troops commanded by Maj. Andrew Williamson and Virginia troops commanded by Col. William Christian.

1 August 1776

NEW YORK CITY. Commodore Parker's fleet of nine warships and thirty transports arrives from Charleston bearing Gen. Clinton and Lord Cornwallis and the 2,500 troops under their command.

2 August 1776

PHILADELPHIA. Only President Hancock and Secretary Thomson had signed the Declaration of Independence distributed for public proclamations. The other members of the Continental Congress now join these two and affix their signatures to a copy of the declaration engrossed on parchment.

3 August 1776

TAPPAN SEA, N.Y. Five small boats commanded by Lt. Col. Benjamin Tupper attack the five British ships that in mid-July passed unscathed up the Hudson River from Staten Island and anchored here. The attack fails.

7 August 1776

PORTSMOUTH, N.H. The American privateer *Hancock* commanded by Capt. Wingate Newman captures the British ship *Reward* and brings it into port to unload the cargo, which includes turtles intended for delivery to Lord North.

16 August 1776

TAPPAN SEA, N.Y. The Americans try again to assault the five British ships at anchor, this time sending fire rafts against them. Again the attempt is unsuccessful, but the commander of

SIGNERS OF THE DECLARATION

Fifty-six delegates to the Continental Congress signed the Declaration of Independence during the summer of 1776, when the body finally voted (after more than a year of open warfare) to take the momentous step of severing ties with Great Britain. All but eight of the signers were born in America; almost all came from Anglo-Saxon stock; and almost all were Protestants. Most were wealthy or at least prosperous. The youngest, Edward Rutledge, was twenty-six; the eldest, Ben Franklin, was seventy. All of them risked charges of treason if the Revolution failed.

John Adams (Mass.)
Samuel Adams (Mass.)
Josiah Bartlett (N.H.)
Carter Braxton (Va.)
Charles Carroll (Md.)
Samuel Chase (Md.)
Abraham Clark (N.J.)
George Clymer (Pa.)
William Ellery (R.I.)
William Floyd (N.Y.)
Benjamin Franklin (Pa.)
Elbridge Gerry (Mass.)
Button Gwinnett (Ga.)
Lyman Hall (Ga.)
John Hancock (Mass.)
Benjamin Harrison (Va.)
John Hart (N.J.)
Joseph Hewes (N.C.)
Thomas Heyward, Jr. (S.C.)
William Hooper (N.C.)
Stephen Hopkins (R.I.)
Francis Hopkinson (N.J.)
Samuel Huntington (Ct.)
Thomas Jefferson (Va.)
Francis Lightfoot Lee (Va.)
Richard Henry Lee (Va.)
Francis Lewis (N.Y.)
Philip Livingston (N.Y.)

Thomas Lynch, Jr. (S.C.)
Thomas McKean (Del.)
Arthur Middleton (S.C.)
Lewis Morris (N.Y.)
Robert Morris (Pa.)
John Morton (Pa.)
Thomas Nelson, Jr. (Va.)
William Paca (Md.)
Robert Treat Paine (Mass.)
John Penn (N.C.)
George Read (Del.)
Caesar Rodney (Del.)
George Ross (Pa.)
Benjamin Rush (Pa.)
Edward Rutledge (S.C.)
Roger Sherman (Ct.)
James Smith (Pa.)
Richard Stockton (N.J.)
Thomas Stone (Md.)
George Taylor (Pa.)
Matthew Thornton (N.H.)
George Walton (Ga.)
William Whipple (N.H.)
William Williams (Ct.)
James Wilson (Pa.)
John Witherspoon (N.J.)
Oliver Wolcott (Ct.)
George Wythe (Va.)

HMS *Phoenix* is alarmed and orders the fleet to return down the Hudson and rejoin the British fleet.

22 August 1776
NEW YORK CITY. With the Howes' efforts to negotiate some sort of peace-

The retreat from Brooklyn Heights, under the direction of General Washington.

ful resolution to the British-American conflict having made no headway, Gen. Howe changes his plans. By now he has nearly 32,000 troops massed for attack (the largest expeditionary force Great Britain has ever shipped out), including 8,000 mercenaries from the German principalities of Hesse, Brunswick, Ansbach, Waldeck, and Anhalt-Zerbst—all referred to by the Americans as Hessians. These British and German soldiers are among the most professional, best trained, and best equipped troops in the world; and they are commanded by the highly experienced generals Howe, Clinton, Lord Percy, Lord Cornwallis, and Philip von Heister. By contrast, mostly untrained, undisciplined, and poorly equipped amateurs (including the officers) comprise Washington's entire force of 19,000. Gen. Howe believes that Brooklyn Heights is the key to the American defense of the city. He now lands 15,000 troops with arms and supplies at Gravesend Bay on Long Island. Learning of their disembarkation, Gen. Washington sends six regiments to reinforce the garrison on Brooklyn Heights and orders Gen. William Heath, who is quartered at the north end of Manhattan Island, to be prepared to send several regiments under his command if necessary.

23 August 1776

LONG ISLAND, N.Y. Near Bedford Pass on Long Island American soldiers commanded by Col. Edward Hand attack a Hessian outpost, forcing Col. Carl von Donop's men to withdraw, but a counterattack forces their own retreat in turn.

24 August 1776

NEW YORK CITY. When Maj. Gen. Nathanael Greene fell ill of fever, Gen. Washington placed Maj. Gen. John Sullivan, recently returned from Canada, in charge of the troops on Long Island. Now he replaces Sullivan with Maj. Gen. Israel Putnam, who unfortunately knows nothing about the topography of Long Island. Having underestimated the size of the British force on the island, Washington now has a total of only about 5,800 troops there for the defense of Brooklyn Heights, two-thirds of them militia. He retains the bulk of his troops on Manhattan, which he expects to be attacked at the same time as the heights.

CROWN POINT, N.Y. Gen. Benedict Arnold sets sail, commanding a fleet of schooners, sloops, and gondolas ready to do battle on Lake Champlain.

25 August 1776

LONG ISLAND, N.Y. Gen. Howe augments his forces on Long Island with two brigades of Hessians under Gen. von Heister.

26 August 1776

LONG ISLAND, N.Y. Washington arrives on Long Island and, realizing now that Howe has positioned most of his force for an attack here, orders more reinforcements for Brooklyn Heights, bringing the force there to 9,000 men. The Americans' fortifications extend around Brooklyn from Gowanus Creek and its salt marshes north to Wallabout Bay, also protected by salt marshes. About a mile in front of this line stretches a forward defense line along the wooded hills of the Heights of Guan, with gaps at Gowanus, Flatbush, Bedford, and Jamaica passes. The access point on the Americans' left flank, Jamaica Pass, is guarded by only five men. By Gen. Howe's orders a force under Gen. Clinton and Lord Percy begins to march after dark to Jamaica Pass.

27 August 1776

LONG ISLAND, N.Y. Moving silently, Gen. Clinton's troops, followed by Percy's main army and artillery, march across a causeway and the narrow Shoemaker's Bridge, where they must move in single file and could easily be delayed by an American attack, but there is no American defense here. Without incident, except for capturing an American patrol, they occupy the heights at the intersection of the Jamaica and Flushing roads before daybreak: They are in control of Jamaica Pass. In the meantime von Heister's Hessians have distracted the Americans with diversionary maneuvers at Flatbush Pass. Concerned about the security of the Bedford Road, Gen. Sullivan takes 400 men to reconnoiter that site and walks straight into Clinton's force—he hastily surrenders. Lord Stirling brings up reinforcements for a successful defense of the American right against an attack led by Gen. James Grant; but Clinton's unopposed troops suddenly pour down upon his men from the rear while von Heister's Hessians press forward the frontal attack. Surprised and outnumbered, most of the Americans flee toward Brooklyn Heights, although about 950 men under Lord Stirling hold fast. Finally overwhelmed by vastly superior numbers and with retreat cut off, Lord Stirling

The Battle of Long Island; the Americans suffered nearly 1,000 casualties.

is forced to surrender to von Heister. By noon the Battle of Long Island ends abruptly. The Americans have suffered 970 casualties and 1,079 men taken prisoner; British casualties number 400. Strangely, Gen. Howe does not push his advantage but halts his troops' advance.

28 August 1776

LONG ISLAND, N.Y. Determined to retain Brooklyn Heights, Gen. Washington ferries across the East River with reinforcements from Manhattan and takes command of strengthening the defenses. A fierce northeaster storm effectively prevents an engagement by the enemy, who are digging in with the intent to unleash an artillery bombardment of the heights.

29 August 1776

LONG ISLAND, N.Y. Following a council of war the night before—his officers agree that the position on Brooklyn Heights is untenable—Washington orders his troops to begin evacuation during the dark of night.

30 August 1776

NEW YORK CITY. Before dawn the evacuation of Brooklyn Heights is complete. Unknown to the British, some 9,500 men plus equipment, horses, and cannon have been transported to Manhattan. Washington writes to the Continental Congress: "The check our detachment sustained . . . has dispirited too great a proportion of our troops and filled their minds with apprehension and despair.

The militia . . . are dismayed, intractable, and impatient to return. Great numbers of men have gone off, in some instances almost by whole Regiments, by half ones, and by companies at a time." He expresses concern that this behavior has infected the rest of the army with insubordination.

The American retreat from Long Island.

2 September 1776

PHILADELPHIA. Sent as an emissary from Gen. Howe, the captured Gen. Sullivan delivers a message from Howe to the Continental Congress requesting a meeting with some of its members as private citizens; he cannot recognize the entire body as official. Debate ensues.

3 September 1776

NEW YORK CITY. Gen. Howe sends an account of the Battle of Long Island to Lord George Germain. He states that the "enemy is still in possession of the town and island of New York, in force,

and making demonstration to oppose us in their works on both sides of King's Bridge." He makes no effort to explain why his troops did not press the advantage, but he does conclude with this "good" news: "The inhabitants of Long Island, many of whom had been forced into rebellion, have all submitted, and are ready to take the oaths of allegiance." The British military plan to sever the states at the Hudson River, requiring the capture of New York City, seems to be advancing. In answer to his query, Washington receives instructions from Congress not to burn the city if he evacuates it; the question of evacuation is left to him to decide.

5 September 1776

PHILADELPHIA. After four days of debate Congress decides that as "representatives of the free and independent states of America" it would be improper for any of its members to meet as private citizens with Gen. Howe

George Washington, after a portrait by Rembrandt Peale.

but that it will send an authorized committee to confer with him.

6 September 1776

PHILADELPHIA. Congress appoints Benjamin Franklin, John Adams, and Edward Rutledge to confer with Gen. Howe.

NEW YORK CITY. David Bushnell of Connecticut gets a chance to try out his submarine vessel, which he calls a "water machine." It is christened the *Turtle* because of its shape. Constructed of oak timbers, caulked, bound with iron bands, and coated with tar to prevent leaks, the craft is operated by a single man, who can submerge it by pulling a hand spring that flushes water into a compartment in the hull and raise it by means of a foot pump that expels the water. Other hand devices are used to propel

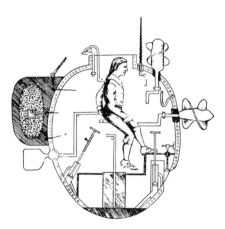

The world's first combat submarine, dubbed the Turtle.

the vessel in four directions. The *Turtle*'s mission is to move underneath an enemy ship and, using a large

screw, to attach a bomb to the ship's hull. The bomb is timed to explode after the *Turtle* has moved to safety. Sergeant Ezra Lee, trained by Bushnell, dives beneath a British ship off of Staten Island and tries to attach the bomb. He fails and is forced to withdraw, setting loose the bomb, which floats into the East River and there explodes harmlessly.

Following up on an order of 4 September in which he exhorted his officers to impose discipline on their troops, Washington now issues an order "to put a stop to plundering ... either public, or private property." Many of his demoralized men have been pillaging the countryside as they desert, just as on Long Island the victorious Hessians have indulged in wanton plundering.

7 September 1776

NEW YORK CITY. Washington calls a council of war to decide the question of evacuating the city. A compromise decision has Israel Putnam's 5,000-man division remaining in the city, with Nathanael Greene commanding five brigades at Turtle Bay and Kip's Bay while William Heath secures Harlem with 9,000 troops.

9 September 1776

PHILADELPHIA. Franklin, Adams, and Rutledge leave on their peace mission. By resolution Congress adopts the name United States of America for the united colonies.

13 September 1776

PHILADELPHIA. The committee returns from conferring with Lord Howe—a three-hour conversation—to report that Howe has stipulated that the colonies must restore their allegiance to the crown, whereupon he could consult with them but could only give them his assurances of the British government's being well disposed toward the colonies. The committee has informed Howe that the Declaration of Independence cannot be rescinded by the Congress because it had been approved in obedience to instructions from the delegates' constituents. There will be no turning back.

15 September 1776
NEW YORK CITY.   In the early morning five British warships take stations at Kip's Bay broadside to the shore. At 10:00 A.M. eighty-five flatboats set out from Long Island carrying British troops. At eleven o'clock the ships open fire on American entrenchments manned by militia under Capt. William Douglas. The patriots flee. The British troops, numbering about 4,000, disembark and meet no resistance. Gen. Washington, alarmed by the sounds of the bombardment, rides south from Harlem and encounters Douglas' men retreating in confusion. Failing to rally them, Washington becomes enraged and flogs both officers

THE CONTINENTAL ARMY

The successful prosecution of the American Revolution was based on the Continental Army—the "regulars" who could, in theory at least, be employed in campaigns to keep the British from regaining control of the American colonies. In fact, the Continental Army was a strange beast, evolving from roots in state militia into a professional force that at its best moments could succeed against the trained armies of Europe. The way was ever rocky, however, and at any one point during the Revolution, the Continental Army may or may not have been an effective fighting force.

The origins of the Continental Army were the state militias of Massachusetts, Rhode Island, New Hampshire, and Connecticut that gathered more or less spontaneously outside Boston after the first violence at Lexington and Concord. Congress adopted this "Boston Army" in the spring of 1775, named George Washington as commander-in-chief, and set up an organization for a national army. Congress copied the British pattern, while bowing to the importance of the individual states. Twenty-six battalions or regiments (roughly the same during this period) were authorized for a total strength of slightly more than 20,000 men. In fact, most of the soldiers were on short-term enlistments, recruiting lagged, and the Continental Army scarcely ever approached that size. Regiments from the New England states formed the first organization, but by the end of the year, regiments were authorized from other states as well. In November 1775, Congress reorganized the army again and specified one-year and privates with his riding cane. The fleeing soldiers leave him behind astride his horse as Hessian troops approach. The commander narrowly escapes being shot or captured only because an aide grabs his horse's bridle and rushes him away. Gen. Putnam rides into the melee and organizes and leads the retreating Americans in an orderly withdrawal up the west side of Manhattan, guided by Aaron Burr, his aide-de-camp. Fortunately, the British forces are hurrying up the east side of Manhattan unaware that they are parallel with their enemy, and the Americans suc-ceed in escaping twelve miles northward to the camp at Harlem Heights. Once again Gen. Howe halts the pursuit. The rout has cost the Americans 367 men lost, nearly all captives of the British, plus abandoned supplies and artillery.

16 September 1776

NEW YORK CITY. An American force of about 10,000 occupies the plateau of Harlem Heights on a neck of land between the Hudson and Harlem rivers, with the army's remaining troops at Kingsbridge farther north. (Washington's army numbers close to enlistments. By September of 1776, with the war in full swing, Congress set three-year enlistments as the standard, raised the quotas (never met) for each state, and authorized a theoretical eighty-eight regiments. In December 1776, Congress also authorized "additional" units above the state quotas and separate from the state-based organization of the rest of the army. The final major reorganization came in 1780, when the bulk of the Continental Line regiments reached the end of their three-year enlistments.

At the heart of the Army were the regiments of the line, in theory the solid basis for putting on a campaign or fighting a battle. The turnover in these line regiments was staggering, however, and only after 1777 did they receive adequate training in the arts of warfare. Unfortunately, by the time training and organization caught up, the financial collapse of the revolutionary government meant that pay and supplies dwindled to the point at which an army could scarcely be supported. From 1778 on, Washington could barely keep a force of a few thousand men intact, although in the end this proved sufficient. To field an army against Cornwallis at Yorktown, however, Washington had to stave off several serious mutinies and a never-ending series of recruiting, supply, and pay problems.

By the end of the Revolution, the Continental Army was close to disintegration, with both officers and men in rebellion or near-rebellion against a Congress that was powerless to meet demands for back pay and retirement benefits.

28,000, but only 16,124 are considered "fit for duty."} The British, encamped two miles to the south, control McGowan's Pass, through which runs the only road connecting Harlem with lower Manhattan. Capt. Thomas Knowlton leads 120 volunteer Rangers on a reconnaisance of the British and is surprised to encounter light infantry at an advance post. They exchange fire. But when a troop of the Black Watch advances against the Americans' left flank, Knowlton gives the order to retreat. The British halt at the base of the Harlem Heights plateau and sound their bugle horns, signaling the end of a fox chase—a musical taunt. Washington sends out one troop for a frontal assault and another to outflank the British. Aware of the flanking movement, the British fall back repeatedly, especially as more Americans rush into the fray—including generals Putnam, Greene, and George Clinton—and drive them from the field of battle. The victory, though small, partially redeems the fiasco at Kip's Bay and uplifts the Americans, although among their casualties are Capt. Knowlton and Maj. Andrew Leitch, two valuable officers.

17 September 1776

PHILADELPHIA. Congress adopts a Plan of Treaties designed primarily to enhance prospects of a treaty with France.

21 September 1776

NEW YORK CITY. Before 1:00 A.M. a fire is discovered in Whitehall at the southern tip of the city. Since the rebel army has carried off the city's bells, no alarm can be sounded. Other fires break out elsewhere, apparently the work of incendiaries, some of whom are captured, according to the British. Lord Howe orders British soldiers and sailors to help fight the flames, but widespread destruction cannot be prevented. The *New York Gazette and Weekly Mercury* reports: "The fire raged with inconceivable violence, and in its destructive progress swept away all the buildings between Broad street and North River, almost as high as the City Hall; and from thence all the houses between Broadway and the North River, as far as King's College, a few only excepted. Long before the main fire reached Trinity Church, that large, ancient, and venerable edifice was in flames. . . . After raging about ten hours, the fire was extinguished." The report commends the behavior of the British soldiers and sailors and condemns the alleged incendiaries as agents of the Continental Congress. "Our distress was very great before, but this disaster has increased it tenfold," it laments. "Many hundreds of families have lost their all, and are reduced from a state of affluence to the lowest ebb of want and wretchedness—destitute of shelter, food, and clothing." However it started, the fire has served the American cause by destroying some of Gen. Howe's supplies and temporarily distracting him.

22 September 1776

NEW YORK CITY. The British hang Nathan Hale for espionage. Following defeat on Long Island, Washington has called for paid volunteers to spy on the British and try to ascertain their plans and tactics. Hale, a Yale-educated schoolteacher and officer from Connecticut, has volunteered out of patriotism. Dressed like a Dutch schoolmaster, he has slipped behind British lines on Long Island, but his identity is revealed when he is recognized at a tavern by a New Hampshire relative, the Tory Samuel Hale. Documents Nathan Hale carries clearly reveal that he is an American spy, and he is arrested on 21 September. Early this morning he confesses and is sentenced to be executed without trial. He writes letters to his brother and a fellow officer but is denied the visit of a clergyman. At 11:00 A.M. he is led to the gallows. With the noose around his neck, he calmly tells the spectators that it is a good soldier's duty to obey any order from his commanding officer. A British officer praises the dignity of Hale's demeanor and says the spy's last words were "I only regret that I have but one life to lose for my country."

23 September 1776

MONTRESOR'S ISLAND, N.Y. From this vantage point, which they occupied on 10 September, the British can land troops above Harlem or can flank the Americans at Kingsbridge. So Brig. Gen. Heath secures Washington's permission to send 240 soldiers under Lt. Col. Michael Jackson to try to retake the island. Jackson and the soldiers in the first boat land near dawn and are attacked immediately. The other two boats withdraw instead of coming to their aid. The Americans suffer fourteen losses. Following their return the two boatloads of "delinquents" are arrested and held for court-martial.

LAKE CHAMPLAIN. Gen. Arnold anchors his fleet in the harbor at Bay St.

Amand, about ten miles south of Valcour Island.

26 September 1776

PHILADELPHIA. Having adopted instructions two days earlier for the guidance of commissioners being sent to France to negotiate a treaty, Congress now appoints Silas Deane, Benjamin Franklin, and Thomas Jefferson as the commissioners (Deane is already in France). They are instructed to make every effort to achieve a treaty in conformance with the Plan of Treaties but are given some discretion to make concessions. They are to promise that the United States will never endorse allegiance to the British crown and that, if France will join the war effort, neither nation shall make peace until six months after notifying the other that negotiations are under way. They are also instructed to request that France immediately supply arms and ammunition and some engineers.

4 October 1776

ST. JOHN'S, CANADA. Gen. Sir Guy Carleton, whose total force has been augmented by 5,000 German mercenaries and now numbers 13,000, sets sail with a fleet of five ships, twenty gunboats, and twenty-eight longboats carrying field pieces and supplies. His guns outnumber Arnold's forty-two to thirty-two and can deliver almost twice the poundage.

11 October 1776

LAKE CHAMPLAIN, N.Y. Near Valcour Island Gen. Carleton's fleet encounters Gen. Arnold's fleet. The two fleets exchange a furious cannonade for several hours. Detachments of Canadian troops and Indians land on the mainland and the island and fire on the Americans from shore. The firing ends at dusk. Arnold's ships sustain serious damage, and he suffers sixty casualties and uses up three-fourths of his ammunition. Realizing that his fleet cannot possibly resume the battle and that he will have to surrender if he remains where he is, Arnold decides to escape during the night. His ships sail off quietly and unseen.

12 October 1776

LAKE CHAMPLAIN. At dawn Arnold anchors five of his ships at Schuyler's Island; the others have sailed farther ahead. He finds two of his ships so badly damaged that they must be scuttled; a third ship runs aground. The two remaining crafts sail in pursuit of the fleet. Surprised and enraged to find the Americans have escaped, Carleton hastens after them. He catches up at Split Rock, where one American ship runs aground and two others are captured. But Arnold's *Congress* sails on to Crown Point, finding the rest of his fleet already there.

NEW YORK CITY. Gen. Howe embarks with most of his army aboard eighty vessels, traverses treacherous Hell Gate, and lands 4,000 troops on Throg's Neck in an effort to outflank the American position on Harlem Heights. But when the soldiers attempt to cross a causeway and a ford to Manhattan, American musket fire from only twenty-five rangers under Col. Edward Hand drives them back. The Americans are reinforced and both sides dig in. Howe's remaining force lands.

14 October 1776

CROWN POINT, N.Y. Arnold and Lt.

Col. Thomas Hartley, commander of the garrison, realize they cannot defend Crown Point, so they burn the buildings and retreat to Ticonderoga. As they arrive British rowboats under a flag of truce deliver 110 captured American sailors, magnanimously paroled by Carleton. Arnold has lost eleven of his sixteen vessels and eighty of his men, but not without some positive effect—Carleton decides he cannot conquer Fort Ticonderoga and withdraws to St. John's, a fateful decision.

16 October 1776

NEW YORK CITY. Gen. Washington calls a council of war to discuss what should be done in response to Howe's efforts to flank the American lines. Gen. Charles Lee, recently returned from Charleston, strongly advises withdrawing to safer positions.

18 October 1776

NEW YORK CITY. Gen. Washington begins the evacuation of Harlem Heights, as his army of 13,000, with artillery, baggage, and supplies moves northward, some to travel as far as White Plains. The 2,000 troops at Fort Washington remain there because Congress wishes navigation on the Hudson to be interdicted for as long as possible. At the same time Howe loads his men on their transports and sets out for Pell's Point, a peninsula on Pelham Bay and a more advantageous site from which to attack the Americans. Col. John Glover with 750 men races to take up a position behind a stone wall in advance of the British troops. Repeatedly falling back and then firing as the British charge, the Americans drive the enemy back several times until night falls. Glover leads his men to Dobbs Ferry, where they make camp. They have suffered twenty-one casualties.

PHILADELPHIA. Congress grants Tadeusz Kościuszko a commission as colonel of engineers. A graduate of the Royal School in Warsaw, Poland, Kościuszko also studied at the school of artillery and military engineering at Mezières, France. He arrived in Philadelphia in August and was hired to help plan forts along the Delaware River.

22 October 1776

WHITE PLAINS, N.Y. The withdrawal from Harlem Heights to White Plains is completed.

MAMARONECK, N.Y. With about 750 men Col. John Haslet attacks Maj. Robert Rogers' 500-man corps of Tories, "The Queen's American Rangers." Though losing the element of surprise, they manage to capture thirty-six of the Tories and some muskets, which they bring to White Plains.

26 October 1776

PHILADELPHIA. Benjamin Franklin departs for France. The commission, on which Arthur Lee now serves in Jefferson's place, has additional orders to procure eight line-of-battle ships from the French court by purchase or loan. They also have been instructed to try to obtain recognition from other European states of the United States as an independent nation.

28 October 1776

WHITE PLAINS N.Y. While Gen. Washington has bolstered his defenses Gen. Howe has encamped at New Rochelle and then at Mamaroneck. Howe launches an assault on

White Plains but is slowed by a 1,500-man advance guard under Brig. Gen. Joseph Spencer firing from behind stone walls. The Americans fall back to avoid being outflanked, cross the Bronx River, and take positions on Chatterton's Hill. They are reinforced by a regiment commanded by Col. Haslet and a brigade under Gen. Alexander McDougall. The British artillery bombards the hill, and troops follow up with a bayonet attack. A cavalry charge by the light dragoons panics some of the American militia, who flee—many of them to die or to surrender. Haslet holds fast while McDougall begins an orderly retreat. Then, as the dragoons re-form for another charge, Haslet joins the retreat, and the Americans fall back into the main encampment at White Plains. Howe's advance temporarily stalls.

31 October 1776

WHITE PLAINS, N.Y. Gen. Washington pulls his army back to North Castle, where the Americans build a new line of entrenchments.

4 November 1776

CROWN POINT, N.Y. Gen. Carleton's fleet leaves for the return to St. John's.

5 November 1776

WHITE PLAINS, N.Y. Gen. Howe, having decided that Washington's position on North Castle Heights is impregnable, moves his army to encampment at Dobbs Ferry on the east bank of the Hudson River. With reinforcements from Manhattan brought by Lord Percy, Howe's force now totals 20,000.

7 November 1776

FORT WASHINGTON, N.Y. Three British ships pass around the sunken hulks and chevaux-de-frise stretching

CAMP FOLLOWERS

The armies of the Revolution included large numbers of women camp followers, or "necessary women" as they were known officially to the British. Contrary to popular belief, most of these women were not prostitutes or drudges, but the wives of noncommissioned officers and private soldiers, and they performed vital duties for an eighteenth-century army.

Both British and American armies lacked much in the way of support services. There were virtually no medical personnel, for example, attached to the armies and few other essential people like cooks or cleaners. The women camp followers took over most of these duties. They tended the routinely ill, of which there were many during the war, especially in the unhealthy wetlands of the South and during the Northern winters, and gave almost the only medical assistance available to wounded on the battlefield. The women also did the laundry, the cooking, the cleaning, and similar chores.

In return, soldiers' wives and other women camp followers were carried "on ration" by the armies and assigned a regular issuance of food. When the British troops moved by ship across the Atlantic, women were assigned space on the transports, and were entitled to stay with their husbands.

At least two married women camp followers on the American side attained renown during the war. When Mary Corbin and Mary Hays stepped forward in battle to take the places of their fallen husbands, they passed into legend as "Captain Molly" and "Molly Pitcher."

There were doubtless some among the women camp followers who were less than virtuous, but records show that the majority were upright and recognized as vital parts of the army.

Somewhat ironically, given the romantic reputation of the French even in the eighteenth century, Rochambeau's French force that landed in 1780 was the only army in America that did not have women attached to it officially.

across the Hudson River that are meant to obstruct navigation. Since these obstructions prove ineffectual, the purpose of Fort Washington and Fort Lee across the river in New Jersey—to protect the obstruction—seems obviated but the garrison remains. Gen. Putnam is convinced that Fort Washington is impregnable, although it has no internal water source, no outworks, no barracks, and only open earthworks.

FORT CUMBERLAND, NOVA SCOTIA. A group of 180 rebels, mostly of New England origin, begins to lay siege to the fort.

8 November 1776
NORTH CASTLE HEIGHTS, N.Y. Gen.

Washington writes to Gen. Nathanael Greene, who is in charge of both Fort Washington and Fort Lee, that he regards the passage upriver of the three British ships as proof of the forts' inefficacy but leaves it to Greene to decide whether to abandon them.

10 November 1776

FORT CUMBERLAND, NOVA SCOTIA. Jonathan Eddy, leader of the rebels, sends Col. Joseph Goreham, commander of the fort, a summons to surrender.

PHILADELPHIA. John Paul Jones, promoted to captain on 10 October, sets sail in the *Providence* intent on taking British ships as prizes in the sea lanes from Nova Scotia to Bermuda.

12 November 1776

FORT LEE, N.J. Gen. Washington visits Gen. Greene to discuss whether to abandon the forts, but no decision is made.

13 November 1776

FORT CUMBERLAND, NOVA SCOTIA. His demand for surrender rejected, Jonathan Eddy launches an attack on the fort. It fails.

16 November 1776

FORT ORANGE, ST. EUSTATIUS. An eleven-gun salute from this Dutch outpost answers the salute of the USS *Andrea Doria*, flying the red-and-white-striped flag of the Continental Congress—the first official salute of the American flag by a foreign nation.

FORT WASHINGTON, N.Y. Early in the morning Washington, on a second visit, rows with generals Greene, Put-

nam, and Mercer to Fort Washington to make a decision on evacuation. They arrive just in time to hear the cannonade signaling Howe's attack on the fort and row back to Fort Lee. The decision has been made for them. The Fort Washington garrison of about 3,000 men led by Col. Robert Magaw is outnumbered at least three to one by the British attacking force.

The *"action"* at Fort Washington, another disaster.

Magaw has three detachments posted in a ring before the fort under Lt. Col. Lambert Cadwalader, Col. Baxter, and Lt. Col. Moses Rawlings. British troops under Lord Percy and Gen. Edward Mathews and Hessians under Gen. Wilhelm Knyphausen attack these three detachments simultaneously. Within three hours the American lines collapse and the troops flee into Fort Washington. Recognizing the hopelessness of his position, Magaw surrenders. The British suffer more than 450 casualties but take 2,858 prisoners and the artillery, ammunition, and supplies, including hundreds of entrenching tools, at the fort. The Americans suffer more than 150 casualties and total defeat. British prospects seem suddenly brighter.

20 November 1776

CLOSTER, N.J. Having crossed the

Hudson River during the night, Lord Cornwallis arrives at daylight with a force of 4,000 British and Hessian troops and immediately marches south toward Fort Lee, intending to cut the Americans off from any escape to Hackensack, where Washington is now encamped with about 3,000 soldiers. An American officer on patrol discovers the advancing troops and rides to warn Gen. Greene. The general sends word to Washington and orders evacuation of Fort Lee. Most of the Americans make good their escape, but more than 100 are captured and several are killed. Lord Cornwallis takes possession of Fort Lee and the supplies abandoned by the fleeing Americans.

21 November 1776

HACKENSACK, N.J. Washington and his small force pull out and march toward Newark. Gen. Charles Lee remains with 5,000 troops at North Castle despite Washington's recommendation that he move his force to the New Jersey side of the river. Gen. Heath has about 3,200 fit troops at Peekskill.

28 November 1776

NEWARK, N.J. After five days of rest Washington's troops break camp and march toward New Brunswick. Cornwallis dogs their heels, occupying Newark.

29 November 1776

NEW BRUNSWICK, N.J. Washington and his bedraggled troops, fatigued and dispirited, arrive and are met by about 1,200 troops under Lord Stirling who are also in a wretched state, some shoeless and shirtless.

FORT CUMBERLAND, NOVA SCOTIA. British reinforcements arrive from Halifax and break the rebel siege. Goreham pardons the rebels, over 100 of whom surrender their weapons and voice regret for the siege.

30 November 1776

NEW BRUNSWICK, N.J. About 2,000 militiamen from Maryland and New Jersey whose enlistments have expired head for home, while some militiamen from Pennsylvania desert. Washington, believing that the entire American cause is in grave danger, has no choice but to continue his flight before the oncoming Cornwallis.

NEW YORK CITY. The Howes, feeling that recent victories have created an opportunity, issue a proclamation promising pardons to Americans who declare their allegiance to the crown within sixty days.

1 December 1776

NEW BRUNSWICK, N.J. Once again Cornwallis nearly catches Washington, who crosses the Raritan River and then destroys the timber supports of the bridge that spans it. Gen. Howe orders Cornwallis to halt at New Brunswick.

2 December 1776

NORTH CASTLE, N.Y. Gen. Charles Lee finally crosses the Hudson River.

3 December 1776

TRENTON, N.J. Washington's troops arrive here at the Delaware River—crossing to the west bank offers hope of safety. Washington has ordered all boats along the river assembled for ferrying his troops across.

4 December 1776

ST. NAZAIRE, FRANCE. Benjamin Franklin arrives on his mission to France and Europe. He has crossed the ocean safely aboard the *Reprisal*, commanded by Capt. Lambert Wickes. Franklin is accompanied by two grandsons, William Temple Franklin (age sixteen) and Benjamin Franklin Bache (seven). William, whose father William Franklin is now under house arrest after being deposed as governor of New Jersey, is to serve as his grandfather's clerk.

5 December 1776

TRENTON, N.J. The Pennsylvania Associators (a military organization of patriots formed before the Revolution) and part of Col. Nicholas Haussegger's regiment of Germans from Pennsylvania and Maryland arrive, strengthening Washington's depleted force.

6 December 1776

NEW BRUNSWICK, N.J. Cornwallis, now joined by Gen. Howe, resumes the pursuit of Washington at Howe's order.

WILLIAMSBURG, VA. The state legislature incorporates the County of Kentucky.

7 December 1776

TRENTON, N.J. Washington, with 1,200 troops, sets out for Princeton but meets the retreating Lord Stirling en route—Cornwallis is coming. The Americans return to Trenton.

TAPPAN, N.Y. A force of Tories and British marauders known as cowboys pillage the town, tormenting local patriots and cutting down their liberty pole.

8 December 1776

TRENTON, N.J. Cornwallis' force marches into Trenton too late. Washington has crossed the Delaware River. His troops have seized all the boats up and down the river for seventy-five miles and destroyed those not needed for the crossing. If he wants to continue the pursuit, Cornwallis must first have boats made. Instead he obtains Howe's permission to halt at the river. On the Pennsylvania side Washington deploys his troops thinly along a front of at least twenty-five miles. Though Cornwallis has halted, panic spreads in Philadelphia, where residents begin to pack their belongings and flee into the countryside. Washington sends Gen. Israel Putnam to fortify the city and impose martial law.

NEWPORT, R.I. Gen. Sir Henry Clinton, under orders of Gen. Howe, who has found Clinton's insistent advice aggravating, sails into Newport with 6,000 soldiers and takes possession of the town.

12 December 1776

PHILADELPHIA. The Continental Congress, anxious that the British might sweep down upon Philadelphia and capture Congress itself, adjourns to Baltimore. Before departure the members pass a resolution stating "that until Congress shall otherwise order, General Washington be possessed of full power to order and direct all things relative to the department, and the operations of war." The resolution gives Washington virtual dictatorial powers. Responding to a recommendation by Washington, Congress authorizes a regiment of light dragoons —the 2d Dragoons, consisting of a Connecticut battalion of light horse already recruited by Washington— and commissions Elisha Sheldon of Connecticut as colonel and commander of the regiment, the first cavalry unit in the American army.

13 December 1776

BASKING RIDGE, N.J. The nearly insubordinate and unresponsive Gen. Charles Lee, who has detained his 5,500 troops in northern New Jersey hoping for a chance to attack Gen. Howe from the rear, is surprised and captured by a British reconnaissance patrol of the Queen's Light Dragoons at White's Tavern. Subaltern Banastre Tarleton orders Lee to surrender or his men will set fire to the tavern and put everyone inside to the sword. Lee attempts to escape. The British kill or wound all his staff officers and take him prisoner. The *Freeman's Journal* comments: "The enemy showed an ungenerous, nay, boyish triumph, after they had got him secure at Brunswick, by making his horse drunk while they toasted their King till they were in the same condition. A band or two of music played all night to proclaim their joy for this important acquisition. They say we cannot now stand another campaign. Mistaken fools! to think the fate of America depended on one man. They will find ere long that it has no other effect than to urge us on to noble revenge."

14 December 1776

TRENTON, N.J. Gen. Howe ends the pursuit of Washington and orders his troops into winter quarters. He and the largest contingent of his British troops head for New York City, while the Hessian troops under Col. Carl von Donop remain in New Jersey in Amboy, New Brunswick, Princeton, and Trenton. The 42nd Black Watch holds Bordentown. Howe gives Lord Cornwallis permission to return to England.

19 December 1776

PHILADELPHIA. Thomas Paine, now serving as a volunteer assistant aide-de-camp to Gen. Nathanael Greene and a member of the American force that fled across New Jersey, publishes the first tract of his *The American Crisis* in the *Pennsylvania Journal*. It begins: "These are the times that try men's souls. The summer soldier and the sunshine patriot will, in this crisis, shrink from the service of his country; but he that stands it now deserves the love and thanks of man and woman. Tyranny, like hell, is not easily conquered; yet we have this consolation with us—that the harder the conflict, the more glorious the triumph. What we obtain too cheap, we esteem too lightly." Paine asserts that God will not abandon the Americans, certainly not in favor of King George, whom he equates with "a common murderer, a highwayman, or a housebreaker." He recounts the conditions of the retreat across New Jersey and the state of the army and praises the steadfastness of Gen. Washington. And he exhorts his readers: "Up and help us; lay your shoulders to the wheel. . . . Let it be told to the future world that in the depth of winter, when nothing but hope and virtue could survive, that the city and country, alarmed at one common danger, came forth to meet and to repulse it."

20 December 1776

BALTIMORE. The Continental Congress reconvenes, but fewer than half the members are present. Gen. Washington writes to the Congress: "I can only say that desperate diseases require desperate remedies; and I with truth declare that I have no lust after power, but I wish with as much fervency as any man upon this wide-extended continent for an opportunity of turning the sword into the plough-share." The words reassure that the commander has no desire to take advantage of the power Congress has granted him except in furtherance of the war effort. He orders up recruits and militia and requests money from state legislatures.

NEWTOWN, PA. Maj. Gen. John Sullivan, who has assumed Lee's command, has crossed the Delaware and arrives at Washington's encampment with 2,000 troops. At the same time Gen. Gates arrives with 500 men from Schuyler's command; Col. John Cadwalader, with 1,000 Philadelphia Associators; and Col. Nicholas Haussegger, with his Maryland and Pennsylvania Germans. Most of the new arrivals, however, are poorly clothed, ill, or otherwise in a sorry state.

NEW YORK CITY. Gen. Howe writes to Germain and proposes a change in strategy. His offer of a pardon has drawn hundreds of New Jersey and Pennsylvania residents to the British side, and this change of allegiances has persuaded him that capturing Philadelphia—within easy striking distance of his forces in New Jersey—

will end the rebellion in the Middle Colonies. So he proposes sending 10,000 men against Philadelphia, but this will mean postponing the planned offensive against Boston from Rhode Island and diverting troops from the New York campaign against Albany. The proposal represents a shift in the strategy in place since Bunker Hill: to break the back of the rebellion in New England by attacking from both Canada and the Atlantic.

21 December 1776

PARIS, FRANCE. Benjamin Franklin arrives to join Silas Deane and Arthur Lee in the effort to negotiate treaties with European nations and to seek loans from France.

24 December 1776

NEWTOWN, PA. Gen. Washington calls a council of war to discuss his plan for a surprise attack, the principal objective being Trenton. Generals Greene, Sullivan, Mercer, Stirling, Roche de Fermoy, and St. Clair attend along with several colonels. They adopt the plan. Washington issues the password for the operation: "Victory or Death."

25 December 1776

MCKONKEY'S FERRY, PA. Three divisions of American troops set out to cross the Delaware River for the attack on Trenton, but the two embarking at Trenton Ferry under Gen. James Ewing and at Bristol under Col. John Cadwalader abandon the effort, discouraged by severe weather and ice floes in the river. Cadwalader, believing it impossible to cross at Bristol, actually marches to Dunk's Ferry and crosses there, but returns to the Pennsylvania side when he cannot get his artillery across. Only Gen. Washington's division, comprised of 2,400 men in two corps commanded by Greene and Sullivan, succeeds in making the crossing as planned, transported by Col. John Glover's Marblehead oarsmen in flat-bottomed Durham boats designed to haul grain and iron ore. Washington and his division assemble at McKonkey's Ferry after dark. Its members include seasoned veterans John Stark and Aaron Burr along with new recruits John Marshall and James Monroe. Col. John Knox's artillery is there with eighteen field pieces—Alexander Hamilton, who provided competent artillery service at the Battle of White Plains, commands one of the batteries. Washington hopes to have his entire force in place on the New Jersey bank by midnight. He crosses with the advance party to await the others, but they proceed laboriously, struggling against snow and sleet and ice chunks driven against the boats by fierce winds.

26 December 1776

TRENTON, N.J. By 3:00 A.M. Knox's artillery has reached the east bank of the Delaware, and Washington's entire force is assembled for the nine-mile march to Trenton through a wind-and-sleet storm. Halfway to Trenton Sullivan's corps continues along the road by the Delaware to enter the town from the south while Greene's corps marches along the Pennington Road to enter the town from the north. Four cannons precede the columns, with others accompanying the reserves. Washington accompanies Greene's corps. About 1,500 men and six cannons comprise the Trenton garrison—Hessian regiments under Col. Johann Rall—but there are no fortifications. By daybreak the Americans enter Trenton. Knox places his cannons at the juncture of King and Queen streets, the main thoroughfares, while Sullivan's and Greene's troops take up positions to seal off other streets and move in to attack.

The Hessians (some, including Col. Rall, rather stupified from celebrating Christmas) awake to a total surprise. Unable to muster an organized defense, they retreat before Americans attacking with bayonets or using muskets as clubs (some have wet firing pans and cannot discharge). Many Hessians are shot by American soldiers firing from houses. As the Hessians flee down Trenton's streets they are decimated by Knox's artillery fire. The Americans take full possession of the town. Col. Rall and some of his men manage to re-form in an orchard on the town's outskirts. While Rall organizes them for a counterattack, Knox trains captured British cannons

THE GERMAN MERCENARIES

Although most often lumped under the single label *Hessians*, the nearly 30,000 German mercenary soldiers who fought for the British in America during the Revolution actually came from six small German states: Hesse-Kassel, Hesse-Hanau, Brunswick, Waldeck, Anhalt-Zerbst, and Anspach-Bayreuth. The troops were not hired individually but by entire unit under contracts between their rulers and Great Britain. The soldiers themselves were highly disciplined, highly trained members of armies organized according to the Prussian precepts of Frederick the Great.

The British had to fall back on mercenary forces because the well of manpower in the British Isles had run virtually dry after the prolonged wars of the preceding decades. The English turned first to the Dutch and the Russians, but could not persuade either to sell the services of troops. The German petty princes and dukes, however, were all too glad to take British gold, and they drove hard bargains. In addition to a payment for each soldier shipped to America, the British also had to ante up large annual subsidies to the German rulers. Parliament appropriated more than 4.5 million pounds for mercenaries.

Most of the Germans were foot-soldiers, but there were also specialized jaeger units of riflemen and units of dragoons (the latter sailing without their horses, however). The Germans supplied their own officers as well, including many competent veterans of the European wars. Baron von Riedesel, for example, who was a native Hessian but commanded the troops of the Duke of Brunswick, was a good soldier whom the British failed to use to best advantage. Jacob Rall, on the other hand, foolishly underestimated his American foes and paid for the mistake with his life at Trenton. On the whole, the Germans fought well and took part in every major battle of the war. Their reputation among Americans for unusual cruelty was probably undeserved.

About 5,000 German mercenary soldiers deserted during the Revolution and added to the ethnic mix of the new nation. Nearly 8,000 died in battle or as the result of wounds or sickness.

---

on the orchard and looses a barrage of grape and canister. Rall falls mortally wounded, and his men flee. The entire battle is over in an hour and a half. Upon rounding up their prisoners, the Americans learn they have captured over 900 of the enemy, have killed 22 and wounded 92; about 400 Hessians have escaped to Bordentown. The Americans have suffered no dead and only a few wounded, including James Monroe and William Washington, the commander's nephew, who were hit by musket balls when charging and capturing a Hessian cannon emplacement.

Washington, realizing that his troops are exhausted, decides that he cannot risk pushing on to Princeton and New Brunswick without Ewing and Cadwalader, and that he must recross the Delaware before Cornwallis sends out an attacking force. He returns to the boats and crosses to McKonkey's Ferry with his troops and their prisoners and captured supplies. *Freeman's Journal* reports: "The men behaved with the utmost bravery . . . rushed like bloodhounds upon the Hessians, who, astonished at their fury, fled or threw down their arms; and it was owing to the ardor of the attack that so little blood was shed." Washington has achieved a stunning victory that unnerves the other Hessian and British outposts. Von Donop immediately withdraws from Mount Holly to Allentown, ordering the Hessians at Bordentown to join him; and the troops at Burlington evacuate that town, some heading for Princeton and the others for New Brunswick.

27 December 1776

BALTIMORE. The Continental Congress, rejoicing over the victory at Trenton, adopts a resolution granting Washington a six-month extension of his "dictatorial powers," spelling them out in more detail, including full power to raise more battalions, infantry, artillery, dragoons, and engineers and to appoint all officers below the rank of brigadier general. The Congress also resolves to raise sixteen new at-large regiments.

BRISTOL, PA. In the morning Cadwalader, having learned of the American success at Trenton, recrosses the Delaware with his 1,800 men to the New Jersey side, where he receives a letter from Washington regretting the failure of Ewing's and Cadwalader's efforts of the previous day and informing him that the army has returned to the west bank. Cadwalader thinks he must be in danger but, persuaded by Col. Joseph Reed that his men want action, decides to push forward. He discovers that the enemy has evacuated Burlington and Bordentown.

30 December 1776

TRENTON, N.J. Gen. Washington, embarking the previous day to recross the Delaware, arrives in Trenton. He learns that Lord Cornwallis and Gen. James Grant have assembled an army of 8,000 and a train of artillery at Princeton and an advance troop is en route to Trenton. He sends for Gen. Mifflin's 1,600 Philadelphia militia now at Bordentown and Cadwalader's 2,100 troops at Crosswicks, raising his force to 5,000 men and forty cannon. But many of his men are untrained, ragged, exhausted, and hungry. Enlistments expire on this day for about half of Gen. Washington's troops. He addresses them and persuades most to stay on for another six weeks, adding the benefit of a ten-dollar bounty for those who volunteer.

BALTIMORE. Congress, responding to the report of a committee appointed on 24 December to study obtaining foreign assistance, now resolves to send commissioners "to the courts of Vienna, Spain, Prussia and the Grand Duke of Tuscany." These and the commissioners already abroad are instructed to seek the European nations' help in preventing Great Britain from sending more troops to America and are to offer sharing the Newfoundland fisheries and any territorial conquests with France and giving the harbor and town of Pensacola to Spain.

★ 1777 ★

A year that will include both buoyant victory and disheartening loss for the Americans begins in triumph as Washington quickly follows up his victory at Trenton with an advance into New Jersey, inflicting another defeat on the British at Princeton. In the space of a few days, Washington has succeeded in pushing the British out of all but a small toehold in New Jersey. Satisfied for the time being, Washington leads the Continental Army into winter quarters at Morristown. Congress reconvenes at Philadelphia in March after meeting briefly in Baltimore.

In May the British begin to implement a strategic plan to seal off the northern and New England colonies. Gen. John Burgoyne lands with an army in Quebec. He is to march south from Canada, through upper New York, and take Albany. Another British army is to meet him after moving northward along the Hudson River, but the plan is imprecise and vague as to timing. Burgoyne takes Ticonderoga in early July, but the pace of his advance is slowed by the rugged terrain and the harassment of a small American army under Schuyler. A second British column, moving independently south from Canada under Barry St. Leger, is derailed by a battle at Oriskany, New York.

Meanwhile, the main British army under commander-in-chief Gen. Howe embarks on its own mission, sailing aboard the fleet from New York Harbor, headed for the Chesapeake and intent on taking Philadelphia. Congress flees first to Lancaster, Pennsylvania, and then York after it receives reports of Howe's movements.

To the north, Burgoyne's campaign begins to unravel. His army is dealt a blow by Vermont militia at Bennington, and the force that was to advance from lower New York to link with him never gets on track. Despite the deteriorating condition of his troops and supplies and against the advice of his subordinates he presses on, however, and comes up against a growing American army now commanded by Gen. Horatio Gates near Saratoga, New York. Two battles seal Burgoyne's fate, and he is forced to surrender his entire army to the Americans by mid-October.

Simultaneously Howe lands his main force and advances on Philadelphia. Washington attempts to block Howe, yet after furious but indecisive battles at Germantown and Brandywine, Howe nudges Washington's army aside and occupies Philadelphia. Washington, his options at an end for the time being, withdraws his exhausted force to winter quarters at Valley Forge.

Congress, functioning in the safety of York, adopts Articles of Confederation. The long-term prospects for the American cause are bolstered in December when France, encouraged by the American victory over Burgoyne, secretly recognizes the new nation.

---

1 January 1777

PRINCETON, N.J. Gen. James Grant arrives with 1,000 men, leaving a guard of only 600 at New Brunswick. Lord Cornwallis also arrives, having ridden fifty miles from New York City; the debacle at Trenton has forced cancellation of his trip to England. Including the 6,000 troops he has brought with him, Cornwallis' command at Princeton totals 8,000 men.

TRENTON. Gen. Washington, who now has a force of about 5,100 men, sends a brigade under Brig. Gen. Roche de Fermoy, a French volunteer, toward Princeton to try to delay Cornwallis' anticipated march to Trenton. Gen. de Fermoy occupies a position south of Maidenhead.

PHILADELPHIA. Emphasizing the importance of negotiations with Spain, the Congress appoints Benjamin Franklin commissioner to that nation's court.

2 January 1777

TRENTON. In the early morning Cornwallis leaves a force of 1,200 men commanded by Lt. Col. Charles Mawhood to guard Princeton and begins the march to Trenton with 5,500 troops and twenty-eight artillery. Deep mud created by heavy rains the previous night slows their progress. At about 10:00 A.M. they come upon the American advance guard, now commanded by Col. Edward Hand, as De Fermoy has returned to Trenton. The Americans retreat slowly, stopping at advantageous positions to skirmish and thus delay the British advance—holding the enemy for three hours at Shabbakonk Creek and for another hour at the north side of Trenton. Finally, firing from behind houses and fences, they fall back to the ridge along the south bank of Assunpink Creek, where Washington has positioned his force behind earthworks. By five in the afternoon a 1,500-man British advance guard reaches the creek. Three times American fire prevents their crossing a bridge. When Cornwallis arrives with the main body of the British force, he decides that Washington, with his back to the Delaware River, is trapped. So Cornwallis withdraws his men to encamp and prepare for attack the following day. The American soldiers light their campfires. Washington calls a council of war. He and his officers choose an audacious plan: to withdraw under cover of darkness, march around the British left flank, skirt Maidenhead, and attack Princeton and then New Brunswick. Washington sets 400 men to deceive Cornwallis by noisily building entrenchments and heaping the campfires with wood—they will remain until daybreak and then sneak off and hasten toward Princeton.

General Washington at Princeton, directing his troops.

3 January 1777

PRINCETON. Washington sets forth from Trenton at 1:00 A.M. Fortunately, a sudden temperature drop has frozen the roads during the night, facilitating the march. With their wheels wrapped in rags, the gun carriages move quietly on the frozen mud. Reaching Stony Brook, Washington leaves 350 men under Gen. Hugh Mercer to hold a stone bridge in the event Cornwallis comes in pursuit. The main army heads for Princeton. But Mawhood is already astride his horse, under orders to march most of his men to join Gen. Leslie at Maidenhead. They cross Stony Brook bridge and see Mercer's men heading for them. Both forces race to take a

position in a nearby orchard. The Americans win the race and, crouching behind trees and hedges, fire on the British. Mawhood orders his men to attack with their bayonets, and the unnerved Americans flee before them. Mercer, trying to rally his men, falls mortally wounded by seven bayonet thrusts. Cadwalader's men, approaching from the same direction as Mercer, enter the fray.

Hearing the firing, Washington and his staff leave Sullivan's division and gallop into the melee. Waving his hat, Washington attempts to rally Mercer's and Cadwalader's retreating men and races ahead toward the midst of the pursuing British. An aide covers his eyes, not wanting to see his commander die, as the British fire a volley at Washington, now within thirty yards of their muskets. But the clearing smoke reveals the commander intact astride his white horse shouting for his men to come on. Many of them rally and, joined by men from Sullivan's division, charge into the British, firing at point-blank range. Mawhood and many of his men break free and retreat toward Trenton, with Washington and a troop of Philadelphia dragoons in hot pursuit. Finally the British scatter and run, throwing away muskets and equipment in their haste to escape. Meanwhile, the 194 men left behind are driven back to Princeton, where they are forced to surrender. The troops who had remained in Princeton have fled to New Brunswick before the American assault. British losses exceed 250; the Americans have 40 killed—including Mercer and Col. John Haslet—and 100 wounded.

It is a stunning victory for Washington, and he is tempted to move on to attack New Brunswick; but, knowing that his men are exhausted and that Cornwallis is probably fast marching to Princeton, he decides to withdraw toward Morristown. Cornwallis' men, forced to ford Stony Brook's breast-deep waters because American soldiers have destroyed the bridge, enter Princeton in time to see the rear guard of Washington's army withdrawing in the distance. Assuming that Washington is headed for New Brunswick, Cornwallis hastens toward that town, intent on securing his supply depot there.

The Army's winter quarters at Morristown, New Jersey.

4 January 1777

PLUCKEMIN, N.J. Washington pauses here to allow his troops to rest. Cornwallis enters New Brunswick after an all-night march.

5 January 1777

PLUCKEMIN, N.J. Hoping to secure some advantage from the victories at Trenton and Princeton, Gen. Washington writes to Gen. William Heath in the Hudson Highlands and instructs him to "move down towards New York with a considerable force, as if you had a design upon the city; that being an object of great importance, the enemy will be reduced to the necessity of withdrawing a considerable part of their force from the Jerseys, if not the whole, to secure the city."

6 January 1777

MORRISTOWN, N.J. Washington's army settles into winter quarters in the Watchung Mountains; from here he can keep an eye on New York City and the roads leading to New England and Philadelphia. American contingents capture Hackensack and Elizabethtown. Now, instead of controlling New Jersey as before, the British forces hold only Amboy and New Brunswick, with 5,000 troops in each town.

9 January 1777

BALTIMORE. The Continental Congress dismisses Dr. John Morgan as director- general of hospitals. Morgan has worked hard to organize an effective medical service for the army, making enemies in the process. No explanation is given for his dismissal.

16 January 1777

WESTMINSTER, N.H. New Hampshire grants Vermont a declaration of independence, and a convention meeting here votes to request recognition from the Continental Congress as an independent state.

18 January 1777

FORT INDEPENDENCE, N.Y. With three divisions under Gen. Benjamin Lincoln, Gen. Charles Scott, and generals David Wooster and Samuel Parsons converging with his own force near

Spuyten Duyvil, Gen. Heath has almost 6,000 troops for an attack on Fort Independence north of Kingsbridge on the approach to Manhattan. The fort is manned by about 2,000 Hessians. The Hessian commander, though taken totally by surprise, rejects Heath's demand to surrender within twenty minutes and unleashes a cannonade against the Americans. Heath considers how to respond.

20–22 January 1777

SOMERSET COURTHOUSE, N.J. British troops advance to this village looking for provisions, resulting in a skirmish with American troops encamped at Morristown. Led by Brig. Gen. Philemon Dickinson, some 400 Continentals drive off the British foraging party and capture some prisoners, wagons, and horses.

25 January 1777

DELANCEY'S MILLS, N.Y. Following several days of ineffectual fighting at Fort Independence, a party of British and Tory soldiers routs Heath's men.

29 January 1777

FORT INDEPENDENCE, N.Y. Hessian troops sally forth and send American troops into flight. Gen. Heath decides to withdraw, returning to Spuyten Duyvil and eliciting the scorn of the Hessians.

2 February 1777

FORT MCINTOSH, GA. A Tory militia force stationed on the Florida–Georgia border attacks this small stockade on the bank of the Satilla River that is commanded by Capt. Richard Winn of the Continentals.

4 February 1777

FORT MCINTOSH, GA. After a two-day

siege Capt. Winn is forced to surrender. The Tories parole all their captives except for two officers taken as hostages to St. Augustine.

15 February 1777

BALTIMORE. Following long intermittent discussions inspired by concern over inflationary prices generated by the excessive but necessary issuance of paper money, the Congress approves the response of a New England convention—recommending the rigid regulation of prices—and encourages the other states to hold conventions and follow the New England lead.

19 February 1777

BALTIMORE. The Congress promotes five men to major generalships: Lord Stirling, Thomas Mifflin, Adam Stephen, Arthur St. Clair, and Benjamin Lincoln. Furious at being omitted from the list, Benedict Arnold submits his resignation but is persuaded by Gen. Washington to withdraw it.

25 February 1777

LONDON, ENGLAND. King George's cabinet, overlooking the king's message to Lord North that Germain will propose Gen. Clinton be put in charge of the Canadian forces and Gen. Burgoyne be sent to join Gen. Howe, approves sending Burgoyne to Canada to assume a dual command with Carleton.

27 February 1777

BALTIMORE. The Continental Congress adjourns, scheduled to meet in Philadelphia on 4 March.

28 February 1777

LONDON, ENGLAND. Gen. Burgoyne, who has been on leave in England and has taken the cure at Bath, presents his plan for the 1777 campaign to Germain. He proposes sending a force of 8,000 men southward from Canada by way of Lake Champlain while a small force moves through Oswego and down the Mohawk River—the two forces to unite on the Hudson River above Albany, the objective of the invasion. He thus rejects the alternative of a strike force from the sea, asserting: "I do not conceive any expedition from the sea can be so formidable to the enemy, or so effectual to close the war, as an invasion from Canada by Ticonderoga." The intent is to take control of the Hudson and seal off New England from the other states, freeing Gen. Howe to attack Philadelphia and southward or to pursue some other alternative plan.

3 March 1777

LONDON, ENGLAND. Lord Germain writes to Gen. Howe approving his plan to attack Philadelphia and southward, although he makes no promises about providing the additional 20,000 troops Howe wants, stating that the reinforcements may amount to only 5,500 men.

12 March 1777

PHILADELPHIA. Unable to form a quorum on 4 March as planned, the Continental Congress now reconvenes, but some of the states are still not represented.

13 March 1777

PHILADELPHIA. The Congress, distracted and annoyed by the problem of large numbers of foreign officers seeking commissions to serve in the Continental Army—many of them presumptively mercenaries with du-

bious motives—orders the Committee of Secret Correspondence to write immediately to "all their ministers and agents abroad, to discourage all gentlemen from coming to America with expectation of employment in the service, unless they are masters of our language, and have the best of recommendations."

14 March 1777

MORRISTOWN, N.J. Plagued by desertions, and with the six-week re-enlistment period Washington persuaded many soldiers to accept at the end of 1776 now ended, his army has dwindled to fewer than 3,000 men; two-thirds of these are militia whose enlistment period terminates at the end of March. The Congress has authorized raising some 75,000 troops on paper and has offered bounties of $20 plus 100 acres of land at the end of the period of service, but so far recruitment lags badly. What few troops he has Washington keeps busy in harassing the enemy, attacking their foraging parties and sentinels, in an effort to make Gen. Howe think the American force is greater than it is. Washington is forced to commandeer supplies from civilians in order to feed his men.

23 March 1777

PEEKSKILL, N.Y. The previous November Gen. Washington had left 3,300 troops here to watch over the Hudson Highlands. Although in the intervening months large quantities of military supplies have been stored at the post, the great majority of the troops are gone and Massachusetts has ignored Washington's request for eight regiments to hold it. The post is manned by only 250 troops under

Gen. Alexander McDougall. Ten British vessels disembark 500 British soldiers for an attack on this storehouse. McDougall withdraws from the town, requesting Col. Marinus Willett to send troops over from Fort Montgomery across the river. The British advance guard burns the American barracks and some military supplies. Willett arrives with eighty men and unsuccessfully urges McDougall to attack. With the general's permission, Willett attacks, firing on the British and then charging with bayonets. The British fall back to their boats and withdraw.

26 March 1777

LONDON, ENGLAND. Lord Germain signs the orders for Carleton incorporating Gen. Burgoyne's plan, sending them to Quebec with Burgoyne; he sends a copy of the orders to Gen. Howe. He also orders Carleton, once the Americans have been driven out of Canada, to retain enough troops there to defend the province and to dispatch the remainder to march south and join Burgoyne's command for the invasion of the colonies. Lt. Col. Barry St. Leger is to lead these troops on a diversionary march through the Mohawk Valley while Burgoyne heads for Albany.

2 April 1777

NEW YORK CITY. Gen. Howe writes to Lord Germain advising him that since the requested reinforcements have been denied him, he will not be able to move overland to attack Philadelphia but instead will load his troops aboard ships in New York Harbor and sail to Philadelphia for an assault from the water. If carried out, this decision will mean that Howe's force will be unavailable to augment the northern campaign—the invasion from Canada—but Germain has not made clear to him the nature of this invasion.

11 April 1777

PHILADELPHIA. Congress names William Shippen, a Philadelphia physician, to replace John Morgan as director-general of hospitals. He has served as director-general of the Continental Army hospital in New Jersey, and in March he submitted a plan for reorganizing the medical service to Congress, which accepted it.

13 April 1777

BOUND BROOK, N.J. British troops under Lord Cornwallis attack the American outpost commanded by Maj. Gen. Benjamin Lincoln. Taken by surprise, Lincoln manages to withdraw most of his 500 men; but the British take some prisoners along with Lincoln's artillery and bring them back to New York.

17 April 1777

PHILADELPHIA. Congress resolves that in the future the Committee of Secret Correspondence will be called the Committee for Foreign Affairs. Congress also appoints Thomas Paine as secretary to the committee.

20 April 1777

FRANCE. Marie Joseph du Motier (the Marquis de Lafayette) and Johann Kalb ("Baron de Kalb"), his mentor, set sail for America with the blessing of Silas Deane to join the Revolution.

25 April 1777

NORWALK, CONN. Under orders from Gen. Howe to destroy an American magazine of supplies at Danbury, William Tryon, now a major general, lands at the mouth of the Saugatuck River with a force of about 2,000 men, including 300 Tories.

26 April 1777

DANBURY, CONN. Encountering no opposition on his march to Danbury, Tryon discovers that the small detachment of Continentals guarding the post has withdrawn, taking some supplies with them. His men begin to destroy what has been left behind.

27 April 1777

DANBURY, CONN. The work of destruction continues into the morning. The British burn nineteen houses, twenty-two storehouses and barns, and quantities of meats, flour, clothing, and tents. Tryon begins the return march to Norwalk.

RIDGEFIELD, CONN. Benedict Arnold, sulking at his sister's house in New Haven because he was passed over for promotion to major general, learns of Tryon's attack on Danbury. He saddles up and rides to Redding, where generals Wooster and Silliman are situated with 600 men. They march to Bethel, arriving in the early morning. Learning that the British will be returning to Norwalk, they divide into two units. Arnold and Silliman head for Ridgefield with 400 men, while Wooster sets out to harass the British rear guard with 200 troops. Wooster skirmishes repeatedly until mortally wounded only two miles from Ridgefield; his men retreat. At Ridgefield Arnold is joined by 100 more militia. They barricade the road at the north of town and fire as the British approach. About to be outflanked, the

Americans retreat. Arnold is nearly captured when he becomes entangled in his stirrups as his horse is shot from under him. Shooting an attacking Tory demanding his surrender, he manages to untangle himself and escape.

28 April 1777

NORWALK, CONN. Tryon makes his way to Compo Hill, close to where he will board his ships. Arnold's men form for an attack, but 400 British troops led by Gen. Erskine charge them with bayonets and the Americans scatter. Tryon's men board ship and sail off. The two-day encounter has cost the Americans about sixty casualties, including twenty dead; the exact British losses are unclear, though they have at least sixty dead.

1 May 1777

PHILADELPHIA. Congress appoints Arthur Lee commissioner to Spain. He replaces Benjamin Franklin in that post.

2 May 1777

PHILADELPHIA. The Continental Congress, praising Benedict Arnold for his "gallant conduct" at Danbury, promotes him to major general, though he remains junior to the five men who were promoted ahead of him on 19 February.

FORT HENRY, VA. Lt. William Linn arrives with a cargo of ninety-eight barrels of powder to aid the frontier fight against Indians and Tories.

3 May 1777

DUNKIRK, FRANCE. Gustavus Conyngham, "the Dunkirk Pirate," appointed by the American commissioners in

Paris at the beginning of March as commander of the *Surprise,* attacks and captures the British packet *Prince of Orange* and brings her into port.

6 May 1777

QUEBEC. Gen. John Burgoyne arrives aboard the HMS *Apollo* to assume command of British forces in Canada. Sir Guy Carleton welcomes him.

7 May 1777

PHILADELPHIA. Congress appoints Ralph Izard commissioner to the court of the Grand Duke of Tuscany. He replaces Franklin in this post.

8 May 1777

MORRISTOWN, N.J. Gen. Washington issues a general order condemning gaming: "... reports prevailing, which it is to be feared are too well founded, that this destructive vice has spread its baneful influence in the army, and ... to the prejudice of the recruiting service, the Commander-in-chief ... forbids all officers and soldiers playing at cards, dice, or at any games ... it being impossible ... to discriminate between innocent play for amusement and criminal gaming for pecuniary and sordid purposes."

9 May 1777

PHILADELPHIA. Congress names William Lee commissioner to the courts of Berlin and Vienna.

10 May 1777

PISCATAWAY, N.J. Hoping to surprise the 42nd Highlanders (Black Watch) posted here, Maj. Gen. Adam Stephen attacks. The Scots rout the Americans, killing twenty-seven and capturing perhaps twice that number, while Stephen's men inflict fewer

than thirty casualties. Gen. Washington is displeased with Stephen.

15 May 1777

MORRISTOWN, N.J. Following Washington's efforts at recruitment, his army now has burgeoned to 9,000. In addition, he has the equipment to outfit them since in March he received 12,000 muskets, 1,000 barrels of powder, 11,000 flints, and clothing sent surreptitiously from France. Washington organizes his army into five divisions under major generals Greene, Stephen, Sullivan, Lincoln, and Lord Stirling.

17 May 1777

THOMAS' SWAMP, FLA. Col. Augustine Prevost leads a motley group of Indians, Rangers, and British regulars against Col. John Baker's small force of 109 Americans. They rout the Americans, killing eight and capturing thirty-one. But then Prevost and his regulars struggle to save the captives when the Indians begin massacring them, killing over half the prisoners before the British gain control.

29 May 1777

MIDDLEBROOK VALLEY, N.J. Concerned about the moves Gen. Howe might make, Washington moves his army south to this site in the Watchung Mountains, where he can keep watch on the roads to New Brunswick and Philadelphia. Washington stations a force under Sullivan at Princeton.

12 June 1777

NEW BRUNSWICK, N.J. Gen. Howe amasses an 18,000-man British force at Amboy with orders to march to

New Brunswick and from there to separate into a column led by Lord Cornwallis to Somerset and a second column led by Gen. Philip von Heister to Middlebrook. Howe's intent is to cut Sullivan off from Washington's main army and to draw the main army into an attack. His strategy fails.

FORT TICONDEROGA, N.Y. Sent by Gen. Horatio Gates, Maj. Gen. Arthur St. Clair arrives to take command of the small garrison—perhaps 2,500 men—at the fort. Serving under him are three brigadier generals: Alexis Roche de Fermoy from France, John Paterson, and Enoch Poor.

13 June 1777

ST. JOHN'S, QUEBEC. For his march south Gen. Burgoyne has an army of over 7,200 men, including about 150 French Quebeckers, 100 Tories, and 400 Indians, the main force being comprised of British (3,724) and German (3,016) regulars. They are augmented by 138 cannon. Burgoyne also has a fleet of nine ships (three of them captured from Arnold), twenty-eight gunboats, and numerous bateaux to transport this force down Lake Champlain. He stages a massive salute to the Union flag by all the guns in the fort and the fleet.

GEORGETOWN, S.C. The Marquis de Lafayette and Johann Kalb arrive in the United States with written agreements from Silas Deane that the Continental Congress will commission them major generals.

14 June 1777

PHILADELPHIA. The Continental Congress authorizes the official flag of the United States in a resolution stating that the flag shall "be thirteen stripes alternative red and white; that the Union be thirteen stars, white in a blue field, representing a new constellation." The Congress also appoints John Paul Jones commander of the sloop *Ranger*.

16 June 1777

CROWN POINT, N.Y. Burgoyne's advance guard commanded by Brig. Gen. Simon Fraser reaches Crown Point.

17 June 1777

SOMERSET COURTHOUSE, N.J. Col. Daniel Morgan, released by the British and given a regimental command by Washington, harasses British troops trying to set up entrenchments at a redoubt.

18 June 1777

CUMBERLAND HEAD, LAKE CHAMPLAIN. Gen. Burgoyne's main army assembles and prepares to move down the lake.

19 June 1777

NEW BRUNSWICK, N.J. With his efforts to lure Washington into open battle bearing no fruit, Gen. Howe withdraws von Heister's troops from Middlebrook to this anchor post. Washington sends Gen. William Maxwell with a detachment to occupy a position between New Brunswick and Amboy to forestall any attempt by Howe to assault the Americans' exposed left flank.

20 June 1777

CUMBERLAND HEAD, LAKE CHAMPLAIN. Gen. Burgoyne issues a proclamation, a bombastic manifesto actually, accusing the American rebels of inflicting on the "suffering" Tories "the completest system of Tyranny that God ever in his displeasure suffer'd for a time to be exercised over a froward and stubborn Generation," comparing this tyranny to that of the Inquisition; and he threatens the rebels with the vengeance of the Indians and the "devastation, famine and every concomitant horror that a reluctant but indispensable prosecution of military duty must occasion." The exaggerated wording of the proclamation opens Burgoyne to ridicule, even by his countrymen. With the rebels now fairly warned, the theatrical general and his troops set sail for Crown Point.

FORT TICONDEROGA. The unpopular Maj. Gen. Philip Schuyler, still in command of the Northern Department, arrives for a council of war with the generals at the fort. All agree that the fort must be held as long as possible but will have to be abandoned, with the garrison to depart in boats for Mount Independence across the lake.

22 June 1777

NEW BRUNSWICK, N.J. Howe starts for Amboy. American troops led by Daniel Morgan and Anthony Wayne attack his Hessian rear guard. Washington, whose generals argue that the British are staging a genuine withdrawal, moves his main army to Quibbletown along Howe's left flank. Howe switches direction, heading for Scotch Plains, hoping to outflank Washington and occupy the ridges above Middlebrook.

23 June 1777

MONTREAL, CANADA. Lt. Col. Barry St. Leger begins his march southward to juncture with Burgoyne at Albany. His force consists of about 2,000 men, half of them Indians, with 340 British and Hessian regulars and at least as many Tories. He takes with him over a dozen artillery weapons.

26 June 1777

WOODBRIDGE, N.J. Howe sends Cornwallis' force through Woodbridge to attempt to outflank the American left while he moves to Metuchen Meeting House, sending still a third detachment to Bonham Town to confront generals Greene and Wayne. On the outskirts of Woodbridge Cornwallis encounters Lord Stirling. Though outnumbered two to one, Stirling's division fights valiantly, suffering perhaps 100 killed. Washington takes advantage of the delay in Cornwallis' advance to withdraw the main army to the protected positions at Middlebrook. Howe's tactics have failed, and he begins to withdraw all of his troops to Staten Island.

CROWN POINT, N.Y. Gen. Burgoyne has set up a magazine and a hospital and issued supplies. Gen. Fraser's advance guard comprised of Indians, Tories, and Canadians sets out for Ticonderoga.

27 June 1777

COAST OF FRANCE. After a successful foray against British merchantmen in the Irish Channel (they captured eighteen ships, destroying ten and keeping eight as prizes) Capt. Lambert Wickes and his two accompanying raiders encounter the British warship *Burford* when almost returned to France. Wickes orders the other ships to scatter while he tries to make good the *Reprisal*'s escape. He stays out of range at first, but the *Burford* catches up and turns to fire a broadside. Wickes turns to prevent his sides being exposed, has some beams sawed from the *Reprisal* to increase the ship's buoyancy, and speeds to safety.

30 June 1777

NEW YORK CITY AND STATEN ISLAND. Howe's entire army has reassembled, leaving all of New Jersey in control of the Continental Army.

FORT TICONDEROGA. Burgoyne's army disembarks at a landing site secured by Fraser's advance guard.

General John Burgoyne, the British commander defeated at Saratoga.

1 July 1777

FORT TICONDEROGA, N.Y. Gen. Burgoyne's army divides, with the British troops on the west side of Lake Champlain and the Hessians on the east; their flotilla nearly covers the mile-wide lake. They disembark and camp on opposite sides of the lake three miles above the fort, which lies on both sides of the lake, though its principal entrenchments on the west bank are in disrepair.

2 July 1777

FORT TICONDEROGA. Burgoyne begins operations against the fort. Maj. Gen. William Phillips leads a force, including Fraser's advance guard, against Mount Hope. The Americans set the post on fire and flee. Meanwhile Baron von Riedesel leads his division to the rear of Mount Independence, where it receives some fire from the Americans.

3 July 1777

FORT TICONDEROGA. Gen. Phillips' men occupy Mount Hope. Burgoyne

sends his chief engineer, Lt. Twiss, to reconnoiter Sugar Loaf Hill (Mount Defiance). Twiss reports that the hill overlooks both Ticonderoga and Independence within range of the British artillery. Burgoyne issues orders to build a road up the hill and move the artillery into position.

4 July 1777

PHILADELPHIA. Here and throughout the states Americans celebrate the first anniversary of independence. The *Pennsylvania Journal* reports that in Philadelphia at midday the armed ships in the Delaware River each set off thirteen cannons in honor of the thirteen states. In the afternoon the Continental Congress dines on an elegant meal in company with various dignitaries and military officers, while the Hessian band captured at Trenton on 26 December plays appropriate music and a group of British deserters fires celebrative fusillades outside at intervals. Toasts followed. "The evening was closed with the ringing of bells, and at night there was a grand exhibition of fireworks . . . on the commons, and the city was beautifully illuminated. Every thing was conducted with the greatest order and decorum, and the face of joy and gladness was universal." The report concludes: "Thus may the fourth of July, that glorious and ever memorable day, be celebrated through America by the sons of freedom, from age to age, till time shall be no more. Amen and amen."

5 July 1777

FORT TICONDEROGA. Gen. St. Clair observes the British placing cannons on Sugar Loaf Hill and calls a council of war resulting in the quick and unanimous decision to abandon the fort.

6 July 1777

FORT TICONDEROGA. Under cover of the early morning darkness St. Clair marches his men across the bridge to Mount Independence after loading ill soldiers led by Col. Pierce Long and supplies aboard bateaux for transport to Skenesboro. From Mount Independence the Americans march southeast to Hubbardton. St. Clair orders Lt. Col. Seth Warner to wait here with 150 men for the rear guard to appear and then to follow after the main body of troops, which he marches on to Castleton, six miles distant. The arrival of the rear guard augments Warner's force to about 1,000. Warner disregards St. Clair's orders and remains the night in Hubbardton. The British, having quickly learned of the American evacuation of Ticonderoga, are in hot pursuit; an advance party

of about 850 men under Gen. Simon Fraser actually encamps within three miles of Warner. Fraser's Indian scouts discover Warner's encampment—he has posted no pickets—and Fraser decides on a surprise attack for the following morning.

SKENESBORO. Arriving at this weak stockade, Long realizes it is untenable. He sets fire to the buildings and three of his transports and hurries toward Fort Anne. Burgoyne arrives and sends men in pursuit.

7 July 1777

HUBBARDTON, VT. Gen. Fraser's troops surprise Warner's force at dawn and a vicious battle ensues. The Americans, though totally unprepared, mount a ferocious defense. After two hours of fighting the British, suffering from heavy losses inflicted by accurate American shooting, are losing when suddenly a detachment of Hessians under von Riedesel arrives and rushes forward to the rescue; they have heard the sounds of battle. (St. Clair also has heard, but the militia he orders to march to the fray refuses to obey.) The Hessians launch two flanking movements and a bayonet attack accompanied by spirited band music. The American flanks cave in, and Warner orders his men to scatter. The Continentals suffer over forty dead and close to 300 taken prisoner. The British have 183 casualties, including thirty-five dead. Informed of the defeats at Hubbardton and Skenesboro, St. Clair sets out for Fort Edward, hoping to save his remaining troops.

8 July 1777

FORT ANNE, N.Y. The British catch up

THE BRITISH ARMY

It was no mere conceit among American patriots when they declared themselves to be fighting against the best troops in the world. The British royal army that served during the American Revolution was indeed among the finest anywhere, despite its deficiencies. Seldom did the British regulars fail on the battlefield; if they did, it was usually due to the mistakes of their commanders. The defeat of the British army came about only in part because of victories by the Americans; in large measure defeat could be laid to the difficulties of fighting so far from home base with too few men and too little resource. So long as it controlled maneuverability by sea, the British army almost never lost during the Revolution—Burgoyne's surrender being the one great exception.

The officer corps was made up almost entirely of amateurs drawn from the aristocracy and gentry of England. Only a few British officers had been trained as professionals. Moreover, they achieved rank not by merit but by purchase. Through the rank of colonel, British officers bought their commissions and sold them like property when they resigned or purchased higher rank. Officers could not hold appointment without the personal approval of the king, who made certain that only politically reliable men commanded troops—there was no police force in Great Britain, so the army was one of the crown's major sources of power and stability. The generals of the British army also were appointed directly by the King, and few made it to the top commands without political connections. Howe, Burgoyne, Clinton, and Cornwallis were all among the twenty-three generals who were also members of Parliament and relied on by the king to help form a ruling majority.

The rank and file of the British army served for life, which meant that recruiting took place mostly among those parts of society that had little to lose: paupers and criminals. The pressures of finding manpower during the American Revolution forced the army to loosen the demands, and shorter-term enlistments were authorized during the war, but the conditions of service remained harsh: punishments of hundreds of lashes were common, for example. Nonetheless, the private British soldier during the Revolution was typically a well-drilled professional whose allegiance was to his regiment and his peers. He fought hard and well during the Revolution.

---

with Long, whose 150 men have been reinforced by the arrival of 400 militia sent by Gen. Schuyler and led by Col. Henry van Rensselaer. The Americans turn back upon their pursuers and give battle. After a two-hour skirmish Long decides that British reinforcements are arriving—he mistakenly believes a single war whoop announces approaching Indian warriors—and withdraws his men. They set fire to Fort Anne and begin the trek to Fort Edward, located on the Hudson River.

WINDSOR, VT. The Vermont Convention adopts a constitution as an independent state, providing for manhood suffrage and abolition of slavery.

NEW YORK CITY. Gen. Howe begins loading his troops aboard ships in preparation for sailing to Philadelphia.

9 July 1777

NEWPORT, R.I. Militia Lt. Col. William Barton conceives a plan to capture Gen. Richard Prescott, commander of the British forces in Rhode Island, and to offer him in exchange for Gen. Charles Lee. During the night, Barton sets out with forty volunteers from his company in five bateaux. They land on the western shore, move a mile inland, enter the general's headquarters, and capture the general and his aide-de-camp.

SKENESBORO, N.Y. Burgoyne arrives and pauses here, having sent his gunboats, artillery, and heavy supplies onward to sail to the head of Lake George. He stations his German troops under von Riedesel at Castleton, confusing the Americans about his intended direction of advance.

16 July 1777

DUNKIRK, FRANCE. Gustavus Conyngham, now a commissioned captain in the Continental Navy and in command of the *Revenge*, sets sail for British waters to prey on the Royal Navy.

17 July 1777

PORTSMOUTH, N.H. Concerned over the fall of Fort Ticonderoga, the General Court accepts John Langdon's reputed offer to fund a militia out of his own pocket and his recommendation to put John Stark in charge. Stark, who had resigned his commission in the Continental Army in a fit of pique over not being made brigadier general in April, agrees—if his command is independent of any orders from Congress. The General Court quickly accedes and commissions him brigadier general.

23 July 1777

NEW YORK CITY. After a long delay Gen. Howe sets sail with 18,000 troops and numerous horses, artillery, and supplies loaded on 260 warships and transports. His fleet passes Sandy Hook and disappears into the Atlantic. His destination is a mystery to the Americans, although most of Gen. Washington's colleagues believe he is headed for Philadelphia. The commander doubts it, but Howe's departure persuades him to order four divisions under generals Sullivan, Lord Stirling, Stephen, and Lincoln, plus Morgan's riflemen and three squadrons of dragoons, to move immediately to Philadelphia.

24 July 1777

PORTSMOUTH, N.H. Only a week after being commissioned by the General Court, John Stark has already raised a force of nearly 1,500 recruits.

25 July 1777

PHILADELPHIA. The Congress commends Lt. Col. William Barton for his daring capture of Gen. Prescott and votes to award him "an elegant sword."

SKENESBORO, N.Y. Burgoyne's men have cleared a passageway, allowing his army to move on to Fort Anne. By now Schuyler has received sufficient reinforcements—not only St. Clair's and Long's detachments, but also 600 Continentals led by Brig. Gen. John Nixon—to swell his total force to nearly 2,900 regular soldiers and 1,600 militia. In addition, Gen. Washington has sent him generals Benedict Arnold and Benjamin Lincoln, but the officers know that Fort Edward cannot be held: The American force is simply too small.

26 July 1777
OSWEGO, N.Y.   Lt. Col. Barry St. Leger begins his southern offensive.

27 July 1777
FORT EDWARD, N.Y.   Jane McCrea, daughter of a Presbyterian minister and fiancée of Tory David Jones, who is with Burgoyne's army, is staying in Fort Edward with a Mrs. McNeil, a cousin of Gen. Simon Fraser, in anticipation of spending time with Jones when the invading army arrives. A group of Burgoyne's Indian detachment arrives as an advance party, captures the two women, and sets out on the return to Fort Anne, where Burgoyne is headquartered. They arrive with Mrs. McNeil and the scalp of Jane McCrea. The circumstances of her death are obscure, but the scalp implicates a Wyandot brave whom Burgoyne cannot punish for fear of losing the Indians' allegiance. The incident creates an exploitable propaganda issue for the Americans, who are horrified by the atrocity and outraged at Burgoyne's lack of control over his Indian cohorts.

PHILADELPHIA.   The Marquis de Lafayette and Johann Kalb arrive. As Kalb has distinguished himself in service with the French Army, the Americans will accept the Bavarian soldier's fraudulent title of Baron de Kalb. Nevertheless, although Silas Deane has promised both men commissions as major generals, the Continental Congress, beleaguered by the influx of foreigners seeking commissions in the Continental Army, is perplexed over whether to honor Deane's promise.

The Marquis de Lafayette; he became one of Washington's closest friends.

29 July 1777
FORT EDWARD, N.Y.   Gen. Schuyler abandons the fort and marches down the Hudson River to Saratoga. His delaying tactics had slowed Burgoyne's advance to a crawl. The natural landscape is hazardous enough, with numerous ravines, fallen trees, and swamps; and Schuyler's men have compounded the difficulties for Bur-

goyne by felling scores of trees, rolling boulders down the hillsides, and digging ditches to create more swampland. Consequently it has taken Burgoyne's army twenty-four days to traverse twenty-three miles. As he approaches Fort Edward the retreating Americans put the torch to crops and grasslands, withdrawing settlers and their cattle as they proceed, to deny the British forage, horses, and meat.

30 July 1777
FORT EDWARD, N.Y. Burgoyne's army occupies the abandoned fort.

PORTSMOUTH, N.H. John Stark starts for Manchester with his militia brigade—all wearing their own clothes and carrying their own weapons.

31 July 1777
PHILADELPHIA. Congress commissions the Marquis de Lafayette a major general without a command.

CORRYELL'S FERRY, N.J. Gen. Washington receives reports that Howe's fleet has been sighted off the Delaware capes. A pilot at Lewes, Henry Fisher, has sent the news by express to Philadelphia the day before. The commander orders his troops across the Delaware River and south to Philadelphia.

1 August 1777
CHESTER, PA. Lafayette meets Washington at the commander's temporary encampment. The commander, greatly taken with the young Frenchman, invites Lafayette to join his staff.

2 August 1777
GERMANTOWN, PA. Washington re-

ceives word from Henry Fisher that Howe's armada has sailed off, destination unknown. The commander guesses that Howe is headed back to the North River intent on joining Burgoyne and sends orders to his generals to reassemble their forces at Peekskill.

FORT STANWIX, N.Y. St. Leger's force arrives to begin the siege of the fort, a garrison of about 750 men commanded by Col. Peter Gansevoort.

3 August 1777
GERMANTOWN, PA. Gen. Washington changes his mind, deciding to wait for certain intelligence that Howe's fleet has returned to Sandy Hook before moving. He orders Sullivan to halt at Hanover, N.J., and holds his main army at the Falls of the Schuylkill River near here.

STILLWATER, N.Y. Gen. Philip Schuyler arrives with his 4,500-man army intact at this outpost on the Hudson River twelve miles below Saratoga.

4 August 1777
FORT STANWIX, N.Y. The Indians in St. Leger's force encircle the fort and begin an unnerving yelling that lasts into the night.

PHILADELPHIA. Congress issues orders that Gen. Horatio Gates is to replace Gen. Schuyler as commander of the Northern Department.

6 August 1777
FORT STANWIX, N.Y. Three militiamen sent by Gen. Nicholas Herkimer from Oriskany manage to sneak through the marauding, yelling Indians surrounding the fort and bring

Gansevoort word that Herkimer is en route with 800 militiamen. Gansevoort signals Herkimer that the message is received, firing three cannons as the general has instructed, and then sends 200 of his own men under Lt. Col. Marinus Willett to distract the British and meet Herkimer. They chance upon one of St. Leger's camps, kill over fifteen of the enemy, and drive the rest off; but the raid exposes their movements and precludes their joining Herkimer. St. Leger sends Joseph Brant with 400 of his Mohawks along with John Butler's Tory Rangers and John Johnson's Royal Greens to prepare an ambush for Herkimer. Herkimer's own Oneida Indians fail to detect the ambush. As Herkimer's troops move along a causeway that crosses a ravine St. Leger's men launch their ambush, firing into the American ranks with devastating effect. Herkimer's leg is shattered; his officers are cut down. Trapped, the Americans fight furiously. After nearly an hour of bloody hand-to-hand combat a thunderstorm terminates the fighting. Butler and the Royal Greens attack the rebels after the rain stops but are beaten back. Rebel losses may total over 200 killed or wounded but British losses have also been severe, especially among the Indians.

7 August 1777

FORT STANWIX, N.Y. St. Leger sends a delegation under a flag of truce to talk with Gansevoort and urge surrender of the fort. His message offers the rebels safe conduct but threatens an Indian massacre of the civilians if the fort must be taken by force—a threat that offends Gansevoort and his officers. Gansevoort refuses to surrender

but accepts the British offer of a three-day truce. During the truce Willett and Maj. Stockwell sneak through the enemy lines in the dark and head for Fort Dayton, fifty miles distant, to seek reinforcements.

8 August 1777

BENNINGTON, VT. Having paused at Manchester, where both Seth Warner and Benjamin Lincoln are posted, Brig. Gen. John Stark marches his men ten miles south to this important depot for American military supplies.

General John Stark, commander of the New Hampshire army.

10 August 1777

STILLWATER, N.Y. Schuyler has learned of the British investment of Fort Stanwix and decides to send a detachment to relieve the embattled garrison. When he asks for a brigadier general to lead these men, Benedict Arnold quickly volunteers. Brig. Gen. Ebenezer Learned is made second in command. The detachment numbers about 900 men.

CORRYELL'S FERRY, PA. Doubts about Gen. Howe's intentions have brought Washington back to this encampment, but he is on the march once again when he learns that Howe's fleet has been sighted off the Maryland coast headed south. He halts, camping thirty miles north of Philadelphia on Neshaminy Creek.

11 August 1777

FORT EDWARD AND FORT MILLER, N.Y. Beset by numerous shortages of supplies, Gen. Burgoyne has been persuaded by Gen. von Riedesel to send a foraging party as far as the Connecticut River Valley to acquire meat and horses. But Burgoyne, over von Riedesel's protests, has decided the expedition should be more ambitious than a foraging operation. He orders the troop unit to push toward Manchester, where he thinks Seth Warner has gone, while trying to enlist Tory and other supporters en route. Lt. Col. Friedrich Baum sets out with about 800 men, nearly half of them Germans, but including also about 300 Tories, Canadians, and Indians. Upon his leaving, Burgoyne changes his first objective to the American depot at Bennington, Vt. How Baum, who knows no English, is supposed to succeed in enlisting sympathizers is not clear. In addition, with their cumbersome uniforms and equipment, his Germans are ill-suited for combat or slogging travel in the dense northern woods. But then Burgoyne is convinced that the Americans will not fight anyhow and that many English sympathizers will come forward to help.

13 August 1777

FORT EDWARD, N.Y. Burgoyne begins to cross the Hudson and head for Saratoga.

14 August 1777

BENNINGTON, VT. Learning that Baum's Indians, in advance of the main detachment, are looting, killing cows, and destroying property, Stark sends 200 men to a mill on Owl Creek to put a stop to the depredations. But Baum's men approach and drive the Americans off. Baum now suspects there are more than the 300 or 400 militiamen Burgoyne believes to be at Bennington; he sends Burgoyne a letter informing him of the capture of flour and other supplies at the mill and assuring him of an attack against the Americans on the following day.

15 August 1777

BENNINGTON, VT. Stark receives 400 reinforcements, Vermont militia led by Seth Warner, increasing his force to about 2,000 men. Rain prevents any action. Baum positions his men and builds breastworks.

16 August 1777

BENNINGTON, VT. Warner and Stark devise a plan of attack: they will completely encircle Baum's force and charge his front, rear, and flanks. By noon the rain has stopped and the Americans move to the attack. As the two detachments sent to outflank Baum to the right and left approach the colonel sees that they are in civilian clothes and assumes they are local Tories come to his aid (he has been assured by guide Col. Philip Skene, not now with him, that local sympathies are strongly pro-British) so he withdraws his guards. With all the Americans in place, the attack begins; John Stark leads the frontal assault. At the Americans' first volley the Tories, Canadians, and Indians in forward positions break and flee. Only the German and British troops, dug in on a hilltop, remain at their post, joined now by some of their retreating comrades. After two hours of fierce fighting, Baum runs low of ammunition; all his command but the dragoons flee. He orders the dragoons to draw sabers and leads their charge into the midst of the American swarm. Baum falls fatally wounded. His men surrender.

Baum's request Burgoyne has sent more Germans under Lt. Col. Heinrich von Breymann to reinforce Baum. They approach the outskirts of the battlefield, confronting some of Stark's men. Skirmishes follow while Stark tries desperately to regroup his scattered men. More of Warner's Vermonters from Manchester appear in time to join the men Stark manages to regroup. Their assault forces von Breymann to retreat. Over 200 of Baum's and von Breymann's men lie dead on the field of battle; 700 are prisoners. The Americans suffer fewer than seventy casualties.

The Battle of Bennington; General John Stark is on horseback.

Promised the spoils, Stark's men scatter to loot Baum's encampments and chase fleeing redcoats. But at

17 August 1777
FORT MILLER, N.Y. Gen. Burgoyne receives the news of the disaster at Ben-

nington. He immediately orders his troops to be in readiness.

19 August 1777

STILLWATER, N.Y.   Gen. Gates arrives to assume command of the Northern Department. He finds about 4,500 soldiers at this camp near the mouth of the Mohawk River.

21 August 1777

FORT DAYTON, N.Y.   Arnold's brigade is reinforced by the arrival of 100 militia. He learns, however, that St. Leger has 1,700 men. He believes reinforcements are necessary.

NESHAMINY CREEK, PA.   Still puzzled about Gen. Howe's intentions, wondering why the British commander does not move north to support Burgoyne, Washington holds a council of war that decides Howe's destination must certainly be Charleston.

22 August 1777

NESHAMINY CREEK, PA.   Learning that Howe's armada is now in the Chesapeake Bay, Washington cancels his orders to move the army toward the Hudson River and issues new orders: Sullivan is to join Washington's main army speedily and Gen. Francis Nash is to make haste to Chester. The commander announces to his troops the news of the victory at Bennington—a boost to everyone's morale.

23 August 1777

FORT DAYTON, N.Y.   Having received word the day before that Fort Stanwix is imperiled, Arnold starts out with part of his force, marching up the Mohawk, to relieve the fort. He soon learns that a subterfuge he devised with a local German, Hon Yost

Schuyler, has succeeded. Schuyler had been sentenced to death for trying to recruit troops for the British, and Arnold had promised he would be pardoned if he traveled to St. Leger's camp and spread rumors that an overwhelming American relief force is approaching. Schuyler had bullet holes shot through his coat and was able to convince St. Leger he had escaped from Arnold's troops (and the gallows) and come to warn him. St. Leger abandoned the siege of Fort Stanwix and began the return march to Montreal on 22 August. Delighted to receive this news from Schuyler, Arnold continues on to the liberated fort.

NESHAMINY CREEK, PA.   Washington's army marches south to Philadelphia. The troops encamp at Germantown for the night.

24 August 1777

PHILADELPHIA.   Washington marches his 16,000-man army through the streets of Philadelphia—down Front Street and up Chestnut Street—with the intention of impressing the local Tories. The army marches in a single column led by Washington on his white horse, Lafayette beside him, and his mounted staff immediately behind. The march has the intended effect: subduing for the Loyalists, bracing for the patriots.

25 August 1777

HEAD OF ELK, MD.   The vanguard of Howe's fleet drops anchor in the Elk River. His troops begin to disembark.

28 August 1777

HEAD OF ELK, MD.   After resting and waiting for rainy weather to clear, Lord Cornwallis, accompanied by

Howe, leads one division of the British army to Elkton, while the second division under Wilhelm von Knyphausen marches to encamp at Cecil Courthouse after crossing the Elk River.

1 September 1777

FORT HENRY (WHEELING), VA. Four hundred Indians lay siege to this fort, named in honor of Patrick Henry. The settlers take refuge in the fort before the Indians attack, but several soldiers die in skirmishes outside the walls before the siege begins. After American reinforcements arrive the Indians burn the settlement, kill livestock, and withdraw. There are no deaths among the fort's defenders.

2 September 1777

PHILADELPHIA. Having struggled with the provisions of confederation for months, the Continental Congress votes down a motion to make the question of confederation part of each day's business.

3 September 1777

IRON HILL (COOCH'S BRIDGE), DELAWARE. About 100 Continentals under Brig. Gen. William Maxwell surprise the vanguard of Cornwallis' division, firing from behind trees at the Hessian and Anspach troops in the forefront. Lt. Col. Ludwig von Wurmb wheels his artillery into position and leads a bayonet charge. The Americans fall back and stop to fire repeatedly but finally take to their heels and flee to the main encampment (Greene's and Stephen's divisions) on White Clay Creek. Each side suffers about thirty casualties. The skirmish is one of many Washington orders to

harass the British, but Howe is not deterred from the pursuit.

6 September 1777

NEWPORT, PA. The Continental Army divisions commanded by generals Greene and Stephen position themselves here, leaving Maxwell's corps on White Clay Creek as a guard.

9 September 1777

RED CLAY CREEK, PA. Believing that Howe is trying to pass around his right flank and move on to Philadelphia, Washington removes his army to Chadd's Ford on Brandywine Creek.

10 September 1777

KENNETT SQUARE, PA. Gen. Howe assembles his entire army on the road to Philadelphia that passes through Chadd's Ford.

11 September 1777

BRANDYWINE CREEK, PA. Washington has strung his army along the east bank of the creek. Troops under Nathanael Greene and Anthony Wayne occupy the center at Chadd's Ford; John Armstrong's men hold the left; and John Sullivan's, Lord Stirling's, and Adam Stephen's commands cover the right. The creek is a natural barrier, crossable only at fords, but Washington's troop deployment leaves Trimble's Ford on the west branch and Jeffrie's Ford on the east branch unguarded. Gen. Howe sends von Knyphausen's German soldiers against the American center at Chadd's Ford. Howe and Cornwallis set out for the two unguarded fords. While von Knyphausen and the Americans engage in an artillery duel at Chadd's Ford, Howe and Cornwallis cross the

The Battle of Brandywine.

creek and are in position on Osborne's Hill by mid afternoon. Washington, who was misled by conflicting warnings about their movement, is outflanked. Sullivan sends Stephen and Lord Stirling to confront the British, but they unwittingly leave a wide gap between their lines. At 4:00 P.M. Howe launches a bayonet attack straight into the gap. Greene's brigade, sent by Washington, races into the breach. A melee of furious fighting, with men and lines swallowed in obscuring smoke from artillery and musket fire, results in the Americans falling back. At the same moment as Howe attacks von Knyphausen surges across the Brandywine and, despite the Continentals' stubborn defense and deadly fire, captures the American artillery and turns it on the retreating defenders. Darkness ends the battle. Washington withdraws to Chester, still between Howe and Philadelphia. But the day's victory is Howe's. He camps on the battlefield. Gen. Greene estimates the American losses at 1,200, a third of them prisoners; the British casualties are fewer than 600.

12 September 1777

BEMIS HEIGHTS, N.Y. Gen. Gates be-

gins to fortify this strategic bluff above the Hudson at a point where the river narrows. Bemis Heights is protected by ravines made by creeks to each side and by heavily forested hillsides. Gates now has a force of over 6,000 men.

General Horatio Gates, commander of the army that defeated Burgoyne at Saratoga.

PHILADELPHIA. Congress receives a dispatch from Gen. Washington about the Battle of Brandywine and the status of his troops—they are "in good spirits." The members immediately send out orders to New York, New Jersey, Maryland, and Pennsylvania seeking reinforcements for Washington, who now moves his army from Chester to the Falls of the Schuylkill near Germantown.

13 September 1777

FORT MILLER, N.Y. Realizing that crossing the Hudson from the east at Albany will be too difficult, Burgoyne decides to cross to the west bank and march south on that side of the river. He creates a bridge of bateaux across to Saratoga and begins to send his troops over.

14 September 1777

ST. MALO, FRANCE. After being detained by the French because of vehement protests by British ambassador Lord Stormont over American privateers using French ports for bases of operation in British waters, Capt. Lambert Wickes is allowed to set sail for America in the *Reprisal*.

GERMANTOWN, PA. Concerned that Howe will once again try to outflank him on the right, Washington moves his army to the White Horse Tavern near Malvern in Chester County with the intention of doing battle.

15 September 1777

PHILADELPHIA. Congress commissions Baron de Kalb a major general and Kasimir Pulaski a brigadier general. A Polish nobleman, Count Pulaski had arrived in Boston in July with a letter from Benjamin Franklin and served as a volunteer aide-de-camp with Washington at the Battle of Brandywine. The commander considers him a good choice to head four recently authorized dragoon regiments since he served in the Polish cavalry and has recommended him to Congress for this post. Consequently, the Congress now also creates the position of Commander of the Horse and appoints Pulaski to the post.

PHILADELPHIA. Ironically, on the very day that Congress commissions two of the many European adventurers who have come seeking appointments another dies accidentally. Phillipe Tronson du Coudray has an extensive background in the French artillery and has made a favorable impression on Beaumarchais and Silas Deane. In an agreement with Deane that he will be made a major general and placed in charge of the American artillery, he has accompanied a shipment of officers and materiel here in May and immediately created headaches. Generals Greene, Knox, and Sullivan threaten to resign if this arrogant Frenchman is made their senior commander. In August Congress makes him a "staff" major general with no authority in the field except to inspect ordnance and hopes with this compromise to forestall the problem. Today Du Coudray rides his nervous mare onto the Schuylkill ferry and stays astride to instruct her. The jittery horse leaps into the river and du Coudray drowns. Congress' problem with him is resolved, to the relief of many. John Adams writes: "This dispensation will save us much altercation."

16 September 1777

WHITE HORSE TAVERN, MALVERN, PA. Howe marches from Chadd's Ford toward White Horse Tavern. The column led by von Knyphausen encounters Wayne and Maxwell, and the Americans withdraw. Washington's and Howe's armies move into positions for battle. The Continental Army occupies an inferior position but avoids possible misfortune when a giant cloudburst terminates the confrontation. The heavy rains ruin hundreds of thousands of the Americans' cartridges, and Washington

CAVALRY

During the fighting in the Northern theater of the War of the Revolution, cavalry played little part. The British sent very few cavalrymen to North America, in part because of severe problems in finding and feeding horses. Transport across the Atlantic was too slow and too inefficient to allow cavalry mounts to be supplied from England or Europe in any significant numbers. The German mercenary units designated as mounted troops all arrived without horses, for example. Moreover, the problems of finding forage for horses during campaigns were usually more than the British were capable of solving.

In fact, there was little for pure cavalry—soldiers who fought from horseback as distinct from dragoons or mounted infantry, who only used horses to move rapidly and fought dismounted—to do on the battlefields of the Northern campaigns, since seldom did the terrain lend itself to the use of cavalry except in the restricted roles of reconnaissance and harassment. There were almost no cases in which cavalry was employed as a striking force during a battle.

The Continental Army made even less use of cavalry than did the British. George Washington was notorious in his disdain of cavalry, and he paid little attention to organizing or employing horsemen. Congress authorized a cavalry corps in 1777, but it was never brought to full strength or used except on minor assignments.

In the campaigns of the South, however, mounted troops were indispensable, although they were almost all dragoons or mounted infantry rather than cavalry in the classical sense. The so-called legions organized by both sides—units that combined dragoons, mounted infantry, and light infantry—were among the most effective forces during the fighting in the Carolinas. American units under Light-Horse Harry Lee and William Washington were in almost every major battle in the South during 1780 and 1781, and often provided the extra edge needed to bring victory or stave off defeat. Banastre Tarleton's Loyalists of the British Legion formed the heart of the British striking forces in the South, and seldom were the British successful without Tarleton's men.

The legions could move very rapidly indeed—the light infantry often rode double with the dragoons in order to cover large distances fast. When they arrived on the battle scene, the dragoons and mounted infantry could either strike as a mounted force or fight dismounted as infantry, making them among the most flexible and effective combat units.

marches in the downpour toward Reading Furnace to acquire replacement ammunition. He stops this night at Yellow Springs.

17 September 1777

READING FURNACE, PA. Washington arrives and camps.

18 September 1777

PHILADELPHIA. Fearful of Howe's army, the members of Congress begin an exodus from the city—they are to reconvene in Lancaster. The Liberty Bell, rung to proclaim American independence on 8 July, is shipped on an army baggage train to Allentown to be hidden in Zion Reformed Church.

VALLEY FORGE, PA. Von Knyphausen has marched from White Horse Tavern to join Cornwallis for the march to Valley Forge, where they find a rebel storehouse of flour, soap, horseshoes, entrenching tools, and other items.

Morgan's riflemen in action.

BEMIS HEIGHTS, N.Y. Burgoyne is inching southward, searching for his enemy, and an American patrol attacks one of his foraging parties. He now has a clearer idea of the American army's location. The American forti- fications, drawn up by Benedict Arnold and Col. Tadeusz Kościuszko, are complete, stretching from Bemis' Tavern near the river to the bluff on the heights, where three-sided breastworks have been built.

19 September 1777

RICHARDSON'S FORD, PA. Having restored his supply of ammunition, Washington marches his men a strenuous twenty-nine miles back to the Schuylkill River and camps on the east side of the river along Perkiomen Creek. Again he is positioned between Howe and Philadelphia.

BEMIS HEIGHTS, N.Y. At 10:00 A.M., with a cannon shot as signal to advance, Burgoyne sends his men in three separate columns against the Americans waiting behind their breastworks. Gen. Gates is content to wait as the British approach, but Gen. Arnold urges him to send troops out to encounter the enemy in the woody terrain and thereby avoid entrapment on the heights by denying Burgoyne the use of his artillery to bombard the American position there. For two hours the British advance while Gates mulls this counsel—he and Arnold are personally at odds. Then Gates accedes, first sending Morgan's men and finally most of Arnold's force to meet the enemy's center column, led by Brig. Gen. Hamilton, at Freeman's Farm a mile north of the heights. Their battle rages all afternoon, with each side successively and repeatedly charging and then withdrawing across a 350-yard clearing that separates them. The British, with Burgoyne in their midst, withstand the heaviest fire most of them have ever experienced. Gen. Fraser's column, sent to the northeast toward the river to search for high ground, is too distant to enter the battle, but part of the third column under von Riedesel struggles up the bluffs from the river in time to prevent the imminent collapse of Hamilton's force. As darkness falls Arnold retreats, leaving the battlefield in British hands, but his men have exacted a terrible toll—556 British casualties. American casualties are 287.

20 September 1777
VALLEY FORGE, PA. Howe establishes a post here.

20–21 September 1777
PAOLI, PA. Washington has sent 1,500 men and four cannon under Anthony Wayne to Warren's Tavern near Paoli to harass the British rear guard and baggage train, but local Tories warn the British of their presence. Howe sends a force under Maj. Gen. Charles Grey to surprise Wayne in his camp at night. They succeed, killing most of Wayne's sentries and sending his men into flight. The Americans suffer about 150 dead and about half that number taken prisoner. Local residents find mangled bodies at the site and immediately term the encounter the Paoli Massacre.

22 September 1777
FATLAND FORD, PA. Washington, still fearful of being outflanked, has moved his troops to Pott's Grove (Pottstown), so Howe changes directions, marches to Fatland Ford, and begins to cross the Schuylkill River.

23 September 1777
NORRISTOWN, PA. With Washington's tired army too distant to threaten opposition, Howe marches

to Norristown. Washington, unable to follow, waits in Pott's Grove, sending Alexander Hamilton into Philadelphia and Clement Biddle through the countryside to acquire blankets and clothing for his men.

PHILADELPHIA. Lord Cornwallis, marching in with four British and two Hessian units, takes possession of the city to the acclaim of Loyalist supporters. The main body of his army encamps at Germantown. Washington moves from Pott's Grove to encamp at Pennybacker's Mill (Schwenksville) on the Perkiomen River. The commander is not deeply dispirited by the loss of Philadelphia and concentrates his energies on restoring his troops.

24 September 1777
DIAMOND ISLAND, N.Y. Having previously captured 300 British troops on the west shore of Lake George, Col. John Brown's Continentals successfully raid this British post south of Ticonderoga, but they are unsuccessful in capturing Fort Ticonderoga itself.

27 September 1777
LANCASTER, PA. The Continental Congress meets here for a single session. Still fearful of Gen. Howe's movements, the members adjourn again and cross the Susquehanna River to reconvene at York.

30 September 1777
YORK, PA. The Continental Congress reconvenes, presumably now at a safe distance from Gen. Howe.

1 October 1777
NEWFOUNDLAND. Near the end of its return voyage to the United States the

Reprisal founders off the Banks of Newfoundland. Capt. Lambert Wickes and his entire crew are lost except for the ship's cook.

2 October 1777

BILLINGSPORT, N.J. Gen. Howe, realizing that the best supply route for his army is the Delaware River, wants obstacles to passage removed from the river. The first of these is a double line of chevaux-de-frise stretching across the river at Billingsport that can rip open the bottom of any ship that passes over. He sends troops to attack the garrison here—the American defenders set fire to the barracks, spike the guns, and flee—and clear the obstacle from the river channel.

3 October 1777

NEW YORK CITY. Sir Henry Clinton, left by Gen. Howe in command of the New York garrison, sends toward Tarrytown the first contingent of a force intended to create a diversion for Gen. Burgoyne. He had been left only 7,000 troops, 3,000 of them Tories, for the defense of Manhattan Island, Long Island, Staten Island, and Paulus Hook, and was reluctant to proceed despite Howe's suggestion of a diversion. But in late September he received reinforcements, increasing his force of British and German regulars to 7,000, so he now commits 4,000 men to this northward thrust—the objectives are Forts Clinton and Montgomery, forty miles upriver from New York.

4 October 1777

GERMANTOWN, PA. Having marched during the night from Skippack Creek, sixteen miles distant, Washington launches an attack at dawn, driving back British advance units of the 9,000-man force Howe has sta-

tioned at his headquarters here. This marks the first time Washington has advanced to attack the major part of the British army and the first time British troops have retreated in open battle with the Americans. Col. Thomas Musgrave, commanding the retreating British 40th Regiment, decides to occupy Benjamin Chew's sturdy stone house. From this fortress his men fire on Gen. Sullivan's Continentals, halting their advance. Washington, persuaded by Gen. Knox that it would be a mistake to bypass the house and push on with the attack, orders an artillery bombardment that proves ineffectual and costs the Americans not only many casualties but also an hour's delay. Meanwhile nearby Gen. Stephen, attracted by the firing but confused by a heavy fog, defies his original orders, changes directions, moves up on the rear of Gen. Wayne's troops, and opens fire, effectively immobilizing both his own and Wayne's units. At the same time Gen. Greene's advance has been delayed, so hope of a coordinated attack is totally lost. Washington orders a general withdrawal. He has lost 673 men, and 400 have been captured, out of a force of 7,000. Howe's force has 535 casualties. Though the British win the day, they find the battle rather demoralizing.

5 October 1777

TARRYTOWN, N.Y. Having assembled his entire force, Clinton launches his convoy of flatboats, galleys, and bateaux with his attack force and arrives at Verplanck's Point, which he quickly seizes when the American defenders withdraw without resistance.

CAPE HENLOPEN, DELAWARE. Admiral Lord Howe's fleet, which left Head of Elk over a month ago, begins to arrive in Delaware Bay.

6 October 1777

FORTS CLINTON AND MONTGOMERY, N.Y. Leaving 1,000 men, mostly Tories, to guard Verplanck's Point, Gen. Henry Clinton crosses the Hudson to Stony Point and marches up the east side of the river. Near Doodletown he divides his troops into two divisions—one led by Lt. Col. Archibald Campbell to march on Fort Montgomery while the other under Clinton himself marches on Fort Clinton. When American Gen. George Clinton refuses to surrender, the British launch simultaneous victorious attacks on both forts in late afternoon. The Americans manage to escape as night falls, but their losses are heavy: some 250 killed, wounded, or missing out of a combined force of a little over 600. The British have fewer than 200 casualties. American vessels in the river fail to escape; the British burn them.

7 October 1777

BEMIS HEIGHTS, N.Y. For over two weeks since their initial encounter Gates and Burgoyne have rested; but the pause is to Gates' advantage, as new recruits have streamed in, swelling his force to 11,000, while Burgoyne has waited in vain for reinforcements and consumed supplies. Against the advice of Fraser and von Riedesel, Burgoyne has refused to retreat. Now he leads a reconnaissance detachment of about 1,500 men to test the strength of the American left. Not finding the enemy, they assemble in formation to wait in a wheatfield. Unexpectedly, American troops led by Enoch Poor and Daniel Morgan attack, with Morgan outflanking the British so that they are nearly sur-

rounded. Although Gates had relieved him of any command several days before and asked him to leave, Benedict Arnold rides into the fray, his recklessness inspiring the men to battle. The Americans charge wildly, repeatedly, and British resistance disintegrates. Trying to cover their retreat, Gen. Fraser receives a mortal wound. Dominant and relentless, Arnold and his men sweep on to Freeman's Farm and capture the redoubt on Burgoyne's right flank; but Arnold takes a wound in the leg, his horse shot from under him, and must be carried from the field—without his brash leadership the charge comes to an end. The American assault, however, leaves Burgoyne's position completely untenable; his casualties number 600, while the Americans' number less than 150. During the night Burgoyne begins to withdraw to Saratoga, abandoning en route tents, wagons, baggage, and even the bodies of his dead to marauding wolves.

YORK, PA. Congress resumes debate of the question of confederation, focusing on "the mode of voting in Congress." The question is resolved with the decision that each state shall have one vote—only Virginia votes against this principle, although some delegations vote for it in order to advance the debates on to other difficult topics, such as taxation.

8 October 1777

FORT MONTGOMERY, N.Y. Replying to a letter from Gen. Burgoyne dated 28 September requesting orders, Clinton expresses the hope that his own success will bolster Burgoyne's—it is already too late, of course, but he does not know that—and advises that only Gen. Howe can order Burgoyne either to advance down the Hudson or retreat. He sends the message in a hollow silver bullet by messenger Daniel Taylor.

NEW WINDSOR, N.Y. The Americans under generals George and James Clinton join Putnam's force at New Windsor.

9 October 1777

SARATOGA, N.Y. Burgoyne's retreating army reaches the heights of Saratoga. Gates is in pursuit, and his advance troops constantly harass the enemy. By now Burgoyne is significantly outnumbered—Gates has 13,000 men, Burgoyne fewer than 5,800.

10 October 1777

PROVINCE ISLAND, PA. The British begin an artillery bombardment of the land side of Fort Mifflin on Mud Island in the Delaware River.

12 October 1777

SARATOGA, N.Y. Gates cuts off any possibility Burgoyne can retreat, blocking his access to the Hudson and forcing the British commander to consider entering discussions on terms of surrender.

13 October 1777

SARATOGA, N.Y. His situation desperate, Burgoyne requests a cessation of hostilities. Gates agrees. Surrender negotiations begin.

14 October 1777

SARATOGA, N.Y. The Americans capture Clinton's messenger, Daniel Taylor, who swallows the silver bullet.

The Second Battle of Freeman's Farm; it marked the end for Burgoyne's army.

The surrender at Saratoga. Burgoyne offers his sword to Gates.

Gen. George Clinton orders administration of an emetic, the bullet is retrieved, and Taylor is executed as a spy.

YORK, PA. After nearly a week of debate on whether taxes under the confederation should be proportional to population or be based on land values or general property values, the Congress decides in favor of land values and their improvements; but the vote is narrowly divided. Congress also decides that each state shall have no fewer than two nor more than seven congressional delegates, whose terms shall be set at three years.

16 October 1777
SARATOGA, N.Y. Gates and Burgoyne meet to agree on final details for the British surrender. The terms of their "Convention" specify that Burgoyne's army will return to England via Bos-

ton and that all persons in Burgoyne's force, regardless of nationality, will be regarded as British citizens. All must pledge never again to be involved in the American war.

KINGSTON (ESOPUS), N.Y. Clinton has sent Gen. John Vaughan with 1,700 troops and a flotilla commanded by Sir James Wallace upriver in an effort to find and support Burgoyne. Having anchored at Kingston the previous day, they now burn the town and move on to Livingston's Manor.

17 October 1777
SARATOGA, N.Y. At 2:00 P.M. the British march forth from their fortifications to the beat of drums, and Gen. Burgoyne surrenders his army to Gen. Gates. The two commanders and their staffs then eat a simple lunch, during which Burgoyne, to everyone's surprise, proposes a toast to Gen. Wash-

ington and Gates responds with a toast to George III.

YORK, PA. Congress adopts a resolution establishing a Board of War of noncongressional members to exercise some supervisory powers over army operations. Critics of Washington see it as a possible means of undermining him.

19 October 1777

PHILADELPHIA. Gen. Howe withdraws from Germantown, concentrating his entire force in Philadelphia.

22 October 1777

FORT MONTGOMERY, N.Y. Clinton, ordered by Howe to abandon his Hudson River expedition and send reinforcements to Pennsylvania, sends orders to Vaughan to withdraw. Vaughan has written that he is unable to contact Burgoyne.

FORT MERCER, N.J. Continuing his efforts to free the Delaware River for British navigation, Gen. Howe sends 2,000 Hessians under Col. von Donop to attack and dislodge the American garrison commanded by Col. Christopher Greene at Fort Mercer at Red Bank, one of the forts whose fortifications have been strengthened under the direction of Chevalier de Mauduit du Plessis. The Hessians cross the river at Philadelphia and march to attack the fort from the land. Col. Greene refuses to surrender and orders his men to hold fire as the Hessians advance. They pass by the abatis (an obstacle constructed of felled trees), cross a ditch, and ascend to the parapets of the fort without drawing fire;

then suddenly they are shattered by murderous musket blasts. The Hessians try to launch a second attack from the south but are hit by fire from galleys in the river. They withdraw, leaving behind the mortally wounded von Donop.

23 October 1777

FORT MIFFLIN, PA. American artillery shells six British ships that have broken through the chevaux-de-frise in the Delaware and moved within range. The *Augusta* and the *Merlin* run aground and are destroyed.

28 October 1777

READING, PA. James Wilkinson, aide to Gen. Gates, stops en route to York to inform the Congress of Gen. Burgoyne's surrender. Thus Gates, in an affront to his commander-in-chief, disdains to properly channel his report through Washington, sending it directly to Congress instead. Compounding the affront, Wilkinson tells Maj. William McWilliams, Lord Stirling's aide, of a letter Thomas Conway has sent Gen. Gates derogating Gen. Washington while praising Gates. Conway, an Irish Catholic by birth but raised mostly in France, is another of Silas Deane's "protégés." Congress made him a brigadier general in May, and he has served well under Gen. Sullivan at the battles of Brandywine and Germantown.

31 October 1777

YORK, PA. John Hancock resigns as president of the Continental Congress. James Wilkinson arrives to confirm rumors circulating in Congress that Burgoyne has surrendered at Saratoga. He simply gives a verbal report, however, requesting further time to "digest and arrange" the written dispatches he has brought with him from Gen. Gates.

1 November 1777

YORK, PA. The Continental Congress elects Henry Laurens of South Carolina president. By this time many of the delegates have departed for home; the remaining delegates continue the discussion of confederation.

2 November 1777

PORTSMOUTH, N.H. Capt. John Paul Jones and his sloop *Ranger* set sail for France.

WHIPPANY TOWNSHIP, PA. As a court of inquiry has determined that Gen. Adam Stephen has acted "unlike an officer" on three occasions—he lied about a skirmish at Piscataway, and he was drunk during the battles at Brandywine and Germantown—Gen. Washington orders a court-martial of the general. Then once again Washington breaks camp and marches his army to encamp at Whitemarsh, twelve miles from Philadelphia.

3 November 1777

READING, PA. Lord Stirling, outraged by what he has learned from his aide-de-camp William McWilliams, writes to Gen. Washington recounting the tale and denouncing Gen. Thomas Conway's "duplicity." And so Washington first learns of the so-called Conway Cabal, whose reputed purpose is to have Washington replaced by Gates as commander-in-chief. The news that two of his subordinates are trying to discredit him shocks the commander.

YORK, PA. Wilkinson presents Gates' official written dispatches about the Battle of Saratoga and the capture of Gen. Burgoyne to Congress.

6 November 1777

YORK, PA. Congress appoints Gen. Thomas Mifflin (recently resigned as quartermaster general), Col. Timothy Pickering, and Col. Robert H. Harrison to the Board of War established on 17 October.

7 November 1777

YORK, PA. With an understanding that the final form of the Articles of Confederation has been agreed upon except for revisions of wording, Samuel Adams and John Adams receive requested leaves of absence to return home.

WHITEMARSH, PA. Gen. Washington writes a two-sentence letter to Gen. Conway stating that he has received a letter which says Conway wrote these words to Gates: "Heaven has been determined to save your Country; or a weak General and bad Counsellors would have ruined it." The intent of the statement is clear.

10 November 1777

FORT MIFFLIN, PA. The river's current having opened a new channel between Mud Island and the Pennsylvania shore, the British have been able to move a floating battery of twenty-two 24-pound cannon within forty yards of the fort. They commence a daylong bombardment of the fort.

11 November 1777

YORK, PA. The committee to which proposals for additions to the Articles of Confederation have been referred reports approval of seven additions—the document's provisions are still not final.

14 November 1777

YORK, PA.   Thomas Conway submits his resignation to the Congress, citing as reasons criticism of his request for promotion; his not being promoted; the unfortunate letter Washington referred to; and the promotion of Baron de Kalb, who had been his junior officer in the French army, ahead of him, which he says will demean his reputation in France. Congress takes no action except to pass Conway's letter on to the Board of War.

15 November 1777

FORT MIFFLIN, PA.   After five days of continuous bombardment from the British floating battery in addition to the shore batteries, the defenders of Fort Mifflin now have only two cannon in service. They have taken many casualties, and much of the fort has been destroyed. Now the British move six ships into firing range to complement the artillery on the shore and the floating battery in a horrendous bombardment—perhaps as many as 1,000 balls hurtle toward the fort every twenty minutes. The punishment levels the fort and its defenses. During the night Maj. Simeon Thayer, who has replaced the wounded Lt. Col. Samuel Smith as commander, puts the torch to the ruins and crosses the river with his men to Red Bank. Out of the garrison of 450 men only 150 have escaped death or wounding. British casualties total only twelve.

YORK, PA.   The thirteen Articles of Confederation are recorded in the journals of the Continental Congress as finally adopted. They provide for sovereignty of the states; a common defense; open borders; nationwide recognition of citizenship; mutual acceptance of all states' court decisions; election of and duties of Congressional delegates; freedom of speech in Congress; congressional approval of treaties between states, military affairs, and wars; a common treasury for war expenses; coinage of money; and admission of Canada to the confederation.

17 November 1777

YORK, PA.   Copies of the Articles of Confederation are sent to the states to be considered for ratification. With them go copies of a circular letter written by Richard Henry Lee describing the articles as best "adapted to the circumstances of all" and urging legislators to examine the provisions with liberality, wisdom, and magnanimity and to reveal themselves "capable of rising superior to local attachments, when they may be incompatible with the safety, happiness, and glory of the general Confederacy." The appeal also requests the legislators to understand that consummation of the union among the states will "confound our foreign enemies, defeat the flagitious practices of the disaffected, strengthen and confirm our friends, support our public credit, restore the value of our money, enable us to maintain our fleets and armies, and add weight to our councils at home, and to our treaties abroad." Believing that the confederation is vital to successful prosecution of the war, the Congress hopes that the ratification process will be speedy and provide a unanimous outcome.

18 November 1777

PHILADELPHIA. Having captured Fort Mifflin—or at least the site the fort once occupied—Gen. Howe sends 2,000 men commanded by Lord Cornwallis to the New Jersey side of the Delaware to attack Fort Mercer a second time. Gen. Washington places Nathanael Greene in charge of the Continentals in New Jersey with orders to try to prevent loss of the fort. Cornwallis lands at Billingsport.

20 November 1777

FORT MERCER, N.J. With Fort Mifflin lost to the British, Fort Mercer appears to be impossible for the Americans to hold because Howe effectively controls the Delaware River to Red Bank. Gen. Greene believes the odds are against the Americans; and Col. Christopher Greene, judging his garrison to be in a hopeless position, evacuates the fort with Gen. Greene's concurrence. The Americans burn the fort's buildings and supplies when they leave. Without a shot being fired, Fort Mercer falls to Cornwallis. Howe now controls the Delaware to Philadelphia. The few American ships upriver are burned to prevent their capture by the British.

WHITEMARSH, PA. Gen. Washington,

agreeing with the findings of the court-martial that Gen. Adam Stephen is guilty of misconduct, dismisses the general from his command.

21 November 1777

YORK, PA. The Continental Congress, reacting to charges made against Silas Deane by Arthur Lee, recalls Deane to the United States to respond to the charges.

25 November 1777

GLOUCESTER, N.J. A reconnaissance force of 300 Continentals led by Lafayette skirmishes with a troop of Hessians in a successful engagement against Cornwallis' position at Gloucester.

27 November 1777

YORK, PA. Congress recommends to the states that they confiscate the property of Loyalists. Since Col. Harrison has declined to serve on the Board of War, Congress appoints three new members—Gen. Horatio Gates, Joseph Trumbull, and Richard Peters—designating Gates president. Trumbull is ill and cannot serve. Since Gates and Mifflin are hostile to Washington and Pickering is lukewarm, the board appears to represent a threat to the commander-in-chief.

28 November 1777

YORK, PA. Congress appoints John Adams to succeed Silas Deane as commissioner to France.

1 December 1777

PORTSMOUTH, N.H. Baron Friedrich Wilhelm Augustus von Steuben arrives from France to offer his services to the Continental Army. A former

CONTINENTAL GENERALS

Most of the major generals of the Continental Army loved high rank. With few exceptions, they fought to get it, and once gained, they protected their positions as senior officers with all the power and fervor they could muster. During the war of the Revolution, Congress appointed twenty-nine major generals, in three rough categories. The first group, commissioned in 1775 at the organization of the Continental Army, were mostly political appointees. Although Congress attempted to include military experience as one of the criteria, the first major generalships (both in 1775 and to a lesser extent during a second round of appointments in 1776) were apportioned to acknowledge the various geographical and political divisions of the colonies—each section had to have its share. A second group of major generals was comprised of European soldiers of fortune or revolutionary sympathizers who presented themselves as prizes for Congress to grab and who expected to begin service with the highest rank possible. Some of them were genuinely important to the American cause—Lafayette, von Steuben, and De Kalb, for example —but at least one, Phillippe Du Coudray, was a total disaster. The third group was made up of officers who achieved major general rank more or less by virtue of meritorious service during the war. Two major generals died on the battlefield during the war; a few expired from illness; and several resigned or retired before the end of the conflict. Many served until the disbanding of most of the army in the fall of 1783. One—Benedict Arnold—deserted to the enemy. Ranking above them all, of course, was George Washington, General and Commander-in-Chief of the Continental Army.

Major Generals (with dates of service)

Artemus Ward (1775–1776, resigned)

Charles Lee (1775–1780, dismissed)

Philip Schuyler (1775–1779, resigned)

Israel Putnam (1775–1783)

Richard Montgomery (1775, killed in action, Quebec)

John Thomas (1776, died of illness)

Horatio Gates (1776–1783)

William Heath (1776–1783)

Joseph Spencer (1776–1778, resigned)

John Sullivan (1776–1779, resigned)

Nathanael Greene (1776–1783)

Benedict Arnold (1777–1780, deserted)

William Alexander (1777–1783, died of illness)

Thomas Mifflin (1777–1779, resigned)

Arthur St. Clair (1777–1783)

Adam Stephen (1777, dismissed)

Benjamin Lincoln (1777–1783)

Marquis de Lafayette (1777–1783)

Phillippe Du Coudray (1777, died in accident)

Johann De Kalb (1777–1780, killed in action, Camden) Robert Howe (1777–1783) Alexander McDougall (1777–1783) Thomas Conway (1777–1778, resigned) Friedrich Von Steuben (1778–1784)	William Smallwood (1780–1783 Samuel Parsons (1780–1782, retired) Henry Knox (1781–1784) Louis Duportail (1781–1783) William Moultrie (1782–1783)

member of Frederick the Great's Prussian general staff, von Steuben has the blessing of Benjamin Franklin, who has sent a letter of introduction to Washington. He also has the blessing of the comte de St. Germain, the French minister of war; and his travel expenses are being paid by Beaumarchais' Hortalez et Cie.

2 December 1777
NANTES, FRANCE. John Paul Jones and the USS *Ranger* arrive.

4 December 1777
VERSAILLES, FRANCE. Jonathan Austin, sent by the Continental Congress, arrives with news of the surrender of the British army at Saratoga and the capture of Gen. Burgoyne. The American commissioners' efforts to secure an alliance with France have foundered since news of the loss of Philadelphia reached France in November, but now those efforts revive with increased French interest.

PHILADELPHIA. Gen. Howe marches forth from the city with most of his army. He intends to surprise Washington at Whitemarsh; but Capt. Allen McLane, who has been continuously scouting, observes Howe's movements and reports to Washington, giving the commander time to make defensive preparations. McLane's cavalry also begins to harass the British front and flank.

5 December 1777
CHESTNUT HILL, PA. Howe encamps only three miles from Washington, who has fortified his position and has fifty-two cannons in place for his defense.

6 December 1777
VERSAILLES, FRANCE. Vergennes sends his congratulations on the American victory at Saratoga to Franklin, Deane, and Lee. More importantly, he invites them to revive their request for a formal alliance between the two countries.

7 December 1777
CHESTNUT HILL, PA. Howe marches to Edge Hill and is now within a mile

of Washington's left flank, but during the night he marches on to Jenkintown.

8 December 1777

WHITEMARSH, PA. The American right and left wings fall back as British troops advance. The American left is in disarray, but Capt. McLane's cavalry drives back a British bayonet attack, and the skirmishing ends. Deeming Washington's position too strong, Howe marches back to Philadelphia.

PASSY, FRANCE. Franklin sends his grandson Temple to Vergennes with a proposal he has drafted the day before concerning an alliance.

11 December 1777

WHITEMARSH, PA. Washington's ar-

By His EXCELLENCY
GEORGE WASHINGTON, Esquire,
GENERAL and COMMANDER in CHIEF of the Forces
of the UNITED STATES OF AMERICA.

BY Virtue of the Power and Direction to Me especially given, I hereby enjoin and require all Persons residing within seventy Miles of my Head Quarters to thresh one Half of their Grain by the 1st Day of February, and the other Half by the 1st Day of March next ensuing, on Pain, in Case of Failure of having all that shall remain in Sheaves after the Period above mentioned, seized by the Commissaries and Quarter-Masters of the Army, and paid for as Straw

GIVEN under my Hand, at Head Quarters, near the Valley Forge, in Philadelphia County, this 20th Day of December, 1777.
G. WASHINGTON.
By His Excellency's Command,
ROBERT H. HARRISON, Sec'y.

LANCASTER: Printed by JOHN DUNLAP

Washington requisitioned supplies for his troops with proclamations such as this.

my leaves Whitemarsh with the intention of crossing the Schuylkill River at Matson's Ford by bridge and proceeding to Valley Forge. Gen. Sullivan's division and half of a second division are already across when the advance unit of a force of 3,500 British regulars led by Cornwallis comes into view. Washington orders his men back across the bridge, which they subsequently destroy. The Continentals and their enemy face each other in battle formations on opposite sides of the river. Cornwallis moves off to forage for supplies. Washington returns to Whitemarsh.

12 December 1777

VERSAILLES, FRANCE. The American commissioners meet secretly with Vergennes, who informs them that France can come into the war openly only if Spain agrees. A courier sent to Madrid will need three weeks to reach there and return with Spain's decision.

13 December 1777

YORK, PA. Congress promotes Thomas Conway to major general, passing over twenty-three other brigadier generals who are senior to him. Congress also approves creation of the post of Inspector General for the Continental Army, which is to be independent of the commander-in-chief and to report directly to the Board of War.

14 December 1777

YORK, PA. With the Board of War having taken no action on Thomas Conway's letter of resignation (14 November), Congress now appoints Conway to the newly created post of Inspector General of the Army—an apparent triumph for the partisans involved in the so-called Conway Cabal.

Benjamin Franklin being presented at the French court.

17 December 1777

PASSY, FRANCE. A French foreign office official brings word to Franklin that Louis XVI's ministers have agreed to a formal alliance—to remain secret until Spain has made a decision. With French recognition of the United States' independence, Franklin is able to reject the appeal of British agent Paul Wentworth to travel with his fellow commissioners to London and there negotiate a cease-fire based on British–American relations before 1763.

19 December 1777

VALLEY FORGE, PA. Following a week's delay resulting from the Matson's Ford confrontation, Washington's army arrives at Valley Forge to establish winter quarters.

23 December 1777

VALLEY FORGE, PA. Washington writes to Congress suggesting that two or three members of the Board of War or a congressional committee visit his encampment for the purpose of discussing and resolving the questions about leadership and organization of the Continental Army being raised by his detractors.

27 December 1777

YORK, PA. Congress, acting as a committee of the whole, resolves that Gen. Burgoyne and his troops—now quartered in Boston awaiting embarkation for England—not be allowed to embark until the convention agreed to at Saratoga is ratified by the crown. At the same time Congress sends instructions to Gen. Heath in Boston to ascertain that the transport ships are adequately provisioned and to liquidate all outstanding accounts—a delaying tactic.

★ 1778 ★

With the signing in February of formal treaties of alliance and commerce, France publicly signals her intent to join the war (open hostilities between Britain and France begin at sea in June). Realizing the importance of America's new ally, the British ministry responds with a plan for conciliation with the Americans. The Cabinet empowers a peace commission to negotiate with Congress and the states, but the talks—doomed from the beginning over the issue of independence and fouled by British attempts at bribery—are to no avail.

Sir Henry Clinton takes over military command from Howe. In the wake of Burgoyne's defeat and the entry of France (which brings a formidable navy into the equation) the British adopt a revised strategy: they hope to separate the Southern colonies, where they believe Loyalist sentiment is strong and American military forces weak, and conduct war in the North only by means of raiding and naval blockades. The threat of French sea power turns British thoughts toward defense of the West Indies.

Accordingly, Clinton decides to abandon Philadelphia and to withdraw his entire force overland to New York City. Washington, his tattered army reorganized and retrained after the winter at Valley Forge, attacks the baggage-laden British column near Monmouth, New Jersey. The British are nearly beaten on 28 June but manage to escape total defeat, owing to poor—some say near-traitorous—generalship by American second in command Charles Lee. Clinton slips away during the night and retreats toward New York City. The battle marks the last major engagement of the war in the North. Washington positions his forces to pin Clinton in New York and plans maneuvers with the French naval fleet, which arrives off Delaware Bay in early July.

In the West, George Rogers Clark captures British frontier posts at Kaskaskia, Cahokia, and Vincennes. After a repulse by the British of a poorly coordinated French and American force at Newport, Rhode Island, in August, the war settles into a lower level of activity, involving mostly small raids. In accord with the British Southern strategy, forces under the enterprising British commander Prevost seize Savannah, Georgia, late in the year.

---

2 January 1778

WILLIAMSBURG, VA. George Rogers Clark, who has been active in fighting the Indians and then the British in the Kentucky Territory, has come to the state capital for the second time to advocate support for his plan to capture control of the vast northwestern territory of the Mississippi–Ohio River Valley. Clark would first secure the defense of the Kentucky frontier against Indian raids, then attack Vincennes, Kaskaskia, Cahokia, and other settlements and forts farther up the Mississippi—the final objective being the British garrison at Detroit. Clark thinks that the French settlements along the Mississippi will rise to the support of the Revolution. He first pressed this plan in Williamsburg in the first year of the Revolution and subsequently in letters to Gov. Patrick Henry. The Virginia government has been reluctant to involve itself in an effort that should properly be the responsibility of the Continental Congress, but the state does claim virtually all of the territory west of the Alleghenies. The fact that in the summer of 1777 the British troops at Kaskaskia withdrew to Detroit favors Clark's proposal, as does Virginians' interest in land speculation and concern about marauding Shawnee and Cherokee Indians. Thomas Jefferson, George Mason, and Richard Henry Lee approve of Clark's plan. Gov. Henry now agrees and places Clark in charge of the proposed expedition with the rank of colonel in the militia, gives him authority to raise seven companies, and provides him some funds and authority to acquire supplies at Fort Pitt. His announced orders are to defend the Kentucky Territory—Henry does not wish to divulge the true purpose of Clark's expedition, as his secret orders are to attack Kaskaskia and, if possible, Detroit.

VALLEY FORGE, PA. After two camp visits by Inspector General Conway in December and an exchange of letters —Washington's coolly phrased, Conway's captious and patronizing—the exasperated and angry commander-in-chief writes to Congress and encloses all of the correspondence, making clear to the delegates what he thinks of Conway in hopes that the "cabal" problem will be resolved.

5 January 1778

PHILADELPHIA. David Bushnell, inventor of the "American Turtle," tries his torpedoes against the British fleet. In the darkness he launches into the Delaware kegs that are filled with powder and equipped with fuses designed to set off explosions when they make contact with the ships—the river's current is supposed to drift them downriver toward the fleet. Unfortunately, icy waters slow their progress and at daylight the British spot them, opening fire until all the torpedoes have been exploded.

8 *January 1778*

VERSAILLES, FRANCE. The comte de Vergennes informs Franklin, Deane, and Lee that his government is ready to form an alliance with the United States.

YORK, PA. Congress completes a resolution stating that the embarkation of Burgoyne's army is postponed until "a distinct and explicit ratification of the convention of Saratoga shall be properly notified by the Court of Great Britain to Congress." Other accompanying resolutions accuse Gen. Burgoyne of failing to fulfill some of the terms of the convention and state objections to the general's contention that the Americans are guilty of breach of faith—indications, the resolutions say, of Burgoyne's true intent to abrogate the convention.

10 *January 1778*

YORK, PA. Responding to Gen. Washington's suggestion, Congress resolves to send to Valley Forge a committee comprised of its own members and three members of the Board of War—Gates, Mifflin, and Pickering.

13 *January 1778*

VALLEY FORGE, PA. Washington's men complete the last of the log huts that will house them for the remainder of the winter. The army at the camp numbers about 11,000, only 8,200 of them fit for duty. They lack adequate provisions of every sort. The commander-in-chief, who promised to share their hardships, has quartered in a tent until many of the huts were finished and then moved into the Isaac Potts house as his headquarters. He sends pleading letters to Congress

The American army at Valley Forge, just north of Philadelphia.

to provide food and clothing. Many of his men lack hats, shoes, and coats; and they go for days without meat, frequently having only firecake (a thin bread of flour and water baked over a campfire) and water, and sometimes even the firecake is lacking.

14 *January 1778*

YORK, PA. Congress sends its resolutions on the Saratoga Convention to Gen. Heath in Boston.

19 *January 1778*

YORK, PA. Gen. Horatio Gates arrives to assume his duties as president of the Board of War and receives a joyous welcome.

20 *January 1778*

YORK, PA. By his own request Gen. Gates is excused from serving on the committee to visit Valley Forge, as also are Mifflin and Pickering—the correspondence with Conway that Washington has sent to Congress is sufficient reason to back out.

21 January 1778

BORDENTOWN, N.J. Inspired by Bushnell's failed torpedoes, Francis Hopkinson, poet, signer of the Declaration of Independence, congressional delegate, and now commissioner on the Continental Navy Board, publishes "Battle of the Kegs" in the *New Jersey Gazette*. The poem begins "Gallants attend, and hear a friend/Trill forth harmonious ditty:/Strange things I'll tell, which late befel/In Philadelphia city."

22 January 1778

YORK, PA. At the very time when the Continental Army at Valley Forge suffers from inadequate clothing, fuel, food, and supplies the Continental Congress envisions an apparently madcap adventure, passing a resolution "that an irruption be made into Canada, and that the Board of War be authorized to take every necessary measure for the execution of the business, under such general officers as Congress shall appoint, and apply for such sums of money as may be thought by them proper and requisite for the expedition."

23 January 1778

YORK, PA. The Board of War selects the Marquis de Lafayette to head the Canada "irruption," with Thomas Conway to be second in command and Brig. Gen. John Stark to serve with them.

27 January 1778

NASSAU, BAHAMAS. Under the command of Capt. John Peck Rathbun, who formerly served under John Paul Jones, the fifty-man crew of the USS *Providence* seizes the two forts at Nassau, raising the Stars and Stripes in place of the Union flag—the first time the American flag has flown over a conquered foreign post.

28 January 1778

YORK, PA. Having received letters from Lafayette in which the marquis expresses his abhorrence of Conway and his refusal to serve with him, President Laurens writes apologetically to Lafayette. A strong supporter of Washington, Laurens now begins to suspect foul play on the part of the "Conway Cabal," especially as Conway, with the approval of the Board of War, has already departed for Albany to begin making preparations for the expedition.

31 January 1778

YORK, PA. Lafayette confronts the Board of War with his objections to serving with Conway, presenting them an ultimatum. Without Lafayette's cooperation, the expedition is presumed dead since he threatens to return to France and take most of the other French officers with him.

4 February 1778

BOSTON. Gen. Heath delivers the Continental Congress' resolutions on the Saratoga Convention to Gen. Burgoyne, thereby preventing the embarkation of the defeated British army and the possibility that, upon their return home, other troops would be substituted for them to prosecute the war in America.

5 February 1778

YORK, PA. Baron Friedrich von Steuben arrives in New York. Congress accepts his offer to serve the Continental Army as an unpaid volunteer for the time being.

6 February 1778

PARIS, FRANCE. The American commissioners and the French government agree to two treaties: the Treaty of Amity and Commerce, by which France recognizes the independence of the United States and publicly sanctions the heretofore clandestine trade with them; and the Treaty of Alliance, to take effect whenever war breaks out between France and England—a prospect the first treaty makes inevitable. Thus the former colonies of Great Britain disavow their traditional hostility toward becoming involved in European rivalries and toward a "papist" nation with former imperial ambitions on the North American continent which they had helped the British thwart during the Seven Years' War. The second treaty specifies mutual guarantees that the United States will recognize French claims in the West Indies and that both nations will recognize the other's territorial gains from the war with the exception that Louis XVI renounces forever any claims to the Bermudas, Canada, and any areas of North America east of the Mississippi River. In addition, neither nation may make a separate peace with Great Britain or cease fighting with the enemy until American independence is secured.

9 February 1778

VALLEY FORGE, PA. Angry and determined to squelch the apparent "Conway Cabal" plot to have him displaced, Gen. Washington sends Gen. Gates a letter rebuking him for writing waffling or ambiguous statements and not making Conway's original letter public in order to clear the air. He describes Conway as "capable

of all the malignity of detraction and all the meanness of intrigue to gratify the absurd resentment of disappointed vanity, or to answer the purposes of personal aggrandizement." This and other scathing letters from the commander-in-chief have the desired effect of bringing to an end the presumed intrigue against him.

16 February 1778

VALLEY FORGE, PA. Gen. Washington writes to Gov. George Clinton of New York about the "dreadful situation of the army for want of provisions." The situation is worse than those not at the camp can conceive, he says. "For some days past, there has been little less than famine in camp. A part of the army has been a week without any kind of flesh, and the rest three or four days." Conditions are deplorable, but his men behave admirably. "Naked and starving as they are, we cannot enough admire the incomparable patience and fidelity of the soldiery that they have not been ere this excited by their sufferings to a general mutiny and dispersion." Nevertheless, Washington enforces a stern discipline, with frequent court-martials and whippings in response to violations.

LONDON, ENGLAND. Responding to a letter received in December from Gen. Howe requesting that he be relieved of his duties as commander-in-chief, Lord George Germain writes to tell the general that his resignation is accepted but that he must remain in America until his replacement arrives.

17 February 1778

LONDON, ENGLAND. Recoiling from the stunning loss at Saratoga and concerned over rumors of a French-American alliance, Lord North presents a plan for reconciliation to Parliament. The plan offers repeal of the Tea Act and the Coercive Acts, the promise of no revenue taxes to be imposed on the American colonies, the appointment of a commission to negotiate a peace settlement with the Continental Congress, and suspension of all acts passed since 1763 if that becomes necessary. Charles James Fox compliments Lord North on having finally come round to Fox's viewpoint and asks whether it is true that France and America have signed a commercial treaty. North is stunned, speechless. Edmund Burke points out that the plan presented is virtually the same as the one Burke had proposed two years before and repeats Fox's question. North equivocates.

19 February 1778

ALBANY, N.Y. Lafayette, sent by Washington to direct the Canada "irruption," has arrived here two days before and now writes to his commander to tell him that the expedition is hopeless. Thomas Conway, who preceded him to Albany, has already reached this conclusion since he has received letters from generals Schuyler, Lincoln, and Arnold telling him that an expedition to Canada is impossible. No soldiers are available. Lafayette is disgusted at having been sent on a wild-goose chase in the dead of winter and also deeply resentful toward the Board of War for having concocted this farcical undertaking that has caused him humiliation. He tells Washington he has sent a full account of the matter to Congress.

23 February 1778

VALLEY FORGE, PA. Baron von Steu-

ben arrives, invited by Washington, with a secretary-translator (the baron speaks no English), two aides, and a German servant. The baron has misrepresented his background—he was not a lieutenant-general in Frederick the Great's army but only a captain who was discharged from the army fourteen years before—but he is knowledgeable and well-trained, instructed by Frederick himself.

Baron Frederick William Augustus von Steuben. A former Prussian army officer, he met Franklin in Paris.

Washington assigns him Alexander Hamilton and John Laurens, son of the president of Congress, as aides.

24 February 1778

VALLEY FORGE, PA. Gen. Washington, now believing that the supposed effort to displace him has been obviated, writes once again to Gen. Gates, who has backed away from any hint of involvement in a plot and blamed his aide Col. James Wilkinson for generating the entire unfortunate misunderstanding. Washington is conciliatory. He describes himself as "averse to controversy" and states: "Your repeatedly and solemnly disclaiming any offensive views in those matters which have been the subject of our past correspondence makes me willing to close with the desire you express of burying them hereafter in silence and, as far as future events will permit, oblivion." The Conway Cabal, if it ever really existed, is dead. "My temper leads me to peace and harmony with all men," the commander-in-chief declares. "And it is particularly my wish to avoid any personal feuds or dissensions with those who are embarked in the same great national interest with myself, as every difference of this kind must in its consequences be very injurious." And so the glorious cause of the Revolution overrides personal disputes.

2 March 1778

YORK, PA. Among its recommendations to Congress on reforming the army, the committee visiting Valley Forge proposes a substantive reorganization of the department of quartermaster general. Congress appoints the highly capable Nathanael Greene as quartermaster general to implement the reorganization. He reluctantly accepts.

7 March 1778

LONDON, ENGLAND. Germain signs orders appointing Gen. Sir Henry Clinton to replace Gen. Howe in command of British military forces in America.

WEST INDIES. HMS *Yarmouth* and USS *Randolph* clash. After a fierce twenty-minute battle the *Randolph*, even though outgunned by more than two to one, appears on the verge of victory but suddenly explodes, killing the already-wounded Capt. Nicholas Biddle and all but four of his 315 officers and crew. Only twenty-seven years old, Biddle had a very successful career as a raider for the American navy in the North Atlantic and the West Indies. His death is a significant loss for the navy and its contribution to the war effort.

8 March 1778

LONDON, ENGLAND. Discouraged especially by Burgoyne's disaster at Saratoga and pressured by George III to conduct a thorough review of strategy, the North ministry has concluded that a land war is not likely to succeed against the Americans and a different strategy is needed. The reassessment results in new orders to Gen. Clinton, now the commander-in-chief, signed today by Lord Germain. Under these orders, Clinton is to cooperate with Adm. Lord Richard Howe in diverting the fleet from support of military operations to enforcement of a blockade augmented by military raids against the American coast from New York to Nova Scotia. In addition, Clinton is to prepare an invasion of the Carolinas and Georgia with the purpose of separating the Southern states from the Northern states. Since this plan means Philadelphia is no longer strategic, Clinton is to pull back the army to New York, though he is given discretion to decide whether conditions warrant maintaining a force in Philadelphia.

12 March 1778

MONTPELIER, VT. A new government elected on 3 March takes office in the independent state of Vermont, which is in fact a free republic.

13 March 1778

YORK, PA. Following the reports submitted by Lafayette, the Congress decides "that the irruption ordered to be made into Canada should be suspended" and authorizes Gen. Washington to order Lafayette and Baron de Kalb to rejoin the main army immediately.

LONDON, ENGLAND. The French ambassador informs Lord Weymouth, secretary of state in the royal government, of the Treaty of Commerce between France and the United States. He does not mention the Treaty of Alliance, but the commerce treaty is tantamount to French recognition of American independence. The North ministry immediately recalls Lord Stormont from Paris and cancels the orders to Gen. Clinton signed by Lord Germain just five days before.

16 March 1778

LONDON, ENGLAND. Lord North's plan of conciliation with the former American colonies is adopted under the title "Royal Instructions to the Peace Commission of 1778." The Earl of Carlisle; the Howe brothers; William Eden, commissioner for trade and plantations; and George Johnstone, naval captain and former governor of West Florida, are to comprise the peace commission, referred to as the Carlisle Commission. They are also to have broad authority to concede or to negotiate every point of contention between the royal government and the former colonies.

18 March 1778

QUINTON'S BRIDGE, N.J. In an effort to counteract Gen. Anthony Wayne's foraging excursions in New Jersey a small force under Col. Charles Mawhood has entered the state on 12 March and now manipulates about 300 militia into a trap. Thinking the British troops are retreating, the Americans restore the planks in the bridge and leave 100 men to guard it while Capt. Smith leads 200 men after the British. Smith's men are suddenly cut off from retreat to the bridge when rangers stationed in a brick house emerge to attack them from the rear. The rebels flee in disarray, and the British exact a heavy toll, perhaps forty dead, while losing only one man.

20 March 1778

VERSAILLES, FRANCE. In a formal act of recognition, Louis XVI receives the American commissioners—Benjamin Franklin, Silas Deane, and Arthur Lee, plus William Lee and Ralph Izard—all dressed in formal court clothes. During a private audience the king speaks warmly, asking Franklin to assure the Continental Congress of his friendship for the Americans. Franklin replies that the king can be certain of the Congress' gratitude and fulfillment of the treaty agreements. Vergennes treats the guests to a sumptuous dinner and afterward introduces them to the royal family. Franklin charms Queen Marie Antoinette.

21 March 1778

HANCOCK'S BRIDGE, N.J. Disappointed that he did not achieve total success at Quinton's Bridge, Mawhood stages an attack at Hancock's Bridge, where 200 militia are stationed. All but twenty of the militia have been withdrawn before the attack, however, and Mawhood's Tory raiders content themselves with killing the sentries, a patrol, and the inhabitants of the Hancock house, who are known to be Loyalists. The ruthlessness of this and the earlier attack at Quinton's Bridge, referred to as massacres by the local residents, stir outrage in New Jersey.

LONDON, ENGLAND. Germain issues new orders to Clinton. Now the main focus is on France, not the rebellious Americans. Germain orders Clinton to send an expedition of 5,000 men to assault the French island of St. Lucia in the West Indies. He is to send another 3,000 men to reinforce St. Augustine and Pensacola in order to secure Florida while providing a base for possibly attacking New Orleans or defending Jamaica. And he is to withdraw the remainder of his army from Philadelphia to New York City, which is considered desirable to hold as an enhancement to the negotiations the Carlisle Commission will presumably be conducting with the rebels; but if New York proves too difficult to hold, then he can maintain the garrison at Newport and move the New York garrison to Halifax, Nova Scotia. The new strategy means that, as in the past, the British see the West Indies as more important commercially than the former American colonies are. British trade with the West Indies is in fact more lucrative, and the involved merchants have pressured the North ministry for protection. If the British can capture St. Lucia and its excellent harbor in the Windward Islands south of Martinique they will have a strong base from which to attack the important French islands in the Lesser Antilles. Of major concern, however, at this time the British navy has only fifty-five ships of the line, while the French

have twenty-one in harbor at Brest and twelve at Toulon. If the French send this total fleet or a contingent of it to the Americas, British naval supremacy there will be seriously challenged; yet blockading the French harbors is now not practicable for the British navy.

26 March 1778

YORK, PA. Two members of the committee sent to Valley Forge, Francis Dana and Nathaniel Folsom, introduce a proposal to provide officers of the Continental Army with half pay for life and their widows with pensions—a proposal worked out by the committee and Washington. Congress erupts with furious debate. Although a slight majority are in favor, opponents raise the issue of fear of a standing army and questions about whether officers are motivated by patriotism or merely self-aggrandizement.

30 March 1778

YORK, PA. After two months of information-gathering and discussion the committee sent to the Continental Army camp at Valley Forge to study means of reforming army procedures with Gen. Washington has finished its efforts. But in the process the committee members have interfered with a plan for a general exchange of prisoners Washington's agents have been negotiating with Gen. Howe, creating consternation and debate in the Congress, which now appoints a committee to prepare instructions for the committee Washington is naming to complete an official agreement on exchanges with Howe. Curiously, the congressional committee's work is finished this same day. Washington is instructed that Gen. Charles Lee must be exchanged for Maj. Gen. Richard Prescott or no exchange can occur without further orders from Congress. There is another requirement: for the exchange of Ethan Allen. In addition, all resolutions of Congress about Tories who have served with the British must be respected (Tories would, for example, be handed over to states to be tried for treason); all exchanges are to be unrelated to rank; and Gen. Washington must approve the terms of the exchange agreement.

31 March 1778

BORDEAUX, FRANCE. John Adams and his ten-year-old son John Quincy Adams arrive.

4 April 1778

VALLEY FORGE, PA. Washington writes to inform President Laurens that in his judgment Gen. Howe can never accede to some of the requirements the congressional committee has mandated for the exchange of prisoners, including vindictive treatment of Tories who have served with the British.

5 April 1778

BOSTON, MASS. Congress allows Gen. Burgoyne and two members of his staff to return to England, but his troops (referred to as the "Convention Army") must remain behind as prisoners.

8 April 1778

PARIS, FRANCE. John Adams arrives in the French capital to assume his duties as Silas Deane's replacement.

9 April 1778

YORK, PA. As part of the effort to re-

form the army Congress appoints Jeremiah Wadsworth to head and reorganize the trouble-plagued Commissary Department. His title is Commissary General of Purchases.

10 April 1778

BREST, FRANCE. John Paul Jones, with a crew of about 140 men, sets sail in the *Ranger*, armed with eighteen six-pounder cannon and six swivel guns, to begin raids in British waters.

VALLEY FORGE, PA. Gen. Washington writes to President Laurens supporting the Dana–Folsom proposal on officers' compensation: "I do most religiously believe the salvation of the cause depends upon it, and without it, your Officers will moulder to nothing, or be composed of low and illiterate men void of capacity for this, or any other business. To prove this, I can with truth aver, that scarce a day passes without the offer of two or three Commissions." He asserts that he has no personal interest in the proposal, as its passage will bring him no benefit—the real benefit will arise from the increased honorableness of army commissions and the resultant order and regularity among officers.

11 April 1778

TOULON, FRANCE. The French fleet harbored at Toulon (eleven ships of the line, one fifty-gun ship, and several frigates) sets sail under the command of Charles Hector Theodat, comte d'Estaing. The British ponder its destination—Brest, to join forces with the fleet there, or America? If the former, then the French navy may threaten the British Isles; consequently, Admiral Augustus Keppel, commander of the home fleet, adamantly opposes dividing the fleet to send ships to America or counter the French at the Straits of Gibraltar. John Montagu, fourth Earl of Sandwich and first lord of the Admiralty, agrees with Keppel. Germain favors stopping the French at the Straits in order to prevent their sailing for America. The dispute presents Lord North and the king with a dilemma: divide the fleet between the English Channel and the Straits and risk invasion or maintain the fleet intact and risk the French sailing to America with the consequent loss of the British naval advantage there.

12 April 1778

LONDON, ENGLAND. The North ministry appoints the final two other members of the peace commission to join Frederick Howard, fifth Earl of Carlisle, and the Howe brothers; Carlisle's friend William Eden, a member of the Board of Trade; and George Johnstone, former governor of West Florida, a partisan of the Americans in Parliament. As Carlisle is a close friend of opposition leader Charles Fox, the commission's composition is expected to be pleasing to the Americans. Unfortunately, the concessions its members are authorized to grant are not likely to be so pleasing, although they are generous: no standing armies in the colonies in peacetime, the Americans to maintain their own military, Congress to continue existing, American charters guaranteed, offices reserved for Americans, and so on. But the sovereignty of Parliament is to be recognized—meaning power to regulate the empire's trade, to forbid American ships of war, to impose taxes on non-British imports into the colonies, to deny an independent American coinage, to require that

Loyalists' estates be restored. The sticking point, of course, is independence; and if the Americans insist on independence, the commissioners are to refer the question to London while negotiating an armistice. Understandably, Lord North is not optimistic about the Carlisle Commission's chances of success. Their efforts will be jeopardized by the fact that they know nothing about the change in British military strategy.

14 April 1778

YORK, PA. At the behest of Congress President Laurens sends Washington a letter, drafted by the Congress after acrimonious debate, that is clearly a rebuke of the general for objecting to the resolutions of Congress respecting an exchange of prisoners. Among other things it states that there will be no agreement on prisoner exchange unless that agreement accepts exchange of Gen. Lee for Gen. Prescott. As it happens, the negotiations with Gen. Howe break down and Washington chooses to ignore the rebuke, instead thanking Congress for reiterating "their confidence."

16 April 1778

PORTSMOUTH, ENGLAND. The Carlisle Commission departs for America aboard the man-of-war *Trident*. With them travel the pregnant Mrs. Eden and Lord Cornwallis, the latter returning to America to be Gen. Clinton's second in command.

21 April 1778

YORK, PA. At Washington's request Elias Boudinot, commissary of prisons, has arranged the exchange of Gen. Richard Prescott for Gen. Charles Lee, who was released on parole on 5 April. After a brief stay at

Valley Forge—where Washington greeted him warmly and Martha Washington prepared an elegant dinner and provided him a room next to her parlor—he visits the Continental Congress, complaining that other officers have been promoted in his absence. His exchange becomes official today, and he sets out for Virginia. Before leaving, however, he tells Boudinot that the condition of the army is worse than he expected and that Washington is "not fit to command a sergeant's guard."

22 April 1778

YORK, PA. The Continental Congress resolves that any individual or group that comes to terms with the Carlisle Commission is an enemy of the United States, effectively precluding any hope of the commission's success before they even arrive in America. Members of Congress have seen a draft of North's speech introducing the conciliatory measures in Parliament and a draft of the bill and are unimpressed by the ministry's change of heart, abandoning the prior adamancy, against negotiating with the Americans. They insist that there can be no negotiations until the British "either withdraw their fleets and armies, or else, in positive and express terms, acknowledge the independence of the said States."

WHITEHAVEN, SCOTLAND. The *Ranger* enters this port on the Irish Sea, and in the dark Capt. John Paul Jones rows ashore with a raiding party of thirty-one volunteers. They spike the cannon at the port's entranceway and set fire to some vessels in the harbor. The inhabitants put out the fire as Jones' party returns to the *Ranger*. Little

harm is done, but the British do suffer some humiliation and consternation as this is the only time a British port has been "assaulted" since 1667.

23 April 1778

ST. MARY'S ISLE, SCOTLAND. Jones lands with the intent of kidnapping the Earl of Selkirk, owner of the island, and taking him to France as a hostage to exchange for American prisoners in England. But the earl is not home, and the only prize seized is Lady Selkirk's family silver.

24 April 1778

CARRICKFERGUS, SCOTLAND. The *Ranger* sails in. The captain of the twenty-one-gun warship HMS *Drake*, at anchor in the harbor, takes her to be a British privateer and sends an officer in a longboat to visit while he prepares to leave harbor. Jones takes the officer prisoner. As the *Drake* leaves harbor and hails the *Ranger* Jones identifies his ship and offers a challenge, firing a broadside. The ensuing battle lasts a little over an hour, when the *Drake*, badly cut up, surrenders. The *Ranger* suffers eight casualties, the *Drake* over thirty, including her captain.

27 April 1778

LONDON. On the basis of intelligence reports received from Paris and confirmed by bankers in Amsterdam, the king, North, and most of the Cabinet—not including Sandwich—decide d'Estaing is heading for America, destination either the Delaware or Boston. Germain, who had argued strenuously for intercepting the French fleet at Gibraltar, foresees all of his efforts in ruins and Philadelphia, Halifax, even Quebec falling to the enemy. He urges North to send part of the home fleet to America at once.

29 April 1778

LONDON. As Sandwich has hesitated, the desperate Germain sends written protests to the king and the Cabinet—with immediate effect. The Cabinet decides to send thirteen ships of the line to America under the command of Admiral John Byron to reinforce Adm. Lord Richard Howe's fleet, and Germain relays the order to the Admiralty. One question remains: how to warn Admiral Howe in time that the French fleet is en route. No such effort has been made, of course, as the Cabinet debated policy.

1 May 1778

CROOKED BILLET, PA. A force of about 450 Pennsylvania militia under Brig. Gen. John Lacey stationed here to harass British forage parties has been reduced to fewer than sixty fit men because of expiring enlistments, and they now find themselves nearly surrounded by a large British force—400 light infantry under Lt. Col. Robert Abercrombie at their front and 300 rangers under Maj. John Graves Simcoe at their back. They withdraw into a woods, hold their ground temporarily, and finally retreat, leaving behind their baggage and suffering thirty-six casualties, including twenty-six dead. The British have nine wounded.

2 May 1778

YORK, PA. Congress adjourns for the Sabbath only to be recalled on this Saturday evening to hear good news: Simeon Deane, brother of Silas, has received copies of the treaties of commerce and alliance brought directly to

him by a messenger from the American commissioners in France. The members hear the treaties read and again adjourn until Monday.

4 May 1778

YORK, PA. Congress reconvenes and ratifies the treaties with France—a unanimous vote—though deciding to request that France rescind two articles.

5 May 1778

VALLEY FORGE, PA. Gen. Washington, like others, views the treaties with France as guaranteeing American independence, foreseeing the *"certain prospect of success."*

YORK, PA. Responding to a 30 April recommendation by Gen. Washington, the Congress confirms Baron von Steuben's appointment as major general and Inspector General of the Army. Beginning with a select company of 100 men, the baron has been instructing Washington's army in military drill and training, including instruction in the use of the bayonet (so terrifying to American troops in

Baron Frederick von Steuben drilling troops at Valley Forge.

the hands of onrushing British and Hessian regulars), with remarkable success. He has also written the army's first military manual, with Alexander Hamilton revising his aide's English translation for clarity, and has imposed standards of hygiene. Among the men at Valley Forge he has become one of the most popular officers.

6 May 1778

VALLEY FORGE, PA. The Continental Army celebrates news of the French treaties with noisy joyfulness, as the Marquis de Lafayette has advocated. The troops march in review, demonstrating to Washington's satisfaction the new precision instilled by von Steuben's training.

8 May 1778

BREST, FRANCE. John Paul Jones and the *Ranger* return with the captured *Drake* and about 200 British prisoners.

YORK, PA. Congress publishes the "necessary" parts of the treaties with France to be disseminated along with copies of an address to the American people composed by Gouverneur Morris that warns of the dangers of accepting a peace with the enemy leading to loss of independence while portraying and excoriating the evils that enemy has perpetrated. It is recommended that ministers read this address to their parishioners following worship services.

PHILADELPHIA. Gen. Sir Henry Clinton arrives from New York to replace Gen. Howe as commander-in-chief of British forces in America.

BORDENTOWN, N.J. A force of over 600 British troops from Philadelphia enters Bordentown with the purpose of destroying American military stores. Essentially unopposed, they burn Joseph Borden's estate, do some plundering, and destroy the stores. They then burn two frigates and some smaller vessels at nearby White Hills.

11 May 1778

LONDON. William Pitt, Earl of Chatham, a longtime advocate of American interests in Parliament, dies.

12 May 1778

REDSTONE SETTLEMENT, MONONGAHELA RIVER. George Rogers Clark sets out downriver to rendezvous at the Falls of the Ohio with men being recruited for his western expedition by Maj. W. P. Smith.

14 May 1778

LONDON. Keppel and Sandwich remain doubtful about d'Estaing's destination; and with their doubts seemingly confirmed by news on the thirteenth that d'Estaing's fleet was sighted off Algiers on 28 April (two weeks after setting sail he is still in the Mediterranean Sea), Sandwich hastily orders Adm. Byron not to sail.

15 May 1778

YORK, PA. After strenuous debate and acceptance of a compromise on the period for half-pay, Congress adopts the officers' compensation proposal. As accepted, the proposal specifies that following the war's conclusion officers will receive half-pay for seven years provided that they continued in service for the duration of the war.

16 May 1778

STRAITS OF GIBRALTAR. Sighted by HMS *Proserpine* and HMS *Enterprise*, the French fleet out of Toulon passes the Straits and heads for the open sea.

18 May 1778

PHILADELPHIA. An extravagant party and mock tournament, or Meschianza, organized by Capt. John André is held in honor of Gen. Howe. Most of the young belles of the city, Tory or otherwise, attend except for the lovely Peggy Shippen, whose father forbids it, even though she has rehearsed a part in the tournament pageant. The setting features a square for jousting with pavilions at two ends, one housing young ladies in Turkish costumes who offer favors for the winning knights. After the mock joust guests proceed through two triumphal arches honoring the Howe brothers and enter a large hall, where they have refreshments. Then into a ballroom for dancing and afterward fireworks erupting outside the now-opened ballroom windows and poetry being declaimed within. The evening terminates with a sumptuous dinner of 1,200 dishes. The lavishness of the party seems in such bad taste in an occupied city with the half-starved American army camped nearby that even Tories express disgust. One, Thomas Jones, decries the Meschianza as "ridiculous, undeserved, and unmerited," and concludes: "Had the General been properly rewarded for his conduct while Commander-in Chief in America, an execution, and not a Meschianza, would have been the consequence."

VALLEY FORGE, PA. Apparently to gratify Lafayette after the Canada "irruption" fiasco and to assuage his desire for meaningful action, Gen. Washington places the marquis in command of a 2,200-man division (one- third of the army) with orders to approach the enemy lines, interdict their foraging parties, gather intelligence, and protect the area between the Delaware and Schuylkill rivers while avoiding being taken by surprise—a dangerous and perhaps pointless exercise, as the company is too small to be effective in providing protection and too large to be effective at spying. Lafayette crosses the Schuylkill and posts his force at Barren Hill, eleven miles from Philadelphia and only two miles from the British outposts at Chestnut Hill.

19 May 1778

PHILADELPHIA. Gen. Clinton has learned of Lafayette's movement and troop deployment almost immediately, and he plans a surprise attack with the intent of capturing the marquis, humiliating him and France. At 10:30 P.M. 5,000 British troops under Maj. Gen. James Grant leave Philadelphia and march toward the intersection of Whitemarsh and Ridge roads, where they can cut off Lafayette's retreat to fords across the Schuylkill and on to Valley Forge. At the same time Maj. Gen. Charles Grey leads over 2,000 men directly down the road to Barren Hill to attack Lafayette's left flank, while another force under Clinton, with Howe accompanying, marches up Ridge Road from the south. When these three forces are in position Lafayette will be effectively encircled, with the river at his back. But the versatile raider Capt. Allen McLane learns of Clinton's approach and sends a company of riflemen to delay Clinton while he hastens to camp to warn Lafayette.

20 May 1778

BARREN HILL, PA. Lafayette's posi-

EIGHTEENTH-CENTURY TERMS OF WAR

Abatis — A defensive obstacle of felled trees around a fort. Trees were cut with branches intact and pointed away from the fortifications, making an assault difficult. A basic feature of most fortified places.

Adjutant — The principal staff officer who assisted a commander by processing orders and seeing to logistical and administrative duties. An adjutant general served an entire army; a deputy adjutant served smaller commands with the help of assistant adjutants.

Aide-de-camp — Junior staff officers attached personally to a commander. They acted as messengers, secretaries, administrative assistants, and surrogates.

Artificer — Technical field soldiers skilled in mechanics who served with engineer or artillery units. They could build, repair, and maintain equipment in the field. Sometimes organized into separate units such as the Continental Regiment of Artillery Artificers.

Bateau — A small, flat-bottomed boat with a very shallow draft used primarily on rivers or lakes to move troops and supplies. Often constructed hastily and crudely, but could be more permanent. Capable of rowing, poling, or sailing and thus flexible. The Continental Army had a unit of bateaux men.

Battalion — A term meaning essentially the same as "regiment" during the War for Independence.

Brig — A class of medium-sized sailing craft with two, square-rigged masts; usually smaller than a ship or a barque.

Canister — Small shot (the size of musket balls) fired from artillery in a metal can that opened on discharge. It was vicious against troops or cavalry at close range.

Chevaux-de-frise — A portable defensive obstacle made of logs or beams bristling with spikes. One of the basic devices of the time, chevaux were used on land as roadblocks or to fill gaps in fortifications. Underwater versions blocked rivers or harbors.

Cutter — A small craft used primarily in sheltered water or along a coastline to patrol. Usually a fast, maneuverable type of craft such as a sloop.

Durham boat — Specialized flat-bottomed, barge-like, high-capacity craft used on the Delaware River to move cargo. Made famous when Washington transported his troops on Durham boats to attack Trenton.

Flank companies — Special companies made up of grenadiers and light infantry. They were usually positioned on the flanks of a battleline of foot soldiers. Presumed to be the best troops in a regiment, flank companies from several units were often combined into a single elite striking force.

Forlorn hope — A small group of picked troops sent to lead an assault, usually relying on speed and surprise. Akin to a suicide squad.

Gabion — A portable wickerwork basket, filled with dirt, used to build field fortifications in a hurry.

Could be constructed on the spot from branches or hauled into place from the rear.

Galley – A class of small war craft, constructed along the lines of a very large rowboat, that could carry troops and a small gun or two (usually swivel guns). Employed extensively on lakes or rivers, galleys might have sails but were often equipped with banks of oars and called row-galleys.

Gondola – A flat-bottomed small boat with pointed ends, used on lakes and rivers and rigged with both oars and two square sails on a single mast.

Grapeshot – Small round-shot fired from artillery against massed foot soldiers, opposing batteries, sailing ships, or light fortifications, and having a shotgun effect.

Grenadiers – Elite troops formed into special companies (or even battalions) and used for the most difficult or dangerous assignments. Originally formed of soldiers of large stature who could throw the heavy hand grenades of the previous century.

Jaeger – Literally "hunter" in German (the same as the French "chasseur"), the term referred to German mercenary units equipped with short-barreled rifles and trained to fight in wooded or rough terrain. Roughly equivalent to American rifleman companies.

Langrage – A specialized form of naval gun projectile consisting of chains and scrap metal, designed to disable the opponent's rigging and render them immobile. Used mostly by the French navy; the British preferred round-shot fired into hulls.

Privateers – Captains of private ships given letters of "marque and reprisal" by a government body, which authorized them to seize vessels of an opposing nation and thus created an officially sanctioned force of pirates. Privateers sold their prizes and split the profits. The American Congress and individual states commissioned thousands of privateers during the Revolution.

Redoubt – An outlying, self-contained fortification forming part of the overall defense of a larger fortress. The most famous were Redoubts No. 9 and 10 at Yorktown, taken by allied storming parties.

Regiment – The basic and largest unit of army organization during the eighteenth century (used interchangeably then with *battalion*). Usually authorized at between 750 and 1,000 men and officers, regiments in the Continental Army were organized primarily by state and seldom had more than a fraction of the numbers ordained. British regiments were designated by sequential numbers and were usually much larger than American regiments. French regiments carried the name of the commander or of the region from which they were recruited. German regiments generally were named for their commanders.

Sappers – Troops trained to tunnel and use explosives. Most often employed against large fortifications.

Ship of the line – The largest class of naval warship, usually carrying at least sixty-four heavy guns and equipped with three

masts. Such vessels were essentially floating gun platforms and were employed in a classic long-line formation for battle at sea.
Sloop – A small sailing craft, probably the most common in the American theater of war, rigged with a single mast and one or two sails fore and aft.

tion seems hopeless, but he prepares for defense and sends out scouts in all directions. One scout returns with the information that there is a second road to Matson's Ford descending the steep slope from Barren Hill so abruptly that Lafayette's troops can be quickly hidden from Grant's view on the heights above. Lafayette feigns an attack on Grant while his troops slip away to Matson's Ford, followed by the marquis and the rear guard. By the time Clinton appears on the scene the Americans are ensconced on a height on the west bank of the river. The British commander gives up in disgust and orders his troops back to Philadelphia.

ALTAMAHA RIVER, GA. Maj. Gen. Robert Howe, with about 550 Continental Army troops plus Georgia militia under Governor William Houston and colonels Pinckney, Bull, and Williamson reaches the Altahama River on an expedition to invade East Florida and attack British Gen. Augustine Prevost. His first objective is St. Augustine, but his plan of attack aborts when the Georgia militia officers refuse to take orders.

25 May 1778

PHILADELPHIA. Gen. William Howe sails for England.

BRISTOL, R.I. British marauders commanded by Maj. Gen. Richard Prescott, recently exchanged for Gen. Charles Lee, raid Bristol and Warren, burning buildings, harassing residents, plundering, and confiscating livestock.

27 May 1778

YORK, PA. Congress adopts proposals for regulating and reorganizing the army proposed by the committee sent to review army operations with Gen. Washington at Valley Forge.

FALLS OF THE OHIO. George Rogers Clark arrives to discover that Maj. Smith has failed to raise the four companies of recruits from the Holston settlements and only part of a company from Holston are joining him. He has four captains in his service—Joseph Bowman, Leonard Helm, William Harrod, and John Montgomery. Clark encamps his frontiersmen on an island in the Ohio River at the Falls and begins to train them before revealing what their true mission is to be.

28 May 1778

VALLEY FORGE, PA. Gen. Washington appoints Benedict Arnold military governor and commander of troops in Philadelphia—if and when the British evacuate the city. Arnold had arrived at Valley Forge weeks earlier to warm greetings and an embrace from his commander. His temper is somewhat mollified by Congress' having restored his rank and seniority, but he still suffers from his leg wound received at Saratoga—the leg is two inches shorter than before—and thus remains incapable of assuming a field command.

31 May 1778

TIVERTON, R.I. Some two dozen defenders hold off Gen. Prescott and his 150 raiders after the British put the torch to several mills.

1 June 1778

COBBLESKILL, N.Y. Tories and Indian warriors led by Mohawk chieftain Joseph Brant burn this settlement of about twenty families on the Susquehanna River west of Albany after driving off Continental troops and killing their commander, Capt. William Patrick. They massacre many of the settlers. Following the defeat at Saratoga the British encourage such frontier raids as their only military recourse. The raids are launched mostly from British posts at Detroit on the western frontier and Niagara and Oswego on the New York frontier.

2 June 1778

FALMOUTH, ENGLAND. HMS *Proserpine* speeds into port with the news that the French fleet has cleared the Straits of Gibraltar and is headed for America.

6 June 1778

PHILADELPHIA, PA. The members of the Carlisle Commission arrive from England.

9 June 1778

PLYMOUTH, ENGLAND. Following a hasty decision by the Cabinet issuing new orders to Adm. Byron on 7 June, the admiral sets sail for New York.

13 June 1778

PLYMOUTH, ENGLAND. The channel fleet, Adm. Augustus Keppel in command, sets sail with orders to protect British ships sailing up from Gibraltar to reinforce the home fleet—they must pass by Brest, where part of the French fleet remains in harbor.

16 June 1778

PHILADELPHIA. The British remove the artillery from all their redoubts around the city and several regiments begin the evacuation, crossing the Delaware at Cooper's Point. The evacuation entails moving 10,000 troops and the army's wagons, horses, artillery, provisions, and supplies—all could be easy prey for the Americans while on the river. Clinton also has to evacuate 3,000 Tories, who leave with their possessions by ship, using space that could have accommodated some of his troops' baggage.

17 June 1778

LIZARD, ENGLAND. Adm. Keppel sights two French frigates off the coast. Both will be safe according to custom if they respond peaceably to his hailing, but one opens fire with a broadside. War between England and France has begun. Following surrender of the French ship, the British find aboard a list of the Brest fleet, indicating twenty-seven ships are ready to sail and five more are in preparation. Keppel turns back to obtain reinforcements.

YORK, PA. After three days of discussion of letters received from the Carlisle Commission outlining the British terms for reconciliation but deploring the American alliance with France, the Congress unanimously adopts a response. It states that Congress is prepared to consider a peace treaty whenever the king evidences his sincerity of intention by "an explicit acknowledgment of the independence of these states, or the withdrawing of his fleets and armies."

18 June 1778

PHILADELPHIA. The last of Clinton's troops leave the city and march to Gloucester Point to cross the river to Gloucester, while the fleet hoists anchor and sails down the river. Philadelphia is ceded to the Americans. A courier brings the news to Washington at Valley Forge, and the commander- in-chief immediately begins to set his army in motion toward Coryell's Ferry. By this time, despite the deprivations of the past winter, the Continental Army numbers more than 13,500 men and officers. And thanks to the competence of Quartermaster General Nathanael Greene and Commissary General Jeremiah Wadsworth, the men are reasonably well clothed and equipped and in improved health. Over 12,000 of them stationed at Valley Forge also constitute a well-disciplined force thanks to Baron von Steuben.

19 June 1778

PHILADELPHIA. Gen. Benedict Arnold enters the city accompanied by a regiment of light horse to establish a military occupation.

20 June 1778

YORK, PA. Congress resumes consideration of the Articles of Confederation with a sense of chagrin and embarrassment that they have not been adopted by the states—legitim-

izing the union of states and the authority of Congress—at a time when a minister from France may be arriving. Thus far only Virginia, New York, and New Hampshire have ratified.

24 June 1778

HOPEWELL, N.J. Washington's entire army has crossed the Delaware at Coryell's Ferry in pursuit of Clinton's force and encamps for the night about fifteen miles northeast of the British encampment at Allentown. In a council of war Gen. Charles Lee once again opposes attack; the majority supports him. It is decided that the 1,300 Continentals under Brig. Gen. William Maxwell and 800 New Jersey militia under Gen. Philemon Dickinson should continue harassing the British flanks.

25 June 1778

ALLENTOWN, N.J. Fearing that Washington will intercept him at New Brunswick and attack his troops as they cross the Raritan River, Gen. Clinton decides on a different route to New York. He divides his force, sending half the army in advance under Lt. Gen. Wilhelm von Knyphausen followed by the baggage train and then the second half under Lord Cornwallis accompanied by Clinton—all now headed for Monmouth Court House and on to Sandy Hook. Washington marches to Kingston. He is displeased with the decision not to attack Clinton; and in hopes of assaulting the enemy's rear he places Lafayette, a strong advocate of attacking, in charge of an advance guard totaling some 4,000 men, including Maxwell's and Dickinson's men. Charles Lee, who first rejected command of this force, now claims it as second in command, and Washington acquiesces. Lee, with an additional 1,000 men, marches off to join Lafayette at Englishtown. During the night Washington moves the remainder of his army to Cranbury.

26 June 1778

FALLS OF THE OHIO. George Rogers Clark, leaving behind about twenty men to defend the supplies and blockhouse on the island, sets out with 175 men in flatboats, shooting the rapids at the Falls during an eclipse of the sun—an omen of good luck, as he sees it. Clark has had to force some of his men to serve, as they tried to desert once they heard what the expedition's objectives were; but most have pledged loyalty to him, swayed by his forceful personality.

27 June 1778

YORK, PA. The Continental Congress adjourns, in compliance with a resolution passed on 24 June, to reconvene in Philadelphia on 2 July and there to hold a public celebration of national independence on 4 July and to attend church en masse on 5 July to give thanks for independence.

ISLE OF WIGHT. Adm. Keppel's fleet drops anchor so that the admiral can plea for reinforcements; but the king and his Cabinet express dismay over his return, believing he leaves the Gibraltar fleet and merchant ships from India and the West Indies to the mercy of French raiders from the fleet at Brest. The Admiralty orders Keppel to return to sea off Brest as soon as he has added four more ships, bringing his force to twenty-six ships against the Brest fleet of twenty-two (five

ships previously harbored there have already set sail).

ENGLISHTOWN, N.J. Washington, now encamped five miles from here, calls his officers together to order an attack on Clinton's rear, placing Lee in command. During the night he sends orders to Lee to dispatch a unit of troops to observe Clinton's force and detect signs of movement, but Lee delays doing so for hours.

28 June 1778

MONMOUTH COURT HOUSE, N.J. At about 4:00 A.M. Clinton orders von Knyphausen's division to start for Middletown. Dickinson observes the movement of the advance column and reports it to Lee and Washington. A few hours later Lee moves haltingly, interrupted by brief skirmishes with British rear-guard troops, toward Cornwallis' division, already in movement following von Knyphausen. Sometime after eleven o'clock Lee's 5,000-man force confronts 2,000 troops in Cornwallis' rear guard; but unfortunately Lee has no plan of attack and sends few or no orders to Gen. Maxwell, Gen. Wayne, Gen. Scott, and Gen. Woodford, leading to uncoordinated actions and confusion. Clinton, realizing that the skirmishing constitutes a larger menace than Dickinson's and Maxwell's harassing tactics, turns about and marches back to do battle. Misconstruing Lafayette's movements, Maxwell and Scott retreat in order to avoid becoming dangerously exposed. The retreat becomes general, as Lee and his entire force march back toward Englishtown.

Washington, with the main army,

The Battle of Monmouth Court House; here Washington rallies the troops.

comes upon the retreating troops and is outraged that what he thinks should have been an easily successful attack on Clinton's rear has disintegrated. He confronts Lee, demands an explanation, and reviles the feckless general—"he swore ...," says Gen. Scott, "till the leaves shook on the trees ... he swore like an angel from heaven!" Washington assumes command, riding up and down the lines, restoring control, inspiring confidence, and turning his soldiers back to the attack. They establish a strong defensive position under Gen. Greene and Lord Stirling on a ridge above West Ravine, placing a morass between themselves and Clinton's troops, and implanting Knox's artillery to their right on Comb's Hill. The ensuing battle lasts all afternoon, with a massive artillery duel and Clinton sending sporadic assaults against the American position that are suc-

Molly Pitcher; legend claims she took over the cannon manned by her fallen husband during the Battle of Monmouth.

cessively beaten back. By six o'clock the weary British withdraw. The Americans rest, sleeping on their arms, Gen. Washington wrapped in his cloak and Lafayette beside him. Washington plans to attack the British in the morning. But Clinton, following Washington's own precedent at Trenton, slips away during the night to Middletown. Although the battle is inconclusive, the Americans lose 356 men, including 72 dead and 132 missing, many disabled by heat exhaustion or sunstroke; the British casualties are 358 men, including 217 dead, perhaps 60 of them from sunstroke.

Soldiers stopping for a drink of water at Monmouth.

30 June 1778

SANDY HOOK, N.J. Clinton's army reaches Sandy Hook, but during the march some 600 of his troops—440 of them Hessians—have deserted.

ALLIGATOR BRIDGE, FLA. Gen. Robert Howe sends American cavalry against a unit of East Florida Rangers, who drive them off, wounding Col. Elijah Clarke.

1 July 1778

SANDY HOOK, N.J. Clinton's army reaches Sandy Hook to await transport to New York City. At the same time Washington begins a series of short daily marches, halting today in New Brunswick. His final destination is White Plains, N.Y.

2 July 1778

PHILADELPHIA. The Continental Congress reconvenes but lacks a quorum.

3–4 July 1778

FORTY FORT, WYOMING VALLEY, PA.

Maj. Sir John Butler's Tory Rangers and their Indian allies, a force of over 1,200 that has descended from Niagara looting and burning in western Pennsylvania, begin an attack on Forty Fort. The fort's defenders, led by Zeb Butler, unlike their comrades at nearby Jenkins' Fort and Wintermot Fort, have refused to surrender, even with assurances that women and children will be kept safe from the Indians. Consequently, Sir John Butler tries a subterfuge, setting fire to Fort Wintermot to make Zeb Butler and his comrades think the Tories and Indians are leaving. The ruse works. Zeb Butler and his men race from the fort in pursuit of the raiders, only to be surprised in the woods by Indians wielding spears and tomahawks. Butler's men flee in panic, some diving into the Susquehanna River, where the Indians kill them in the water. The Indians also overtake and kill others fleeing to their forts, taking some men captive to be tied to trees and burned alive. Outrage against the Tories and Indians erupts among the frontier settlements as news of this "Wyoming Valley Massacre" spreads.

4 July 1778

KASKASKIA. George Rogers Clark, with his 175 frontier recruits from Kentucky, Tennessee, and western Pennsylvania, captures Kaskaskia without bloodshed. To maintain the advantage of surprise Clark has abandoned the river at Fort Massaic, where he has hidden his boats, and has trekked 120 miles overland through dense forests and across open prairies. Having learned that the local militia has disbanded when rumors of his coming could not be verified, Clark procures boats, crosses the Kaskaskia River, sends half his troops to surround the village, and with the rest marches through an open fort gate straight to the house of the commandant, the Chevalier de Rocheblave, a French officer in the British service, who immediately surrenders. Clark then sends Capt. Bowman with thirty men to Prairie du Rocher and Cahokia, which also surrender without resistance. Not a single shot is fired during the entire operation.

BRUNSWICK, N.J. In response to a series of letters written on 30 June and sent by Charles Lee complaining of his treatment by Washington, demanding reparations, and finally requesting a court-martial, the commander-in-chief grants the final request. The court-martial opens with Lord Stirling presiding as president. Lee is charged with disobeying orders by not attacking at Monmouth Court House, misbehavior in the same battle evidenced by a disorderly and shameful retreat, and disrespect for the commander-in-chief revealed in the series of letters.

6 July 1778

SANDY HOOK, N.J. British navy ships transport Clinton's army and all its supplies, wagons, horses, and baggage to New York City.

7 July 1778

PHILADELPHIA. Congress only now manages to muster a quorum of delegates.

8 July 1778

CAPES OF DELAWARE. Comte d'Estaing's fleet of sixteen men-of-war, delayed in crossing the Atlantic by unfavorable winds, finally arrives off the coast—several days too late to intercept Admiral Howe's fleet and cut off his exodus to New York. (Howe has nine ships with 534 guns, D'Estaing twelve ships with 834 guns.)

Sir Henry Clinton, British Commander-in-Chief in America.

9 July 1778

PHILADELPHIA. Congress receives the newly engrossed Articles of Confederation. Delegates representing eight states sign their names, acknowledging their states' ratification. North Carolina and Georgia, which have authorized ratification, have no delegates at Congress now. Delegates from New Jersey, Maryland, and Delaware have not yet received authority to sign. So the articles remain unadopted.

10 *July 1778*

BREST, FRANCE. Adm. d'Orvilliers sets sail with thirty-two ships, although three of them are unfit for fighting. He has been ordered to cruise for a month but not to search for or attack the British fleet.

11 *July 1778*

SANDY HOOK, N.J. d'Estaing's fleet arrives.

14 *July 1778*

KASKASKIA. Impressed by George Rogers Clark's humaneness and forcefulness, many of the French settlers promise him support. Father Pierre Gibault, having agreed to seek surrender of Vincennes and its Fort Sackville on Clark's behalf, sets out with some other Frenchmen for Vincennes with letters addressed to that settlement's French residents from Clark (all the British regulars have been withdrawn from Vincennes).

15 *July 1778*

HAVERSTRAW, N.Y. Washington's army arrives at Haverstraw to prepare for crossing the Hudson and marching on to White Plains.

18 *July 1778*

ANDRUSTOWN, N.Y. Indians led by Joseph Brant burn and plunder this settlement of seven families, massacring many of the inhabitants.

20 *July 1778*

VINCENNES. Persuaded by Father Gibault and the letters from Clark, residents agree to shift their allegiance to Virginia and give Clark their support. Once again Clark secures a surrender without a single shot being fired.

21 *July 1778*

PHILADELPHIA. North Carolina ratifies the Articles of Confederation.

22 *July 1778*

SANDY HOOK, N.J. Having been unable to attack Admiral Howe's fleet because a sandbar extending from Staten Island to Sandy Hook renders the water too shallow for passage of his ships, d'Estaing, after agreeing on a strategy with Washington, hoists anchor and sets sail for Newport, R.I. Washington directs Gen. John Sullivan, in command of 1,000 troops at Providence, to request Rhode Island, Massachusetts, and Connecticut urgently to raise 5,000 men to join him and also to acquire boats and pilots for an assault on Newport coordinated with d'Estaing's fleet. Washington sends Lafayette to Providence with two brigades; 6,000 New England militia under Maj. Gen. John Hancock are also en route—thus Sullivan's force should burgeon to 10,000 men.

23 *July 1778*

USHANT ISLAND. About sixty-six miles off the west coast of this outermost of the French islands in the English Channel Adm. d'Orvilliers sights Adm. Keppel's fleet. He maneuvers to avoid engagement with the British ships.

24 *July 1778*

PHILADELPHIA. Georgia ratifies the Articles of Confederation. Maryland,

A view of West Point in 1780.

New Jersey, and Delaware continue to hold out. Maryland is especially obdurate, demanding before signing that all states with western land claims cede them to the United States.

27 July 1778

USHANT ISLAND. After three days of D'Orvilliers' maneuvering out of reach, working to windward, the wind shifts to his disadvantage, allowing Keppel to close on his rear. D'Orvilliers turns about to confront the British fleet. Two of his ships have sailed away during the previous night, leaving him with twenty-seven ships with 1,950 guns against Keppel's thirty ships with 2,280 guns. D'Orvilliers wants to avoid close action, so the two fleets pass each other in opposed directions while firing their guns. The French discharges of langrage shatter the masts of the British ships, effectively immobilizing them and making it impossible for Keppel to give chase as D'Orvilliers withdraws during the night. Although both sides claim victory, the French casualties outnumber the British casualties by 736 to 408; and Keppel is left possessing the battle scene, suggesting that the British fleet will be capable of controlling the Channel and thus obviating the French threat to mainland England.

28 July 1778

PHILADELPHIA. Silas Deane, only recently returned from France, requests an audience with Congress to report on the commissioners' activities in Paris and Versailles and to defend his own conduct, as Arthur Lee has accused Deane of undertaking excessive commercial ventures to profit himself, misusing public funds, and advocating the view that the supplies secretly provided to America by Beaumarchais should be paid for rather than accepted as gifts. Lee has pressed Congress to investigate Deane, who has had a difficult time—his wife died while he was in France, and his finances are presently shaky.

29 July 1778

NEWPORT, R.I. d'Estaing's fleet arrives off the coast, but Sullivan's troops are not yet assembled. Newport, held by the British since December 1776, is now occupied by 3,000 troops commanded by Sir Robert Pigot. They control the large island between the Sakonnet and Middle passages of the Providence River on whose southern tip the city stands.

30 July 1778

WHITE PLAINS, N.Y. Washington's army arrives and encamps, initiating a land blockade of the British army in New York City.

NEWPORT, R.I. d'Estaing's fleet begins to enter Narragansett Bay.

1 August 1778

CONANICUT ISLAND, R.I. d'Estaing lands a small number of his troops on this island west of Newport.

5 August 1778

NEWPORT, R.I. Gen. John Sullivan's force has now assembled, 10,000 strong, with Gen. James Varnum's Rhode Island troops and Gen. John Glover's Marblehead troops forming the core of the army. Sullivan and d'Estaing have agreed on their strategy, though tension exists between them—the son of Irish indentured servants makes remarks that rile the French nobleman. Nevertheless, initiating their strategy, Adm. Pierre André de Suffren, under d'Estaing's command, sails two frigates up the Sakonnet Passage of the Providence River, creating great panic among the British that results in destruction of their river fleet. The British run four of their ships aground and then destroy them, while scuttling several vessels in an effort to block the French fleet's entry into Newport Harbor.

6 August 1778

NEW YORK CITY. Gen. Henry Clinton, receiving word that Newport is under siege, orders Adm. Lord Howe's fleet, now augmented to twenty ships by the arrival of four ships from Adm. John Byron's fleet, to set sail for Newport to confront d'Estaing's fleet of sixteen ships. Howe's fleet boasts 914 guns to the French fleet's 834.

8 August 1778

NEWPORT, R.I. Gen. Sullivan's Continentals, assembled at Tiverton, await the arrival of militia forces before beginning an attack coordinated with the French and planned to begin on the morrow. But discovering that the British have abandoned defenses at the north end of Newport's island and fearing they may return, Sullivan crosses the river immediately. His precipitate action, carried out without first consulting d'Estaing, angers the French admiral and further endangers the effectiveness of the two men's cooperation.

9 August 1778

NEWPORT, R.I. Adm. Lord Howe's fleet arrives off the coast, much to the relief of the British defenders of Newport. Adm. d'Estaing orders French troops posted on the island to reboard their ships in preparation for battle with the British fleet.

10 August 1778

NEWPORT, R.I. With the wind now in his favor, Adm. d'Estaing moves out of Newport Harbor under fire from the shore batteries and heads out to sea, full sails set to the wind, to engage Adm. Lord Howe, who avoids contact while hoping for the wind to shift.

AUGUSTA, GA. The state of Georgia has foundered with no effective government, and so some members of the state assembly meet and elect nine men to comprise an executive council with John Wereat as their head. Wereat immediately appeals to Gen. Benjamin Lincoln for help, pleading for money, supplies, and Continental soldiers before British troops join with the Indians to overrun the state.

12 August 1778

NEWPORT, R.I. After two days of maneuvering by the French and British fleets that forestalls conflict, a sudden, furious wind disperses ships of both fleets from their formations.

PARAMUS, N.J. Climaxing the court-martial of Gen. Charles Lee, the tribunal finds the general guilty on all charges and sentences him to be suspended from command for one year.

15 August 1778

NEWPORT, R.I. Gen. Sullivan moves his 10,000 troops closer to the British lines, builds entrenchments, and sets up two batteries of artillery, forcing Brig. Gen. Sir Robert Pigot to move his outposts back into his main lines. Both sides exchange cannonades with little effect.

PHILADELPHIA. Silas Deane appears for his first hearing before the Congress. The resulting discussions quickly reveal that there is strong partisan sentiment divided into two camps favoring Deane or favoring Arthur Lee.

16 August 1778

WHITE PLAINS, N.Y. Without added comment, Gen. Washington forwards to Congress for review the results of the court-martial of Gen. Charles Lee.

20 August 1778

NEWPORT, R.I. After several days of scattered fighting between individual ships of the French and British fleets, Adm. d'Estaing's fleet reassembles off Newport. (Adm. Howe has gathered his fleet and returned to New York City for refitting.) Gen. Sullivan requests d'Estaing's aid according to their original plan—Sullivan to attack from the east and d'Estaing from the west—but the French admiral, still piqued by Sullivan's behavior, turns down the American general, protesting that his orders and the counsel of his officers oblige him to sail for Boston to have his ships refitted before the severe hurricane season begins.

21 August 1778

NEWPORT, R.I. Rejecting the appeals of his countryman the Marquis de Lafayette, who believes Newport can be taken in two days with the French fleet's support, d'Estaing sets sail at midnight. With him, of course, go 4,000 French troops.

23 August 1778

PORTSMOUTH, ENGLAND. Adm. Keppel's fleet sails out again to seek the French fleet at the entrance to the English Channel in hopes of inflicting a decisive blow. But Adm. d'Orvilliers is now in the Bay of Biscay and eludes detection.

26 August 1778

PHILADELPHIA. With the Carlisle Commission having encountered a stone wall, commission member George Johnstone has tried to remove the obstacle by offering bribes to congressmen Joseph Reed, Robert Morris, and Francis Dana. Exposure of this quite unsuccessful machination forces his resignation from the commission.

27 August 1778

PHILADELPHIA. John Berkenhout, an English agent, arrives to continue the dirty work undertaken by George Johnstone and introduces himself to Richard Henry Lee as a friend of Arthur Lee. As he passed through Elizabethtown en route from New York City, however, he aroused the suspicions of Gen. William Maxwell, who has forewarned Richard Henry Lee.

28 August 1778

NEWPORT, R.I. Discouraged by the withdrawal of d'Estaing's fleet, the militia in Gen. John Sullivan's force have deserted, cutting his strength by half and precluding any possibility of attacking Brig. Gen. Sir Robert Pigot's well-entrenched British garrison of 6,000 men. Consequently, Sullivan begins to withdraw, but Pigot sends troops to follow him.

29 August 1778

NEWPORT, R.I. With his main lines spread across the north end of the island and a strong position established at the tip of Butt's Hill, Sullivan is in full retreat when attacked by the British. Although the British force out-

flanks their position on Quaker Hill, the Americans persistently repulse the British advances, even though several British frigates have moved up the river and opened fire on the American positions. Finally at about four in the afternoon the British begin to withdraw. Gen. Nathanael Greene, whose men have steadfastly held off the enemy's attacks on Sullivan's right flank, sallies forth in a counterattack and routs the retreating British and Hessian troops.

30 August 1778

NEWPORT, R.I. Gen. Sullivan receives word that Gen. Clinton is sending 5,000 British troops to relieve the garrison at Newport and realizes his own force is in peril. Under cover of darkness Sullivan begins ferrying his men across the river to Bristol and Howland.

31 August 1778

BRISTOL, R.I. As anticipated, a fleet of 100 British ships appears off the coast carrying the 5,000 reinforcements commanded by Clinton and Maj. Gen. Charles Grey. But by early morning Sullivan's entire force has crossed the river and escaped to safety. The experience at Newport, however, does not augur well for French–American cooperation in joint military ventures.

3 September 1778

PHILADELPHIA. With Congress having learned from a London newspaper that John Berkenhout and Sir John Temple, his colleague still in New York, are agents of the British government, the Council of Pennsylvania questions Berkenhout and has him jailed.

5 September 1778

NEW BEDFORD, MASS. Having returned to New York City after deciding d'Estaing cannot be successfully attacked at Boston, Gen. Clinton sends Gen. Charles Grey to raid the coast of Massachusetts. Grey lands at Clark's Neck and moves against Bedford and Fair Haven, burning seventy vessels in the Acushnet River and many buildings in both towns. He then sails for Martha's Vineyard.

7 September 1778

BOONESBOROUGH, KY. Indian and Tory raiders attack the fort. Daniel Boone, only recently escaped from the Shawnees, who had taken him to Detroit, has returned in time to warn of the attack and help secure the fort's defense.

DOMINICA, LESSER ANTILLES. While Adm. Samuel Barrington's fleet, sent from England in May to protect the British Leeward Islands, lingers at Barbados awaiting an expedition supposedly being sent by Admiral Howe, the governor of the French island of Martinique takes advantage of his absence. The governor lands a force of 2,000 men on Dominica, garrisoned by only sixty men, who have no choice but surrender. With Dominica added to their network of islands, the French have a solid wedge between the British-controlled islands to the north and south.

8 September 1778

MARTHA'S VINEYARD. Gen. Grey's raiders invade the island, confiscating thousands of sheep and cattle, public moneys, and militia weapons. They also destroy vessels and equipment, a loss that cripples the local whaling industry.

13 September 1778

GERMAN FLATS (HERKIMER), N.Y. Joseph Brant leading 150 Indians and Capt. William Caldwell commanding 300 Tories raid the settlement. They kill three men; burn over 100 houses, barns, and mills; and lead away hundreds of horses, cattle, and sheep. But they apparently commit no atrocities against women and children, as had occurred at the "Wyoming Massacre." Actually, Joseph Brant reportedly deplores such atrocities—he is well-educated and a devout Anglican and has helped translate the Bible into the Mohawk language.

14 September 1778

PHILADELPHIA. The Council of Pennsylvania paroles John Berkenhout. The Continental Congress, following up on a unanimous decision reached on the eleventh that the United States needs a minister plenipotentiary to represent the nation at the French court, names Benjamin Franklin to this post. Franklin will thus replace the cumbersome three-man commission that has previously served as the American emissary.

16 September 1778

SAW MILL RIVER (WESTCHESTER), N.Y. On another of their numerous raids in New York, British troops under Lt. Col. John Simcoe attempt to surprise and surround American soldiers commanded by Col. Mordecai Gist, but the Americans escape.

19 September 1778

NEW YORK CITY. Berkenhout returns,

his mission a failure, having managed only to further convince the Congress not to deal with the Carlisle Commission.

22 September 1778

PHILADELPHIA. After weeks of intermittent testimony from Silas Deane and others, Congress reaches the conclusion that dissensions among the commissioners to France were detrimental to their mission there and decides to investigate.

26 September 1778

PHILADELPHIA. Without consulting Gen. Washington, the Congress appoints Gen. Benjamin Lincoln commander of the Continental Army in the South. He replaces Gen. Robert Howe, who remains in command of the Savannah garrison.

28 September 1778

OLD TAPPAN, N.J. As part of Washington's plan to harass foraging parties led by Lord Cornwallis on the west side of the Hudson and Gen. von Knyphausen on the east, Gen. Anthony Wayne has posted New Jersey militia here under Lt. Col. George Baylor. Cornwallis sends troops under Gen. Charles Grey to attack them. Under cover of darkness they surround three barns in which over 100 of the militia are sleeping and then charge in with bayonets, killing thirty and capturing fifty. Ten of the prisoners are officers, including Baylor.

3 October 1778

PHILADELPHIA. The Carlisle Commission attempts to bypass the Continental Congress and appeal directly to the American people. The Earl of Carlisle and William Eden publish a proclamation offering a general pardon of disloyalty to all Americans and a full pardon to all military or civil officeholders who accept the offer within forty days.

6–7 October 1778

CHESTNUT CREEK, N.J. Set ashore from ships, British troops raid Chestnut Creek, a base for American privateers. The soldiers burn the local sawmills and saltworks and plunder the houses.

7 October 1778

DETROIT. George Rogers Clark may have been easily victorious thus far, but with his small band of frontiersmen and meager supplies he is in serious danger if attacked by Indian or British forces. He has been negotiating with Ottawa, Chippewa, Miami, and Fox warriors at Cahokia in an effort to gain their neutrality. But now the danger becomes substantive as Lt. Gov. Henry Hamilton of Detroit, wishing to retake Clark's conquests, sets out from Detroit with 175 troops, mostly French, and sixty Indians to attack Vincennes.

6–8 October 1778

UNADILLA, N.Y. Lt. Col. William Butler leads his 4th Pennsylvania Continentals and a group of Daniel Morgan's sharpshooters and some rangers against Joseph Brant's base of operations in a reprisal for Brant's raid on German Flats on 13 September. As the Mohawks have fled, the troops encounter no opposition. They burn all but one of the stone-and-frame houses, a sawmill, and a grist mill—Unadilla was formerly a white settlement, abandoned after Brant confiscated the settlers' crops and cattle. With this destruction culminating over two weeks of attacks on Indian sites in the area, the soldiers return to their base at Schoharie, N.Y.

14 October 1778

LITTLE EGG HARBOR, N.J. Three British sloops and six smaller vessels attack this favorite port of American privateers from the water while Capt. Patrick Ferguson leads 300 regulars and Tories against it by land. The British burn ten privateering ships and several houses and storehouses. Informed by a French deserter from Count Kasimir Pulaski's Legion (a corps independent of the Continental Army) that the count and his force are encamped on nearby Mincock Island, Ferguson and 250 of his men set out in rowboats during the night and land on the island in preparation for an attack on Pulaski.

15 October 1778

MINCOCK ISLAND, N.J. Before daybreak Ferguson's men enter three houses where Pulaski's legionnaires are sleeping and kill fifty of them, including two French officers, with their bayonets. Made aware of the attack, Pulaski brings up his dragoons and, supported by the legion's infantry survivors, drives off Ferguson's men, who manage to reach their boats, escaping under fire.

19 October 1778

WHITE PLAINS, N.Y. Alexander Hamilton, sharing Gen. Washington's disgust for civilian war profiteers—and in particular congressman Samuel Chase of Maryland for taking advantage of his position in order to profiteer in grains needed by the French

fleet—writes to the *New-York Journal* deploring such conduct and advocating rigorous punishment: "When avarice takes the lead in a state, it is commonly the forerunner of its fall. How shocking it is to discover among ourselves, even at this early period, the strongest symptoms of this fatal disease." Referring to Chase, although not by name, Hamilton asserts that there is ". . . no punishment the vengeance of the people can inflict, which may not be applied to him with justice." And he concludes that the congressman ought to be ". . . detested as a traitor of the worst and most dangerous kind."

23 October 1778

PHILADELPHIA. The Congress finally takes up discussion of the findings of Gen. Charles Lee's court-martial tribunal. Lee himself, having remained with the army until September, is now in Philadelphia.

26 October 1778

PHILADELPHIA. The Congress completes the letter of credence and instructions to Benjamin Franklin as minister plenipotentiary to the French court. Franklin is to assure the court that the United States appreciates French assistance and is committed to pursuing freedom and fulfilling the purposes of the alliance. He is also to solicit French financial aid and to advocate French attacks on Halifax and Quebec in order to destroy the British fisheries off the banks of Newfoundland. But he may not commit the United States to any stipulations without the consent of Congress.

28 October 1778

PHILADELPHIA. The Committee for

Foreign Affairs dispatches Congress' completed instructions to Franklin and also writes to John Adams, whose role as commissioner to France now terminates, of course. They encourage him to focus on the problem of improving American finances.

31 October 1778

PORTSMOUTH, ENGLAND. Having failed to find and engage Adm. d'Orvilliers' fleet and plagued by the problems of his own ill health and of sickness afflicting 1,000 of his seamen, Adm. Keppel returns to Spithead to harbor his fleet for a winter refitting.

4 November 1778

BOSTON. With the ill-conceived plan for a proposed French-American naval attack on Halifax and Newfoundland now abandoned, Adm. d'Estaing sails for the West Indies. He fails to inform Gen. Washington of his destination.

6 November 1778

CHERRY VALLEY, N.Y. Col. Ichabod

WARTIME MANUFACTURING

The mercantilist economic policies of Great Britain during the pre-Revolutionary period had aimed at keeping manufacturing at a low level in the American colonies, so when the war began Americans had only a limited capacity to make needed goods for themselves. During most of the war the great majority of manufactured goods had to be imported, usually through the West Indies; however, the rebellious states were able during the first years of the Revolution to manufacture some classes of vital materiel.

When the war broke out, the American colonies produced nearly 14 percent of the world's iron, and Congress and state governments moved rapidly to encourage American iron mining and foundries. Cannon were cast in the states as early as 1775, and for a time, iron production and cannon manufacture boomed. The Brown brothers of Rhode Island claimed to have cast 3,000 cannon at their Hope works, and the state-run iron foundry at Stirling, N.Y., forged the 180-ton chain that was strung across the Hudson at West Point to deter British ships.

The production of gunpowder was much more of a problem, since the states lacked the means to manufacture saltpeter, one of the key ingredients. Most of the gunpowder used by the Americans during the war came from overseas.

There were, of course, many skilled gunsmiths in America, but seldom was small-arms manufacturing put on a scale sufficiently large to meet the Continental Army's demand for muskets. Armories were established in several cities, notably Springfield, Mass., early in the war, but most were out of business by 1777 or 1778.

Overall, the collapse of the American economy and the rampant inflation after 1778 undermined the successful early efforts of Americans to establish a manufacturing sector to support the war.

Alden, in charge of 250 members of the 7th Massachusetts Regiment, here to protect the settlers, receives warning from Fort Stanwix that a force of Indians and Tories plans to attack the settlement and the fort recently completed by Alden's men.

10 November 1778

CHERRY VALLEY, N.Y. Col. Alden makes no preparations for defense against attack and rejects settlers' requests to be allowed into the fort or to have their belongings taken inside for protection. He does, however, send out reconnaissance teams. Seneca and Mohawk Indians led by Joseph Brant and Tories led by Capt. Walter Butler (son of John Butler, who led the "Wyoming Valley Massacre") capture one team while they sleep and learn from them of the disposition of troops in houses around the fort.

11 November 1778

CHERRY VALLEY, N.Y. Joseph Brant's Indians attack local houses where Alden and his officers are billeted, killing Alden. But after several hours of skirmishing they fail to take the fort

British troops and Indians with an American prisoner.

and withdraw to attack the local settlers in their homes, massacring over thirty, mostly women and children. Capt. McDonnell leads a sortie from the fort, rescuing settlers hidden in the nearby woods. Brant and Butler make off with seventy-one prisoners.

12 November 1778

CHERRY VALLEY, N.Y. After releasing most of his prisoners, Walter Butler withdraws toward Niagara. He takes along two women and their seven children as hostages possibly to be exchanged for his mother and aunt and the wives of Tory officers being held prisoner in Albany.

19 November 1778

SPENCER'S HILL, GA. Lt. Col. James Mark Prevost leads a British plundering expedition on the south Georgia frontier that Col. John Baker's American troops hope to harass. But as the Americans are marching toward Prevost's position British troops led by Lt. Col. M'Girth, Prevost's subordinate, ambush them, wounding Baker and forcing the Americans to retreat.

24 November 1778

MEDWAY CHURCH, GA. Lt. Col. James Mark Prevost's troops skirmish with American troops led by Col. John White and burn the church and other buildings in the settlement.

26 November 1778

PHILADELPHIA. The New Jersey delegates ratify the Articles of Confederation. Maryland still holds out.

27 November 1778

SANDY HOOK, N.J. Under orders from Gen. Clinton, Col. Archibald Campbell sets sail with 3,500 troops—regulars, Hessians, and Loyalists—to join forces with Gen. Augustine Prevost for an attack on Savannah, Ga. They are transported by a squadron commanded by Commodore Hyde Parker. (Since Adm. Sir Richard Howe relinquished command and left for England in September the British fleet at New York has been under command of Adm. John Byron.)

PHILADELPHIA. Accepting failure of their mission, the members of the Carlisle Commission board the *Roebuck* and set sail for England.

30 November 1778

MIDDLEBROOK, N.J. Gen. Washington has been redeploying his troops, formerly concentrated near White Plains. He now has units in winter quarters at West Point and Fishkill in New York, Danbury in Connecticut, and Middlebrook, Elizabeth, and Ramapo in New Jersey; he is headquartered in Middlebrook. So the Continental Army is deployed in a semicircle around New York City within a radius of about forty miles to observe movements of British troops and to protect the American north-south interstate communication routes.

4 December 1778

CHARLESTOWN, S.C. Gen. Benjamin Lincoln, recently appointed commander of the Continental Army in the South, arrives. He is too late to forestall the planned British assault on Savannah.

5 December 1778

PHILADELPHIA. Congress finally orders the carrying out of the sentence recommended for punishment of Gen.

Charles Lee by the court-martial tribunal nearly four months earlier—he will be relieved of command for twelve months.

10 December 1778

BRIDGETOWN, BARBADOS. While replenishing here after cruising off Martinique, Adm. Samuel Barrington is finally joined by the promised force from New York, which sails into Carlisle Bay with a fleet commanded by Commodore William Hotham. Gen. James Grant, under orders from Gen. Clinton, has brought 5,800 troops. Now the British offensive against St. Lucia can begin.

PHILADELPHIA. John Jay, a delegate from New York just re-elected, becomes president of the Continental Congress.

11 December 1778

MARTINIQUE, LESSER ANTILLES. Adm. d'Estaing's fleet arrives from Boston.

12 December 1778

ST. LUCIA, LESSER ANTILLES. The expedition of admirals Barrington and Hotham and Gen. Grant anchors off the island prepared to attack. Hotham lands Grant's all-British force flawlessly and they begin to sweep the island.

13 December 1778

NEWPORT, R.I. After his wretched fleet has been turned back or scattered and delayed twice by storms at sea, Adm. John Byron ("Foul-weather Jack"), who has succeeded Adm. Sir Richard Howe as commander of the British navy in American waters, sets sail for the West Indies in a much-belated pursuit of d'Estaing.

ST. LUCIA. The British secure their control of the island by capturing the French naval base—but a mere hour before d'Estaing arrives from Martinique with a force of 9,000 troops and a fleet that outnumbers the British fleet by three to one. The British force of 5,800 divides into three units and digs in at the Vigie peninsula on the harbor's north side and at Morne Fortune mountain and at Cul-de-Sac.

17 December 1778

VINCENNES. As he has marched southward from Detroit Lt. Gov. Henry Hamilton has been joined by Indians, now 500 strong. He has also captured small parties sent out for scouting by Capt. Leonard Helm, left in command of the fort at Vincennes by George Rogers Clark. Helm's garrison now consists of only one soldier; and, since the local French offer no help, he is forced to surrender to Hamilton. So Vincennes falls back into British control without a shot being fired.

18 December 1778

ST. LUCIA. Though outnumbering the British fleet by three to one, d'Estaing has failed to penetrate Adm. Barrington's defense of Cul-de-Sac Bay, and so he lands his troops at Anse de Choc to attempt overrunning the British defenses at Vigie Point and opening the bay to his ships. But the British repulse two attacks and take a huge toll—in three hours d'Estaing's force suffers 1,200 wounded and 400 dead. The 1,300 British troops defending the point suffer 13 killed and 158 wounded.

21 December 1778

MIDDLEBROOK, N.J. Gen. Washing-

ton leaves for Philadelphia to confer with the Congress.

23 December 1778

TYBEE ISLAND, GA. The squadron commanded by Commodore Hyde Parker arrives with Lt. Col. Archibald Campbell's force at Tybee Island at the mouth of the Savannah River, fifteen miles below Savannah. Gen. Augustine Prevost, under orders to join Campbell, has not yet arrived. Gen. Robert Howe marches from Sunbury to Savannah with 700 Continentals and 150 militia to defend the city. Savannah's fortifications, constructed twenty years before, are now in ruins and unsuitable for staging a defense.

25 December 1778

TYBEE ISLAND, GA. Lt. Col. Campbell sends Capt. Sir James Baird ashore with a company of light infantry. Baird learns that Howe has only a small force but that Gen. Benjamin Lincoln can be expected to join him as soon as possible after he discovers the British have come. He also learns that to defend the city Howe has placed his men on the road to Girardeau, where both of their flanks are protected by swamps. Campbell decides to attack rather than wait for Prevost, who will be in command once he arrives.

28 December 1778

ST. LUCIA. After a pause of ten days Adm. d'Estaing withdraws and sails for Martinique. The French garrison surrenders. The British control St. Lucia.

SAVANNAH, GA. Campbell orders Parker downriver to Girardeau's plantation. Parker scares off two American galleys, but the tide turns, forcing him to wait until morning to land troops.

29 December 1778

SAVANNAH, GA. The American commander, Gen. Howe, assumes that, because of the swamps at his flanks, the British can attack him only head-on, giving his outnumbered force a fighting chance. But by accident Campbell has discovered a slave named Quamino Dolly, who tells him of a secret trail through the swamp. Campbell sends Baird up this trail to attack Howe's flank while he leads a simultaneous attack against Howe's front. The assault succeeds, forcing the Americans to retreat across the causeway over Musgrove's Swamp and to swim Musgrove's Creek, where many drown or are taken prisoner. British troops chase the fleeing remnants of Howe's troops through Savannah, putting many to the bayonet. The British capture 453 American officers and soldiers along with forty-eight cannon, twenty-three mortars, ammunition stores, and the ships in the harbor. And they inflict ninety-four casualties, including eighty-three dead, while suffering only twenty-six casualties.

During the Boston Massacre on 5 March 1770 a mob of citizens armed with clubs confronts a small group of British soldiers near the Customs House. Five of the mob die when the panicked soldiers fire into the crowd. *(Courtesy of the Anne S.K. Brown Military Collection, Brown University Library)*

Massachusetts militiamen during the afternoon of 19 April 1775 inflict hundreds of casualties on the British column retreating toward Boston after the skirmishes at Lexington and Concord. *(Courtesy of the Anne S.K. Brown Military Collection, Brown University Library)*

Left: After three costly assaults, the British finally overrun the patriot fortifications on Breed's Hill in the misnamed Battle of Bunker Hill on 17 June 1775. *(Courtesy of the Anne S.K. Brown Military Collection, Brown University Library)*

Below: Threatened by new American artillery emplacements on Dorchester Heights, Gen. William Howe supervises the evacuation of Boston in March 1776. *(Courtesy of the Anne S.K. Brown Military Collection, Brown University Library)*

The British fleet under Adm. Sir Peter Parker futilely bombards a
half-finished fort on Sullivan's Island at the mouth of Charleston Harbor on
28 June 1776. The sand-and-palmetto-log fort absorbs the British round shot.
*(Courtesy of the Anne S.K. Brown Military Collection, Brown University
Library)*

Washington's stunning attack on the Hessian garrison at Trenton on
26 December 1776 ends a long string of American failures and takes 900
prisoners. *(Courtesy of the Anne S.K. Brown Military Collection, Brown
University Library)*

Above: Visiting the troops on Christmas 1777, Martha, his wife, joins commander-in-chief George Washington during the difficult winter at Valley Forge. *(Courtesy of the Anne S.K. Brown Military Collection, Brown University Library)*

Right: American general Hugh Mercer dies from enemy bayonet thrusts during the early stages of the Battle of Princeton on 3 January 1777, an engagement ultimately won by Washington. *(Courtesy of the Anne S.K. Brown Military Collection, Brown University Library)*

The second Battle of Saratoga on 7 October 1777 is fought near the American strongpoint on Bemis Heights. The defeat forces British Gen. John Burgoyne to surrender ten days later. *(Courtesy of the Anne S.K. Brown Military Collection, Brown University Library)*

The second British expedition against Charleston, led by Sir Henry Clinton, succeeds in May 1780 after American Benjamin Lincoln's army is bottled up and brought under siege. *(Courtesy of the Anne S.K. Brown Military Collection, Brown University Library)*

Gen. Johann de Kalb, a foreign volunteer in the American cause, falls mortally wounded by multiple gunshots and bayonet thrusts after American militia break and run at the disastrous Battle of Camden on 16 August 1780. *(Courtesy of the Anne S.K. Brown Military Collection, Brown University Library)*

Mounted dragoons clash at the Battle of Cowpens on 17 January 1781. American Daniel Morgan inflicts a devastating defeat on Banastre Tarleton by clever tactics and skillful deployment. *(Courtesy of the Anne S.K. Brown Military Collection, Brown University Library)*

Above: The surrender of the British army under Lord Cornwallis at Yorktown on 19 October 1781 ends the war. Cornwallis cannot face the humiliation and sends Brig. Gen. Charles O'Hara to offer his sword in submission. *(Courtesy of the Anne S.K. Brown Military Collection, Brown University Library)*

Left: America's finest combat general, Benedict Arnold, shown in front of Quebec, which he failed to take in 1776-1777, well before his decision to betray his country. *(Courtesy of the Anne S.K. Brown Military Collection, Brown University Library)*

Virginia planter George Washington, commander-in-chief of the Continental Army and Father of His Country. *(Courtesy of the Anne S.K. Brown Military Collection, Brown University Library)*

★ 1779 ★

The war in the North stagnates, but the British strategy in the South begins to bear fruit during the year. Augusta, Ga., falls to Gen. Augustine Prevost in late January, although he fails later to capture Port Royal, S.C. Americans under Andrew Pickens beat the British at the Battle of Kettle Creek in Georgia, but cannot retake Augusta. Across the Atlantic, John Paul Jones takes command of a decrepit ship donated by the French, which he names *Bonhomme Richard* in honor of Franklin.

The British advances continue in the South during the spring, with raids on Portsmouth and Norfolk, Va. Prevost continues to advance on Charleston.

In the North, Sir Henry Clinton sends a force to capture West Point, a key position on the Hudson, but the advance is stalled at Stony Point, N.Y., which is retaken by Gen. Anthony Wayne in a daring raid in July. The British never again threaten seriously to break out of their major base in New York City. A large American force under Sullivan launches a scorched-earth campaign against the Indian villages in the Genesee Valley of upper New York state during the summer. Clinton wearies of command and asks to be replaced but meanwhile plans a new offensive to take Charleston and deny the Americans another vital Southern port city.

On 23 September Jones' *Bonhomme Richard* meets the British *Serapis* in the most celebrated confrontation of British and American ships during the Revolution.

The Americans open a siege at Savannah in September, but the British repulse the attack within weeks. With Savannah securely in British hands, Clinton embarks a large army from New York, headed toward Charleston.

At the same time, Washington leads the Continental Army into winter quarters at Morristown, N.J.

1 January 1779

BOSTON. After much wrangling and congressional assertions that Gen. John Burgoyne has been guilty of a breach of faith respecting the terms of the so-called Saratoga Convention (Congress, of course, believes the terms are too liberal and would free British troops for deployment in the United States), Gen. Henry Clinton, under instructions from the king, has assured Congress that the convention is ratified. Nevertheless, Congress disputes Clinton's word, contends the king's signature may be a forgery, and reneges on fulfilling the terms of the convention. Burgoyne's troops, detained in Boston for all these months, now are sent to Rutland—with Virginia their final destination.

PHILADELPHIA. As a result of the conferences between members of Congress and Gen. Washington a recently discussed plan to "emancipate" Canada is abandoned. The idea of bringing Canada into the Union had been revived the previous summer, when William Lee of the Committee for Foreign Affairs received word from Nova Scotia that the province desired to be "adopted" by the United States, and when the French treaties provided an ally for such an expedition. Union with Canada has great appeal for the New England congressional delegates, but Washington and President Laurens oppose becoming involved in an invasion with the French (an idea proposed by the Marquis de Lafayette) for fear that the French will retain control of Canada when the war ends, which would not be in the best interests of the United States. Their view prevails.

2 January 1779

PHILADELPHIA. Congress resolves to cancel some of the previously issued bills of credit and substitute for them a new issuance of fifty million dollars.

6 January 1779

FORT MORRIS (SUNBURY), GA. Gen. Augustine Prevost with about 2,000 men, including some Indians, attacks Fort Morris during his march to join Col. Archibald Campbell at Savannah. Maj. Joseph Lane, left in command when Gen. Robert Howe departed for Savannah, tries to defend the fort with only 200 men.

9 January 1779

FORT MORRIS (SUNBURY), GA. Gen. Prevost moves his artillery into place to bombard the fort, and Maj. Lane surrenders. Lane has eleven casualties, Prevost four. The British confiscate twenty-four guns and the Americans' supplies. With this victory and the capture of Savannah, the British effectively gain control of eastern Georgia.

10 January 1779

PHILADELPHIA. Conrad Alexandre Rayvenal de Gerard, French minister to the United States, in acquainting himself with the ways of the Continental Congress and its members has discovered opposition to the alliance with France. Consequently, he has been seeking a declaration of positive commitment from the Congress, and he once more urgently requests issuance of such a declaration.

11 January 1779

PHILADELPHIA. Congress having acquiesced to his October request to return to France and examine opportunities for service there or in Canada, the Marquis de Lafayette sails for his homeland aboard the American ship *Alliance* commanded by his countryman Capt. Pierre Landais, the only Frenchman to command a warship in the Continental Navy. Landais has orders to join John Paul Jones in France.

14 January 1779

PHILADELPHIA. The Congress complies with French minister Gerard's request, unanimously passing a resolution that pledges the United States "will not conclude either truce or peace with the common enemy, without the formal consent of their ally first obtained."

23 January 1779

PHILADELPHIA. Congress adopts a proposal made by Gen. Washington to spur the effort to raise enlistments for the Continental Army, voting to award a bounty (not to exceed $200) to all who re-enlist and also bounties to all new recruits in amounts decided by the general (again, not to exceed $200). A problem likely to impede success of the plan is the competitive bounties offered by individual states, but Congress decides not to address this problem now.

LONDON, ENGLAND. With a strategy for the campaign of 1779 worked out, Lord Germain sends orders to Gen. Clinton in New York. The strategy rests on the concept of restoring in at least one of the former colonies a government swearing allegiance to the king and Parliament by severing it from the others and reconstituting its citizenry's loyalty. The concept pre-

Mohawk chief Joseph Brant.

sumes a majority of Loyalists and British sympathizers in the target colony or colonies; and a variety of advisers, including the exiled renegade congressman Joseph Galloway and Gen. James Robertson (returned from New York), have convinced the North ministry that such is the case in Pennsylvania, New Jersey, and New York. The military objective, then, is to engage Washington's army, drive him into the upper Hudson Highlands, and sever New York from the other colonies, making it possible for the "majority" Loyalists to re-establish a royal government in New York, which then could be the stage for spreading the same eventuality to the Middle Colonies. To fulfill this objective Germain assumes the need for an army of 29,000 men in New York and Rhode Island. Clinton has only 22,000 men, but 1,000 will be brought from Halifax and the remainder sent out from England.

29 January 1779

AUGUSTA, GA. After joining forces

with Col. Archibald Campbell at Ebenezer, Gen. Augustine Prevost sends Campbell to take Augusta. The colonel and his men, joined on their march by Tory troops from South Carolina, occupy the town without opposition, as it has been abandoned. Since Augusta became the seat of the state government in 1776, its occupation means the British and their Loyalist allies now control Georgia. Many patriots flee to South Carolina; those who remain behind sign the oath of allegiance to the king or see their property seized or put to the torch.

31 January 1779
PHILADELPHIA. After five weeks the conferences between Gen. Washington and a committee of the Continental Congress conclude. Washington begins preparations to leave for Middlebrook.

2 February 1779
PHILADELPHIA. Gen. Washington departs to rejoin his army at Middlebrook, while Martha Washington remains in the city as a guest in the home of Henry Laurens.

3 February 1779
PHILADELPHIA. Joseph Reed, Gen. Washington's former aide, former member of Congress, influential patriot, and president of the Pennsylvania Council, on behalf of the council and the state brings charges against Gen. Benedict Arnold before Congress. The ostentatious luxury characterizing Arnold's mode of life offends many Philadelphia residents, as do his arrogance, ambition, and tactlessness in conducting his official duties. There are also rumors that he has profited from his position through speculation and misuse of equipment,

workmen, and facilities available to him as military commander in the city. Nor has his socializing with wealthy Philadelphians who hold Tory sympathies, including the beautiful Peggy Shippen, helped his image. Nevertheless, the eight charges brought against him are vague, and his commander Gen. Washington staunchly defends Arnold, as do many members of Congress. Thomas Burke of North Carolina, for example, accuses the Pennsylvania Council of being "peevish, and childish." Arnold himself demands an immediate investigation to clear his name.

BEAUFORT, PORT ROYAL ISLAND, S.C. Maj. Gen. Benjamin Lincoln has sent Gen. William Moultrie to prevent conquest of the island by two companies of British troops led by Maj. Gardiner under orders of Gen. Augustine Prevost. With 300 Charleston militia and only ten Continentals and three field pieces Moultrie occupies Beaufort and stations his men on both sides of the road by which Gardiner's force approaches. A cannon blast sends the British scurrying for cover in a nearby woods. After nearly an hour of fighting the Americans run out of ammunition but realize the British are retreating. Some American dragoons chase after them, taking a few prisoners. The Americans suffer thirty casualties; British casualties are uncertain.

PHILADELPHIA. Only a month after authorizing over fifty million dollars in new bills of credit the Congress orders issuance of another five million.

4 February 1779
PHILADELPHIA. Following Gen. Washington's return to his winter quarters

at Middlebrook, the Continental Congress resolves that he should "proceed in such manner as he shall judge expedient" to reform and enhance the Continental Army. He is also given authority to resolve all questions of officer rank below that of brigadier but in doing so must adhere to the rules established in a congressional act of 24 November 1778.

PARIS, FRANCE.   After nearly a year of waiting while being lionized and enjoying food, wines, and the company of women, John Paul Jones finally secures a ship. Encouraged by Benjamin Franklin, he has lobbied Gabriel de Sartine, French minister of marine, who informs him today that an East Indiaman named the *Duc de Duras* has been purchased for his use.

George Rogers Clark; his epic march through flooded wilderness gave the Americans control over what is today Ohio, Indiana and Illinois.

5 February 1779

KASKASKIA.   George Rogers Clark, whose force has dropped to about a hundred men as a result of expired enlistments, has survived because for some reason Lt. Col. Henry Hamilton has not marched his British troops from recaptured Vincennes against him. So Clark, having regained the support of the French with the help of Father Gibault, decides to move against Hamilton. He sends Lt. Col. John Rogers in command of a crew of forty men up the Ohio and Wabash rivers in the *Willing*, a row-galley armed with two four-pounder cannon and four swivel guns. Their assignment is to prevent a British retreat down the Mississippi River.

6 February 1779

KASKASKIA.   Clark begins an overland march with 127 men, almost half of them French, to attack Vincennes, about 180 miles distant.

PHILADELPHIA.   The Continental Congress fetes Reynaval de Gerard, the French minister to the United States, on the first anniversary of the alliance between the two countries with a public entertainment and a banquet.

8 February 1779

PHILADELPHIA.   Congress resumes an earlier discussion of whether to request the comte d'Estaing's aid in defending Georgia and South Carolina and whether the United States should compensate France for such aid. Gerard brings the startling secret news to President Jay that Spain seems likely to join the alliance between France and the United States.

10 February 1779

CARR'S FORT, GA.   Col. Andrew Pickens, with a combined force of his South Carolina militia and Capt. John Dooley's Georgia militia, a total of about 350 men, attacks a force of 200 Loyalists led by the highly regarded Lt. Col. John Hamilton, a Scottish patrician and veteran of the Battle of Culloden. The patriots are winning when they learn that Tory Col. Boyd approaches with 700 men—he has been marching from North Carolina to join Hamilton. Pickens breaks off engaging Hamilton and marches to attack Boyd.

13 February 1779

KETTLE CREEK, GA. Col. Boyd crosses the Savannah River and camps, unaware that Col. Pickens has made a complete circle, crossed the river, and moved in behind him.

VINCENNES. George Rogers Clark and his men, after marching through swamps and across muddy prairies, are within twenty miles of their destination.

14 February 1779

KETTLE CREEK, GA. With Pickens in the center, Capt. Dooley on the right, and Lt. Col. Thomas Clark on the left, the patriots launch a surprise attack on Boyd from three directions simultaneously. Despite their unpreparedness, the Tories form and hold fast for nearly an hour, when Boyd receives a mortal wound and his men break and run. The Tory losses are forty dead and seventy-five taken prisoner; patriot casualties number thirty-two.

15 February 1779

PHILADELPHIA. In a meeting with the committee of the whole of Congress, French minister Gerard presses the Congress to decide upon what definitive peace terms the United States desires, calling particular attention to

the questions of navigation rights on the Mississippi River and the future status of the Floridas—two major concerns of Spain as a potential ally.

18 February 1779

VINCENNES. Having taken two days to ferry across the Little Wabash River and then being slowed by heavy rains, floods, and hunger, George Rogers Clark's expedition arrives at the Wabash River.

19 February 1779

PHILADELPHIA. Once again Congress authorizes issuance of five million dollars in bills of credit.

23 February 1779

VINCENNES. Weary and half-starved, George Rogers Clark's men reach the lake at Horseshoe Plain. Clark urges them forward, plunging into the shoulder-deep waters of the lake, while Capt. James Bowman brings up the rear with twenty-five men and orders to shoot anyone who refuses to continue. Two miles from Vincennes they rest, build fires, and dry their clothes. From a captured Frenchman Clark learns that Lt. Col. Henry Hamilton, British commander at Vincennes, remains unaware of the Americans' approach but has been reinforced by 200 Indians. Clark sends the French captive to Vincennes with this message: Residents who favor the United States should remain in their homes, those who favor Britain should join Hamilton in Fort Sackville, because Clark's troops will overwhelm the fort tonight. As his force is outnumbered, Clark hopes to frighten the British and their Indian allies into surrender. At sunset he deploys his men in two divisions to march toward Vincennes in a manner that gives the impression of greater strength than he has. His message and march ruses work. The townspeople remain indoors or bring Clark ammunition to support his assault, many of the Indians take flight while others offer to join the Americans, and Clark marches straight through town to begin the attack on the fort. The Americans maintain a steady fire throughout the night.

PHILADELPHIA. The committee appointed to examine the matter of defining terms for a peace settlement reports to Congress. Members of the committee are Gouverneur Morris of New York, Thomas Burke of North Carolina, John Witherspoon of New Jersey, Samuel Adams of Massachusetts, and Meriwether Smith of Virginia. They delineate Great Britain's recognition of American independence as an absolute condition, and they define six other stipulations as ultimatums: establishing minimum boundaries, evacuation of British forces from the United States, granting of fishing rights off Newfoundland, free navigation on the Mississippi as far as the southern boundary of the United States, free commerce with one or more ports to the south of that boundary, and the ceding of Nova Scotia to the United States if the allies so request. The committee also recommends six negotiable points. Congress begins discussion of the committee's report.

24 February 1779

VINCENNES. The accuracy of the firing by Clark's Long Rifles has killed or wounded so many British soldiers that cannons at the bastions in Fort Sackville rest silent by dawn, while only one American has been wounded. At about 9:00 A.M. Clark demands Hamilton's surrender. Well supplied with ammunition and food, Hamilton refuses. The firing resumes until eleven o'clock, when Hamilton agrees to surrender if the terms are right. Clark rejects this offer, but the two men agree to confer at the French church. With no progress made, the talks recess while Hamilton returns to the fort to consult with his officers. In the interim a raiding party of British Indians returns to town with two American captives and some scalps; Clark's men kill or capture the entire party. Clark has the prisoners, including a son of Pontiac, brought to a site in clear view from the fort and there executed with tomahawks—an unnerving demonstration for the Indians in the fort. Realizing that his Indian allies are now probably undependable and that he can expect no support from the French residents of Vincennes, many of whom had joined in firing on the fort, Hamilton decides to return to the negotiation of terms. Hamilton writes: "Colonel Clark, yet reeking with the blood of these unhappy victims, came to the esplanade before the fort gate, where I had agreed to meet him and treat of the surrender of the garrison. He spoke with rapture of his late achievement, while he washed the blood from his hand stained in this inhuman sacrifice." Clark detests Hamilton, who is known on the frontier as The Hair Buyer because of the American scalps he supposedly buys from the Indians, and insists on unconditional surrender or the alternative of a merciless attack by Clark's force. At the end of the day Hamilton capitulates.

25 February 1779

VINCENNES. Hamilton surrenders himself, his men, and Fort Sackville to Clark. With this stunning victory Clark assumes effective control of the entire Illinois Territory.

26 February 1779

HORSENECK LANDING, CONN. Governor William Tryon leads 600 troops on a raid against the village, unsuccessfully defended by only two cannons and 150 militia commanded by Gen. Israel Putnam. Losing only two men killed and twenty captured, Tryon succeeds in destroying the salt works, three vessels in the port, and a store and plundering the village, confiscating nearly 200 cows and horses. He also nearly captures Putnam, who barely escapes by riding breakneck down a hill so steep that the British troops are afraid to follow.

3 March 1779

BRIAR CREEK, GA. Emboldened by the American victories at Beaufort and Kettle Creek, Maj. Gen. Benjamin Lincoln has sent troops under Gen. Andrew Williamson to the eastern bank of the Savannah River opposite Augusta, under Gen. Griffith Rutherford to the Black Swamp, and under Gen. John Ashe to Briar Creek for the purpose of mounting an attack on Augusta in hopes of recapturing the city from the British. Ashe's force consists of 1,400 North Carolina militia, 100 Georgia Continentals, and 200 lighthorse militia. The threat from the Americans has caused Lt. Col. Archibald Campbell to withdraw his troops from Augusta, cross the Savannah River, and head for Savannah, burning a bridge at Briar Creek to deter Ashe's

pursuit. Ashe is rebuilding the bridge when a force of 900 infantry, grenadiers, dragoons, and militia sent by Gen. Augustine Prevost crosses the creek above Ashe's camp to prepare an attack on the rear of the Americans. As the British attack begins Ashe's Continentals open fire, alarming the American militiamen, who flee. Realizing they are deserted, the Continentals also retreat in disorder. Most of the fleeing Americans throw down their weapons and seek escape in the river, where many drown. Over 150 American troops die, and the British capture eleven officers and 162 other men, plus seven cannon, other weapons, and ammunition, while experiencing only sixteen casualties. A British report of the skirmish published in the *New York Gazette and Weekly Mercury* declares of the patriots: "The panic occasioned by the terror of the bayonet, left them no alternative but that of plunging into the water . . . few would have escaped if night had not come on soon." This disaster precludes any possibility that the Americans can regain control of Georgia in the foreseeable future.

9 March 1779

PHILADELPHIA. As the problem of state bounties impedes enlistments in the Continental Army, as feared, Congress amends its resolution of 23 January, repealing the sections on new enlistments and re-enlistments and substituting an across-the-board $200 bounty for anyone who enlists for the duration of the war. States that award an equivalent or higher bounty will receive credit for the congressional bounty. Congress also encourages the states to raise recruits through drafts, while adopting a resolution that eighty battalions should be raised by the states—each state having a quota—for the infantry.

12 March 1779

PHILADELPHIA. President John Jay sends to the states copies of the resolutions adopted on 9 March with a letter optimistically asserting that the campaign of 1779, "if successful, will be the last," and therefore the states should happily do whatever is necessary to ensure the campaign's success and the achievement of independence.

14 March 1779

PHILADELPHIA. Alexander Hamilton, Gen. Washington's aide-de-camp, sends a letter to president of the Congress John Jay addressing the concern over reversals in the South and the inability of the Continental Army to send reinforcements to the region. To buttress the patriot forces in Georgia and the Carolinas he advocates arming the slaves, who he believes "will make very excellent soldiers." He recognizes that prejudice and self-interest will oppose this proposal, as people misperceive the nature of the blacks and their owners will not want "to part with property." But he suspects that if the patriots do not procure the blacks' services, then the enemy might. Essential to his plan, Hamilton concludes, is to give the slaves "their freedom with their muskets. This will secure their fidelity, animate their courage, and I believe will have a good influence upon those who remain, by opening a door to their emancipation. This circumstance, I confess, has no small weight in inducing me to wish

the success of the project; for the dictates of humanity and true policy equally interest me in favor of this unfortunate class of men."

23 March 1779

PHILADELPHIA. Having more or less settled what boundaries the United States would want specified in a peace treaty, the Congress now bogs down in attempting to draft a resolution dealing with fishing rights off the Newfoundland banks—delegates from the New England and Southern states hold conflicting views.

29 March 1779

PHILADELPHIA. Congress urges South Carolina and Georgia, where the struggle for independence seems fatefully imperiled, to enlist 3,000 slaves, proposing that their owners be paid a thousand dollars per slave and that the slaves, if they perform well, be granted their freedom and paid fifty dollars at the end of the war. The governments of the two states are unreceptive.

1 April 1779

PHILADELPHIA. Still once more Congress authorizes the issuance of five million dollars in bills of credit.

CLINCH RIVER (TENNESSEE). After a series of devastating raids conducted from the summer of 1775 through the summer of 1777 by militia from Virginia, Georgia, and the Carolinas, the Cherokee had signed treaties in 1777 ceding all their lands east of the Blue Ridge Mountains and north of the Nolichucky River to those states. But many Cherokee rejected the treaties: Chief Dragging Canoe and other chieftains and warriors removed to Chickamauga and continued to wage war; others, including Creeks, joined them and created new settlements. Their resistance has endangered the southern frontier, and so Virginia and South Carolina send a force of 900 men commanded by Col. Evan Shelby against them. Shelby begins a month-long series of raids on Indian villages along the Clinch, Powell, and Tennessee rivers, driving off the Indians and destroying their settlements.

3 April 1779

MADRID, SPAIN.   Spanish foreign minister conde Floridablanca offers Great Britain the service of mediating between Britain and France in exchange for Gibraltar as the price of Spanish neutrality, but the offer indicates that without the cession of Gibraltar, Spain will ally herself with France.

8 April 1779

PHILADELPHIA.   Following an ardent courtship by the would-be groom, Benedict Arnold and Peggy Shippen are married in the Shippen home. Because of his injured leg Arnold must be supported by a soldier during the ceremony.

12 April 1779

ARANJUEZ, SPAIN.   Ministers of Spain and France sign the Convention of Aranjuez, by which both nations commit themselves to pursue the war with Great Britain until George III's government cedes Gibraltar to Spain. The convention also specifies other war objectives—France is to recover Senegal and Dominica, be awarded Newfoundland, and be returned to India—and forbids either power to make a separate peace with Great

Britain. In accepting this alliance, however, Spain does not recognize the independence of the United States. The fact is that Floridablanca regards American independence as menacing to Spain because an independent United States might begin to occupy Spanish possessions in Louisiana and Mexico and also because of the unfortunate example it might set for Spain's colonies, inspiring them to seek independence. Spain's financial support of the United States, very modest compared to that of France, results from her desire for vengeance against Britain; and her entrance into the war is a potential means of regaining Gibraltar, Florida, Jamaica, and other territories lost to England in earlier wars.

21 April 1779

ONONDAGA CREEK, N.Y.   With the approval of Gen. Washington, an expedition of 550 Continental troops and officers commanded by Col. Gose Van Schaick arrives at the creek after a 180-mile march to attack the Onondaga Indians. They destroy the Onondaga Castle of about fifty houses, kill over twenty warriors, and take thirty-seven prisoners, including a white man, although most of the Indians flee into the woods. A report in the *New York Packet* says ". . . the destruction of all their settlements was complete." The Americans capture 100 guns and plunder the settlements, destroying whatever they cannot carry, and then return to Fort Schuyler.

23 April 1779

PURYSBURG, S.C.   The disastrous losses in Georgia have generated fears of a British attack among South Carolinians, leading Governor John Rutledge, awarded nearly dictatorial powers to protect the state, to bolster the militia. Gen. Benjamin Lincoln now has about 4,000 men; he crosses the Savannah River and marches on Augusta.

24 April 1779

TORBAY, ENGLAND. After numerous delays Admiral Marriot Arbuthnot, who is to assume command of the American fleet from Admiral John Byron, starts for New York with British and German troop reinforcements for Gen. Clinton. Lord Germain realizes that the delays mean Arbuthnot will arrive too late to be of much assistance in carrying out the royal government's war strategy for 1779.

29 April 1779

PURYSBURG, S.C. In order to counter Lincoln's move and draw him back out of Georgia, Gen. Prevost crosses the Savannah River with a force of 2,500 men, apparently intent on attacking Charleston. Col. Alexander McIntosh, posted at Purysburg with only 220 men for its defense, quickly withdraws and joins Gen. William Moultrie, in command of 1,000 men at Black Swamp. Prevost follows. Moultrie, believing Black Swamp indefensible, withdraws to Coosahatchie Bridge.

5 May 1779

NEW YORK CITY. British forces under the command of Adm. Sir John Collier and Maj. Gen. Edward Mathew embark on an expedition to raid ports along the Virginia coast in order to interrupt that state's supplies of com-

modities to the rebels and shipments of tobacco used to undergird foreign credit.

9 May 1779

HAMPTON ROADS, VA. The expedition of Adm. Collier and Gen. Mathew arrives. The British quickly conquer Fort Nelson, built for the protection of Portsmouth and Norfolk and the navy yard at Gosport. The fort's garrison of 100 soldiers under Maj. Thomas Matthews hastily evacuates and heads for the Dismal Swamp.

10 May 1779

NEW YORK CITY. Joseph Stansbury, a Philadelphia Tory and owner of a china shop, meets with Maj. John André, aide to Gen. Henry Clinton. Stansbury represents Gen. Benedict Arnold, who has solicited him to convey to the British, "under a solemn obligation of secrecy," word of Arnold's intention to offer his services to the British commander-in-chief. Arnold requests and receives assurances that the British intend to prosecute the war to victory. Clinton accepts Arnold's offer of service, indicating that he can best serve for the time being by remaining in his current post.

11 May 1779

PORTSMOUTH, VA. The Collier–Mathew expedition descends upon Portsmouth, Norfolk, Gosport, and Suffolk without any opposition from the rebels. The invaders capture large quantities of naval supplies, ordnance, and tobacco. They also capture, burn, or destroy 137 vessels and numerous privateers, inflicting an estimated two million pounds' worth of damage. Their expedition successfully completed without the loss of a single life, the British set sail for New York.

CHARLESTON, S.C. Gen. Augustine Prevost, countering Gen. Benjamin Lincoln's offensive move against Augusta, Ga., crosses the Ashley River and thrusts toward Charleston with a force of 900 men. He has been hard on the heels of Gen. William Moultrie's troops as they retreated in successive stages to the city. Moultrie now has only about 600 troops, but Gov. John Rutledge has also arrived with some militia to join Moultrie. They find the Charlestonians in a state of high terror over the approaching British. To this point Prevost's purpose has been to distract Lincoln and halt his advance; but, encouraged by meeting no resistance during his two-week march, he now appears to threaten an attack on Charleston itself. In the afternoon Count Kasimir Pulaski, just arrived, leads a small force of infantry and cavalry against Prevost, hoping to entice him into an ambush. But the men Pulaski has stationed behind earthworks for the ambush become overeager, sally forth too soon, and negate the surprise, forcing Pulaski to withdraw to the city. Prevost's force bottles up Charleston, and the general demands the city's surrender. During the negotiations the governor's council pledges the state will be neutral for the duration of the war if the British withdraw and never return. Prevost rejects the offer. During the early morning hours Gov. Rutledge, without informing Gen. Moultrie, sends out troops under Maj. Benjamin Huger to repair and reinforce the abatis protecting the patriots' front line. Moul-

A contemporary caricature of General Charles Lee; it was said to be a good likeness.

tire's troops assume them to be the enemy and open fire, killing Huger and twelve of his men. The governor's council awards the enraged Moultrie full command of Charleston's defense. During a council of war, reacting to the gloomy indecisiveness of the governor's council, Moultrie decides there will be no surrender: "I am determined not to deliver you up as prisoners of war—we will fight it out."

12 May 1779

CHARLESTON, S.C. Moultrie sends Prevost an early-morning message canceling the negotiations; he anticipates that the British will attack at dawn. But the message remains undelivered, for Prevost has learned from an intercepted letter that Gen. Lincoln has moved back into South Carolina. Not wanting to be pinned between Moultrie and Lincoln, Prevost has withdrawn his troops during the night to James Island, about two miles south of Charleston.

13 May 1779

JAMES ISLAND, S.C. In the early morning hours Prevost withdraws to Johns Island, adjoining James Island. He begins to construct fortifications at Stono Ferry on the mainland.

21 May 1779

PHILADELPHIA. The American financial problem has become so acute that the Congress is devoting three days per week to working on solutions, and today the members pass a resolution calling upon the states to fulfill their quotas of $45 million—requesting payment to the treasury by 1 January 1780.

23 May 1779

PHILADELPHIA. Benedict Arnold sends Gen. Clinton information on Gen. Washington's movements, indicating the seriousness of his own intentions and assisting Clinton's efforts to evaluate the American commander's plans.

26 May 1779

PHILADELPHIA. Realizing that their resolution of 21 May requesting the states to fulfill their monetary quotas requires that the states impose burdensome taxes—a cause of the Revolution itself—the Congress now adopts a persuasive address drafted by John Dickinson to accompany the copies of the resolution being sent to the individual states. The address concludes: "Rouse yourselves, therefore, that this campaign may finish the great work you have so nobly carried on for several years past. . . . Persevere, and you ensure peace, freedom, safety, glory, sovereignty, and felicity, to yourselves, your children, and your children's children. . . . Fill up your battalions . . . place your several quotas in the continental treasury . . . and may you be approved before Almighty God worthy of those blessings we devoutly wish you to enjoy."

28 May 1779

PHILADELPHIA. Uncertain how the states will respond to their request for money, the Congress appoints a committee to report upon the best way to negotiate a foreign loan and to decide how large the amount should be and how the money should be used.

KINGSBRIDGE, N.Y. At this site, where the Post Road crosses the Spuyten Duyvil Creek, Gen. Clinton assembles 6,000 of his best troops—a force comprised of British and Hessian grenadiers, light infantry, and dragoons and regiments of Tory troops, including Simcoe's Queen's Rangers. Clinton intends to move up the Hudson River and attack West Point.

30 May 1779

KINGSBRIDGE, N.Y. Clinton's offensive force embarks on the Hudson in seventy sailing vessels and 150 flat-bottomed boats.

1 June 1779

STONY POINT AND VERPLANCK'S POINT, N.Y. The British force sent out by Clinton captures the unfinished fort on the west bank of the Hudson at Stony Point without opposition, as the forty Americans stationed there torch the blockhouse and flee. From this vantage point and from their ships in the Hudson the British unleash a cannonade on Fort Lafayette at Verplanck's Point across the river. Though defended by palisades, abatis, and a double ditch, Fort Lafayette is garrisoned by only seventy North Carolina troops commanded by a single captain—they are forced to surrender. The conquering British immediately begin work to complete the fortifications at Stony Point. With control of these two vantages on the Hudson the British command Kings Ferry, twelve miles below West Point, a vital link in the Americans' east-west communications system and the gateway to the strategic Hudson River Highlands.

11 June 1779

PHILADELPHIA. Concerned over the Congress' struggle to raise money for the war and even more over the tenuous value of the vastly overminted issues of Continental currency, Richard Henry Lee comments, "The inundation of money appears to have overflowed virtue, and I fear will bury the liberty of America in the same grave. . . . The demon of avarice, extortion, and fortune-making seizes all ranks." War profiteers, speculators, and luxury-seekers appear to be endangering the glorious cause.

12 June 1779

PHILADELPHIA. Congress, reconsidering its earlier compromise resolution on lifetime half-pay for Continental Army officers (providing payments for only seven years after the war ends), receives a memorial from a group of officers strongly supporting the lifetime-compensation proposal that Gen. Washington originally recommended. The memorial's forceful tone prods the Congress to vote unanimously to send it to the Committee of Conference with instructions "to report speedily" about further provisions for the army.

NEW WINDSOR, N.Y. Gen. Washington instructs Maj. Henry Lee to gather intelligence about the strength of the British forces and fortifications at Stony Point.

16 June 1779

JOHNS ISLAND, GEORGIA. Gen. Prevost begins evacuating his troops to Savannah, leaving behind a rear guard of 900 men under the command of Lt. Col. John Maitland.

LONDON, ENGLAND. As the Channel fleet sails out to search for the French the Spanish ambassador brings a declaration to Lord Germain. It lists numerous alleged grievances, deplores the "rejection" of Spanish offers to mediate the war, and concludes that Spain is now forced to use whatever means are available to procure "justice." Though the statement employs veiled wording, Germain and his ministry associates understand that it is tantamount to a declaration of war, the way having been prepared by the Convention of Aranjuez, the offensive alliance arranged between the French and Spanish in April.

17 June 1779

LONDON, ENGLAND. Lord John Cavendish, in response to the Spanish ambassador's declaration, moves for a resolution by Parliament that all of Great Britain's forces be assembled for war with Spain and France. The resolution fails by an overwhelming two-to-one-vote margin, but other members of Parliament join Cavendish in urging abandonment of the conflict in

America to face this new peril of war with the allied Bourbon nations.

18 June 1779

ST. VINCENT, WEST INDIES. Adm. d'Estaing captures St. Vincent in preparation for an attack on Barbados.

20 June 1779

STONO FERRY, S.C. Gen. Benjamin Lincoln, commanding 6,500 troops in Charleston, leads a force of about 1,200 troops out of the city after midnight for an assault on Maitland's garrison on James Island. After crossing the Ashley River, he marches eighteen miles to stage a dawn attack, assuming that Gen. William Moultrie will be attacking Johns Island at the same time to prevent Maitland from moving reinforcements across Stono Inlet. Lincoln organizes his attack force into two wings: on the right Carolina militia under Jethro Sumner; on the left Continentals under Isaac Huger. They encounter fierce resistance from two Scottish Highlander companies and subsequently a German regiment, yet manage to struggle their way to the abatis circling Maitland's fortifications. Lincoln orders a bayonet attack, though his troops are poorly trained for such a maneuver. The American attack falters as Maitland's troops rally and he brings reinforcements over from Johns Island. In addition, Gen. Prevost's troops approach to reinforce the British resistance. Lincoln orders a retreat. Maitland sends his men forward to attack the withdrawing Americans, but Col. Mason leads a brigade of Virginians to thwart their advance and the Americans make good their escape. The operation, ineptly pursued by Lincoln, results in 146 casualties and 155 missing troops, mostly deserters,

for the Americans, while Maitland suffers 129 casualties with only one missing soldier.

21 June 1779

LONDON, ENGLAND. In an effort to rouse Lord North to meet the threat posed by the French and Spanish alliance, King George III summons his Cabinet. His challenge to his ministers invokes the memory of the Spanish Armada, as the king hopes to inspire the vigorous response Queen Elizabeth had mustered two hundred years earlier. Conceding only two errors—changing his ministry in 1765 and agreeing to the repeal of the Stamp Act—the king defends his choices of generals Howe, Burgoyne, and Clinton to prosecute the war in America; he voices confidence that God is on his side; he reaffirms his duty to preserve the empire; and he advocates steadfastness by the ministers, offering to bring new blood to their ranks if so desired. But his message is to no avail: Lord North remains distracted and indecisive.

23 June 1779

STONO FERRY, S.C. Following the unsuccessful American attack Maitland, who had already decided on 15 June to withdraw his troops but lacked the necessary ships, now begins a retreat to Beaufort (Port Royal Island).

WYOMING, PA. Maj. Gen. John Sullivan arrives with his troops en route to meet Brig. Gen. James Clinton at Tioga, where they are to combine their men into a single force of 3,700 to march north into the territory of the Six Nations.

28 June 1779

HICKORY HILL, GA. American troops

led by Col. John Twiggs capture an entire force of forty British grenadiers commanded by Capt. Muller.

30 June 1779

MARTINIQUE. Commodore la Motte-Picquet arrives from Brest with five ships, providing the French naval superiority in the Leeward Islands.

OTSEGO LAKE, N.Y. Gen. James Clinton sends word to Gen. Sullivan that his entire force, including all needed supplies and boats, is assembled at the lake, where he awaits further orders from Sullivan concerning their rendezvous at Tioga. Sullivan lingers at Wyoming, asserting that he is delayed by inadequate provisions for his men.

2 July 1779

POUND RIDGE, N.Y. Lt. Col. Banastre Tarleton leads a raid at Pound Ridge, twenty miles northeast of White Plains. His goal is to capture patriot Maj. Ebenezer Lockwood (there is a reward for his arrest) and to defeat Col. Elisha Sheldon and his ninety troops of the 2nd Continental Dragoons encamped near the village. Tarleton's force of 360 comprises troops of the Light Dragoons, his own British Legion, Simcoe's Queen's Rangers, hussars, and Germans. Apprised of Tarleton's approach by an American spy, Sheldon forms his men but is forced to retreat as Tarleton advances. Local militiamen come to the rescue, firing on Tarleton's men from behind fences and buildings; and Tarleton turns back, with Sheldon following. The British burn the church and some houses in Pound Ridge and capture Sheldon's colors found in one of the houses. They suffer two casualties and the Americans ten.

3 July 1779

WHITESTONE, N.Y. Gen. Clinton assembles a fleet of transports to be convoyed by four ships of war and embarks a force of 2,600 troops—one division of guards and jaegers under Brig. Gen. Garth and a division of Royal Welch Fusiliers, Hessians, and Tories under Gen. William Tryon—for punitive raids against Connecticut, whose people have been supplying the Continentals and harassing British commerce from their whaleboats and fishing vessels.

4 July 1779

GRENADA, WEST INDIES. The comte d'Estaing captures this British island while Adm. Byron is away on convoy duty.

OTSEGO LAKE, N.Y. Gen. James Clinton marks the day of independence by a salute with thirteen cannon and three successive musket volleys.

5 July 1779

NEW HAVEN, CONN. The expedition sent by Clinton anchors in New Haven Harbor. Garth's division disembarks with four cannon and marches on the town, meeting moderate opposition. Tryon's division lands at East Haven and routs the opposition.

EAST HAVEN, CONN. Garth's division joins Tryon's. Garth wishes to torch New Haven but instead plunders the town, taking about forty prisoners. The British then return to their ships to sail for Fairfield.

6 July 1779

GRENADA. Reinforced by Adm. de Grasse, who has arrived with a squadron from France, d'Estaing prevents

the outnumbered British fleet from re-
taking the island in an inconclusive
battle.

8 *July 1779*

FAIRFIELD, CONN. The British raiders
land and occupy the village, already
abandoned. They plunder the houses
and set fire to two churches, eighty-
three houses, over a hundred barns
and storehouses, two schools, the jail,
and the courthouse.

9 *July 1779*

PHILADELPHIA. In a modest effort
to address the issue of reforming
procurement procedures, Congress
passes a resolution requesting the ex-
ecutives of the various states to examine the conduct of all persons
involved in any way with the supply
departments and, if there is any suspicion of misconduct, to remove the
suspected persons or have them prosecuted at the expense of the Continental government.

10 *July 1779*

NEW WINDSOR, N.Y. Gen. Washington has recalled Brig. Gen. Anthony
Wayne from home leave, placing him
in command of the recently organized
Light Infantry; both generals have
made personal reconnoiters of the
British fortifications at Stony Point.
Gen. Lee has even managed to get his
able scout, Capt. Allen McLane, inside the fort on the pretext of gaining
permission for an American woman
to visit her sons, who are prisoners in
the fort. McLane, never blindfolded,
provides details on the state of the fortifications, including the observation
that the central redoubt is incomplete. Wayne also stations some soldiers under McLane in hiding near the

*"Mad" Anthony Wayne, nicknamed
by a deserter's complaint.*

fort to observe the garrison's daily
routine for several days. Local residents inform the Continentals of the
existence of a sandbar, two feet underwater and unknown to the British,
that will permit troops to cross the
marsh separating the Point from the
mainland. About three- fourths of the
promontory, effectively an island,
rises 150 feet from the Hudson—the
marsh is the only means of access.
Convinced by their findings that the
Light Infantry can retake Stony Point
with a night bayonet attack, Washington now sends instructions to
Wayne to make the needed preparations and orders the attack. Gen.
Wayne reportedly responds: "General,
if you give me permission, I'll storm
Hell itself for you."

NEW ORLEANS, LA. Soon after the
king's exhortation to his Ministers
Lord Germain had sent orders to Gen.

John Campbell in Pensacola, Fla., to capture New Orleans, with whatever aid Admiral Parker at Jamaica might be able to render him, and thus to secure navigation on the Mississippi River. Now the Spanish government authorizes Bernardo de Galvez, the twenty-three-year-old governor of Louisiana and Florida, to conduct raids on the British colonial towns along the Mississippi in order to weaken Great Britain's presence in the West.

11 July 1779

NORWALK, CONN. Having ravaged Green's Farms in passing, the British raiders now descend on Norwalk, futilely opposed by only fifty militia. They loot the town and set fire to 130 houses, over 100 barns and storehouses, two churches, over twenty shops and mills, and five vessels. Their hateful mission completed, the British return to New York.

15 July 1779

STONY POINT, N.Y. While McLane's and other units have hidden near the Point to intercept anyone approaching the fort, Gen. Wayne's main force has mustered and marched to Donderberg, where in the late afternoon Wayne for the first time reveals to his colonels the purpose of their march. He gives orders that the soldiers wear slips of white paper in their hats for identification in the dark, that no men may carry loaded guns except those so designated by himself, and that none may remove his musket from his shoulder under threat of death. Anyone who retreats or hesitates is to be killed by the nearest officer, as Wayne insists the success of the mission depends on total obedience and discipline. As a positive incentive for his men Wayne offers cash prizes starting at $500 to the five men who are first to enter the fort on Stony Point. Wayne's troops, numbering about 1,350, must force their way past two lines of abatis and several artillery batteries and then dislodge the fort's 625 defenders commanded by Col. Henry Johnson. To accomplish this improbable victory the resolute Wayne (some already call him "Mad Anthony") divides his force into two main columns: the right column led by Lt. Col. Christian Febiger, Col. Return Jonathan Meigs, and Maj. William Hull; the left by Col. Richard Butler and Maj. Hardy Murfree. The right column, Wayne accompanying them, will attack the fort from the southerly side; the left from the northerly side, with Murfree's men (they alone have loaded muskets) detaching themselves from the column to attack the center with sustained fire in order to make the defenders believe the Americans are coming straight on as a body. At the head of the right column will march 150 hand-picked men under Lt. Col. François de Fleury, and at the head of the left column a similar number of hardy men under Maj. John Stewart—these men armed with axes to demolish the abatis in advance of the attacking columns. Accompanying each group of axemen will be twenty fearless souls led by Lt. George Knox on the right and Lt. James Gibbons on the left whose assignment is to surge through the openings the axemen make and rush upon the British foe in hand-to-hand combat. The advance begins at half past eleven. By midnight the patriots reach the morass below the Point.

NEWFOUNDLAND. Three American frigates—the *Providence* commanded by Commodore Abraham Whipple, the *Queen of France* commanded by Capt. John Rathburn, and the *Ranger* commanded by Lt. Thomas Simpson—become lost in dense fog off the coast of Newfoundland and find themselves in the midst of a British squadron of 150 merchant ships convoyed by a single ship of the line with seventy-four guns and several smaller vessels. Capt. John Rathburn of the *Queen of France* passes his ship off as a British man-of-war and captures several of the merchant ships. The other American ships follow his lead. The *Providence* fires several broadsides at the *Holderness*, one of the escort ships, which surrenders, providing Whipple a rich booty of rum, sugar, coffee, and allspice. Altogether the Americans secure eleven captive ships with a cargo worth a million dollars for the return to Boston.

16 July 1779

STONY POINT, N.Y. The Americans' right column proceeds up the muddy road crossing the marsh, while the left column struggles over the hidden sandbar, discovering it to be waist-deep and in places even neck-deep. Murfree's men open fire before the columns are in position to attack, but the ruse works anyhow, as Col. Johnson leads a large body of troops down from the fort to confront Murfree. Though slowed by the mud, the right American column, led by Wayne and Febiger, surmounts the first barrier and races toward the second before Johnson realizes what is happening. In the confusion of darkness Johnson loses control of his men. At the sec-

ond abatis Wayne falls, his head grazed by a bullet; but at his urging two officers hoist him and half-carry him up the hill. Febiger, a survivor of the march to Quebec, takes a bullet through his nose and cheek but leads his men forward, undaunted by the blood spurting into his mouth. The troops find the gap in the British defenses reported by McLane and race through at the same time as Butler's column on the left, having encountered little opposition, reaches the redoubts. Butler's men are temporarily halted by the parapets, but Francis McDonald climbs up on a comrade's shoulders and pulls himself over the top, leaping into the midst of the British. He unbolts the heavy gate, and the Continentals rush in to capture the summit and raise the American flag. Their triumphant shouts apprise Johnson that his defenses have failed. He gathers whatever men he can find and hastens back up the hill; but, encountering the bloody-faced Febiger, he accepts reality and surrenders his sword and his soldiers. One British soldier manages to escape by diving into the Hudson; he swims to the HMS *Vulture* with the news of the fort's capture. The Americans turn the fifteen cannon of Stony Point on Verplanck's Point and the *Vulture*. Their victory has cost fifteen dead and eighty wounded, while their bayonets have exacted sixty-three dead and seventy wounded among the enemy. They have captured 543 prisoners, thirty-one tents, and numerous stores. Wayne sends Gen. Washington a simple note: "The fort and garrison with Col. Johnson are ours. Our officers and men behaved like men who are determined to be free." François de Fleury wins the prize for being first

The storming of Stony Point, on the Hudson, 35 miles north of New York City. This was one of the most daring feats of American arms of the war. Wayne's men achieved complete surprise and overwhelmed the British garrison.

inside the fort, and George Knox comes in second. They donate their prize money to the enlisted men.

17 July 1779

STONY POINT, N.Y. After inspecting the captured fort, Gen. Washington concludes that defending it will require too many men, so he orders Wayne to remove all the guns and stores and then destroy the fortifications. Gen. Clinton, alarmed by the loss of Stony Point, terminates the destructive raids along the Connecticut shore, assembles all available men-of-war, and sails up the Hudson to retake the Point.

18 July 1779

STONY POINT, N.Y. Having destroyed the fortifications on the Point, Gen. Wayne abandons the site, leaving Gen. Clinton free to reoccupy and refortify it.

19 July 1779

OQUAGA, N.Y. Joseph Brant sets out down the Delaware River with a band of Mohawks and Tories for raids against river villages. He posts the main body of this force at Grassy Brook and proceeds with sixty Indians and twenty-seven Tories toward Minisink.

20 July 1779

MINISINK, N.Y. During the early morning Brant's force enters the village and begins torching buildings. The sleeping inhabitants awake and flee, abandoning the village to Brant's men. They take several prisoners, loot the houses and barns, round up all the cattle, and head back to Grassy Bank with their plunder.

21 July 1779

CASTINE, ME. During June Col. Francis MacLean with about 800 British troops from Halifax has been building a base here in order to secure lumber for the Halifax shipyards, interdict patriot invaders threatening Nova Scotia, and launch marauding expeditions in the nearby countryside. Now Massachusetts, without consulting Congress or Continental Army commanders, sends an expedition against MacLean. Generals Solomon Lovell and Peleg Wadsworth start out with 1,000 militia, while Capt. Dudley Saltonstall of the Continental Navy sets sail in command of a flotilla of three navy ships, three brigantines, thirteen privateers, twenty Massachusetts transports, and a New Hampshire vessel. This flotilla carries 2,000 men.

22 July 1779

MINISINK, N.Y. Col. John Hathorn

and a group of his men join forces with 149 militia called together by Lt. Col. Benjamin Tusten the day before to go in pursuit of Joseph Brant's force. They come upon a recently abandoned campsite revealing that Brant's force is greater than anticipated. Against Hathorn's and Tusten's objections, the men decide to push on. They discover Brant's men moving their loot toward a ford across the Delaware River and try to intercept them. Brant outmaneuvers Hathorn's force, isolating and killing a third of the militiamen, and circles behind the remaining attackers. The Americans retreat to high ground and hold fast for several hours. But Brant discovers a weak point in their line, breaks through, and unleashes a massacre. Forty-five Americans meet death. Only thirty of the original militia force survive, including Hathorn.

25 July 1779

CASTINE, ME. The Penobscot expedition under Lovell, Wadsworth, and Saltonstall reaches its destination, but MacLean's British troops manage to hold them at bay.

28 July 1779

CASTINE, ME. Gen. Lovell's troops land on the southwest side of the peninsula extending into Penobscot Bay in preparation for attacking the British fort. But, as Saltonstall refuses to provide naval support until the militia actually captures the fort (an impossible task), the American operation stalls while the British strengthen their fortifications.

31 July 1779

WYOMING, PA. Still under orders from Gen. Washington to inflict "to-tal destruction and devastation" on the Six Nations of the Iroquois Confederation, to destroy their settlements, and to capture as many prisoners as possible "of every age and sex," Gen. John Sullivan finally sets out with his force of 2,300 men to meet Gen. Clinton at Tioga and from there to launch this vengeful expedition.

2 August 1779

NEW YORK CITY. Gen. Washington's view that the victory at Stony Point will boost the Americans' morale seems borne out by the *New York Journal's* report that the triumphant Continental soldiers had been "Spurred on by their resentment of the former cruel bayoneting which many of them and others of our people had experienced" and by the recent British plundering raids, to enter the fort "with the resolution of putting every man to the sword. But the cry of 'Mercy! mercy! Dear Americans, mercy!...' disarmed their resentment in an instant, insomuch that even Colonel Johnson, the commandant, freely and candidly acknowledges that not a drop of blood was spilled unnecessarily. Oh, Britain, turn thy eye inward, behold and tremble at thyself." And the *New Hampshire Gazette* declares the victory "demonstrates that the Americans have soldiers equal to any in the world, and that they can attack and vanquish the Britons in their strongest works. No action during the war, performed by the British military, has equalled this *coup de main*." The American victory, along with the British government's failure to provide reinforcements, has in fact demoralized and depressed Gen. Clinton, who tries to resign and relinquish command to Lord Cornwallis.

3 August 1779

BOSTON. A French frigate arrives bearing the Chevalier de la Luzerne, the French minister to the United States, and his staff; and also John Adams, returned home from his sojourn as commissioner at the court of France. The minister and his staff are lodged at the home of Gen. John Hancock.

5 August 1779

MORRISANIA (BRONX), N.Y. At this home seat of the Morris family, located within British lines, Brig. Gen. John Glover leads his cavalry and local militia troops in a skirmish with Oliver De Lancey's Loyalists and takes fifteen prisoners.

11 August 1779

PITTSBURGH, PA. Col. Daniel Brodhead, conjoining with Sullivan's expedition, leaves Pittsburgh with 600 men to march up the Allegheny River Valley and devastate Indian villages on the Pennsylvania frontier.

TIOGA, PA. Gen. Sullivan's army, artillery, baggage, and provisions reach the site of the rendezvous with Clinton.

13 August 1779

CASTINE, ME. Sir George Collier arrives from New York with ten vessels and 1,600 troops to bolster the British garrison, rendering the Americans' position untenable. After a council of war the militia reboard their ships to retreat up the Penobscot River, abandon and torch their ships, and flee into the Maine woods. The Americans lose 474 men, the British only thirteen. In addition, the Americans lose all their ships. The Penobscot expedition proves a dismal failure as a result of reluctant leadership.

14 August 1779

L'ORIENT, FRANCE. John Paul Jones puts out to sea with his flotilla of ships funded by France and largely commanded by French officers who resent being subordinate to him. The fleet flies the American flag, with Jones aboard his command ship the *Bonhomme Richard*, named in honor of his benefactor Benjamin Franklin, whose *Poor Richard's Almanac* enjoys great popularity in France. Accompanying the *Bonhomme Richard* are the American frigate *Alliance*, commanded by a Frenchman, Pierre Landais; and three French ships, the frigate *Pallas*, the brig *Vengeance*, and the cutter *Le Cerf*. They are headed for the west coast of the British Isles.

PHILADELPHIA. After months of debate centering largely on the issue of protecting the New England fisheries, Congress approves instructions to the minister (still unnamed) who will negotiate the peace settlement with Great Britain. The instructions avoid an ultimatum on the fisheries issue but do stipulate that, with the consent of France, any truce arrived at must include the immediate withdrawal of enemy troops from the United States. Significantly, the instructions empower the minister to abide by "the advice of our allies, by your knowledge of our Interests, and by your own discretion, in which we repose the fullest confidence."

15 August 1779

ALLEGHENY VALLEY. Brodhead's expedition into the Indian territory confronts opposition as his advance guard under Lt. Harding encounters over thirty Indians traveling downstream in canoes. Harding's men drive off the Indians, killing five of them.

18 August 1779

PARAMUS, N.J. Maj. Henry ("Light Horse Harry") Lee, Jr., inspired by "Mad Anthony" Wayne's victory at Stony Point, has scouted the British outpost at Paulus Hook, a sandy peninsula in the Hudson River across from New York City, and has persuaded Gen. Washington to let him attack it. Except for its low elevation, the Hook resembles Stony Point in being cut off from the mainland by salt marshes, making it accessible only at low tide and by a deep ditch spanned by a single drawbridge—thus the Hook is a virtual island. The British redoubts here comprise a central circular area, 150 feet in diameter, fortified by the ditch, abatis, and six heavy cannon; a larger, oblong area to the northeast defended by four large cannon and a blockhouse; a blockhouse by the drawbridge and another to the southeast by the river. Two hundred British troops and forty-eight Hessians man this strong position, commanded by Maj. William Sutherland. Lee's attack force consists of 100 members of Woodford's Virginia brigade under Maj. Jonathan Clark on the right; two Maryland companies under Capt. Levin Handy in the center; and 100 of Muhlenberg's Virginians and Capt. Allen McLane's dismounted dragoons on the left led by Lee. (The enterprising scout for the

Stony Point battle, McLane has also been in charge of scouting Paulus Hook.) A "suicide" squad like that used at Stony Point is to hack a route through the abatis—they are to be led by lieutenants Mark Vanduval, Philip Reid, and James Armstrong. Capt. Nathan Reid commands a reserve detachment. Lee leaves Paramus at ten-thirty in the morning, accompanied by wagons to feign a foraging expedition, to join McLane and the Virginia troops, hoping to stage an assault after midnight on the nineteenth; but their guide misleads them into a lengthy detour, causing a three-hour delay; and about half of the Virginians under Maj. Clark, who is disgruntled at being subordinate to Lee, become disaffected and abandon the march.

19 August 1779

PAULUS HOOK, N.J. With his expedition delayed and his force depleted, Lee arrives for the attack at 4:00 A.M., his hopes for success now also jeopardized by the approach of daylight. Lee orders a bayonet attack, with muskets loaded but unprimed; now Clark and the residue of his Virginians man the right, with Capt. Robert Forsyth, McLane's men, and the rest of the Virginians on the left. Handy's men are in reserve; the "suicide" squad is led by Lt. Michael Rudolph and Lt. Archibald McAllister. As they wade the marsh their splashing alerts the British, whose musket fire does not deter the swift work of Rudolph's and McAllister's men. With the way opened, Clark's troops surge through the abatis and into the circular redoubt. Forsyth and McLane also press on. The Americans capture a blockhouse and the commanding officer and his soldiers. Without firing a single shot, Lee's men triumph, bayoneting fifty of the defenders and taking 158 prisoners, while suffering only two killed and three wounded. But Maj. Sutherland and over forty Hessians barricade themselves in a blockhouse and continue their fire, refusing to surrender. Since the garrison in New York has already been alerted by the alarm guns, Lee has no choice but withdrawal, leaving behind barracks and cannon intact and any booty. Marching off with his prisoners, he heads for Douwe's Ferry, where Capt. Henry Peyton has assembled boats to convey Lee's Legion to safety. But since Lee is hours late, Peyton has assumed the attack was called off and has left for Newark with the boats before Lee arrives. Now in a desperate position, as all his men's ammunition is wet and Col. Abaram van Buskirk's Loyalists are hot on his tail, he orders his tired men on to New Bridge and sends a rider ahead to have Lord Stirling, waiting there with 300 men, come to his aid. Capt. Thomas Catlett arrives with fifty of the Virginians who had abandoned the expedition, and a detachment sent by Stirling also arrives—just in time to repulse an assault on Lee's left by Van Buskirk. By one o'clock Lee reaches safety at New Bridge with all of his prisoners. Though hardly a great military victory, the Paulus Hook expedition provides the Americans with another morale boost, as Stony Point had.

22 August 1779

TIOGA, PA. Clinton joins Sullivan to begin their expedition against the Indians. While awaiting his arrival, Sullivan has been raiding nearby Iroquois villages—some consisting of log houses with glass windows—burning them to the ground, their inhabitants already having fled before his troops' arrival.

25 August 1779

NEW YORK CITY. After months of delays caused by weather, accidents, and battle alarms, the British fleet bearing 3,000 troops to reinforce Gen. Henry Clinton that was to have sailed from Portsmouth at the end of February but did not clear the English Channel till 4 June, finally drops anchor in New York Harbor. Adm. Marriot Arbuthnot, under orders to succeed Adm. Byron as naval commander in America, commands the fleet.

26 August 1779

TIOGA, PA. Leaving most of their heavy baggage behind with 250 men to defend the base, Sullivan and Clinton begin a march up the Chemung River.

27 August 1779

NEW ORLEANS, LA. Governor Bernardo de Galvez, advancing Spain's involvement on the side of the French and the Americans, sets out with a motley army of Spanish regulars, militia, Americans, and Indians to attack British outposts on the Mississippi River at Manchac Post, Baton Rouge, and Natchez.

29 August 1779

CHEMUNG RIVER, N.Y. Although thus far during their march Sullivan and Clinton have come upon villages already abandoned by the Indians, they now encounter opposition. The Iroquois and their British cohorts have erected a hidden breastwork on a hill-

Robert Morris, the Philadelphia financier who helped keep the finances of the Continental Congress above water during the war years.

top above the path the Americans are following along the riverbank; from this vantage they plan to ambush the expedition and then attack it front and rear. The breastwork is held by Capt. Walter N. Butler commanding two battalions of rangers, a detachment of the 8th Regiment, about 200 Tories, and about 500 Indians led by Joseph Brant. Their plan of action falters when the American advance, led by Maj. James Parr and three companies of Morgan's riflemen, discovers their position and returns to halt the American column. The Americans decide to unleash their artillery against the foe while a force under Brig. Gen. Enoch Poor circles behind them to cut off their retreat. After a brief skirmish the British and Indian forces, effectively surrounded, flee into the woods, leaving behind a dozen dead and two prisoners. The Americans

have three killed and thirty-nine wounded. They scalp their dead foes and skin the legs of two Indians to make boot legs for Lt. William Barton and his commanding major. They then press on to lay waste a nearby village and the Iroquois settlement of Newtown, destroying the orchards and all crops in the fields.

1 September 1779
PHILADELPHIA. After months of struggling with the problem of financing the war through emissions of bills of credit that continue to depreciate, the Congress finally embraces fiscal responsibility, resolving that "on no account whatever" will it authorize emitting bills of credit in excess of $200 million overall. To date emissions total $160 million, making possible $40 million more.

3 September 1779
PHILADELPHIA. Congress now resolves not to authorize emission of even the $40 million more in bills of credit made possible by the 1 September resolution unless absolute necessity so demands. French minister Gerard sends Congress an address announcing his intention to leave his post. His successor, Chevalier Anne-Cesar de la Luzerne, has arrived in Boston in August.

COAST OF SCOTLAND. Having gone off on their own earlier, the *Alliance* and the *Pallas* now rejoin John Paul Jones. The squadron turns to head south, with plans to attack Leith, the port of Edinburgh, and Newcastle-on-Tyne, the great coal-shipping port.

4 September 1779
CHEMUNG RIVER, N.Y. Having de-

stroyed Catherine's Town and two Iroquois villages and their surrounding croplands, Sullivan's expedition continues its scorched-earth rampage through Six Nations territory, burning Appletown and pushing on toward Kindaia.

5 September 1779

LLOYD'S NECK, LONG ISLAND, N.Y. Maj. Benjamin Tallmadge leads 150 dismounted dragoons in a surprise raid against 500 Tories sited at Lloyd's Neck. Capturing most of the garrison without losing a single man, he returns with his prisoners to his base at Shippan Point near Stamford, Connecticut.

7 September 1779

MANCHAC POST, LA. Galvez captures Manchac Post (Fort Bute), established by the British in 1763 at this northern boundary of the Isle of Orleans, and thus controls a water route by way of the Amite River and through lakes Maurepas, Ponchartrain, and Borgne into the Gulf of Mexico.

8 September 1779

SAVANNAH, GA. Responding to the urgings of the Marquis de Bretigny and of Southern patriots, especially John Rutledge and William Moultrie, that only he can save Charleston, Adm. d'Estaing has hastily returned from cruising in the West Indies. He arrives at the mouth of the Savannah River with a fleet of twenty-two battleships, ten frigates, and other vessels bearing 4,000 troops. The French admiral actually has appeals from Gen. Washington's headquarters requesting his aid in attacking Newport or New York, but for his own reasons he chooses to intervene in the South instead.

10 September 1779

CANANDAIGUA, N.Y. Sullivan's expedition destroys this major Iroquois settlement, noteworthy for its twenty-three frame houses. The cornfields and fruit orchards are so extensive that Sullivan's men need two days to effect their destruction. The work completed, Sullivan heads for Genesee, the "grand capital" of the Six Nations.

13 September 1779

GENESEE, N.Y. Maj. John Butler and his troops ambush Sullivan's advance guard of twenty-six men under Lt. Thomas Boyd as they approach to reconnoiter the Indian capital. Butler's men kill twenty-two of the Americans, taking Boyd and an Oneida guide named Hanyerry prisoners. The Iroquois with Butler hack Hanyerry to pieces and torture Boyd to death after he has been questioned.

SAVANNAH, GA. Adm. d'Estaing lands 3,000 troops at Beaulieu to prepare for a siege of Savannah.

PHILADELPHIA. Congress unanimously approves a circular letter drafted by President John Jay to accompany copies of the resolutions restricting emission of bills of credit to be sent to the states. Jay's letter forcefully defines and defends the credibility of the confederacy and its future ability to reimburse purchasers of the bills, while also arguing the certainty of the revolution's success. Congress, he asserts, will never breach its faith by reneging on its debts. The Congress authorizes printing 200 copies of the letter in English and 200 in German.

14 September 1779

PITTSBURGH, PA. Col. Daniel Brodhead and his men return to Pittsburgh after a month of raids in the Iroquois territory complementing Sullivan's expedition. They have marched 400 miles, burned ten villages, destroyed crops, and brought back furs and booty.

GENESEE, N.Y. Sullivan's expedition enters the abandoned Iroquois capital, an old town of 128 houses, "most very large and elegant," as Sullivan describes them. His men torch the entire town and destroy all the crops. Since this is the Six Nations' central granary, its destruction foretells a bleak winter for the Iroquois. Realizing that Brodhead will not be rendezvousing with him, Sullivan abandons plans to march against Niagara and begins to withdraw, heading back to Wyoming through the Cayuga Indian territory by way of Lake Ontario's southern shore.

16 September 1779

SAVANNAH, GA. A force commanded by Gen. Benjamin Lincoln joins d'Estaing; Gen. Kasimir Pulaski and his legion have also arrived. The American troops—from Georgia, Virginia, and South Carolina—number 1,350. Convinced that victory is certain, d'Estaing requests Gen. Augustine Prevost to surrender. Prevost responds by asking for a twenty-four-hour truce to prepare capitulation articles. D'Estaing grants the request, and Prevost uses the time to strengthen his fortifications greatly. In addition, the truce gives Col. John Maitland time to enter the city with reinforcements from Port Royal. With his defenses now augmented, Prevost sends d'Estaing word that he intends to defend Savannah "to the last extremity."

21 September 1779

BATON ROUGE, LA. Bernardo de Galvez captures this former French outpost that reverted to the British in 1763 as part of West Florida. In surrendering, the British also cede Natchez and other posts on the Mississippi River.

FLAMBOROUGH HEAD, ENGLAND. John Paul Jones captures two English brigs and learns that there is a large fleet of merchant ships accompanied by a British frigate at the mouth of the Humber River.

PHILADELPHIA. Chevalier de la Luzerne arrives to succeed Gerard.

23 September 1779

SAVANNAH, GA. Lincoln, Pulaski, and d'Estaing begin the siege of Savannah. D'Estaing has brought ashore heavy cannon from his ships in order to bombard the British garrison. The success of the allied effort is threatened by quarrels between the French admiral and the Americans and by the approaching hurricane season.

FLAMBOROUGH HEAD, ENGLAND. John Paul Jones, commanding the *Bonhomme Richard* and accompanied by the French cruisers *Pallas* and *Alliance*, sights forty-one merchant ships heading north and gives chase. Spotting their attackers, the merchantmen head for shore, leaving their convoy ships, HMS *Serapis* and HMS *Countess of Scarborough*, to do battle. The *Pallas*, joined by the *Alliance*, engages the *Countess of Scarborough* as the *Bonhomme Richard* and the *Serapis*, commanded by Capt. Richard Pearson, confront each other. The *Serapis*, a new, double-decked, copper-bottomed frigate, carries fifty-four cannon, including twenty eighteen-pounders, and thus outguns the *Bonhomme Richard* by a ratio of about three to two. The British guns blast the *Bonhomme Richard*'s rigging and hull, silencing Jones' battery of twelve-pounders, while two of his nine-pounders explode when fired, killing most of their crews. The two ships maneuver, each trying to cross the other's bow and fire into it. Pearson's miscalculation allows Jones' crippled ship to ram his stern. As the *Serapis* wheels about a sudden gust of wind pivots both ships and drives them together, stern to bow and bow to stern. The *Serapis'* jibstay breaks

away and hurtles to the deck of the *Bonhomme Richard*, where Jones and his helmsman Stacy rope it to the mizzenmast while Jones' crew struggles to lash the ships together with grappling hooks. Fierce combat ensues, interrupted periodically as the crews race to extinguish fires that sweep through the rigging of both ships. Nearness prevents using the two ships' main batteries, but four of the *Serapis'* bow guns fire point-blank with horrendous effect. Belowdecks the *Bonhomme Richard*'s bulkheads gather spattering blood and torn flesh, while the wounded and dying agonize, fearing both bursts of flame and water

WAR ON THE WATER

The British Royal Navy controlled the sea along the American coastline during most of the Revolution, allowing free movement of armies and supplies. But the British could not make seapower a decisive advantage. The late appearance of the French navy—not a very good navy, but just good enough in the circumstance—gave George Washington a chance to trap and subdue the British army at Yorktown.

When the Revolution began, the British Royal Navy was the largest and most powerful in the world, boasting 131 large ships of the line (each with at least sixty-four guns) and even more smaller vessels. However, the fleet had fallen into a sorry state of disrepair under the inept and incompetent Lord Sandwich, who headed the Admiralty from 1771 onward, and the fleet commanders

were a mediocre group. Moreover, British admirals and captains were hampered by the rigid *Fighting Instructions* that required them to make set-piece engagements no matter what the circumstances. Individual captains were aggressive, and they sailed better ships than their foes, but their logy admirals and rigid battle instructions seldom allowed them full rein. The Royal Navy also faced terrible strategic problems that required maintaining fleets at home, off French ports, in defense of Gibraltar, in the West Indies, and along the American coast.

American naval forces were minuscule compared to the Royal Navy. There were hundreds of able seafarers among the colonists of the American coastline, but no warships and few resources with which to build any. The Continental Navy, pouring through the ship's gaping hull. Night descends and the battle rages on under a full moon. Suddenly the *Alliance*, having provided meager help to the *Pallas*, looms off the *Serapis'* bow, ostensibly coming to Jones' rescue. But instead of attacking the *Serapis*, the erratic Capt. Pierre Landais, despite frantic signals from his sister ship, fires repeated broadsides into the *Bonhomme Richard's* stern, apparently intentionally, killing nearly twenty men and further damaging the ship's hull. Acknowledging their hopeless condition, Jones' officers urge surrender. At this perilous moment an American sailor lobs a grenade into a hatchway on the *Serapis* that ignites powder on the gundeck, creating a huge explosion that destroys twenty men and shakes the ship's mainmast. Convinced the battle is lost, Capt. Pearson strikes his colors. John Paul Jones' stubborn will triumphs. The four-hour battle has cost the lives of half of the *Bonhomme Richard's* crew of a little over 300, while the *Serapis* has suffered forty-nine dead and sixty-eight wounded out of a crew of similar size. In no previous naval battle in history has a commander sustained such extensive casualties as Jones and still claimed victory. Within minutes of Jones' suc-

launched in 1775, consisted of a few small frigates, a class of fighting ship that would have barely made the sixth rate in the British fleet. They were all captured or destroyed by the war's end despite the valiant work of American naval heroes like John Paul Jones, John Barry, Nicolas Biddle, Lambert Wickes, and Joshua Barney. David Bushnell's innovative submarine was nothing more than an ineffective curiosity. The most important American naval threat came from the thousands of privateers that raided British shipping (Massachusetts alone commissioned more than 600) and the successful commerce raiders like Gustavus Conyngham. British shipping suffered considerably from these small-ship raiders, and at times even the small navies authorized by eleven of the states effectively harassed the enemy's movements. Overall, however, American naval efforts were seldom more than an annoyance to the British.

The French navy, which finally became decisive in 1781, was comprised of fine ships (the result of a superb rebuilding program after the Seven Years' War), but the quality of French sailors was dismal. Time after time, French admirals and captains either sailed away from confrontation with the British or were satisfied with inconclusive engagements. Timidity ruled the French outlook with few exceptions, and the Battle of the Capes off the Chesapeake in September 1781 (which left Cornwallis to his fate) was not so much a French victory as a standoff illustrative of the general war at sea.

John Paul Jones shooting a sailor who had attempted to strike his ship's colors during battle. (It is most likely that this event never happened.)

cess the *Countess of Scarborough* surrenders to the *Pallas*.

25 September 1779
FLAMBOROUGH HEAD, ENGLAND. Jones' carpenters repair the *Serapis* but find the *Bonhomme Richard* too devastated to be salvaged. The Americans abandon and sink the forlorn hulk.

27 September 1779
PHILADELPHIA. Congress appoints John Jay minister to Spain, charging him with the mission of negotiating treaties of alliance and of amity and commerce. Hope prevails that Spain might also be amenable to providing a loan to the United States. In a spirit of compromise between adherents of Jay and John Adams, Congress concurrently names Adams to be chief negotiator of treaties of peace and commerce with Great Britain in the aftermath of the Revolution.

28 September 1779
PHILADELPHIA. Congress elects Samuel Huntington of Connecticut to succeed John Jay as president.

FLAMBOROUGH HEAD, ENGLAND. Jones sets sail for Holland in the *Serapis* accompanied by the *Pallas* and the *Countess of Scarborough*.

30 September 1779
WYOMING, PA. Having ravaged the Indian towns around Cayuga Lake during his march homeward, Sullivan arrives at Wyoming. Though he has returned without a single hostage, he reports having laid waste forty towns, an estimated 160,000 bushels of corn, and huge quantities of other vegetables and crops, including vast orchards. The Sullivan expedition's ruinous tactics have effectively destroyed the Iroquois civilization beyond any hope of restoration.

3 October 1779
TEXEL, HOLLAND. Hampered by rough weather and hunted by eight British warships during its flight, John Paul Jones' little squadron arrives safely and drops anchor in Texel's port.

4 October 1779
LICKING–OHIO RIVERS, KENTUCKY. The infamous Simon Girty, a former interpreter for the American army who defected to the British the previous year, ambushes Col. David Rogers on the Ohio River. He and his Indian band kill fifty-seven of the seventy men under Rogers and seize 600,000 Spanish dollars, blankets, and

other supplies Rogers was taking to Fort Pitt from New Orleans.

SAVANNAH, GA. After twelve days in which the American sappers have dug trenches, slowly thrusting forward, and have emplaced three battering cannon and fourteen mortars, the allies begin the bombardment of the British garrison in Savannah. The ferocity of the cannonade prompts Gen. Prevost to request a truce in order to evacuate women, children, and the aged; but, disillusioned by their past experience, d'Estaing and Lincoln refuse.

6 October 1779

PHILADELPHIA. Congress decides to levy an assessment of $15 million monthly on the states from 1 February until 1 October 1780 and to charge interest on any deficient payments.

9 October 1779

SAVANNAH, GA. The American cannonfire has mostly gone over the heads of the British and devastated the city, while Adm. d'Estaing has grown impatient and Gen. Prevost, confident of his artillery and extensive fortifications, anticipates—even hopes for —an allied attack. Against Gen. Lincoln's counsel, d'Estaing demands an immediate attack or he will lift the siege. The allied force begins a predawn attack on Prevost's right across a swamp while militia strike at his center—3,500 French troops join 600 Continentals and 350 Charlestown militiamen for the assault. The British right, commanded by Maitland, responds with ravaging grapeshot and musket fire. Count Pulaski, at the head of the advancing Continentals with his cavalry, reaches the British

abatis but falls mortally wounded by a canister shot. Lt. Col. John Laurens leads his men into a ditch before Maitland's redoubt but finds the sides too steep to climb. Maitland's grenadiers drive him out while Gen. Lachlan McIntosh's Continentals advance. D'Estaing receives an arm wound; he tries to regroup his French troops by sending McIntosh farther to the left. Pulaski's men join Laurens in hasty withdrawal, and McIntosh's men become mired in Yamacraw Swamp, where Maitland's artillery pounds them remorselessly. The allied troops, repulsed and shattered, break off the assault and withdraw. They count 700 French and 450 American dead and wounded. The British have fewer than 150 casualties out of a total force of 3,200.

The wounding of Kasimir Pulaski at Savannah. He died two days later.

11 October 1779

NEW YORK. Reacting to the presence of d'Estaing's fleet at Savannah, Gen. Henry Clinton orders the withdrawal of the small British force (3,000 men) stationed at Newport, R.I.

SAVANNAH, GA. Following ineffectual surgery to remove grapeshot from his groin, Count Pulaski dies aboard the USS *Wasp*.

20 October 1779

SAVANNAH, GA. d'Estaing and his remnant force reboard their ships and embark, leaving Lincoln no alternative but retreat to Charleston.

WEST POINT, N.Y. Gen. Washington writes to the Marquis de Lafayette declaring himself pleased over "the entire destruction of the Country of the Six Nations" and convinced that Sullivan's expedition has "humbled" the Indians.

21 October 1779

PHILADELPHIA. Congress selects Henry Laurens as the government's agent to negotiate a loan from Holland.

22 October 1779

KINGSTON, N.Y. The Provincial Congress approves an act mandating the forfeiture and sale of property owned by Loyalists and declares Gov. Lord Dunmore, Gen. Tryon, Oliver De Lancey, and fifty-seven others public enemies. About 15,000 New Yorkers serve with the British army, and 8,000 more serve in Loyalist militias.

1 November 1779

PHILADELPHIA. Congress gives Henry Laurens the added duty of negotiating treaties of amity and commerce with Holland.

7 November 1779

JEFFER'S NECK, N.Y. The Marquis de la Rouerie Tuffin, known to the Americans as Col. Charles Armand, a French aristocrat volunteer who has served commendably at Brandywine and Whitemarsh and assumed command of the Pulaski Legion after the count's death, surprises and captures Maj. Mansfield Bearmore and five other Tories.

25 November 1779

LONDON, ENGLAND. Parliament convenes. The king's opening speech pleads for unity, derides the Americans for an "unprovoked war," and solicits financial and popular support for his ministers and their prosecution of the war. Opponents reject the plea. In the House of Lords Rockingham deplores the ruinous conditions of the empire, Lyttleton denounces policies toward Ireland, and Shelburne excoriates the government for losses in the West Indies. Others join the attack. In the Commons opponents criticize failures in the Caribbean and the Mediterranean and the war in America; and Charles James Fox accuses the king of improperly exercising ministerial authority. The beleaguered North ministry, however, manages to survive no-confidence votes in both houses.

1 December 1779

MORRISTOWN, N.J. Gen. Washington arrives to establish winter quarters and sets up his headquarters in the home of Mrs. Theodosia Ford, recently widowed. "A very severe storm of hail and snow" persists throughout the day.

5 December 1779

MORRISTOWN, N.J. Washington's guard arrives, occupying huts southeast of the Ford house, and troops begin to arrive and to fell trees for constructing huts.

23 December 1779

MIDDLEBROOK, N.J. After months of delay the court-martial of Gen. Benedict Arnold reconvenes. By this time three of the original fourteen jurors—generals William Smallwood, William Woodford, and William Irvine—have been replaced by William Maxwell and Mordecai Gist, and only two colonels remain. Col. John Laurence is in charge of the prosecution, and Arnold conducts his own defense. Since known documents do not support many of the original charges, the court is able to accuse the general of only minor offenses and three more serious offenses for which clear proof is lacking.

26 December 1779

NEW YORK CITY. Believing that, following the British victory in Savannah, the time is ripe for conquest in the South, Gen. Henry Clinton confers command of a garrison of 10,000 British troops in New York upon Lt. Gen. Wilhelm von Knyphausen and, with Lord Charles Cornwallis as his second in command, sets sail for Charleston, S.C., with the rest of his army. His expedition involves ninety transports carrying eight British and five Hessian regiments and five corps of Tory troops—8,500 men in all—along with artillery and cavalry. The convoy comprises five ships of the line and nine frigates with a total of 650 guns and 5,000 crewmen under the command of Adm. Marriot Arbuthnot.

★ 1780 ★

The deepening economic crisis affects Washington's army in winter quarters in New Jersey: It faces a food shortage, few clothes, and no pay. Severe cold makes matters worse. A mutiny, soon quelled, breaks out among Massachusetts troops over terms of enlistment. Supplies improve slightly in late January. Fortunately, there is little fighting in the northern theater; in fact, there is never again a major engagement north of Virginia.

The focus of the war during the year continues in to be on the South, where the British follow up their success at Savannah with an attack on Charleston, a city they had failed to take four years earlier. Benjamin Lincoln and his entire army are bottled up in the city by Sir Henry Clinton, who has sailed his force from New York in yet another demonstration of the potency of controlling the sea lanes. Charleston's seaward defenses have crumbled and lightning attacks by Banastre Tarleton, soon proven one of Clinton's most effective subordinates, close off Lincoln's possible escape routes. American militia bands prove no match for Tarleton's Loyalist British Legion. With British control of the harbor and no escape or relief possible by land, it is only a matter of time before Charleston must fall to siege. Lincoln is harassed by both Clinton and city and state officials. By mid-May he surrenders, turning over great numbers of prisoners and supplies to Clinton in the worst American defeat of the war. The British Southern strategy is working, and they now virtually control South Carolina as well as Georgia. The last remaining American force is wiped out by Tarleton at Waxhaw's Creek.

In the North, Knyphausen sallies into New Jersey but accomplishes little, except to burn buildings. In upstate New York, John Johnson and Joseph Brant renew raids in the Mohawk and Schoharie valleys.

Meanwhile, the comte de Rochambeau lands unmolested at Newport with 6,000 first-rate French troops. Washington's army is too weak however to take immediate advantage of the French presence.

In June Congress appoints Horatio Gates to command in the South (without consulting Washington). He meets his army in North Carolina, taking over from De Kalb, who has been in temporary command. The "hero of Saratoga" decides to confront Clinton and orders a march into South Carolina. Careless and incompetent, Gates forces a battle near Camden in mid-August. The American militia breaks during the first moments of battle, and the British sweep to victory, killing De Kalb and completely routing their enemy with severe losses. Gates himself turns tail and abandons the army, ending the day sixty miles to the rear.

Patriots are further stunned when General Benedict Arnold, now commanding at West Point, is revealed as a traitor and flees to the British just ahead of capture. His British contact, Maj. John André, is caught and hanged as a spy.

The first bright glimmer for the American cause comes in October, when a band of Western patriots defeats Patrick Ferguson's Loyalists at King's Mountain, S.C. This victory and the success of Francis Marion and Thomas Sumter in a partisan campaign force Clinton into winter quarters. Congress asks Washington to name a new commander for the Southern Department, and he chooses Nathanael Greene—who takes over the shattered army and plans a new campaign, relying on the help of Daniel Morgan. Green divides his army and sends Morgan west to draw out the British.

---

1 January 1780

WEST POINT, N.Y. A mutiny breaks out among members of the Massachusetts regiments that make up part of the garrison at West Point. The men had enlisted originally for three-year terms, and many erroneously believe that their time is up. About 100 men gather their equipment and march off toward home, but they are pursued and brought back to West Point. Most are pardoned and returned to duty.

2 January 1780

MORRISTOWN, N.J. Washington's troops continue to suffer from severe weather and lack of supplies while es-tablishing their winter quarters. Most of the men have built log huts, but shelter for the officers is still not finished. The movement to Morristown has been extremely difficult for many of the troops, and they arrive poorly fed and clothed. Moreover, the winter weather is the worst in many years with record-breaking cold that further saps energy and stamina. Surgeon James Thacher notes in his journal that all the baggage of his unit had to be left behind for want of transport, and "the snow on the ground is about two feet deep and the weather extremely cold; the soldiers are desti-tute of both tents and blankets and some of them are actually barefooted and almost naked."

9 January 1780

MORRISTOWN, N.J. Washington appeals to the governments of surrounding states to send food for the army, but the meager response fails to meet the need. Conditions in winter quarters deteriorate rapidly, and the men begin to forage for food among nearby communities. Washington writes: "They have been at last brought to such dreadful extremity that no authority or influence of the officers could any longer restrain them from obeying the dictates of their own sufferings. The soldiery have in several instances plundered the neighboring inhabitants even of their necessary subsistence."

10 January 1780

PHILADELPHIA. Congress moves to dismiss Maj. Gen. Charles Lee from the service of the United States. After his court-martial and suspension from command in 1778, Lee had retreated to his estate in the Shenandoah Valley. When his year's suspension expired in December 1779, he wrote to Congress about rumors of his permanent dismissal. The letter is so offensive that Congress decides finally to rid the army of his influence. Lee moves to Philadelphia and plays no further role in the Revolution.

14 January 1780

STATEN ISLAND, N.Y. Lord Stirling leads a raid against the British at Staten Island by moving 2,500 men across the ice and snow from Elizabeth Point by sled. The intent is to surprise the garrison, but the British detect the movement and retreat into

John Jay, the American Minister to Spain.

their fortifications. Stirling's force is unable to make an effective attack and spends the night exposed to sub-zero temperatures and deep snow. New Jersey civilians who came along as militia loot and ransack farms on Staten Island. The result of the raid is slight: seventeen prisoners and seizure of a small amount of food, tents, and arms. In return, six Americans are killed.

17 January 1780

MORRISTOWN, N.J. Provisions continue to dwindle for the army in winter quarters. Maj. Patten of the Delaware Regiment reports that the men must get by for five days on a ration of a half pound of salt beef and a half pint of rice, "without any other kind of support whatever."

25 January 1780

NEWARK AND ELIZABETH, N.J. The British raid in retaliation for the American attack on Staten Island ten days before. They burn the academy at Newark and the courthouse and meetinghouse in Elizabeth.

26 January 1780

PHILADELPHIA. The court-martial of Benedict Arnold on charges of financial speculation and misuse of his civilian powers while in charge of Philadelphia delivers a sentence that formally finds him guilty on two minor charges and dismisses two others. This is a virtual vindication of Arnold and carries only the slimmest penalty—a reprimand from the commander-in-chief, Washington. Arnold, however, is incensed that he has not been completely exonerated. He expected a complete acquittal after conducting his own defense.

27 January 1780

MORRISTOWN, N.J. Supplies of food improve for the army after Washington reorganizes the system of requisition from New Jersey. He divides the state into eleven districts, each of which must contribute an allotment of food. Officers are dispatched to collect grain and cattle under threat of force. The scheme works, and the plight of the army is relieved immediately. Washington writes to Congress: "The situation of the Army for the present is, and has been for some days past, comfortable and easy on the score of provisions."

28 January 1780

TENNESSEE. A fort is established on the Tennessee River, called Fort Nashborough (modern-day Nashville), as part of a system of defenses against Indian attacks. Tennessee is part of the western lands claimed by North

POPULATION

The estimated population of the thirteen colonies in 1770, before the Revolution, was slightly over 2 million, including around 500,000 black slaves. By 1780, it is estimated that the population had grown to nearly 2.8 million. This provided a military pool of approximately 175,000 men from which the armed forces of the rebellion were drawn, including Loyalists who fought on the British side. The historical estimates for the thirteen states, plus Vermont, Maine and the Western territories of Kentucky and Tennessee in 1780 are:

Connecticut 206,701	New Jersey 139,627
Delaware 45,385	New York 210,541
Georgia 56,071	North Carolina 270,133
Kentucky 45,000	Pennsylvania 327,305
Maine 49,133	Rhode Island 52,946
Maryland 245,474	South Carolina 180,000
Massachusetts 268,627	Tennessee 10,000
New Hampshire 87,802	Vermont 47,620

Carolina, but the state can do little to support settlers in the West since the British threaten all along the coast. The westerners name their fort after North Carolina Gov. Abner Nash, who is nonetheless powerless to help them.

1 February 1780

SAVANNAH, GA. The British expedition under Gen. Henry Clinton arrives aboard ships commanded by Adm. Marriot Arbuthnot. The force is headed toward Charleston. The British strategy to pry Southern states loose from the American cause will take another step forward with the imminent assault on Charleston, a major seaport hitherto held firmly by the patriots, who had valiantly fought off a British attack four years before. The seaward approaches to Charleston are a web of islands and channels that should have been easy to defend, but the forts in the harbor have been allowed to deteriorate. To the landward side, the city stands between two rivers, with only a few certain routes in and out. Gen. Benjamin Lincoln of Massachusetts, the commander of American forces, has concentrated his troops in the city. He has comparatively few regulars—800 Continental infantry and about 380 survivors of Pulaski's Legion—and 2,000 militia from North and South Carolina, and he vacillates between escaping to fight another day and preparing to withstand a siege. Quick footwork might save his army, but Lincoln is under strong political pressure from Gov. Edward Rutledge, Lt. Gov. Christopher Gadsden, and Charleston officials to defend the city.

3 February 1780

YOUNG'S HOUSE, N.Y. In an engage-ment typical of the limited but nasty fighting in the North during the winter, a large British force under Lt. Col. Chapple Norton issues from Fort Knyphausen (formerly Fort Washington) in an attempt to catch Lt. Col. Joseph Thompson's five Connecticut companies (supported by more troops from Massachusetts) that are on roving patrol in Westchester County. Thompson incautiously allows Norton's advance units to approach too closely, and his outposts are captured. A tough, brief fight follows. The British surround the Continentals, some of whom take refuge in the house of Joseph Young before retreating. The British losses are five killed and eighteen wounded; fourteen Americans are killed, thirty-seven wounded, and seventy-six taken prisoner.

9 February 1780

PHILADELPHIA. Congress asks the states to furnish 35,000 more men to the revolutionary cause by draft before 1 April and to contribute $1.2 million monthly to the national treasury. The campaigns in the North and the prolonged and deepening financial crisis demand solutions, but the states—as usual by this stage of the Revolution—are either powerless or unwilling to comply. While still for the most part committed to the cause, individual states and regions are weary of war and disruption and look increasingly to solving their own difficulties rather than to the needs of Congress. Washington writes in despair: "One state will comply with a requisition of Congress, another neglects to do it, a third executes it by halves, and all differ in the manner, the matter, or so much in point of time, that we are always working uphill."

10 February 1780

SAVANNAH, GA. Clinton's force leaves anchorage in the Savannah River and sails toward Charleston. A few troops move overland, but most of Clinton's army is aboard ship, eager to see land after a difficult, stormy voyage from New York.

11 February 1780

CHARLESTON, S.C. Clinton sails into North Edisto Inlet and lands his expedition on Johns Island at the mouth of Charleston Harbor. The landing is unopposed, and the troops rapidly begin preparations to move. The initial force includes around 8,500 British regulars and Loyalist units, vastly outnumbering Lincoln's garrison in the city.

12 February 1780

CHARLESTON. Lincoln's defenses against direct assault over land are strong. The complex system of waterways makes the approaches hazardous, even though they also make escape difficult for the defenders. The fortifications are anchored between the Ashley and the Cooper rivers, with marshes, strong earthworks, and gun positions in between.

14 February 1780

CHARLESTON. Clinton begins a leisurely series of moves to hem in the Americans. He pushes forward to establish a base at Stono Ferry above the city and occupies all of James Island. He begins to build up his supply base ashore and waits for Arbuthnot to enter the harbor and provide heavy guns for the siege.

23 February 1780

SOUTH CAROLINA. The British Legion of Lt. Col. Banastre Tarleton surprises a small force of patriot militia, killing ten and taking four prisoner. The legion is made up of Loyalist heavy dragoons and mounted infantry. Their regular-army leader is soon to become the most feared British commander in the Southern campaign, known for his daring, energy, and implacable cruelty. Tarleton welcomes the victory and the horses captured from the American militia since his own mounts died during the long voyage south and he needs fresh animals for his troopers.

26 February 1780

ASHLEY RIVER, S.C. Tarleton's legionnaires meet Col. William Washington's horse troops along the banks of the river and are pushed back. The Americans take several prisoners, but withdraw to join other forces near Monck's Corner.

29 February 1780

ST. PETERSBURG, RUSSIA. Empress Catherine declares the formation of the League of Armed Neutrals. Russia, Denmark, and Sweden are to form a treaty alliance of neutrals whose ships may not be seized or boarded by belligerents. Eventually joined by other European nations, the Armed Neutrality attempts to keep commerce flowing without hindrance (and to make money for its own merchants). The principles laid down in the treaty include free navigation, free passage of cargo on neutral ships, limited definition of blockades, and legal disposition of prizes taken on the seas. Britain ignores the Armed Neutrality, but France and the United States accept it wholeheartedly. Although an important precedent in establishing the principles of neutrality on the seas during wartime, the league has little actual effect during the War of the Revolution.

1 March 1780

PHILADELPHIA. A Pennsylvania act calls for the gradual emancipation of black slaves. From the beginning of the war, both slaves and free black men have enlisted in the Continental Army and fought well in the Northern campaigns. Many free blacks have volunteered, but most slaves are sent to serve as substitutes for their white masters. The Southern states, however, refuse to allow black slaves to be used as armed troops in that region.

3 March 1780

CHARLESTON. Benjamin Lincoln's forces are increased by the arrival of 700 North Carolina Continentals, sent overland on a march of three months through winter weather to stiffen the defense of the city. Unfortunately, an equal number of North Carolina militia leave at the same time. Lincoln's total manpower stays the same.

5 March 1780

CHARLESTON. Workers continue to build and improve the defenses of the city. Gov. Edward Rutledge has requisitioned the services of 600 black slaves to construct more earthworks. The main defensive point is a redoubt surmounted with stonework, called The Citadel.

14 March 1780

MOBILE. Bernardo de Galvez, the energetic Spanish governor of Florida and Louisiana, captures the British post at Mobile. With only a few ships but nearly 1,400 men, Galvez attacks the 300-man British garrison under Elias Dunford. A British relief column from Pensacola fails to reach Mobile in time, and Dunford surrenders after two days of fighting. The outpost had been established by the British in support of its naval base on Jamaica.

18 March 1780

PHILADELPHIA. Congress finally is forced to acknowledge the severe depreciation of the value of its currency and sets the ratio of paper to specie at forty to one. Congress will now retire the paper money in circulation by accepting it as payment for levies due from the states at only one-fortieth of its face value. In fact, specie (hard money) is by this stage practically nonexistent in the national treasury, and Continental dollars are headed toward complete worthlessness. Inflation reaches a wartime high, with prices nearly three times higher than the previous year and nearly a hundred times greater than in 1776.

19 March 1780

CHARLESTON. Gen. Sir Henry Clinton learns that the resignation he had submitted earlier has been rejected. He hoped to hand over command to Cornwallis and return to England, but he now understands he must play out the hand and take Charleston. He has delayed vigorous action for five weeks since landing. He orders more troops south from Savannah to join him.

20 March 1780

CHARLESTON. The only American naval force, a small fleet that had been purchased from French admiral d'Estaing, withdraws up the mouth of the Cooper River under the command of Commodore Whipple. He cannot hope to resist the British squadron, so most of the ships and small boats are sunk in the channel in order to obstruct British navigation on the river. On the same day Arbuthnot finally forces a crossing of the bar in Charleston Harbor and has his ships in position to support the British attack on the city.

22 March 1780

HACKENSACK, N.J. German Gen. Knyphausen, left in command of New York when Clinton sailed for the Carolinas, crosses into New Jersey for a pillaging raid on Hackensack with a force of 400 mixed British troops and German mercenaries. The city is undefended, and the troops break into homes and carry off booty before setting fire to the courthouse and several private houses.

25 March 1780

CHARLESTON. Reinforcements for Clinton arrive overland, and he is also joined by Tarleton's Legion and Ferguson's American Rangers, a Loyalist infantry unit.

27 March 1780

PENSACOLA. Galvez, fresh from the capture of the British fort at Mobile, sails past the British post here—the seat of British government in West Florida—but is unable to attack.

28–29 March 1780

CHARLESTON. During the night, Clinton's troops cross the Ashley River by boat and take up positions unopposed across the peninsula leading to Charleston. This effectively cuts off Lincoln's main line of retreat

and almost seals the American garrison into the city, although a slim route still is open along the Cooper River, north to Biggin's Bridge. However, Clinton is now free to move south and begin siege operations.

1 April 1780

CHARLESTON. Clinton breaks ground within 800 yards of the American fortifications to begin the siege approach works. The defenders can only look on helplessly as the British engineers begin digging a series of trenches that will almost inevitably result in taking the city.

6 April 1780

PHILADELPHIA. Commander-in-chief George Washington sends an official letter of reprimand to Maj. Gen. Benedict Arnold, as required by the terms of Arnold's conviction by a court-martial. Washington declares that he considers Arnold's conduct "reprehensible both in a civil and military view" as well as "imprudent and improper."

CHARLESTON. Gen. William Woodford arrives with 750 Virginia Continentals to reinforce Lincoln's garrison. The men have marched 500 miles in only twenty-eight days and slipped past the British into the city.

8 April 1780

CHARLESTON. Eight of Arbuthnot's frigates and an additional six supply transports run past the defenses of Fort Moultrie with little damage and anchor between James Island and the city. The British suffer six dead, but now control almost all approaches to Charleston.

10 April 1780

CHARLESTON. With his first parallel of siege works nearing completion, Clinton calls on Lincoln to surrender. The American commander could still manage a retreat up the Cooper River but decides to remain in the city. His refusal to surrender means the siege will proceed.

12 April 1780

CHARLESTON. Tarleton and Ferguson begin to move their troops up the Cooper River into position for an attack against the last remaining American forces outside the city, those under the command of Gen. Isaac Huger near Monck's Corner.

13 April 1780

CHARLESTON. The British unleash a major bombardment of the city from batteries on James Island. Red-hot shot sets fires in Charleston, and the aerial bombs damage many buildings, although there is little loss of life. Lincoln calls a council of war with his officers but declines once again to leave the city without more reflection. He asks his officers to consider a while longer.

14 April 1780

MONCKS CORNER, S.C. Lincoln's last hope is snuffed out when Tarleton and Ferguson sweep down on the Americans at Monck's Corner, catching them unawares and unprepared to fight. Huger has failed to set out patrols or adequate sentries, and the British achieve complete surprise. Tarleton seizes 400 mounts for his dragoons as well as forty-two wagonloads of supplies. The Americans suffer twenty killed or wounded and

sixty-seven are taken prisoner. Maj. Pierre Vernier, now in command of Pulaski's Legion, is killed in the battle, and Huger and William Washington barely escape through the swamps. The British lose only two casualties. More important, they now block the last escape route for Lincoln's garrison in Charleston.

17 April 1780

WEST INDIES. A French naval squadron under Adm. Luc Urbain de Guichen engages a British squadron under Adm. George Rodney off Martinique. The British handle the battle poorly, and Guichen's ships escape the inconclusive contest.

18 April 1780

CHARLESTON. Lord Rawdon arrives with more men for Clinton, who now has a total of nearly 10,000 troops on land and 5,000 more seamen aboard ships in the harbor.

19 April 1780

CHARLESTON. With Clinton's trenches now within 250 yards, Lincoln calls another council to consider surrender and saving his force for later campaigns, but North Carolina Lt. Gov. Gadsden insists Lincoln stay and fight. Gadsden threatens a civilian insurrection if Lincoln attempts to surrender. The military commander is stymied with Clinton to his front and the civilian authorities to his rear.

21 April 1780

CHARLESTON. Realizing that resistance is futile, Lincoln proposes a surrender to Clinton despite the pressure from Gadsden and the city fathers. Clinton refuses the terms, however, and continues the siege.

23–24 April 1780

CHARLESTON. The Americans try a half-hearted night sortie against the British. Led by Lt. Col. Henderson, troops from Virginia and the Carolinas attack the first line of British works with bayonets, but are halted and pushed back at the second line. The attempt accomplishes little except the death of several American and British soldiers.

27 April 1780

CHARLESTON. The British reach a flooded ditch just in front of the American defenses. They now employ 200 workers at a time, round the clock, to dig forward, and they man the trenches with 1,200 troops.

28 April 1780

BOSTON. The Marquis de Lafayette lands after more than a year's absence in France. He has helped work out the terms of French military assistance to the Americans, and he brings with him French commissions for Washington as both a lieutenant general and a vice admiral. Lafayette hopes the formal rank will assist Washington in dealing with Rochambeau and the other French commanders who are due to appear later in the year.

6 May 1780

LENUD'S FERRY, S.C. Tarleton springs again, routing a ragtag American force that had tried to rally at this river crossing near the Santee. Without loss to themselves, Tarleton's men kill or wound forty Americans and capture more horses. Col. William Washington is again sent scrambling for escape from Tarleton's green-coated dragoons.

7 May 1780

CHARLESTON. The British land troops on Sullivan's Island in the harbor and capture the remaining garrison of Fort Moultrie, about 200 Americans left behind when the fort was essentially abandoned.

8 May 1780

CHARLESTON. Clinton issues another summons to Lincoln to surrender, but the American commander rejects it and continues to press for better terms.

9 May 1780

CHARLESTON. A horrendous nighttime barrage of artillery fire from both sides terrifies the civilians of the city, who finally petition Lincoln to surrender.

12 May 1780

CHARLESTON. Lincoln accepts Clinton's terms and surrenders the garrison and city. It is the greatest defeat of the war for the Americans. All of Lincoln's troops march out with colors cased to lay down their arms. The British capture nearly 5,000 men, almost 400 guns, close to 6,000 muskets, and thousands of rounds of ammunition. Lincoln has been forced to agree that his regular Continentals will become prisoners of war, although the militia are allowed to return to their homes under parole. It is also agreed that many revolutionary leaders are to be held as prisoners and effectively removed from further involvement in the war or politics—only Gov. Rutledge escapes the British triumph. Actual casualties on both sides have been comparatively light, but the defeat is a

PRISONERS OF WAR

The treatment and handling of prisoners of war during the American Revolution were significant problems for both sides. Neither anticipated when the war began the large numbers of prisoners they would have to deal with. Aside from the normal small-scale surrenders during six years of warfare, there were also several incidences of large-scale capture.

The normal practice was to arrange for parole and exchange whenever possible. A captured soldier, most often an officer rather than privates or noncoms, might be freed after giving his parole to not serve against the captor until properly exchanged. This freed the captor from the burdens of feeding, housing, and transporting prisoners. The later exchange was a simple switch of prisoners between sides. In the case of high-ranking officers, the exchange usually had to be on an equal level, but in 1779 a ratio of officers to private soldiers was worked out so a sergeant could be exchanged for two privates; an ensign for four; a lieutenant for six; a captain for sixteen; a major for twenty-eight; a lieutenant colonel for seventy-two; a colonel for 100; a brigadier general for 200; a major general for 372; and a lieutenant general (of which the Continental Army had none) for 1,044.

The conditions for prisoners not exchanged were generally gruesome. The British were unable to care adequately for most of the Americans they captured, and thousands died in horrible circumstances—especially aboard the prison ships in New York, where many of the more than 4,000 American prisoners taken in the campaign of 1776 were held. No accurate records exist, but estimates run as high as 11,000 prisoner deaths in New York alone. More than 5,000 Americans were captured in 1780 at the fall of Charleston and held for thirteen months, some of them in a dungeon beneath the Old Exchange.

British who fell into American hands fared better on the whole. The 5,000 prisoners captured after Burgoyne's surrender at Saratoga became the famous "Convention Army" under the terms of the unusual document of surrender. They were to have been evacuated from Boston under a mass parole, but Congress disputed the terms and retained the prisoners, marching them through New England, Pennsylvania, and Virginia over the next four years. Other large contingents, such as the nearly 1,000 German mercenaries taken at Trenton, were allowed to escape and join the general farm population of the middle states.

disaster for the American cause. South Carolina now lies open to the British.

14 May 1780

SOUTH CAROLINA. Abraham Buford's regiment is now the only American force left at large in the entire state of South Carolina. He is ordered to retreat toward Hillsboro in order to save a remnant of a fighting presence.

18 May 1780

SOUTH CAROLINA. Lord Cornwallis sets out in pursuit of Buford from Huger's Bridge. He moves rapidly up the Santee River but cannot gain on the fleeing Americans. He halts his march and turns the task of catching Buford over to the swift Tarleton.

19 May 1780

BOSTON. At 10:00 A.M. a blotting of the sun strikes fear into residents. In the words of the *Boston Country Journal*: "Many persons were much frightened at the sudden darkness, and some thought that judgment-day had come." Others made scientific observations, noting that the darkness extended until well into the afternoon. One group in Ipswich dined by candlelight at 2:00 P.M. Men of "liberal education" conclude that a pall of smoke from a nearby forest fire has caused the phenomenon.

21 May 1780

JOHNSTOWN, N.Y. Sir John Johnson with 400 Loyalists and 200 Indians attacks the settlements here after sailing up Lake Champlain to Crown Point and then moving undetected across land. His well-organized raid comes in response to the depredations of Sullivan's campaign the year before.

22 May 1780

JOHNSTOWN AND CAUGHNAWAGA, N.Y. With half of his forces holding Johnstown, Johnson dispatches the rest to Caughnawaga, where they burn houses and kill settlers along the way. The Mohawk Valley is aflame again.

23 May 1780

MOHAWK VALLEY, N.Y. Johnson's split force reunites and marches on, leaving more destruction in its wake. Every property not belonging to a Loyalist is destroyed, and many settlers are killed. Johnson finally reaches Crown Point and withdraws.

25 May 1780

MORRISTOWN, N.J. Still ill-fed and with their pay five months in arrears, the Continental troops in Washington's winter quarters have nearly reached their limits. Two regiments from Connecticut decide to leave in search of food. One man hits Col. R. J. Meigs when the acting brigade commander tries to stop them, but order is restored by the appearance of the Pennsylvania Line. The Connecticut dissidents return to their huts, and a few are arrested. No action is taken against them, however.

26 May 1780

ST. LOUIS. The Spanish fort at St. Louis (called San Luis de Ylinoises) is attacked by a mixed force of British regulars and Indian auxiliaries from Michilimackinac. The Spanish, under commander Capt. Fernando de Leyba, repulse the attack although there are only a small number of soldiers among the inhabitants.

29 May 1780

WAXHAWS CREEK, S.C. After an incredibly rapid movement through hot weather with tired men and horses, Tarleton catches up with Abraham Buford's force of Virginia Continentals and mixed cavalry at Waxhaws Creek near the North Carolina border.

Tarleton has about 230 of his Loyalists and 40 men from the 17th Dragoons. Buford outnumbers the British but is caught on the move and is ill-prepared to turn and fight. When Tarleton sends a demand for surrender under flag of truce, Buford dithers but decides to make a stand. Tarleton manages the battle skillfully, and his mounted troops smash the American dispositions—a cavalry charge breaking the line when Buford foolishly withholds fire until too late. Those Americans not killed or wounded try to surrender, but Tarleton's men cut them down with sword and bayonet, leading to subsequent claims that the aftermath of the battle was a massacre and giving rise to the ironic term *Tarleton's quarter*. The American losses are 113 dead and 203 captured, most of them wounded. Tarleton has lost only nineteen dead and wounded. With the victory, Tarleton extinguishes the last organized resistance to British power in South Carolina.

2 June 1780

CARIBBEAN. The thirty-gun United States frigate *Trumbull* under Captain James Nicholson meets the British privateer *Watt*, commanded by John Coulthard, in the waters off Bermuda. The ships are evenly matched and fight a fierce ship-to-ship battle. Both are badly damaged but neither can gain the advantage. After two and a half hours they disengage and head for port. Nicholson reports eighteen killed and twenty-one wounded. Coulthard suffers thirteen dead and seventy-nine wounded.

2–9 June 1780

LONDON. Mobs of up to 60,000 take to the streets with massive violence over the issue of the political rights of Roman Catholics. Lord George Gordon, an Irish peer, has formed a Protestant Association to oppose the introduction into Parliament of a bill to remove restrictions against Catholics. His agitation sets off large-scale riots in which Catholic homes and chapels as well as public buildings are destroyed over several days and nights of pillaging. The House of Commons is besieged by the mob, and members of Parliament have to be rescued by the police. Finally quelled by the army, the Gordon Riots point up the basic hostility of the mob toward government and throw British politics into momentary disarray.

6 June 1780

DE HART'S POINT, N.J. Knyphausen decides to move in force into New Jersey after he hears reports of the sorry condition of Washington's army at Morristown. The German general, temporarily in command of all British forces in New York, hopes to either win over the mutinous soldiery of the Continental Army or strike a blow to their fighting ability. He lands 5,000 men on the Jersey shore and begins to march the next day.

7 June 1780

CONNECTICUT FARMS, N.J. Knyphausen discovers resistance on the road from a regiment of Continental infantry under Col. Elias Dayton, supported by local militia—the latter fact giving the lie to Knyphausen's intelligence about disaffection. Washington, however, is so weak that he can do little but encourage Dayton to hold since no force is immediately available. Knyphausen's men attempt to cross the Rahway River but are turned back by American fire. After burning several farms, the British and Germans withdraw again to De Hart's Point, where they begin to dig in.

8 June 1780

CHARLESTON. Gen. Henry Clinton, satisfied with his capture of Charleston, prepares to return to New York, leaving Cornwallis in command of the Southern campaign. Clinton writes optimistically to Lord George Germain in England: "I may venture to assert that there are few men in South Carolina who are not either our prisoners or in arms with us."

13 June 1780

PHILADELPHIA. Congress unilaterally appoints Horatio Gates to command of the army in the Southern Department. The members neglect to consult Washington, who much prefers Nathanael Greene to Gates, a man who had tried to unseat the commander-in-chief three years previously. Congress is convinced, however, that the "hero of Saratoga" is just the general to redeem American fortunes in the Carolinas. Washington's stock is low among delegates. Gates, on the other hand, enjoys great popularity with Congress, although members have scarcely any idea of his real military abilities.

20 June 1780

RAMSUR'S MILL, N.C. A vicious, if disorganized, battle takes place between North Carolina Loyalists and patriot militia. Neither side is a trained or disciplined military force, and there is more than a tinge of settling old local scores to the encounter. The Loyalists have been assembled by Col. John Moore, who had served under Cornwallis during the preceding months in South Carolina. He is under instruc-

tions to delay any Loyalist uprising, but he moves precipitously and gathers nearly 1,300 men, many unarmed. In response, 1,200 patriot militia assemble under Col. Francis Locke, determined to nip the Loyalist threat before it can be backed up by Cornwallis' army. The patriots attack the Loyalist camp, and a unorganized battle ensues with much hand-to-hand scuffling and confused movements. Moore's forces are routed and flee the scene, thus severely damaging Cornwallis' ability to draw on Loyalists during his forthcoming campaign into North Carolina.

21 June 1780

HILLSBORO, N.C. Maj. Gen. Johann de Kalb arrives with 1,400 men—Smallwood's Marylanders and Gist's Delaware Continentals—some of the best American troops of the war. They have marched rapidly all the way from Morristown to buttress the defenses of Charleston, but the city is already lost. They arrive tired and ill-nourished. De Kalb's appeal to local authorities for food and supplies goes unanswered.

23 June 1780

SPRINGFIELD, N.J. Washington has watched warily for weeks while Knyphausen's troops hold their entrenched positions on the Jersey shore across from Staten Island. Worried over possible new British offensives up the Hudson, the commander-in-chief positions first-rate troops under Nathanael Greene to oppose Knyphausen, should the German general attempt a move. British commander Sir Henry Clinton, returned from his triumph in South Carolina, orders Knyphausen to advance into New Jersey as an attempt to draw Washington's strength away from New York. Greene, however, is in Knyphausen's path, and his troops—backed by New Jersey militia—are ready. When Knyphausen divides his force near Springfield, the flanking movement is stymied by Lee's horse and Dayton's New Jersey infantry. A frontal assault against Greene fails, and Knyphausen is forced to withdraw all the way to Staten Island after burning and destroying property in Springfield. Losses to both sides are impossible to determine, but appear to be light considering the size of the forces involved—at least 5,000 on the British side. The upshot is to clear New Jersey of British troops once again.

10 July 1780

NEWPORT, R.I.   A French fleet of eight ships of the line, two frigates, and two bomb vessels arrives off Newport, more than seventy days out of Brest. Aboard are the comte de Rochambeau, appointed commander of French forces in America, and nearly 6,000 first-line troops. They make up the first division of the promised French army that is to assist the faltering American military cause. Rochambeau is a veteran soldier of France, promoted to lieutenant general for this assignment. Unfortunately, the balance of his designated force—nearly 2,000 more men—has been left behind for lack of transport and never reaches America.

11 July 1780

NEWPORT, R.I.   Rochambeau and his entourage of officers come ashore by cutter to find the streets of Newport nearly empty and no American welcoming party to greet the allies: "No

one about in the streets; only a few sad and frightened faces in the windows," as Rochambeau later writes. He searches out local officials and identifies himself. Finally, Gen. William Heath arrives on the scene as Washington's representative and takes matters in hand.

Comte de Rochambeau, the French commander.

12 July 1780

WILLIAMSON'S PLANTATION, S.C.   A motley patriot militia force of about 350 men (150 more stray from the scene and play no role in the day's activities) under a disorganized group of officers with Gen. Thomas Sumter more or less at its head, moves against Capt. Christian Houk's 400 Loyalists and dragoons. Houk has been sent out to organize Loyalists and suppress patriot militia. Despite their lack of unified command, the Americans manage at dawn to get into position between the Loyalists and their picketed horses. They blast the opposition, killing Houk. The Loyalists flee the scene, leaving thirty to forty dead and fifty wounded. The Americans suffer only one casualty.

13 July 1780

SANDY HOOK, N.Y. Adm. Thomas Graves arrives off New York with a powerful British squadron, but he is too late to intercept French admiral deTernay's ships that have already reached Newport and unloaded the French expedition. Sir Henry Clinton had learned previously from Benedict Arnold that Rochambeau was to land in Rhode Island, but coordination of British land and sea operations is faulty and the commander can do nothing to prevent the addition of the French troops to the American cause.

25 July 1780

COXE'S MILL, N.C. Gen. Horatio Gates arrives from his plantation in Virginia and assumes command of the Southern Department. De Kalb, who even though a foreigner has been nominally in command, gratefully turns over responsibility to Gates on the assumption the new commander can wrest food and supplies for his troops from the local authorities—a task that has defeated the Bavarian. Gates confirms De Kalb in command of the Delaware and Maryland troops and a few survivors of Armand's Legion. Gates grandiloquently designates his relatively small force as the "grand army" and determines to move on the British at Camden.

27 July 1780

NORTH CAROLINA. Gates begins to march south, taking a direct route toward Camden that will bring him quickly into range of the enemy but

that also leads through picked-over territory that cannot support his already sick and ill-fed troops.

30 July 1780

(FORT ANDERSON) THICKETY FORT, S.C. Western colonel Isaac Shelby, an Indian fighter from the Tennessee region, surrounds a Loyalist post near Cowpens and induces the defenders to give up without a shot.

1 August 1780

ROCKY MOUNT, S.C. Thomas Sumter has gathered more militia after his victory at Williamson's Plantation and now wants to hit the British lines of support while Gates moves toward Camden. Sumter leads 600 militia men against a miniature fort at Rocky Mount held by Loyalists as an outpost to protect the British army at Camden. The defenders are few, mostly northern Loyalist troops, but they retreat into their strong log fortifications and Sumter's attempts to burn them out fail. He is forced to withdraw.

2 August 1780

MOHAWK VALLEY, N.Y. Joseph Brant and his Loyalist allies continue to raid settlements in New York throughout the late summer.

3 August 1780

MASK'S FERRY, N.C. Gates' army crosses the Pee Dee River and is joined by a handful of Virginia militia who have eluded the British since the fall of Charleston. An odd-looking colonel with a ragged band of twenty followers also turns up—Francis Marion and his men are laughed at by Gates' regulars, but they shrug off the derision and return to South Carolina to scout.

5 August 1780

WEST POINT, N.Y. Maj. Gen. Benedict Arnold is appointed to command this important American post on the Hudson. Arnold has been in treasonous correspondence with British headquarters for more than a year, and he has maneuvered himself to get a significant command in order to hand it over to the enemy. He demands a 10,000-pound payment from the British for his information and double that amount if he can deliver a substantial body of troops and a key American post.

LYNCHES CREEK, S.C. Former governor Richard Caswell, who has been roving the state with a force of over 2,000 well-supplied North Carolina militia, joins Gates, and the combined army continues toward Camden. Despite the provisions brought in by Caswell, the general state of the troops is low. Most had begun the march after weeks of poor food and scant rest, and they find little along their route to sustain them. Green corn and peaches, plucked from the fields and orchards along the line of march, cause "the usual physical results."

6 August 1780

HANGING ROCK, S.C. Sumter is determined to renew attacks on Loyalist-defended outposts, and he moves against this stronghold, which is manned by members of the British Legion as well as portions of North and South Carolina Loyalist regiments. Sumter has considerable infantry on foot and good mounted troops. His initial attack is highly successful, and many Loyalists are cut down outside their defensive perimeter during the first early-morning engagements. While hotly pressing the Loyalist center, Sumter's men are flanked but turn and repulse the attack. The Loyalist resistance all but collapses, and Sumter's men begin to loot the camp's supplies. A small but effective force of Loyalist mounted infantry happens on the scene and renews the battle. Sumter is unable to rally his militia men from their looting and is forced to break off and withdraw. The Loyalists have lost 192 casualties, Sumter only twelve killed and fifty-one wounded.

11 August 1780

LITTLE LYNCHES CREEK, S.C. Gates finds Lord Rawdon opposing the crossing and attempts to move to the right and flank the British. The maneuver is clumsily executed, however, and Rawdon withdraws toward Camden, only fifteen miles distant. Gates has little choice but to press on toward the city, where the British are concentrating their forces. The Americans continue to find little food along their march, and Gates must either turn toward Waxhaws, where supplies may be found, or move on to engage the main British army.

13 August 1780

CAMDEN, S.C. Lord Cornwallis reaches Camden and takes command from Lord Rawdon. The British have called in troops from outposts and now number about 2,200. Almost all are proved and effective troops: either British regular units, such as the 23rd Regiment of the Royal Welch Fusiliers, the 33rd West Riding Regiment, and Fraser's 71st Highlanders, or tested Loyalists like Tarleton's British Legion. Cornwallis knows, however, that he is badly outnumbered. Nevertheless, he resolves to give battle to Gates.

14 August 1780

NEAR CAMDEN, S.C. Seven hundred more militia from Virginia join Gates' army. He now has about 4,100 men assembled, although many are in poor physical condition. Oddly, Gates thinks his army numbers 7,000 and refuses to believe Otho Williams' report that only half that many are fit and ready to fight. "There are enough for our purposes," he tells his aide.

15 August 1780

WATEREE FERRY, S.C. Sumter continues to raid the British supply lines after being reinforced with a hundred of Gates' Maryland Continentals and 300 North Carolina militia. He hits a post at Wateree Ferry and carries off food, clothing, rum, and prisoners, and later in the day captures a supply train headed for the British army at Camden.

NEAR CAMDEN, S.C. Gates cannot benefit from Sumter's success as he attempts to prepare his troops for battle. He makes an ill-advised decision to issue a ration of molasses since there is no rum. The men discover to their dismay that the mixture of molasses and poor food causes severe gastric distress. Deputy adjutant Williams reports most were forced to fall out of ranks for relief during the night and were "much debilitated" by morning.

16 August 1780

CAMDEN, S.C. During the night, Gates begins a march down the main road toward the town. Nearly simultaneously, Cornwallis moves out on

The American defeat at the Battle of Camden, South Carolina.

the same thoroughfare, intent on finding Gates' army. At about 2:30 A.M. the two forces meet and the first shots of battle are fired. The scene of conflict is a wide, sandy space littered with pines and hemmed in on both sides by swampland. Both forces cease fire after the first engagement and await the morning light. Gates holds a slightly advantageous position, and Cornwallis' rear is dangerously close to a creek. Lt. Col. James Webster commands the British right, made up of the Royal Welch Fusiliers, the Volunteers of Ireland (Irish deserters from the American army), and North Carolina Loyalist militia. To the British left are the 71st (Fraser's) Highlanders under Rawdon. Tarleton's men form up in reserve behind the Highlanders. Gates' disposition puts his militia on his left, opposite British regulars, and concentrates his best troops—Maryland and Delaware Continentals under Gist—on the right under the command of De Kalb. Smallwood's 1st Maryland is to the rear in reserve. Gates himself takes a position hundreds of yard to the rear, and after a few initial comments, issues no further orders and takes no active part in the battle. The burden of battlefield command falls to Ortho Williams, De Kalb, and a few other enterprising officers. Nearly as soon as the British launch against the American left wing, the Virginia and North Carolina militia panic, throw down their loaded arms, and run for the rear. Half of the American line collapses almost before the battle begins. As Williams describes the panic: "The best disciplined troops have been enervated and made coward by it. Armies have been routed by it, even where no enemy appeared to furnish an excuse." Despite the disaster, the seasoned Americans on the right wing disregard the flight of their amateur colleagues and prepare to fight. The Marylanders and Delaware troops meet Rawdon's attack and hold steady, despite pressure on their left flank from Williamson's wheeling fusiliers. Williams takes command of the Maryland reserve and tries to rally, but after two valiant stands, he is swept away. De Kalb holds firm, but he suffers from several wounds and his position is now hope-

The wounding of Baron de Kalb at Camden; he had come to America with Lafayette.

less, his men attacked from all points: the British infantry hit the front and sides of the American formation, and Tarleton strikes from the rear. De Kalb finally falls, mortally wounded by multiple gunshots and saber cuts. Only a small number of the Maryland and Delaware troops manage to retreat. What is left of the army flees northward, with Tarleton's horseriders in deadly pursuit. Losses on the American side are horrendous: only 700 of the original 4,100 reach safety at Hillsboro three days later, and the rout is so complete no accurate casualty figures can be compiled. It appears likely that 800 to 900 Americans have been killed and nearly 1,000 more taken prisoner. The British lose 68 killed and about 350 wounded. The British victory is total, and Gates' army has been virtually destroyed. Small groups with no cohesion struggle toward Hillsboro. Gates himself is nowhere to be found. When the left wing collapses during the first moments of the battle, he turns to the rear and flees. At Rugeley's Mill he requisitions a fast horse and gallops for his life away from Camden. By nightfall of the same day he is in Charlotte, sixty miles distant from the battlefield, and he arrives in Hillsboro—a full 120 miles more—three days later.

18 August 1780

FISHING CREEK, S.C. Tarleton completes the British triumph by surprising Thomas Sumter literally asleep and recapturing all the stores Sumter had seized during the week before. Swooping down on Sumter's unguarded camp, Tarleton's men kill 150 Americans and take 300 prisoners.

MUSGROVE MILLS, S.C.   To the west, Isaac Shelby and Elijah Clarke engage Loyalists on the Enoree River and succeed in killing sixty-three.

3 September 1780

OFF NEWFOUNDLAND.   The British capture the American brig *Mercury*. On board is Henry Laurens, on his way to Holland to replace John Adams as American representative and hoping to negotiate a ten-million-dollar loan for the United States. Laurens, a wealthy merchant and one of South Carolina's most prominent revolutionaries, served as president of the Continental Congress until he resigned in late 1778 over the Silas Deane affair. He had been appointed to the Dutch post in November 1779 but did not sail until 13 August 1780. As the British approach, he throws his papers overboard, but they are retrieved by the British and subsequently play an important role in the British decision to declare war on the Netherlands. Laurens is taken to London as a prisoner of war.

15 September 1780

AUGUSTA, GA.   Conflict between patriot and Loyalist irregulars continues in the South. The Loyalists have established a strong post at Augusta, which patriots under Col. Elijah Clarke and Lt. Col. James McCall decide to attack. They recruit about 400 men between them and approach Augusta on the night of 14 September. There are also large numbers of Indians in the area, and one of the patriot columns surprises an outlying Indian camp, which rouses the town's defenders. The rebels take two fortified buildings in Augusta and turn to concentrate on the principal stronghold,

where the Loyalists and Indians under Col. Thomas Browne have gathered. A brief siege fails, but the Americans retreat with a good deal of plunder. Little is accomplished except to inflame partisan passions further.

20 September 1780

HARTFORD, CT.   Gen. Washington and the comte de Rochambeau meet formally to discuss joint plans. Washington benefits from a nearly universal reaction to him by the French: Rochambeau is impressed with Washington's dignity and demeanor. Moreover, Rochambeau has previously written to Washington to place himself at the American's service. "I come," he writes, "wholly obedient and with the zeal and veneration which I have for you and for the remarkable talents you have displayed in sustaining a war which will always be memorable." Nonetheless, Washington stalls the French commander on the matter of actual operations, speaking only in generalities. In truth, the Continental Army is so weak at the moment that Washington fears the French might return to Europe if they learn the full story.

21 September 1780

HAVERSTRAW, N.Y.   Maj. Gen. Benedict Arnold, commander of the American fort at West Point, meets secretly with Maj. John André, Clinton's adjutant general. André has been assigned to deal with the American traitor and is responding to Arnold's urgent requests for a face-to-face meeting. Clinton instructs André to not cross American lines, to remain in uniform, and to carry no documents, but the the theatrical young officer cannot resist donning a disguise. He travels to the meeting aboard the armed sloop *Vulture* and slips ashore on the American side to parley with Arnold, who wants to nail down his fee for turning West Point over to the enemy.

22 September 1780

HAVERSTRAW, N.Y. To André's dis-

may, the *Vulture* has come under fire during the night and sailed away, stranding him ashore. He hides during the day at the house of Joshua Hett Smith, hoping the ship will return.

23 September 1780

HAVERSTRAW, N.Y. Arnold urges André to forget the river and make his

THE FRENCH ARMY

Active participation of the French army in the war was crucial to the ultimate American victory. A force of 4,000 French soldiers from the West Indies served temporarily in America in 1779 during the siege of Savannah. The largest French contingent—nearly 6,000—came with the comte de Rochambeau in 1780 and was stationed for a year in and around Newport, R.I., before marching south with Washington's Continentals to confront Cornwallis at Yorktown in 1781. Four thousand more Frenchmen stationed in the West Indies joined the allied army in Virginia; in fact, the majority of troops on the allied side at Yorktown were French.

While the French troops were good and their officers on the whole well-trained and experienced, the French command and logistical systems sometimes failed to come up to the mark.

All officers in the French army were required to have impeccable aristocratic family connections. If an officer could not prove titled ancestors on each side, he was usually denied a commission. This, of course, tended to limit the pool of talent, but

was compensated to some degree by the higher reliance of the French on formal training for officers. The French had particularly good military engineers and artillery officers, two areas shown to good advantage at the siege of Yorktown.

The French troops were far and away the best-equipped and best-uniformed army in the war. They were splendidly turned out in fancy uniforms and well armed. By the time the French arrived in strength late in the war, the Continental troops, never natty in the best of times, looked like a ragged mob by comparison, and even the once-spruce British army was tattered by 1780 and 1781.

The French army in America also included many units made up of foreigners. Elements of the Regiment Dillon, which was comprised entirely of Irish–Catholic expatriates, served at Savannah and with Rochambeau. Irishmen of the Regiment Walsh fought at Savannah. And, the famous Regiment Royal Deux-Ponts that played a prominent role at Yorktown was filled with German-speaking troops from the Palatinate.

escape overland through the disputed and partisan-ravaged region above New York City. André sees no other course, so he dons civilian clothes and hides in his boot documents in Arnold's handwriting that detail the weakness of West Point. He mounts a horse and sets out with Smith as a guide. They cross the river and settle for the night in a rural farmhouse.

24 September 1780

NEW YORK STATE. When morning breaks, André travels on alone, hoping a pass from Arnold in the name of John Anderson will see him safely through the American lines. Near Tarrytown he is stopped by three scruffy American militiamen, whom he mistakes for British partisans. He reveals he is British, but realizing his mistake tries to use the phoney pass.

The capture of Major John André. The offending documents were found in André's boots.

The trio search him and discover the documents. They turn their captive over to an officer, who conveys André to Lt. Col. John Jameson. Somewhat

confused by the passes and letters signed by Arnold, Jameson sends the documents to Gen. Washington, who is coincidentally traveling in the area on his way to West Point. At the same time, Jameson orders André to be taken to West Point with a letter telling Arnold of the capture. At the last minute, the order to move the prisoner is countermanded, but the letter continues on its way to Arnold.

Benedict Arnold. He was going to betray the Fort at West Point and its' 3,000 man garrison.

25 September 1780

WEST POINT, N.Y. The warning letter reaches Arnold at his breakfast table as he prepares to receive Washington later in the day. He rises calmly, draws his wife Peggy aside to tell her the bad news, and slips out the door. He goes immediately to the river and rows his barge to safety aboard a British sloop. Meanwhile, Peggy fakes a hysterical fit to divert attention. Washington, whose fearful suspicions have been aroused by the spurious documents, arrives just too late to catch Arnold. By the end of the day,

Arnold sends his former commander a letter confirming his treason. André, his identity revealed, remains in American hands.

26 September 1780

CHARLOTTE, N.C. Nipping at Cornwallis' army, a small American troop of dragoons and militia set up behind a stone wall outside the small village of Charlotte. They fire on the approaching British columns and hold up their advance for several hours, but eventually they must turn and retreat.

29 September 1780

TAPPAN, N.Y. Under the rules of war Maj. John André can be summarily executed as a spy: he has been caught behind enemy lines in disguise and with incriminating documents. However, Washington decides to convene a board of general officers to review the evidence. They reject appeals from Clinton that André was only acting under orders, and Clinton refuses to exchange Arnold for the young officer. The board sentences André to death by hanging.

1 October 1780

GILBERT TOWN, N.C. Armed men from the Western settlements—principally Wautaga—have gathered for weeks under such leaders as Isaac Shelby, John Sevier, Arthur Campbell, and William Campbell. They intend to rid their settlements of the threat of Loyalist attacks. While only loosely organized, they are formidible fighters with an abundance of frontier skills, including marksmanship. Their numbers are now swollen to over 1,000. Their object is to defeat a large Loyalist force led by British Maj. Patrick Ferguson, who has recruited heavily in the region around Ninety-Six, S.C., to supplement his well-trained Loyalist American Rangers. On 1 October the Western patriots ask Gates to appoint Daniel Morgan to command them, but the revered leader is not available for the duty. They elect William Campbell temporary leader.

Major John André in a sketch he made of himself the night before he was to be hanged.

2 October 1780

TAPPAN, N.Y. Major John André is hanged as a spy. He appeals to Washington at the last minute for death by firing squad, a mode of execution more befitting a soldier, but the commander-in-chief refuses. André exhibits a calm nobility at his death that earns the admiration of his American captors.

HILLSBORO, N.C. Daniel Morgan, who withdrew from participation in the war in the summer of 1779, is spurred by the American defeat at Camden to return to active duty. He arrives at Gates' headquarters in Hillsboro and is appointed to command of a special corps of light troops.

His reputation and known abilities provide rallying points for American hopes depressed by the recent defeat at the hands of Cornwallis. Morgan is especially popular among militia and Western troops, who admire his unorthodox style of fighting.

4 October 1780

THE CAROLINAS. Although commissioned by Clinton to do little more than consolidate British gains in South Carolina, Cornwallis wants to stamp out all rebel resistance and secure North Carolina as well. He is politically strong in London and allowed to communicate directly with the government there, circumventing Clinton in New York. Cornwallis plans to unite and organize the Loyalists of the Carolinas while pursuing the ruins of the American army, which now licks its wounds after the devastation of Camden. Cornwallis directs Patrick Ferguson to operate against American partisans as part of this scheme. Ferguson blusters and then backs away from the army of American frontiersmen from the Western settlements. During the first days of October, Cornwallis turns his army east toward Charlotte while Ferguson moves in the directon of King's Mountain.

5 October 1780

PHILADELPHIA. The Congress orders an investigation into Gates' conduct during and after the battle at Camden. Many members are embarrassed that their hand-picked commander appears to have fled the fighting in panic, and the illusions about his previous victory at Saratoga are finally laid to rest. Despite Gates' wishes to have the inquiry finished, the inves-

tigation drags on and Gates lingers in semi-disgrace.

6 October 1780

PHILADELPHIA. The Continental Congress formally asks George Washington to designate a new commander in the South. The body has previously gone over Washington's head, with miserable results. The legislators had chosen Robert Howe, who lost Savannah, Benjamin Lincoln, who surrendered Charleston, and Horatio Gates, who ran away at Camden. They now resolve "that the Commander-in-Chief be and is hereby directed to appoint an officer to command the southern army, in room of Major General Gates."

LONDON. Henry Laurens is lodged in the Tower of London. The British are delighted at his capture, but officials are not certain how to treat him, whether as a prisoner of war or as a traitor. They confine him in harsh conditions, and his health deteriorates.

7 October 1780

KING'S MOUNTAIN, S.C. Maj. Patrick Ferguson brings his Loyalist troops to this high, roughly wooded hill, which commands the surrounding region. He has served the British army well in the earlier campaigns in the North, including his invention of a breech-loading rifle as a means to offset the accuracy of the vaunted American frontier riflemen, and he is second only to Tarleton as a leader of Loyalist troops. He now believes he can crush the frontier rebel militia. Ferguson sends a message to Cornwallis, asking for reinforcements, and prepares to engage the Americans. The men from the West have other ideas, however. They slightly outnumber the Loyalists, but their greatest advantage comes from Ferguson's failure to secure the slopes of the hill. He trusts to the rough country to protect the approach to his main camp, which is pitched in an open spot on top of the hill, yet this plays to the strengths of the rebel frontiersmen, who quietly creep up the sides of King's Mountain to within yards of the enemy. Shelby's men attack from one side and William Campbell's from the other. Scrambling to reply, Ferguson orders a bayonet charge down on the rebels, but they easily evade the plunging Loyalists and shoot them down from the dense cover of the hillsides. Ferguson's remaining men are pushed back to their open camp area and surrounded by the riflemen, who pour in a deadly and concentrated fire. Ferguson is conspicuous in a gaudy hunting shirt and is struck down and killed by at least six bullets. As the rebels close in from all sides, the Loyalists collapse and surrender—many of them cut down after raising white flags. Rebel casualties are light: twenty-eight killed and sixty-four wounded. One hundred fifty-seven Loyalists are killed, 163 wounded, and nearly 700 captured. The battle is significant, since it eliminates the Loyalists of the Carolinas as an effective part of Cornwallis' plan of campaign. The British commander later calls King's Mountain "the first link of a chain of evils that followed each other in regular sucession until they at last ended in the total loss of America."

PHILADELPHIA. Congress appoints Gen. Nathanael Greene to command of the Southern Department, on Washington's recommendation. Greene, a self-taught soldier from Rhode Island, has been one of Washington's strongest and most steadfast subordinates, and he currently commands West Point in place of the traitor Arnold. He has recently been quartermaster for the Continental Army and understands the logistical needs of an army in the field.

8 October 1780

GILBERT TOWN, S.C. The victorious rebel militia show the vicious side of the war in the South when they convene an ad hoc court to try some of their prisoners from King's Mountain as war criminals. Many patriots have seen family and friends hung by the British. The court sentences twelve Loyalists who are hung on the spot. Hundreds of other prisoners are turned over to the ill-organized American civil governments of the Carolinas. Most of the Loyalists eventually escape but never again constitute an organized force in the region.

11 October 1780

FORT GEORGE (FORT WILLIAM HENRY), N.Y. A strong force of Loyalists and Indians under Johnson and Joseph Brant continues to sweep through upper New York. They take this formerly important post at the southern end of Lake George but soon move on to renewed raiding of American settlements.

13 October 1780

PHILADELPHIA. Congress finally appoints Daniel Morgan to the rank of brigadier general. Despite his impressive, perhaps decisive, roles in the campaigns against Canada and especially at Saratoga, Morgan has been denied signifigant rank and command. Stung by the insult, he withdrew from the war on a plea of ill health in 1779. He is now active again, despite nearly crippling arthritis.

14 October 1780

SOUTH CAROLINA. Cornwallis learns of Ferguson's defeat at King's Mountain and fears an attack on his rear by the victors. He decides to retreat to winter quarters at Winnsboro, S.C., and orders his army to begin the march. Rain turns the roadways into mire, and the surrounding swampland becomes impassable. The troops lack provisions and are harrassed by illness and American militia, who constantly raid the British baggage train. Cornwallis himself contracts a fever and is out of action for days.

PHILADELPHIA. Congress passes a resolution of thanks to Gist, Smallwood, Porterfield, Armstrong, and Armand for their roles in the Battle of Camden—a small gesture in the face of Gates' monumental failure.

16 October 1780

NEW YORK. Maj. Gen. Alexander Leslie sails toward the south with 2,500 men to reinforce Cornwallis. Lord George Germain supports Cornwallis' plan to take North Carolina, and Leslie's troops will support the campaign.

SCHOHARIE VALLEY, N.Y. Sir John Johnson's large raiding party besieges the valley's Middle Fort but is unable to attack effectively since it has no artillery. Nevertheless, the American commander, Maj. Melancton Woolsey, attempts to surrender. Frontiersmen in the fort, lead by the famous rifleman Timothy Murphy, prevent

General Nathanael Greene; he replaced Horatio Gates as commander of the Southern army in December, 1780.

Woolsey from sending out a white flag. Johnson gives up the task and moves on into the Mohawk Valley.

17 October 1780

SCHOHARIE VALLEY, N.Y. Fires set by Johnson's men take hold in the fields and destroy crops and farms throughout the valley, thereby cutting off a major source of grain for the American cause.

19 October 1780

FORT KEYSER, N.Y. Col. John Brown leads a foray out of Stone Arabia against Johnson, who is advancing up the Mohawk Valley. The badly outnumbered Americans are crushed, and Johnson destroys Stone Arabia by the end of the day. Gen. Robert Van Rensselaer with a force of nearly 850 militia is in close pursuit. The Americans catch up with Johnson near Klock's Field, and a battle ensues. The British forces are hard-pressed but withstand a flanking attack and withdraw the next morning.

20 October 1780

NEW YORK. Washington sets on foot a plan to recapture Benedict Arnold, now safe in the hands of the British in New York City, in order to return the traitor to face "public punishment." Washington instructs Henry Lee to select a noncommissioned officer who will slip into the city and kidnap Arnold. Lee dsignates Sergeant-Major John Champe, a reliable Virginian. Champe fakes a desertion the same day and steals away through the British lines. According to his later story, he nearly brings off the abduction, but is foiled at the last minute. Champe is forced to remain with the British in the guise of a deserter and is even shipped off to Virginia under Arnold's command later in the month.

21 October 1780

PHILADELPHIA. After a protracted campaign, Washington finally convinces Congress to extend half-pay to Continental officers for life. The issue is important to the morale and continued service of all the officers in the army who hold commissions from Congress, but the body has been reluctant to grant retirement half-pay for more than seven years after the end of the war. Washington persistently lobbies for extending half-pay, however, and in a growing atmosphere of crisis, many individual officers add petitions of their own to his urgings. Congress caves in and grants half-pay for life.

26 October 1780

TEARCOAT SWAMP, S.C. Col. Francis

Francis Marion; known as the "Swamp Fox," he led a small but effective guerilla force in South Carolina.

Marion, known ever after as the Swamp Fox, has superbly organized a hit-and-run partisan campaign against Cornwallis' rear and against Loyalist attempts to support the British. Marion and his men—seldom more than

Francis Marion and some of his "irregulars" in a South Carolina swamp.

a few hundred—operate from hidden swamp camps and never stay in one place long enough for the British to find them. Speed and daring are Marion's main weapons. On 26 October he strikes at a gathering of Loyalist militia under Col. Samuel Tynes. The Americans capture prisoners, horses, and supplies, and they suppress any further Loyalist uprising in the area.

4 November 1780

PHILADELPHIA. The Congress asks states for higher war-support quotas. One of the major problems facing Congress and the army is the system that relies on individual state governments to provide supplies. Few states have adequate administrative organization, several are in the hands of the British, and others are simply reluctant to squeeze their own citizens for the good of the united cause. Four and a half years of war have worn down the will and ability of some states to contribute.

9 November 1780

FISH DAM FORD, S.C. Thomas Sumter, the Gamecock, has also taken up a partisan campaign of harrassment and raiding against the British. Now a brigadier general of South Carolina militia, Sumter hopes to deplete British strength by nipping at the heels of the army. Cornwallis sends out a force of mixed infantry and horesemen under Maj. Wemyss to track down Sumter's band. Wemyss finds Sumter's camp on 9 November and launches what he hopes is a surprise attack. Sumter's men are alert, however, and give the British a bloody repulse, capturing Wemyss in the bargain.

Mid-November 1780

NEWPORT, R.I. The French troops under Rochambeau settle in to a long wait for action. Many of them find the quiet seaport a dreary and boring place. As one aide to the French commander writes home: "Our position here is a very disagreeable one. We are vegetating at the very door of the enemy in a most disastrous state of idleness and uncertainty." Other Frenchmen adapt themselves better to conditions and take advantage of local hospitality.

15 November 1780

GEORGETOWN, S.C. Marion attacks the British garrison of this coastal town, hoping to catch it understrength. Loyalist reinforcements have arrived before Marion, however, and after several days of skirmishing, the Americans withdraw.

20 November 1780

BLACKSTOCKS, S.C. Cornwallis turns Tarleton loose to find and destroy Sumter, who has become more than a nuisance. Tarleton has seldom failed to quash rebels in his path and sets off with most of his British Legion plus elements of the 63rd Regiment. Sumter learns of the danger from a deserter and forms his 450 men at Blackstock's plantation, which is on high ground and skirted by thick brush and undergrowth. Tarleton splits his force and attacks the main body of Sumter's troops, but in fierce fighting the British cannot take control. Sumter is badly wounded in the battle, but Tarleton must withdraw without a victory—leaving Sumter's force intact. The Americans lose only three dead, the British nearly 50.

22 November 1780

BROOKHAVEN, N.Y. In the last real military engagement in the North,

Maj. Benjamin Tallmadge of the 2nd Continental Dragoons leads an attack on a fortified house in Brookhaven on Long Island. Tallmadge's eighty men cross to Long Island by boat the day before, wait out a storm, and attack in three parties at dawn. They overwhelm the British garrison, capture fifty-four, and return safely to the American lines.

27 November 1780

HILLSBORO, N.C. Nathanael Greene arrives at Hillsboro on his way to take command of the Southern Army. All along his journey from the North he has stopped to ask for supplies and assistance from state governments but receives little beyond good will.

30 November 1780

NORTH CAROLINA. Not yet twenty-four years old, Henry "Light-Horse Harry" Lee is promoted to lieutenant colonel and his corps of three mounted infantry troops is augmented by three foot companies to form Lee's Legion. This well-equipped and well-trained body becomes an important part of the American army in the South. The men are specially selected by the officers and drawn from all units in the Continental army—forming a select band that proves capable of matching Tarleton's dragoons.

2 December 1780

CHARLOTTE, N.C. Nathanael Greene reaches Charlotte, where Gates has established headquarters after Cornwallis' pullout to winter quarters in October. The new American commander and the old treat each other with punctilious respect, providing (in the words of Otho Williams) "an elegant lesson of propriety exhibited on a most delicate and interesting occasion."

3 December 1780

CHARLOTTE, N.C. Greene assumes command of the Southern Department. Although he has never been in the South before, Greene has consulted extensively with experienced officers—especially his Virginian commander-in-chief—about conditions in the region. He has also shrewdly assessed the capacity of the Southern states to supply his army with food, clothing, and fresh troops. On reaching his new headquarters, he observes the deplorable state of the army. He reaches several conclusions. Greene realizes he will likely be unable to organize an army powerful enough to consistently challenge Cornwallis on the battlefield, especially since the British troops from New York under Leslie have now reached the theater to reinforce Cornwallis. The new American commander resolves to take full advantage of the partisan leaders at his disposal, and he communicates with Sumter and Marion, urging them to continue their depradations against the British lines of supply and to persist in forestalling gatherings of Loyalists. As to his own situation, Greene sees an opportunity to weaken Cornwallis by a daring strategy. He will divide his small army, giving command of one section to Daniel Morgan, and hope to confuse the British with threats from two directions. If Cornwallis can catch either part of the American army, the British may be able to crush it, but Greene does not intend to be caught. If Cornwallis commits himself in either direction, the remaining American force can strike from the rear. Greene prepares to take his own portion of the army into quarters near Cheraw for refitting and training. He also directs Edward Carrington to reconnoiter the roads and river crossings to the north in preparation for rapid movements in the direction of North Carolina.

4 December 1780

RUGELEY'S MILL, S.C. Col. William Washington, a distant cousin of the commander-in-chief, whose dragoons now form part of Morgan's command, surrounds a body of Loyalists under Col. Henry Rugeley who have taken refuge in a fortified barn. Washington lacks artillery, but he makes a fake cannon from a log and wheels it into position, calling on the Loyalists to surrender. Rugeley falls for the ruse and surrenders his force of a hundred men.

16 December 1780

CHARLOTTE, N.C. Greene orders Morgan on the march. The Old Wagoner, as he is known to his troops, is to cross the Catawba River, gather North Carolina militia under William Davidson, and begin operations between the Broad and Pacolet rivers. Morgan is free to make offensive demonstrations or even fight if the odds are right, but if Cornwallis moves on Greene at Cheraw, Morgan is to attack the British rear or rejoin the main American army. Morgan takes with him about 600 of Greene's total effective force of fewer than 2,500 troops.

19 December 1780

SOUTH CAROLINA. Greene begins his move. The army is is poor condition and rains make the going difficult. His baggage train must stop frequently to rest the draft horses.

20 December 1780

PHILADELPHIA. Impressed with the formation of the League of Armed Neutrality, Congress appoints an envoy to Russia. The delegates choose Francis Dana, a Massachusetts lawyer who had served in Congress and as secretary to John Adams in Europe. The mission proves fruitless.

LONDON. Great Britain declares war on the Netherlands. Tacit Dutch support of the Americans and French has finally proved too much for the British, who decide they have nothing to lose by outright belligerence. The embassy to Holland of captured Henry Laurens, whose papers revealed the extent of Dutch sympathy for the Revolution, proves the final straw. The British navy is now free to attack Dutch commercial outposts and to capture Dutch ships.

SANDY HOOK, N.Y. A British naval squadron clears for Virginia. The commander of the expedition is none other than Benedict Arnold, who is now a brigadier general in the British army. His goal is to land in Virginia, which has been spared warfare for several years, and seize or destroy rebel property and supplies. Arnold has with him about 1,600 troops, including Lt. Col. John Simcoe's Loyalist Queen's Rangers. A major objective of the campaign is to deprive Greene of supplies.

26 December 1780

CHERAW, S.C. After a difficult march, Greene's army arrives to establish a base camp at a site chosen by the best American engineer of the war, the Polish expatriate Kościuszko. Greene hopes to gather strength while in camp, although he must be ready to strike at Cornwallis if the British move toward Morgan or into North Carolina.

27 December 1780

WILLIAMSON'S PLANTATION. Morgan dispatches William Washington's dragoons along with mounted militia to attack Loyalists near Hammond's Store and Williamson's Plantation. They destroy a force of Loyalists on 27 December and move on to capture Fort William. Cornwallis sees the action as a threat to his rear and sends Tarleton out to eliminate Morgan.

30 December 1780

HAMPTON ROADS, VA. Arnold's expedition lands after a difficult voyage. He has 400 fewer troops than when he departed from New York, but the remainder move up the James River toward American posts.

★ 1781 ★

The climactic year of the Revolution opens on a low note for the American cause, when serious mutiny breaks out among troops of the Pennsylvania Line. Rejecting pleas from their officers, they leave Morristown and march toward Philadelphia. The mutiny is eventually resolved by negotiation.

In the Carolinas, Gen. Daniel Morgan scores one of the great victories of the war at the Battle of the Cowpens, where he virtually annihilates Tarleton. Francis Marion, Henry Lee, and others continue successful partisan warfare as Greene draws Cornwallis through the countryside. The battle of Guilford Courthouse in mid-March is a tactical defeat for Greene, but the British army is so weakened as to be out of action for months. Lord Cornwallis eventually withdraws to Virginia to take control of British forces there, which have been temporarily under the command of traitor Benedict Arnold while raiding American towns and supply points. Washington dispatches a small army under Lafayette to contain the British in Virginia. Meanwhile, Greene attacks British outposts in the Carolinas, and retakes Augusta in June but fails in a siege of the British garrison at Ninety-Six, S.C. He later loses another battle at Eutaw Springs but inflicts devastating casualties on the British army of Lord Rawdon.

While briefly considering a joint plan to attack Clinton in New York, Washington and Rochambeau learn that a French fleet will sail from the West Indies in force. Washington gambles on catching Cornwallis in Virginia and orders both the American and the French armies to march promptly south. Cornwallis incautiously withdraws to Yorktown, Va., confident the Royal Navy will keep him supplied and reinforced. French Adm. De Grasse arrives in the Chesapeake Bay ahead of the British fleet and repulses Graves in a sea battle on 5 September. Cornwallis is trapped.

Washington and Rochambeau arrive, join Lafayette and French reinforcements, and lay siege to Cornwallis in Yorktown. Lord Cornwallis fails to evacuate, and he surrenders his entire army on 19 October, effectively ending the British armed attempts to reclaim the American colonies.

1 January 1781

MORRISTOWN, N.J. The fabric of the Continental Army is torn when the regiments of the Pennsylvania Line mutiny. The men have suffered through yet another winter of cold, inadequate food, and poor housing. Moreover, they have not been paid for months. The biggest point of contention, however, is enlistments. Many men feel that their three-year original terms are now up, and they do not think they are obligated to serve for the duration of the war. During the morning of New Year's Day, about half the 2,500 Pennsylvania Continentals fall out in full gear and prepare to leave camp. Gen. Anthony Wayne tries to dissuade them, but they brush his arguments aside. The dissidents try to recruit more men for the uprising while the officers try to stop them. In the confusion, several officers and enlisted men are wounded. The mutineers finally form up and move out, headed for Philadelphia to present their case directly to Congress. They halt for the night at Bernardsville.

2 January 1781

NEW JERSEY. As the mutinous members of the Pennsylvania regiments continue their march, Gen. Wayne tries to recover control. He issues a formal order, promising to plead the men's case if they will return to duty. The mutineers ignore him.

3 January 1781

PRINCETON, N.J. The column of Pennsylvania mutineers enters the town and settles in on the college campus. The sergeants have formed a board to deal with Congress and their officers. Wayne trails the column and goes to a tavern in Princeton where a guard of sergeants stands watch. Washington, too far away to reach the crisis, can do little to affect its outcome.

HOOD'S POINT, VA. Arnold's force reaches this fortified point on the James River, near Jamestown, and receives fire from an American battery on shore. The British run past the guns and send a force of 130 under Simcoe to take the position, but the

American defenders have fled by the time the British arrive.

4 January 1781
PRINCETON, N.J. Lafayette, Arthur St. Clair, and John Laurens visit the mutineers' camp, but the men refuse to listen. They want to deal only with Wayne or the Congress. Meanwhile, British commander Sir Henry Clinton in New York learns of the mutiny and immediately plans to take advantage of the unrest. He orders troops to prepare for a march into New Jersey, and he selects agents to offer the mutineers pardon, money, or both.

RICHMOND, VA. Arnold marches from Westover, where his troops have put ashore, and takes Richmond with little bother. American militia abandon the only defensive positions, leaving the city open to the British. Simcoe is dispatched to destroy an iron foundry, gunpowder factory, and machine shops at Westham, six miles upriver. Arnold sends a letter to Virginia governor Thomas Jefferson, offering to spare Richmond if the British are allowed to seize tobacco unmolested. Jefferson refuses, and Arnold ransacks Richmond, burning and destroying houses, public buildings, and the state's official papers. The main British force then withdraws to Portsmouth and begins to dig in.

6 January 1781
MAIDENHEAD, N.J. Joseph Reed has been appointed by Congress to deal with the Pennsylvania mutineers. He arrives at this village near Princeton and sends letters to Wayne, who is still in the tavern more or less under guard. During the evening Clinton's agent, John Mason, and a guide named

Ogden arrive with the British offer to the sergeants.

7 January 1781
PRINCETON, N.J. The mutineers immediately reject the British overtures and take Mason and Ogden into custody. The Pennsylvanians turn the two agents over to Reed, easing fears that the mutineers intend to go over to the enemy. Reed and Wayne (whom the mutineers have allowed to travel to Maidenhead) decide to go to Princeton to talk with the sergeants' representatives. Wayne is aghast at the mutiny, but not entirely without sympathy for the plight of the troops. He writes: "Our soldiers are not devoid of reasoning faculties, nor are they callous to the first feelings of nature; they have served their country with fidelity for near five years, poorly clothed, badly fed and worse paid." At an evening meeting, the mutineers present their case about enlistments to Reed, who promises on behalf of Congress to redress the problems of enlistment and allow any soldiers who have fulfilled the terms of their original bargains to depart.

8 January 1781
PRINCETON, N.J. The mutineers of the Pennsylvania Line accept Congress' terms and agree to final negotiations. Each case is examined individually over the coming weeks, and many are discharged. Ironically, a large number re-enlist. The entire Pennsylvania Line is furloughed until March, and the mutiny ends.

CHARLES CITY COURTHOUSE, VA. Col. Simcoe's Queen's Rangers corner an American militia contingent under Colonel Dudley and rout the Virginians by ruse as much as force. Twenty Americans are killed and eight captured. Simcoe then rejoins Arnold.

10 January 1781

PHILADELPHIA. After a long gestation period, legislation is approved by Congress to establish the first in a series of executive government offices, that of foreign secretary. The purpose, in the words of delegate Joseph Jones, is "to place at the head of the foreign affairs . . . some respectable persons to conduct the business and be responsible. . . ." Until the growing governmental crisis of 1780–1781, the Congress has been reluctant to establish any form of executive office, relying first on special committees and then standing committees to handle all the political, diplomatic, and administrative affairs of the new nation. The result has been (in various degree) inefficiency and ineptitude. The foreign secretary will be charged to carry on correspondence with ministers of the United States to foreign courts and with ministers of foreign powers, to inform Congress about foreign relations, and to attend Congress. Political rivalries prevent the delegates from naming anyone to the post immediately.

11 January 1781

PRINCETON, N.J. Mason and Ogden, Sir Henry Clinton's ambassadors to the mutinous Pennsylvania troops, are hanged as spies.

14 January 1781

THICKETY CREEK, S.C. Daniel Morgan knows that Tarleton is on his trail and withdraws to get the sense of how great is the British force and what are Tarleton's intentions. Tarleton hopes to catch the Americans on the move and cut them down with a lightning stroke as he has so many times in the past year. His troops number close to 1,100, including nearly all of his famous British Legion.

Daniel Morgan, shown here in characteristic uniform.

16 January 1781

COWPENS, S.C. Morgan reaches this elevated meadow, long used—as the name suggests—as a grazing patch for livestock. The ground is good for defense and the sort of battle Morgan intends to wage. His basic force consists of 600 light infantry, including many Maryland and Delaware Continentals who had survived Camden, and 200 veteran Virginia riflemen. About 500 more militia from Georgia, North Carolina, and South Carolina join him, making up a slightly larger force than will face him on the British side. Morgan knows, however, that the militia will not withstand a prolonged battle in open ground, so he devises one of the great tactics of the war: He will place his militia troops in two front ranks but tells them they are to do no more than fire two accurate volleys and then run up the hill past the solidly planted regulars. Morgan believes the militia can do serious damage and bait Tarleton into a precipitous assault, which will come up against the rock-hard Continentals from Maryland and Delaware. Throughout most of the night, Morgan hobbles from campfire to campfire, making certain each militia unit knows exactly what is expected. "Just hold up your heads, boys," he tells them, "give them two fires and you're free."

A later view of the Battle of the Cowpens. The Americans are driving the British back with bayonets.

17 January 1781

COWPENS, S.C. Eager to catch Morgan, Tarleton rouses his men and has them on the march by 3:00 A.M. (as a consequence, most reach the battlefield exhausted). He soon learns that Morgan has come to ground, and he prepares to attack. The first to go forward are dragoons, who are picked apart at long range by the Carolina militia. Tarleton then arrays his infantry and orders the advance. The first line of American militiamen have already fled, and the second delivers its two volleys as planned and retreats also. The militia have severely damaged Tarleton's force, but with their flight to the rear the British

An early engraving depicting the Battle of the Cowpens.

sense a rout and press forward and around the American flank, chasing retreating militia. Morgan's own dragoons and cavalry emerge from hiding and take the British riders from the rear, smashing their formations and driving them from the fight. Meanwhile, Tarleton's advancing infantry comes up against the Continentals and is shocked by volley after volley of disciplined fire. A change of position causes momentary confusion among the Americans, but Morgan steadies the lines and waits. When the British again surge forward, still anticipating a rout, their ranks are withered with fire and the American dragoons hit their flank. A bayonet charge from the Continentals breaks the British attack, and the battle turns into a surrender. Tarleton himself tries to rally 200 of his own Legion cavalry, but they have seen enough and turn tail to ride away as fast as horses will carry them. Tarleton has no choice but to flee himself, after a dramatic horse-to-horse fight with William Washington. He reaches the safety of the main British camp the next day. Morgan, leaving others to gather up captured stores and booty,

THE MILITIA

Each state had its own militia organization during the Revolution, based in similar local, part-time military units formed during the colonial wars of the preceding decades. During the Revolution, the militia of each state formed, dissipated, and re-formed. Sometimes militia units were attached to the regular forces of the Continental Army and fought in major battles—this was the only way Washington and other American commanders could assemble a large force—and at other times the militia operated independently, usually to the despair of people like Washington.

As befitted a nation fighting for independence, the state militias were little interested in discipline or training. They usually elected their own officers with little regard for military competence. Their commanders held rank separately from commissions granted by Congress. Thus a colonel in command of a state militia regiment might have no standing at all in relation to the Continental Army and might refuse orders from Continental commanders. Most states appointed brigadier or even major generals to have charge of the entire militia force from that state.

The great advantage of the militia forces was the flexibility they afforded. When the war moved into a specific region, militia forces could be recruited quickly and used to bulk up whatever army Washington or other Continental generals could bring to the scene.

The other side of the equation, however, was the generally poor performance of militia throughout the war. In many key engagements, militia—being essentially untrained and inexperienced soldiers—broke and ran when attacked by British regulars. The debacle at the battle of Camden was the worst case, when Gen. Horatio Gates was so incautious as to put militia in a key position on the front of the battleline: they threw down their guns and ran at the first volley, leaving the regulars to be flanked and nearly massacred.

The militia did have moments of glory, however. The untried militia soldiers at Bunker Hill, fighting from behind barricades, nearly destroyed the cream of the British army before they ran out of ammunition and succumbed to a final bayonet attack (if the thousands of militia in reserve had come forward, however, the battle might have been a complete triumph instead of ultimately a defeat). When used with an eye toward their best points, as at King's Mountain, militia could be a huge asset on the battlefield. Daniel Morgan understood that militia could shoot well and would stay in place until brought under pressure from regulars. His tactic of telling the militia to fire two volleys and run was enough to start the destruction of Tarleton's opposing force.

withdraws most of his men across the Broad River and into camp by afternoon. The battle, brief as it is, costs the British 100 killed, 229 wounded, and 600 captured—nearly eight out of ten of Tarleton's original force are eliminated. The Americans lose only twelve killed and sixty wounded. Moreover, the victory is priceless to the American cause over and above the numbers and the immediate strategic advantage. Morgan's triumph buoys American hopes and reverses a long trend of British victories in the South. It is, perhaps, the greatest feat of the war by militia, save only Bunker Hill.

20 January 1781

POMPTON, N.J. Members of the New Jersey Brigade, who have followed closely news of the mutiny of the Pennsylvania Line, conclude they have the same grievances. Ignoring their officers, they march out of camp toward Chatham.

21 January 1781

NEW JERSEY. Washington has had enough of mutiny and details Gen. Robert Howe to take 500 troops and suppress the dissidents.

22 January 1781

MORRISIANA, N.J. An American force under Lt. Col. William Hull raids into Westchester County against the Loyalists, especially James De Lancey. The raiders take large numbers of cattle and horses and destroy forage.

24 January 1781

GEORGETOWN, S.C. Lee and Marion cooperate to attack this coastal city in a cleverly planned operation. They

sneak close to the outskirts of the town and dash in, only to find the British garrison buttoned up inside buildings throughout the town. The Americans cannot force them out and withdraw.

25 January 1781

RAMSUR'S MILL, S.C. Lord Cornwallis, deprived of Tarleton's quick striking arm, decides to pursue Morgan into North Carolina on his own with the entire army. The British commander orders almost all the army's food and baggage burnt: the men are to carry only a limited amount of equipment and victuals on their own backs. Cornwallis hopes to convert his entire force into a mobile army that can catch Morgan or turn quickly to find Greene. It is a daring move to strip an eighteenth-century army of its tents and supplies in the midst of winter.

26 January 1781

POMPTON, N.J. Howe and commander-in-chief Washington himself advance on the New Jersey mutineers, who have now returned to their original camp. The loyal troops under Howe surround the camp and bring the ringleaders to the front. Two are sentenced and shot on the spot, and the mutiny is at an end.

30 January 1781

CATAWBA RIVER, S.C. Greene and Morgan reunite their armies and begin a rapid retreat north with Cornwallis in pursuit.

1 February 1781

COWAN'S FORD, N.C. Cornwallis' chase of Morgan and Greene is complicated by the series of rivers and streams running perpendicular to his route. If the British can cross the Catawba quickly enough, the army may be able to get on Morgan's flank, so Cornwallis goes to Cowan's Ford and sends his men across. On the other side are Gen. William Davidson and several hundred North Carolina militia; however, the ford is two-pronged and they have selected the wrong branch to guard. The British struggle across the river, losing many men and horses in the rough going and strong current, but they emerge on the far bank virtually unopposed. They then turn on the surprised Davidson with an attack that scatters the militia and leaves Davidson himself dead. Fortunately for the American cause, Morgan has already withdrawn and cannot be caught this day. Nathanael Greene, who has been waiting alone to rendezvous personally with Davidson, is cut off from his army, but a solo night ride brings him to safety.

TARRANT'S TAVERN, N.C. After crossing at Cowan's Ford, Tarleton moves rapidly to Tarrant's Tavern, ten miles distant, and easily routs a band of militia. Taking to the road again, he narrowly misses capturing Nathanael Greene.

PHILADELPHIA. Congress agrees to a plan to establish more executive offices, including secretaries for finance, war, and marine affairs.

3 February 1781

ST. EUSTATIUS, WEST INDIES. British Adm. George Rodney captures the Dutch trading port, which since the beginning of the war has served as a major point of supply for the Americans. The Dutch operation here has been a thorn in the side of the British for years, but little could be done until the recent declaration of war by Great Britain against the Netherlands. Rodney seizes a fortune in goods—equal to millions of pounds—and hopes to realize a huge personal gain. He sells some of the goods and ships the rest to England (most of the treasure is recaptured by the French before it reaches port).

PHILADELPHIA. Thomas Burke, delegate from North Carolina and long a proponent of a weak central government, reverses his stand and introduces a plan to give Congress the power to levy a 5 percent import duty. Such a measure, if carried out, would solve many of the government's financial woes. Burke has changed his views on the necessity for centralized economic power after observing the effects of the British military success in the South. His attempt is ultimately foiled, however, by the refusal of Rhode Island to agree.

NORTH CAROLINA. A race begins between Greene and Cornwallis. The American commander hopes to lead Cornwallis north over a difficult, river-strewn route that will weaken the British army. The trick for him is to not let Cornwallis catch the American army while crossing one of the several rivers. Greene moves out but dispatches some parts of his small army to feint Cornwallis away from the main route of march. Over the coming week, Cornwallis comes close to making the right guesses, but never quite corners Greene before the Americans ford another river and set off again. Greene's ultimate goal is the Dan River marking the border of Virginia. As the race begins, Daniel Morgan, crippled and lame from arthritis, turns over his command and leaves for home. Greene gives Otho Williams command of the light infantry and mounted troops, including Lee's Legion, that will screen the American army as it marches north.

6 February 1781

PHILADELPHIA. Congress establishes a department of finance as a half-way measure and appoints wealthy and influential merchant Robert Morris to the post of superintendent. Morris is the best financial mind in the states and is one of the few to understand the complexities of national finance. Since the economic crisis is the most pressing problem for Congress, Morris assumes a large role in national affairs. Previous attempts by Congress to deal with finance have been flawed by incompetence and semi-graft.

10 February 1781

NORTH CAROLINA. Greene decides to make for the lower crossing of the Dan River and begins a dash with Cornwallis close behind.

12 February 1781

FORT ST. JOSEPH. A small Spanish force of militia and Indians under Capt. Eugenio Pourre captures this British post in what is now Michigan. Sent northward in retaliation for the earlier British attempt to take St. Louis, the Spanish expedition scores an easy victory when the British garrison surrenders without resistance. The Spanish hold the fort only a day

and then depart, but they subsequently use the action as a basis for territorial claims.

14 February 1781

DAN RIVER CROSSING, N.C. Greene reaches the river and begins to push his army across. His men have outdistanced Cornwallis' pursuit. With the American army safe in Virginia, Greene will be able to resupply, refit, and prepare for a new offensive. Cornwallis arrives to find the river swollen with winter floods and all the available boats on the American side. Greene has won the race.

18 February 1781

DAN RIVER CROSSING, N.C. Greene sends Lee and Pickens back across the river to mount a harassment campaign against Cornwallis. The British have depleted their few remaining stores (most were burned at Ramsur's Mill) during their pursuit of Greene's army, so they are ripe for partisan raiding. Cornwallis marches his men to Hillsboro for rest and recuperation.

23 February 1781

DAN RIVER CROSSING, N.C. Greene himself recrosses the Dan and returns to North Carolina. Many of his militia have left with the end of their enlistments, but he still has a solid core of Continentals who are now rested and ready for a new campaign. Greene also expects fresh drafts of militia from Virginia and North Carolina to join him in time to confront Cornwallis. The American army begins a march in the general direction of the British camp at Hillsboro, but moves often to confuse Cornwallis. During the next two weeks, the main American force marches 230 miles, back and forth, while Lee and Pickens nibble at the edges of the British.

25 February 1781

HAW RIVER, N.C. After playing tag with Tarleton for several days, Lee learns that 400 mounted Loyalists under Col. John Pyles are on their way to join the British. Lee approaches the column on the same road and pretends to be Tarleton himself (both Lee's Legion and Tarleton's men wear green dragoon coats). The Loyalists obligingly draw aside, ground their weapons, and allow Lee's men to ride up with sabers drawn. The result is a massacre: Ninety Loyalists are killed and most of the rest wounded. Not an American is hurt.

PEEKSKILL, N.Y. Washington directs Lafayette to take command of 1,200 light infantry from New England and the New Jersey Continentals and march south to confront Arnold in Virginia. The force is hastily assembled and begins the journey. Rochambeau agrees to send 1,200 of his French troops by sea to join Lafayette. In the meantime, Washington has sent Gen. Friedrich von Steuben, the German drillmaster who since the winter of Valley Forge has served Washington as a trusted administrator, into Virginia to recruit militia. Von Steuben has little success, and his incessant appeals to local government are rebuffed. He writes to Washington: "I am not less tired of this state than they are of me. I shall always regret that circumstances induced me to undertake the defense of a country . . . where every farmer is a general, but where nobody wishes to be a soldier."

1 March 1781

PHILADELPHIA. The final ratification of the Articles of Confederation brings the Continental Congress to an end and begins a new chapter in the history of the United States. The Articles have been up for ratification by the individual states since late 1777, but final adoption has stalled due to disputes over Western land claims. The new government is known as the Confederation Congress. When the act is announced at noon, the city celebrates with bells, cannonfire, and fireworks. A Philadelphia newspaper rejoices: "Thus America, like a well-constructed arch, whose parts harmonizing and mutually supporting each other, are the more closely united the greater the pressure on them, is growing up in war into greatness and consequence among the nations."

2 March 1781

CLAPP'S MILL, N.C. Lee's men again encounter advance units of the British army, skirmishing with some of Tarleton's men.

3 March 1781

HEAD OF ELK, MD. Lafayette reaches the waterway leading to the theater of action. His men embark on boats for Annapolis, where they intend to meet the French forces that are coming by sea.

6 March 1781

WETZALL'S MILL, N.C. Cornwallis attempts to catch Otho Williams' force of mixed light infantry and mounted troops, which has been on a campaign of harassment. The British push out with Tarleton's riders and Col. James

Webster's light infantry in the lead. Williams retreats across the river at Wetzall's Mill and scurries for the main American army camp, leaving Lee, Washington, and Col. William Campbell to occupy the British. The Americans make a sharp encounter of it when the British cross the river under fire, but then slip away.

NEWPORT, R.I Washington rides in to confer with Rochambeau on general strategy. The French commander has prepared an expedition for Virginia, but its start has been delayed by the need to repair some of the transport ships of Destouches' fleet.

8 March 1781

NEWPORT, R.I. The French set sail with the entire fleet and a considerable number of infantry. If they can reach the Chesapeake unmolested, Arnold and his raiding British army in Virginia will be trapped. With unaccustomned energy, British Adm. Marriot Arbuthnot gives chase to the French and actually arrives in the bay ahead of them.

9 March 1781

PENSACOLA, FLA. A powerful Spanish squadron of thirty-five ships, laden with nearly 7,000 soldiers, sails in to begin a siege of the British fort. Bernardo Galvez has been determined to take control of Pensacola since his previous triumph over the British at Mobile. The garrison is a ragtag of worn-out troops, criminals, and deserters under Brig. Gen. John Campbell, but it puts up a determined defense. Galvez finds no easy victory and settles in to bombard the fort into submission.

14 March 1781

GUILFORD COURTHOUSE, N.C. Nathanael Greene's army is now as strong as it can get. He has received reinforcements of militia from Virginia and North Carolina, and the general can count over 4,000 men. Unfortunately, only a few are battle-tested, and Greene knows most of the raw militia will not stand up to British veterans. Nonetheless, Greene resolves to fight Cornwallis at a place of his own choosing, which is this isolated courthouse surrounded by woods. He makes his dispositions and awaits Cornwallis.

15 March 1781

GUILFORD COURTHOUSE, N.C. Cornwallis sets his army in motion early in the day to cover the last twelve miles to Guilford Courthouse. He knows little of the battlefield and he is badly outnumbered. He has no more than 1,900 troops, but they are all veterans and some may rightly be called the cream of the British army. Cornwallis feels the odds are still in his favor. The British advance units emerge from the woods to find Greene's army set up in a fashion similar to Morgan's deployment at the Battle of King's Mountain. Almost all of the untried militia are set forward in two lines, the first behind a log fence and the second just inside the first line of trees. Behind them and to the flanks are the American veterans, including the ever-redoubtable Marylanders and a company of Delaware Continentals. Lee and Washington's dragoons guard the flanks. Greene's plan is similar to Morgan's previous tactic of letting the militia fire off a volley or two and then retreat behind

American dragoons under the command of Henry Lee at the Battle of Guilford Courthouse.

the successive lines. Unfortunately, the distance between lines is too great and there is little possibility to coordinate movements. Moreover, Greene has no reserve to throw forward at a crucial moment. Cornwallis, on the other hand, has to operate blindly, since he cannot see most of Greene's disposition of troops. The battle begins with encounters between Tarleton and the American mounted infantry on the flanks and an ineffectual bombardment from Cornwallis' three light field guns. The center of the British force forms up and advances on the line of militia behind their fence. The Americans deliver a withering volley that nearly, but not quite, halts the British advance, but then they take to heels and run pell-mell for the rear. They do not stop to form up behind the second line, but keep going until they are almost all well clear of the battlefield. The British pause to attack the American flanks and prepare to move again against the second militia line at the edge of the woods. A fierce fight ensues, but the second American line is finally thrown back. The American flanks also begin to collapse. When the British try the middle again, they find the Marylanders waiting. The Continentals fire into the advancing redcoats and then follow with a bayonet charge. The British assault is thrown back for at least the moment. The reserve comes forward, however, and renews the advance. A regiment of green American troops turns and runs, leaving the British room to come to arm's length of the defensive lines. Seeing the confused melee, Cornwallis orders his artillery turned on the entire mass, killing friend and foe alike. The Americans are driven back, and the British prepare for a final assault. The power of their advance is too much for the remaining Americans to withstand. Having no reserve to throw into the battle, Greene orders a retreat and the Americans quit the field. Greene marches in good order to a previous camp on Troublesome Creek, and Cornwallis occupies the battlefield for the night. While the British have won whatever honors attach to the battle, they take terrible losses—532 in all. The American casualties are lighter, with seventy-eight killed and 183 wounded. Cornwallis' force is so depleted by his "victory" that he can only retreat to Wilmington. While Greene's battlefield tactics never seem to win him a triumph, his overall strategy is working—the British no longer have a fit army in North Carolina.

16 March 1781

CHESAPEAKE CAPES. Arbuthnot catches Destouches off the capes before the French fleet can land the troops sent to support Lafayette. The two naval forces are almost evenly matched—eight ships apiece—but the British have slightly heavier guns. Neither commander is more than mediocre, and the short engagement is close to a draw, with a slight advantage going to the French. Destouches, however, sails off to return to Rhode Island while Arbuthnot enters the bay and finds Arnold. Lafayette remains unreinforced.

18 March 1781

NORTH CAROLINA. Cornwallis' army, although technically victorious in the battle three days before, is in bad straits. Most of the troops have had little or no food since before the march to Guilford Courthouse and there are virtually no medical supplies. Cornwallis decides to make for Wilmington, 200 miles distant, and he leaves his wounded, packs up the army, and departs.

20 March 1781

SANDY HOOK, N.Y. Maj. Gen. William Phillips, a pioneer artilleryman in the British army, sails with 2,000 men to take command form Arnold of the British forces in Virginia. Sir Henry Clinton, the British commander-in-chief, has never trusted the turncoat and wants his own man in charge on the spot. Clinton does not, however, intend to make Virginia a major theater but prefers to prosecute the war in the Carolinas.

26 March 1781

NEWPORT. Destouches returns to his base, having achieved virtually nothing in the voyage to the Chesapeake. Lafayette, fearing Arnold has been reinforced by Arbuthnot, leaves Annapolis and returns to Head of Elk.

30 March 1781

PORTSMOUTH, VA. Phillips arrives in Virginia and takes command. Meanwhile, Lafayette has marched to Baltimore, where he refits his command, and thence to Alexandria and Fredericksburg.

1 April 1781

NORTH CAROLINA. Greene now sees opportunity to seriously weaken the British position in the entire Southern theater if he ignores Cornwallis and moves back on the offensive. He writes to Washington: "I am determined to carry the war immediately into South Carolina. The enemy will be obliged to follow us, or give up their posts in that state. If the former takes place, it will draw the war out of this state [North Carolina] and give it an opportunity to raise its proportion of men. If they leave their posts to fall, they must lose more there than they can gain here." With luck and energy, Greene might be able to rid South Carolina and even Georgia of British power. While the British commander in South Carolina, Lord Rawdon has a total of many troops—more than 8,000—most are scattered in a series of ten relatively small outposts all across the state. Greene has only 1,500 men, but they are almost all Continentals (the feckless militia having departed after the battle at Guilford Courthouse). In addition, the partisans of Marion, Sumter, and Pickens are still loose in the countryside. There is a good chance Greene can pick off the British outposts in detail if he can avoid defeat in a pitched battle with Rawdon.

6 April 1781

VIRGINIA. Washington orders Lafayette to advance on Richmond and to hold the city against whatever British forces come against him. Lafayette's New England and New Jersey troops, however, are fed up with marching and countermarching through the hot Southern spring. They begin to desert. Lafayette hangs one recaptured deserter, then confronts his men with an order saying they head for danger and if any wish to depart they may. He later writes: "From that hour on, all desertions ceased, and not a man would leave."

7 April 1781

WILMINGTON, N.C. Cornwallis' depleted army arrives. It is now a long way from the main action and will be effectively out of the coming Carolina campaign.

15 April 1781

FORT WATSON, S.C. Light Horse Harry Lee and Francis Marion combine forces to invest this small British stronghold, a fortified stockade. They have no artillery or digging tools, but Col. Hezekiah Maham invents a unique siege machine on the spot. He builds a tall rectangular box of logs from the nearby woods, places a crude platform on top, and provides riflemen with clear fields of fire over the walls of the stockade. A hundred fourteen British surrender when the "Maham Tower" leaves them defenseless.

18 April 1781

PORTSMOUTH, VA. Arnold with an army of 2,500 men leaves his camp at Portsmouth, intent on raiding more Virginia towns and countrysides.

24 April 1781

WILMINGTON, N.C. Cornwallis departs from Wilmington, headed for Virginia. He leaves Rawdon to deal with Greene and the partisan forces in the Carolinas.

PETERSBURG, VA. Phillips and Arnold have combined forces and approach Petersburg, which is defended by 1,000 militia in good positions under the command of Col. J. P. G. Muhlenberg, a Lutheran clergyman and veteran Continental officer. The militia discourage the British from a frontal assault and hold out most of the day. Eventually, British artillery and a flanking movement force withdrawal, but the Americans set up their own guns to cover the retreat and do considerable damage to the pursuing redcoats. Phillips and Arnold, however, march into Petersburg and burn tobacco stores and several small boats.

HOBKIRK'S HILL, S.C. Greene has brought a force of 1,200 Continentals and 200 militia to the top of this hill a few miles from Camden, where Rawdon's army is waiting. Greene believes he may be able to gain the upper hand over Rawdon but hopes reinforcements from Sumter and Lee will join him before a battle. The American army is comfortably in camp, feasting on recently arrived rations, when Rawdon springs a surprise attack with a 900-man force cobbled together from the garrison of the town. Greene's outposts hold off the British advance long enough for the Continentals to deploy in line at the top of the hill. Since Rawdon has attacked with a narrow front, Greene believes his men can envelop the British advance and he orders a bayonet charge down the hill. Rawdon quickly extends his line, but the American assault seems bent on victory. At the last minute, the elite 1st Maryland regiment falters, and its commander Col. John Gunby, orders it to withdraw from the battle line in order to re-form. The opening is all the British need and they swarm forward. The usually solid Continentals break and run. Only luck and the timely arrival of William Washington's dragoons saves the Americans from a complete disaster. Greene manages to organize a retreat. Rawdon leaves the field and goes back to Camden, which allows the American cavalry to rescue the wounded. Victory has again slipped from Greene's hand at the last minute. He has lost nineteen killed, 115 wounded, and 136 men are missing. The British lose 258 killed, wounded, and missing. As at Guilford Courthouse, the victory is costly to the British. Rawdon's force is further depleted and he has missed the chance to score decisively against Greene. The American general seems to lose battle after battle but is winning the campaign. As he writes to the French ambassador after the battle: "We fight, get beat, rise and fight again."

27 April 1781

CHESTERFIELD COURT HOUSE, VA. Phillips marches out of Petersburg to this village and burns barracks and a large store of flour. No one offers any resistance.

OSBORNE, VA. The same day, Arnold swoops down on this James River town and captures a small rebel supply fleet. He burns the ships, including four brigs and several small vessels, and takes 4,000 hogsheads of tobacco.

29 April 1781

RICHMOND, VA. Lafayette arrives just ahead of Phillips and occupies the city, which Arnold had previously sacked.

WEST INDIES. A strong French fleet under DeGrasse brushes aside British resistance and enters the harbor at Front Royal, Martinique. He tries to catch Hood's squadron the next day, but fails.

30 April 1781

MANCHESTER, VA. Phillips and Arnold destroy more tobacco on their way back to Portsmouth. They have been frustrated at Richmond by Lafayette's quick arrival.

7 May 1781

PHILADELPHIA. Citizens in Philadelphia tar an unfortunate dog, plaster its body with worthless Continental currency, and parade the animal through the streets in protest of the deteriorating state of the American economy. Merchants also threaten to close their shops unless paid in gold or silver.

9 May 1781

PENSACOLA. The British garrison falls to Galvez. Brig. Gen. John Campbell has made a remarkable resistance, considering that his motley 1,600-man force faced almost 7,000 Spaniards. Galvez's artillery bombardment explodes the main British powder magazine, which finally persuades the British commander that further fighting is useless. Spain now can claim all of both East and West Florida.

10 May 1781

CAMDEN, S.C. Rawdon withdraws

from Camden and orders other British garrisons around the state to evacuate. Greene sets off in cautious pursuit.

11 May 1781

ORANGEBURG, S.C. Thomas Sumter surrounds the British garrison, which got Rawdon's order to evacuate too late, and captures fifteen British regulars and seventy militia. Sumter has been more interested in following his own agenda than taking orders from Greene, neglecting to send any reinforcements before the battle at Hobkirk's Hill.

12 May 1781

FORT MOTTE, S.C. Marion and Lee besiege the strongly fortified house here that is a key British post. They learn Rawdon is marching this direction and they must hasten the proceedings. The Americans fire flaming arrows onto the shingle roof of the mansion, forcing the 150 British inside to surrender.

13 May 1781

PETERSBURG, VA. Gen. William Phillips dies of typhoid fever, leaving Benedict Arnold again in temporary command of the British forces in Virginia.

14 May 1781

PHILADELPHIA. Robert Morris formally accepts the post of superintendent of finance. He has driven a hard bargain with Congress, insisting on complete control of fiscal affairs and the power to name all his subordinates. In addition, he demands the right to continue to conduct his private business on the side. Congress hates and fears the idea of giving total financial power to one man, but it has

little choice. The finances of the national government are so desperate that extraordinary measures must be taken.

CROTON RIVER, N.Y. A group of Loyalists attacks the American outpost here and kills Col. Christopher Greene. Some reports say they mutilate his body.

FRIDAY'S FERRY, S.C. Lee pens in a group of Loyalist troops led by Maj. Andrew Maxwell, known for his plundering of American property. Lee announces that all "private property" will be allowed to pass if the Loyalists surrender. Maxwell promptly gives up and drives off with two wagonloads of goods toward parole in Charleston.

20 May 1781

PETERSBURG, VA. Lord Cornwallis arrives in Petersburg with 1,500 troops from Wilmington. He has come to assume command in Virginia and pursue his own strategy somewhat in defiance of Sir Henry Clinton's wishes. Within days, reinforcements push the British numbers to 7,200 men.

WESTERFIELD, CT. Washington orders Gen. Anthony Wayne south with a force of 1,000 men to aid Lafayette. Washington is in Connecticut to meet Rochambeau for a strategic conference.

21 May 1781

FORT GALPHIN, S.C. Yet another British outpost in South Carolina falls when Henry Lee swoops down on the headquarters of George Galphin, the British deputy superintendent of Indian affairs. After a quick fight, the

Americans seize all of the year's supply of trading goods sent from England, including blankets, clothing, small arms, medicine, and ammunition.

21–22 May 1781

WESTERFIELD, CT. After so many disappointments in working with the French allies, Washington hopes to devise a plan with Rochambeau (with whom the American commander-in-chief is on good terms) to make effective use of the 6,000 troops that have been in Newport since the preceding fall. A new French naval commander, the comte de Barras, is now on the scene, for example, and may provide more cooperation than previous French admirals. Moreover, Rochambeau and Washington know that De Grasse is in the West Indies with a significantly larger French fleet than has been available hitherto. The key to allied strategy is whether or not the French can break the British control of the sea lanes along the eastern coast of the United States. Sir Henry Clinton still holds New York with an overwhelmingly large force, and Arnold seems to have control over Virginia. Greene is making headway in the Carolinas, but appears unlikely to win any significant battle victories. The British can continue to operate at will so long as they can move troops and supplies by sea. De Barras proves to be little more cooperative than his predecessors, however, and refuses to act in conjunction with the land forces. The best plan that Washington and Rochambeau can come up with is to make demonstrations against New York City, but Clinton is too strong for the allies to try a real assault. There is still a hope of reinforcing the Americans in Virginia, however, if De Grasse should decide to come north and challenge the British Navy.

NINETY-SIX, S.C. Nathanael Greene brings his main force—about a thousand Continentals from Maryland, Delaware, and Virginia—to this important British post. The fortifications are among the strongest of all the British outposts, and they are manned entirely by Loyalists, many of them veterans from the North, including a large number of New Yorkers under Col. John Cruger. If Greene can take the fort, he will eliminate a powerful British position, but he has no artillery and must conduct a siege with pick and shovel. Cruger is a good soldier, however, and sends out quick sorties that disrupt the American's attempts to begin digging approaches.

24 May 1781

VIRGINIA. Lord Cornwallis leaves Petersburg, crosses the James River, and camps at Hanover Junction. Benedict Arnold leaves Virginia for New York.

26 May 1781

PHILADELPHIA. Congress accepts a plan by Robert Morris to incorporate a national bank, a badly needed institution if the nation's finances are to prosper. The body delays, however, in taking action. The immediate cash crisis is eased by a six-million-livre subsidy from France. The money is entrusted to Morris.

YORK, PA. Gen. Anthony Wayne departs for Virginia with troops to aid Lafayette. His force is drawn mainly from the Pennsylvania regiments reorganized after the mutiny, and several of the men voice dissatisfaction again over pay. Wayne has no patience with more unrest among his troops, and he has seven men shot. The nascent mutiny is quelled.

1 June 1781

NEW YORK AND VIRGINIA. Sir Henry Clinton, although still commander-in-chief of British forces in America, is in a difficult position regarding Lord Cornwallis. Clinton fully expects he will be relieved at any moment in favor of Cornwallis, and the latter has the ear of Lord George Germain in London. Clinton can do little to impose his will on Cornwallis, and he is rather astounded that Cornwallis has moved into Virginia and taken command—Clinton would have preferred Cornwallis to stay in the Carolinas. Given the new situation, Clinton proposes that Cornwallis either move his army north into the region of the Delaware River, where Clinton will meet him, or Cornwallis should withdraw by sea and return most of his army to New York for operations against Washington and Rochambeau. Cornwallis disagrees with both of Clinton's suggestions and decides instead to establish a strong base in Virginia, relying on the navy to keep him supplied and supported. Clinton acquiesces reluctantly.

2 June 1781

WEST INDIES. French admiral De Grasse seizes Tobago from the British after a short siege. Despite his local superiority, De Grasse declines during the coming weeks to engage the British naval squadron.

3 June 1781

NEW YORK. Letters from George Washington are captured and turned over to Sir Henry Clinton. The documents reveal the outlines of the allied "Westerfield Plan," but Clinton is suspicious of a ruse and acts cautiously on the information.

4 June 1781

CHARLOTTESVILLE, VA. Tarleton regains some of his reputation for speed and impudence with a lightning-quick raid on the state government of Virginia. With members of his British Legion and mounted troops from other regiments he dashes toward Charlottesville, hoping to bag the state legislature and Gov. Thomas Jefferson. Capt. John Jouett of the Virginia militia gallops just ahead of the British column to spread the alarm. The legislature flees to Staunton. A detachment of Tarleton's dragoons heads for Monticello, where Jefferson is entertaining the speaker of the assembly, but Jouett gets there before the British. Jefferson makes his escape by horseback, barely minutes ahead of Tarleton's men. After a brief skirmish, Tarleton enters Charlottesville and seizes military supplies and tobacco.

5 June 1781

AUGUSTA, GA. The British fort in Augusta have been under attack off and on since April by a changing variety of American partisan forces, including those of Pickens and Elijah Clarke. Lee joins the rebels and begins a determined siege, using the Maham Tower tactics. The British garrison finally surrenders on 5 June, and another British Southern outpost falls.

POINT OF FORKS, VA. Gen. von Steuben is outfoxed by British Col. Simcoe. The German has skillfully withdrawn a large store of supplies to safety across the Fluvanna River, but when Simcoe deploys his few troops to look like the vanguard of the entire British army, Steuben retreats—allowing Simcoe to cross the river and seize the supplies.

9 June 1781

NEWPORT, R.I. Rochambeau begins the movement of his troops to join Washington for demonstrations against New York. The French infantry marches twenty-five miles to Providence.

10 June 1781

VIRGINIA. Wayne's reinforcements reach Virginia and he links with Lafayette. Despite their mutinous tendencies, the new troops are seasoned veterans and greatly strengthen the American presence in the state. Lafayette should now be able to slow the hitherto unhampered raiding by the British against American towns and supply points.

11 June 1781

PHILADELPHIA. Congress decides to appoint a commission to handle future peace negotiations. Until now, John Adams has been responsible for discussions with the French on the issue. The problem is how to accommodate the French views on conditions for peace with Great Britain. French foreign minister Vergennes has brought almost irresistible pressure on Congress to give up nearly all preconditions of its own and to accept whatever terms the French can work out. Seeing little way around the need for French troops, ships, and money, Congress gives in and instructs the commission to insist only on recognition of American independence, leaving the French to decide all other

matters. In the coming weeks Congress appoints Benjamin Franklin, John Jay, Henry Laurens (who is still lodged in the Tower of London), and Thomas Jefferson (who declines to serve) to the commission, along with Adams.

12 June 1781

MECHUNK CREEK, VA. Lafayette moves to take a position that will allow him to forestall British movements against Charlottesville or Staunton.

15 June 1781

HEAD OF ELK. Blocked in his movements by Lafayette's new position, Lord Cornwallis begins to move his army back toward Richmond.

19 June 1781

NINETY-SIX, S.C. With the approach of Lord Rawdon and a larger British force than his own, Greene abandons the unsuccessful siège of Ninety-Six. A series of violent assaults has failed to take the stronghold, and to wait longer will invite disaster.

20 June 1781

VIRGINIA. Cornwallis leaves Richmond and moves toward Williamsburg, still seeking the best spot to establish a strong base that can be supplied from the sea.

24 June 1781

PEEKSKILL, N.Y. George Washington camps here, waiting for Rochambeau's force to join him.

26 June 1781

SPENCER'S TAVERN, VA. An American detachment under Col. Richard Butler and Col. William McPherson trys to intercept Simcoe, who has been sent by Cornwallis to destroy rebel stores while the main British force continues to Williamsburg. The Americans catch Simcoe's men only six miles from Williamsburg but cannot best Simcoe in a brief, sharp battle—much of it hand-to-hand between mounted opponents. The Americans withdraw after killing or wounding thirty-three and taking thirty-one casualties of their own.

A typical cavalry battle.

29 June 1781

NINETY-SIX, S.C. Deciding the fort cannot long be defended despite the recent failed American siege, the British evacuate the post at Ninety-Six.

3 July 1781

KING'S BRIDGE, N.Y. Washington, impatient to begin action against Clinton, hatches a plan to seize British outposts in northern Manhattan. The scheme is complex, calling for Maj. Gen. Benjamin Lincoln (the hapless defender of Charleston) to take 800 troops down from the Hudson to capture King's Bridge and then raid Fort Knyphausen. If foiled in this, Lincoln is to join the duc de Lauzun's French cavalry in attacking the De Lancey Loyalists at Morrisania, N.Y. The ad-

venture goes wrong almost from the start. The British have a strong mobile force outside Fort Knyphausen and a warship in the river nearby. The first option is gone, so Lincoln moves to implement the second; however, his advance guard meets a British foraging party that gives the alarm, and the local garrisons button up inside their fortifications. Lauzun's cavalry arrives too late, exhausted by a long ride in hot weather. Lincoln withdraws, having accomplished nothing.

6 July 1781

DOBBS FERRY, N.Y. Rochambeau joins Washington's force in preparation to move toward New York City.

GREEN SPRING, VA. Cornwallis nearly deals Lafayette a mortal blow at this crossing point on the James River. The British commander decides to move from Williamsburg and cross the river but he knows Lafayette is close behind. Cornwallis hides his main force in a wooded area near the swampy crossing and sends a few troops to the other side to deceive Lafayette into believing only a rear guard is left. Anthony Wayne moves close to the crossing with 500 men of the advance American guard. Cornwallis has nearly 7,000 hidden on the field, but he waits, hoping to draw Lafayette's entire army forward into the trap. Wayne skirmishes most of the day with the edges of the British army, which Wayne still believes to be only a small force. Lafayette arrives late in the afternoon, personally reconnoiters, and discovers the true state of the British dispositions. He is too late to warn Wayne, however. Cornwallis attacks Wayne with the full weight of the British force. Caught in a terrible predicament, Wayne takes the desperate option of attack—leading his men into the face of grapeshot, musket fire, and overwhelming odds. The tiny American force charges the British battle line, and its furious assault stops the redcoat advance. Lafayette is able to withdraw Wayne's remaining men and forms an orderly retreat. Night falls before Cornwallis can organize pursuit. The Americans lose twenty-eight killed, ninety-nine wounded, and twelve missing. The British have seventy-five killed and wounded.

9 July 1781

CURRYTOWN, N.Y. A mixed force of Loyalists and Indians surprises the settlers here, killing several and burning twelve buildings.

15 July 1781

QUINBY'S BRIDGE, S.C. Cracks appear in the alliance among American partisans after Thomas Sumter badly mismanages a bloody running fight with British Lt. Col. John Coates. Sumter ignores the advice of Francis Marion, Henry Lee, and Col. Thomas Taylor (a veteran militiaman) and causes unnecessary casualties in what turns out to be an inconclusive engagement. Taylor is outraged and tells Sumter he will never again serve with him. Lee and Marion both leave the next day, disgusted with the ever-willful Sumter.

21 July 1781

NEW YORK. Behind a screen of 5,000 troops, Rochambeau and Washington look over the defenses of New York City and Clinton's dispositions. They decide that an attack on the city would require a full-scale siege, something they lack the men and equipment to do.

26 July 1781

PHILADELPHIA. Congress continues to struggle with the problems of national finance. Even though the deflated Continental currency was called in at a ratio of forty to one more than a year before, much remains in circulation. In some parts of the country it is exchanged at 300 or 400 to one, giving origin to "not worth a Continental."

5 August 1781

YORKTOWN, VA. After considerable indecision, Cornwallis selects Yorktown as his base for further operations in Virginia. He occupies the town and its fortifications, as well as Gloucester Point opposite on the river. Both places must be held to make the base secure, and Gloucester Point affords the only certain means of supply by land or escape if needed. Yorktown itself is not particularly well suited for defense. The fortifications are reasonably strong, but the outer works are too close to the inner fort and there is no spot for elevated fire from the defenders. A determined and skilled siege will be fatal. Cornwallis has at his disposal, however, a large force of some of the best troops in the world. His garrison includes the Brigade of Guards, the 23rd, 33rd, and 71st foot regiments, and many more well-trained and seasoned units such as Tarleton's Legion and four German mercenary contingents. He also has 200 artillerymen, supplemented by naval gunners.

8 August 1781

ATLANTIC. Capt. James Nicholson in

command of the *Trumbull* engages the British ship *Iris*. Most of the American captain's crew is made up of British deserters who refuse to fight. After an hour and a half, Nicholson surrenders.

13 August 1781

HAITI. French Adm. De Grasse sails for the Chesapeake Bay. He is authorized to lend assistance to Rochambeau and Washington as they desire, but he is under orders to return to the West Indies by October 15, when the hurricane season will make naval operations impossible. He commands a powerful fleet and has aboard 3,000 troops and a train of siege cannon.

14 August 1781

NEW YORK. Rochambeau receives a letter from De Grasse, detailing the admiral's plan to sail directly to the Chesapeake. When Washington hears the news, the commander-in-chief makes the pivotal decision of the war: The American and French armies will abandon operations in New York and march immediately south to Virginia. If they arrive in time and if De Grasse can gain control of the sea approaches, Cornwallis will be trapped and overwhelmed. Washington orders Lafayette to keep Cornwallis bottled up in Yorktown. He also instructs Gen. William Heath to take half the Continental Army and hold Clinton in New York until too late for the British commander to send troops to Cornwallis' aid.

21 August 1781

NEW YORK. Washington and Rochambeau start the march south. They cross the Hudson, divide into three columns, and take a roundabout path in order to persuade Clinton that New York is still their object. Once the armies turn south and make the direction of their march known, however, they must move swiftly—if Clinton reacts in time, he may send an army to Cornwallis by sea before Washington and the French can march the 450 miles to Yorktown.

NEWPORT. Adm. De Barras prepares to sail southward to meet De Grasse. The admiral has only reluctantly been persuaded to aid the allied effort in Virginia. He prefers a naval expedition against shipping off Newfoundland and wants to avoid fighting under the command of De Grasse, who is technically his junior. Nonetheless, Washington has prevailed and De Barras will head toward Chesapeake Bay.

26 August 1781

VIRGINIA CAPES. De Grasse has eluded Rodney's squadron in the West Indies and arrives off the Virginia coast. The northern British fleet under Admiral Thomas Graves is slow to stir, and De Grasse controls the approaches to Yorktown for the time being. He makes contact with Lafayette and begins plans to land his troops.

28 August 1781

CHATHAM, N.J. Washington and Rochambeau halt temporarily to further decoy Clinton.

30 August 1781

PHILADELPHIA. The race southward is on. Washington and Rochambeau ride ahead of the armies and enter Philadelphia.

31 August 1781

JAMESTOWN, VA. The First French

General Charles Cornwallis, the British commander at Yorktown.

phia, they demand a month's pay in hard money. Washington implores Robert Morris for funds, but the only recourse is for the superintendent of finance to borrow the money from Rochambeau's well-stocked war chest. Satisfied, the army moves on toward Head of Elk.

NEW YORK. Sir Henry Clinton, whose mind may be preoccupied by his difficulties with Cornwallis and the government of Lord North, finally realizes where Rochambaeau and Washington are headed. He can do little to stop them, and he understands the extreme danger Cornwallis is in.

troops from the West Indies land from De Grasse's ships at Jamestown to reinforce Lafayette.

2 September 1781

PHILADELPHIA. The French and American armies reach Philadelphia on their journey south. They scarcely pause, but the stop is long enough for the Continental troops to practice a little blackmail against Congress. The army is relatively small—comprised of two New Jersey regiments, Scammell's light infantry, the Rhode Island regiment, Moses Hazen's "Canadian" regiment, two New York regiments, light infantry from Connecticut, John Lamb's artillery regiment, and various units of engineers, sappers, and miners—numbering in total around 2,000 men. The reconstituted Pennsylvania Line has gone on ahead and is with Wayne and Lafayette in Virginia. Most of these Northern troops have suffered grievously for lack of pay, food, and supplies, and they are not keen on being hustled now to fight in the South. Before leaving Philadel-

The meeting of the French and British fleets off Cape Henry.

5 September 1781

CHESTER, PA. Washington, traveling overland to where the armies will embark for the water leg of the journey to Virginia, meets an express rider who brings him news that De Grasse's fleet has arrived safely. Until this moment, the commander-in-chief has been in the dark as to whether the French navy will actually turn up at the right place and at the right time. Washington is ecstatic and turns back to find Rochambeau, who is traveling by water to Head of Elk. When the Frenchman's boat arrives at the wharf, Washington, usually the most dignified of men in public, stands on the jetty, waving his hat furiously and shouting the news.

CHESAPEAKE BAY. Washington's elation would be even greater could he peer down the bay and out onto the waters off the outer islands of Virginia. Adm. De Grasse, who so often has been cautious when facing the British navy, sails out of his anchorage this morning when the sails of a British fleet come in sight. He intends to give battle to the combined force of British admirals Graves and Hood. De Grasse's flagship, the *Ville de Paris*, carries 110 guns and is probably the largest warship afloat. The rest of the French fleet includes twenty-four ships of the line, ranging from sixty-four to eighty guns, and six frigates. The British have only nineteen ships of the line and seven frigates. The action is joined at 4:00 P.M. The British have the advantage of wind and position, but the heavier and more numerous guns of the French ships more than compensate. After a two-hour battle, the British are forced to draw off with many ships badly damaged. De Grasse returns to the mouth of the bay. After inconclusive maneuvers, the British admirals decide to head back to New York. They sail away, leaving Cornwallis in Yorktown with no hope of rescue or reinforcement. His fate is sealed by the French naval victory.

6 September 1781

HEAD OF ELK. Advance units of the American army arrive to be taken by

boat down the Chesapeake to Williamsburg. The men have marched the hundreds of miles from New York in only a little over two weeks. Other elements take ship at Baltimore and Annapolis for the last leg of the journey.

NEW LONDON, CT. In a nasty last bit of business, Benedict Arnold lands an amphibious force of regulars and Loyalists at this seaport, close to his old home. The British raiders, aided by local Loyalists, successfully overcome the few American defenders and sack the town, doing nearly a half-million dollars' damage. Several American officers are brutally killed after they have surrendered. Although Arnold's reputation among patriots could hardly sink lower, this cruel episode cements forever the view of the traitor. Soon after, he leaves for England.

8 September 1781

EUTAW SPRINGS, S.C. In what proves the last major stand-up battle of the Revolution, Nathanael Greene's Carolina army meets the British in one of the hardest-fought engagements of the entire war, and one that costs the British a high rate of casualties. Lt. Col. Alexander Stewart, now in command of the British army after the departure for England of the young Lord Rawdon two months before, is camped with about 2,000 men on the Santee River. Greene sees an opportunity for surprise and approaches cautiously with force similar in size to the British. The American army includes the familiar Continentals from Maryland, Delaware, and Virginia, as well as Lee's Legion, William Washington's horse troops, partisans under Marion and Pickens, and militia.

The Battle of Eutaw Springs, in South Carolina; it was the final battle of the Southern campaign before Yorktown.

Greene's advance units surprise an early-morning party of British foragers (sent to gather sweet potatoes) and take several captives. Maj. John Coffin, a Boston Loyalist, moves out with his South Carolina cavalry to scout and rides into an ambush. He escapes, however, and hurries back to alert Stewart that Greene's army is in the field. The British hurry into line of battle in front of their camp, with a strong contingent under Maj. John Marjoribanks on the right in a thicket and the rest of the army between the river and a ravine on the left. The battle is joined as the Americans advance. The American militia perform superbly—firing at least seventeen volleys without flinching. The British finally break the militia, however, by bringing on the reserve infantry and cavalry. Behind the American militia are the doughty Marylanders and Virginians, who move into the center and drive the British back to their own camp with a bayonet attack. Stewart's army is on the verge of collapse when the Americans stop to plunder among the British tents. Lee and William Washington try to rally the army, but when their horsemen attack Marjoribanks' force in the thicket, many American dragoons are shot down, and Washington is badly wounded. Marjoribanks, the British hero of the day, leads his men in a mad race for a brick house, reaching safety only yards ahead of the Americans. Once in the house, the British turn a devastating musket and swivel-gun fire on their enemies. The Americans grab British soldiers and officers left outside when the door was slammed shut and use them for shields to retreat. More British rally to the house and the garden nearby, and Marjoribanks leads them in a sortie that sweeps among the looting Americans at the campsite. The gallant major is killed in the action, but he has furnished a victory for the British. Greene is forced yet again to withdraw from a battle that he seemed on the edge of winning. The toll of the engagement is brutal—especially for Stewart, who cannot replace losses. The British take the highest rate of loss of any army during the entire Revolutionary War —losing 693 killed, wounded, or missing out of a force of probably less than 2,000. The American casualties are 500. Stewart retreats toward Charleston.

HEAD OF ELK. The French army from Rhode Island reaches the head of Chesapeake Bay and begins to embark for Williamsburg.

9 September 1781

CHESAPEAKE BAY. De Barras' fleet arrives at the mouth of the bay to join the ships of De Grasse. The French now have complete control of the Chesapeake and will be able to land all the additional troops and guns needed to invest Cornwallis at Yorktown.

MOUNT VERNON. Gen. George Washington detours to visit his home for the first time in six years. Since 1775, he has commanded the American forces from posts in the North. Tonight he sleeps in his mansion on a bluff high above the Potomac.

13 September 1781

HILLSBORO, N.C. In a daring action, Loyalist Col. David Fanning organizes and carries out a raid on the patriot government in Hillsboro. Fanning assembles a Loyalist force of nearly a thousand men, and after a quick all-night march, they take Hillsboro and capture Gov. Thomas Burke along with the council and several Continental officers and men. They withdraw about noon. On their march away from Hillsboro, they are attacked by Continentals under Gen. John Butler. The following battle is fierce, with the Loyalists and the patriots each taking over 100 casualties. Fanning himself is badly wounded and left on the field while the remainder of his force flees with the prisoners in tow.

15 September 1781

WILLIAMSBURG, VA. The allied forces assembling here in preparation for launching the siege against Yorktown give Washington and Rochambeau a grand military review. Afterward, American officers go in a body to visit Washington, as Lt. Ebenezer Denny of a Pennsylvania brigade describes in his journal: "Officers all pay their respects to the Commander-in-Chief. . . . Those who are not person-ally known, their names given by General Hand and General Wayne. He stands in the door, takes every man by the hand. The officers all pass in, receiving his salute and shake." There are nearly 16,000 men in the allied armies surrounding Lord Cornwallis. The Virginia army of Lafayette has joined the troops who marched south with Washington, and the entire American force is organized into three divisions under Lafayette, Benjamin Lincoln, and Von Steuben. Rochambeau's French army includes four regiments that traveled south from Rhode Island and three ferried from the West Indies by De Grasse, in addition to Lauzun's cavalry, 600 artillerymen, and 800 marines. To defend Yorktown Cornwallis has about 6,000 men, most of them British regulars or German mercenaries, with a few marines and Loyalist militia. Part of Cornwallis' force, including Tarleton's Legion, is posted across the river to hold the landings at Gloucester. The rest is bottled up inside the main Yorktown fortifications.

17 September 1781

WILLIAMSBURG, VA. Washington and Rochambeau meet De Grasse aboard the latter's flagship. Their plan to take Yorktown is relatively simple, if De Grasse stays in the area and controls the seaward approaches. Siege warfare is one of the best understood of all military operations—only if the attackers make a major mistake or if the besieged can either escape or be relieved by outside forces will the final outcome be in doubt. So long as the attacking allies make the proper, almost ritualistic, moves Cornwallis is finished. The plan is to encircle Yorktown and bombard it with heavy siege

SIEGE WARFARE

It was very hard to completely destroy an eighteenth-century army in the field—a point proved by George Washington and Nathanael Greene many times over—but entire armies could be captured through siege warfare if their commanders were so incautious as to pen themselves up inside fortifications with no prospect for escape or relief by an outside force. The decisive "battle" of the war at Yorktown was in fact a siege, conducted along lines well known to all the combatants.

The principles of siege warfare had been laid down generations before by the great French military engineer, the Marquis de Vauban, and were still valid in the 1770s. The success of a siege was almost inevitable if operations were placed in the hands of competent commanders equipped with the necessary artillery and manpower. By the time of the American Revolution, all military commanders knew that the odds were so in favor of the besiegers that seldom did a fortified and encircled army attempt to hold out to the last extremity.

After assembling a sufficient force, the attackers began to dig long trenches. The first was usually parallel to the main line of fortifications and placed about 600 yards away (at the extreme effective range of artillery of the day). Working under cover of their own long-range guns, the diggers excavated as rapidly as possible. When the first parallel was finished, the workers turned to digging trenches that approached the fortifications at angles (to prevent enfilade fire from the defenders). As they moved forward, infantry occupied the trenches behind them, ready to repulse a sudden foray by foot soldiers from the fort. When the angled approaches reached to within 300 yards or so, a second long parallel was begun. The attackers moved in heavy siege artillery and mortars to begin to pound down the walls of the fortifications and to drop explosives into the middle of the defenders. More angled approaches were dug from the second parallel and the attack brought ever closer to the walls. Occasionally, defensive strong points were attacked by assault and the captured positions then turned into more sites for siege guns. Eventually, the defenders had to surrender.

The British took Charleston in 1780 with just such tactics, and Cornwallis' fate at Yorktown was sealed when the mass of allied troops and a train of heavy siege guns arrived.

During smaller engagements along the upper New York frontier and in the South, the techniques of siege were cruder and less effective. The fortifications were usually small, perhaps only a stout brick house or a log enclosure, but the attackers seldom had the artillery needed to batter down the walls nor the time to dig elaborate trenches. The attackers in such cases sometimes used ancient techniques such as fire arrows to drive the defenders out into the open, but makeshift sieges often failed.

guns landed from De Grasse's ships. The allied engineers will dig trenches at angles to approach the fortifications and mount new artillery batteries in forward positions as soon as possible to batter the defenders. Strong points of the defense may be taken by storm, and the army inside the fortifications may sally out in quick raids to delay the digging, but without the operation of some outside force, the siege will inexorably triumph by digging. The defenses of Yorktown extend in a circle with seven redoubts (strong points) and six artillery batteries connected by trenches. Other batteries and redoubts support the main works. At Gloucester, the village is protected by a line of trenches.

23 September 1781

NEW YORK CITY. Sir Henry Clinton twists and turns but can devise no certain plan to save the army at Yorktown. Today he receives a letter from Cornwallis that predicts "If you cannot relieve me very soon, you must be prepared to hear the worst."

28 September 1781

WILLIAMSBURG, VA. The allied armies move out at dawn from Williamsburg and advance to take positions around Yorktown. The British outposts withdraw as the allies approach. By nightfall the Americans and French are in position.

30 September 1781

YORKTOWN, VA. Cornwallis orders the outer works to be abandoned during the night. He believes his only hope is to await relief by sea—he hears that Clinton intends to set sail from New York within days—and he wants to conserve his force. The allies

scramble forward to occupy the deserted places and begin to entrench. They now can begin the siege operations from within a few hundred yards of the main fortifications. There are nasty encounters as the allies drive in outlying British detachments. Washington sends Gen. de Choisy across the river with Lauzun's cavalry to keep Tarleton's men bottled up in Gloucester.

1 October 1781

YORKTOWN, VA. American batteries mounted in the outer works abandoned by the British pound Yorktown, and British guns fire in return on the attackers. Although the siege is a sort of stylized dance, much different than an open-ground battle between armies, it is still a dangerous enterprise—dozens of men are killed by artillery fire or brief, sharp clashes outside redoubts. The allies have many of their heavy guns in position, and the men have been busy making wickerwork baskets and stakes needed for the advancement of the parallel trenches.

3 October 1781

GLOUCESTER, VA. De Choisy moves closer to the British trenches at the same time as a British foraging party comes out to gather food. Lauzun's troopers and Tarleton's dragoons fight a quick skirmish in a country lane after the forage party is surprised by the allies marching toward the town. Pushing the British back inside the fortifications, De Choisy takes a position close by and prevents further forays.

6 October 1781

YORKTOWN, VA. Gen. George Washington ceremonially breaks ground for the first approach trench. The allies begin digging 600 yards from the main British fortifications; soon 1,500 men are at work with picks and shovels. They throw up an embankment on the side toward the British to protect themselves from fire. As soon as the head of the trench moves forward, armed troops occupy the ditch. The French attack the outermost British redoubt to prevent sorties. The digging continues without pause.

9 October 1781

YORKTOWN, VA. More allied cannon are in place and the bombardment of the city begins in earnest. Washington himself fires the first shot from a new American battery on the right of the defenses. A French battery opposite the British-held Fusiliers' Redoubt opens fire with four twelve-pounders as well as howitzers and mortars. The shells can now reach the Gloucester side, and a bombardment drives off one of the two remaining British frigates in the river.

10 October 1781

TREADWELL'S NECK, N.Y. A Loyalist post called Fort Slongo is attacked by Continental dragoons under Maj. Lemuel Trescott. The Americans take the fort with no losses, burn the blockhouse, and withdraw across Long Island Sound.

YORKTOWN, VA. More allied guns come on line and step up the bombardment, while the Americans and French reinforce the trenches against attack by British raiding parties. Redhot shot from French guns sets afire a British brig and two transports on the river.

11 October 1781

YORKTOWN, VA. The first allied approach trench reaches a thousand yards length, and a second is begun at another angle, only 300 yards from the main works. The barrage from allied artillery has nearly silenced British guns in the fortifications. Cornwallis writes to Clinton: "We have lost about seventy of our men and many of our works are considerably damaged; with such works on disadvantageous ground, against so powerful an attack, we cannot hope to make a very long resistance." By nightfall, the new parallel is 750 yards long.

Behind the American lines at Yorktown.

14 October 1781

YORKTOWN, VA. In order to extend the approaching trenches to the river, the allies must take two redoubts. Attacks are made during the night by Americans under Alexander Hamilton and by the French under Col. de Deux-Ponts. The Americans bash through the barriers in front of the redoubt on the right and overwhelm the defenders with a furious bayonet charge. The French also succeed, forcing the surrender of the German mercenaries defending the redoubt on the left. By morning, the diggers have extended the trenches and incorporated the captured redoubts into the allied system of strong points.

16 October 1781

YORKTOWN, VA. Cornwallis sends out a sortie against the second allied line of trenches. A force of 350 men dashes out of the fort and briefly overruns the forward allied batteries. They spike the guns but are forced back by French genadiers under the comte de Noailles. The guns are back in action within hours. Cornwallis has one last hope—to evacuate his army across the river and break out on a forced march to the Delaware River and thence to New Jersey. If he can evade the allied armies around Yorktown, nothing will stand between him and Clinton's base in New York City. Shortly before midnight, he sends the Guards and units of light infantry across the river to Gloucester in boats with the rest of the army to follow; however, a storm blows up and the boats cannot return to the Yorktown side. Escape is impossible, and the troops return to Yorktown the following morning.

17 October 1781

YORKTOWN, VA. As Lt. Denny of Pennsylvania awaits his relief from duty in the trenches at about 10:00 A.M., he has "the pleasure of seeing a drummer mount the enemy's parapet and beat a parley, and immediately an officer, holding up a white handkerchief, made his appearance outside their works. The drummer accompanied him, beating. Our batteries

Americans burning an Indian village. Sporadic border conflict continued throughout the war.

ceased. An officer from our lines ran and met the other and tied the handkerchief over his eyes. The drummer was sent back, and the British officer conducted to a house in the rear of our lines. Firing ceased totally." The officer is taken to Washington and asks for an armistice and appointment of commissioners to discuss terms of surrender. Washington grants a two-hour cease-fire and demands a proposal from Cornwallis in writing. The British commander asks for his troops to be paroled and returned to England, but Washington demands unconditional surrender. By nightfall, Cornwallis agrees.

NEW YORK. Sir Henry Clinton tardily prepares to sail to Cornwallis' rescue. He learns of the surrender before his ships arrive, however, and turns back.

19 October 1781

YORKTOWN, VA. The allied troops assemble in a double line a mile long, the Americans on the right and the French on the left. Washington is at the head of the American line, mounted on his horse. Rochambeau is opposite. Finally after an hour's wait, the British begin to march out of the fort with colors cased. Cornwallis pleads illness in order to avoid the ignominy of surrender to the despised Americans. The splendidly uniformed British can scarcely bear the idea of giving up to the Americans and most officers and men display, according to one observer, "much arrogance and ill-humour" while ignoring the American presence and keeping their eyes fixed on the French troops. The British throw down their arms and stand in sullen defeat. Gen. Charles O'Hara presents Cornwallis' sword to Washington in token of surrender, but Gen. Benjamin Lincoln, who had been forced to give up at Charleston, steps forward to ceremonially accept the gesture of defeat. Across the river, Tarleton surrenders to De Choisy. The allies take more than 7,000 prisoners. The men are marched off to prison camps, but Cornwallis and his principal officers are paroled and sent back to New York. The War of the Revolution is won.

The surrender at Yorktown. Washington watches as General Charles O'Hara relinquishes General Cornwallis' sword to General Benjamin Lincoln.

20 October 1781

PHILADELPHIA. Robert Livingston of New York takes office as secretary of foreign affairs. Although it established the office in January, the Congress has been unable for most of the year to select a candidate. Livingston is a distinguished member of Congress and has served on many important committees since the first days of the Revolution. At the same time, Robert Morris becomes secretary of finance.

22 October 1781

PHILADELPHIA. Tench Tilghman, an aide-de-camp to George Washington, rides into Philadelphia with the news of the victory at Yorktown. He arrives at three in the morning and goes immediately to President Thomas McKean's house to tell the presiding officer of Congress. The night watchman, who takes Tilghman to McKean, begins to cry in the streets: "Past three o'clock and Cornwallis is taken!" Euphoria prevails as the city awakens to the news—after six and a half long years, the British are defeated. Elias Boudinot, a congressman from New Jersey, writes to his brother that it is "a day famous in the annals of American history . . . would to God that a deep sense of gratitude may follow this remarkable smile of Heaven at the critical era." There is no money in the national treasury to pay Tilghman's expenses, so individual congressmen donate a dollar each to cover the costs of his journey from Virginia. The entire city is lit up in celebration, and cannon boom out salutes. As the news spreads to other cities, similar celebrations erupt. A New York paper reports: "At Fishkill . . . the glorious victory was observed with exuberant joy and festivity. A roasted ox and plenty of liquor formed the repast; a number of toasts were drunk. . . . French and American colors were displayed, cannon fired, and in the evening, illuminations, bonfires, rockets and squibs gave agreeable amusement."

24 October 1781

PHILADELPHIA. Washington's official dispatch about the surrender of Cornwallis reaches Congress. The body goes to the Lutheran Church for a service by one of the chaplains of Congress, attended also by all the government officials of Pennsylvania and Philadelphia as well as Luzerne, the minister of France. President McKean writes officially to Washington with profuse congratulations.

25 October 1781

JOHNSTOWN, N.Y. A sharp encounter takes place between Loyalist raiders and American militia.

30 October 1781

PHILADELPHIA. Congress appoints Gen. Benjamin Lincoln secretary at war. It also implores the states for eight million dollars immediately to meet the costs of the army and the government. A South Carolina delegate writes home: "On the general subject of supplies we need hardly inform you that our army is extremely clamorous, we cannot pay them—we can hardly feed them. There is no money in the treasury and we are obliged to draw upon the foreign loans before they are perfected."

5 November 1781

YORKTOWN, VA. Despite Washington's pleas to remain and mount further campaigns to retake Savannah and Charleston from the British, Adm. De Grasse sails with his fleet for the West Indies. He has already overstayed his original commitment and he has a secret agreement with the Spanish that he will winter in the Caribbean.

10 November 1781

YORKTOWN, VA. The Americans fill in the siege trenches they have so recently dug in order to prevent a future enemy from using the approaches. The American army also begins to disperse—Gen. St. Clair leading a force of Continentals south to reinforce Greene in the Carolinas and Washington's men back to the Hudson to stand guard against the thousands of British soldiers still in New York City. Rochambeau's French remain in Virginia.

18 November 1781

WILMINGTON, NC. The British garrison evacuates the city.

20 November 1781

PARIS. French foreign minister Vergennes summons Franklin and gives him the news of the British defeat at Yorktown.

25 November 1781

LONDON. The awful news of Cornwallis' surrender reaches London. A packet boat from Paris brings the first dispatches, and a letter from Clinton arrives at the same time to confirm the story. Lord Germain goes to Downing Street to tell Lord North, who takes the news "as he would have taken a ball in the breast." North paces the room, exclaiming: "Oh God! it is all over." Gloom envelops the entire government, and Anthony Storer writes: "What are we to do after Lord Cornwallis' catastrophe? God knows, how any body can think there is the least glimmering of hope for this nation surpasses my comprehension." On the face of things, the single defeat should not spell disaster for the British cause in North America. There are still more than 30,000 British troops active, and they hold all the major American ports save Boston. However, the blow comes at a crucial moment: The British will to fight in America has ebbed low, and there is an overwhelming fear of the combined French and Spanish fleets—a fear only reinforced by De Grasse's victory off the Chesapeake. And the huge debt from the war is nearing crisis proportions. Peace with America seems the only solution.

WEST INDIES. The French recapture the Dutch trading post of St. Eustatius from the British.

1 December 1781

DORCHESTER, S.C. Nathanael Greene pushes up against the main British force, which is under the temporary command of Maj. John Doyle. Relatively light fighting sends the British in retreat to Charleston, where they remain bottled up.

6 December 1781

PHILADELPHIA. The great victory at Yorktown cannot change the grave financial crisis still facing Congress. In fact, many fear that when the British threat dissolves, the union of the states will disintegrate entirely. Alexander Hamilton writes: "There are dangerous prejudices in the particular states opposed to those measures which alone can give stability and prosperity to the Union. There is a fatal opposition to Continental views. Necessity alone can work a reform." Today, Congress dispatches a delegation to Rhode Island, the last holdout, to urge again that state's acceptance of the 5 percent national duty on imports—a measure long stalled that would do much to solve the financial impotence of the Congress. Before the delegation is well on the road, however, word comes that Virginia has rescinded its previous approval and the issue is dead.

GLORIOUS NEWS.

PROVID$\tilde{\text{E}}$CE, October 25, 1781.

Three o'Clock, P. M.

THIS MOMENT an EXPRESS arrived at his Honour the Deputy-Governor's, from Col. Chriftopher Olney, Commandant on Rhode-Ifland, announcing the important Intelligence of the Surrender of Lord Cornwallis and his Army, an Account of which was printed This Morning at Newport, as is as follows, viz.

Newport, October 25, 1781.

YESTERDAY afternoon arrived in this Harbour Capt. Lovett, of the Schooner Adventure, from York-River, in Chefapeak-Bay (which he left the 20th Inftant) and brought us the glorious News of the Surrender of Lord CORNWALLIS and his Army Prifoners of War to the allied Army, under the Command of our illuftrious General, and the French Fleet, under the Command of his Excellency the Count de GRASSE.

A Ceffation of Arms took Place on Thurfday the 18th Inftant, in Confequence of Propofals from Lord Cornwallis for a Capitulation. His Lordfhip propofed a Ceffation of Twenty-four Hours, but Two only were granted by His Excellency General WASHINGTON. The Articles were completed the fame Day, and the next Day the allied Army took Poffeffion of York-Town.

By this glorious Conqueft, NINE THOUSAND of the Enemy, including Seamen, fell into our Hands, with an immenfe Quantity of Warlike Stores, a forty Gun Ship, a Frigate, an armed Veffel, and about One Hundred Sail of Tranfports.

PRINTED BY EDWARD E. POWARS, in STATE-STREET.

"Broadsides" spread the word of the British surrender.

20 December 1781

LONDON. A brief session of Parliament comes to an end. During the sitting, members have debated the issue of continuing the war in America, with the general conclusion that the nation can no longer afford the costs. Lord North tries to make the point to the king, but George III is adamant that Britain can never give up the struggle or else it will lose its place among the great powers of the world. Lord George Germain attempts to resign, but the king insists that either he remain or someone willing to pursue the war take his place. North and the king are at an impasse for the time being, but all support for the American war has collapsed in Parliament and among the armed forces. It is only a matter of time until the king must agree to peace.

22 December 1781

BOSTON. The Marquis de Lafayette takes ship to return to France, his service to the American cause now at an end.

31 December 1781

PHILADELPHIA. Congress reluctantly grants a charter to the national bank first approved the previous spring. Many doubt that Congress has the power to enact such a charter, but subscribers to the bank and Finance Secretary Morris insist.

AFTERMATH OF REVOLUTION:
★ 1782-1783 ★

The Revolutionary War was over when Lord Cornwallis' army marched out of the battlements at Yorktown to stack its arms in defeat.

Sir Henry Clinton could not mount a new offensive in either the Northern or Southern theaters—especially in light of the French naval threat—nor did he want to. In London, there was no longer a will to fight, except in the mind of George III. His support in Parliament evaporated, however, and his own ministers urged peace on the king. After resisting for a few months while the parliamentary majority of Lord North's government declined, the king was forced to give in. The actual peace process took almost another two years before it was final, but the outcome was inevitable after October 1781.

Lord George Germain resigned in February 1782, and in March the government of Lord North fell after having prosecuted the war for more than six years. No politicians would agree to take office in a coalition, so the king bitterly turned to the opposition and asked the Marquis of Rockingham to form a new government. Rockingham insisted on peace with America as his price. The new prime minister named Lord Shelburne secretary of state for America and instructed him to begin talks with the American peace commissioners in Paris. The government also appointed Sir Guy Carleton the new British commander-in-chief in North America and told him to begin evacuation of British bases in the United States. Richard Oswald, the Cabinet's envoy, crossed the Channel and began informal negotiations with Franklin, the only American commissioner in place. The talks continued through the summer. After Rockingham's sudden death in July, Shelburne became prime minister and pressed for an agreement. The Americans in Paris recognized that France was more interested in supporting Spanish claims in the New World than in a peace on American terms. Eventually Franklin, along with John Adams and Jay (who joined the work of the commission by early fall), reached agreement with Oswald, and preliminary terms were signed in November 1782. These formed the essential clauses of the final treaty, which was not signed until September of the following year.

Except for a few minor skirmishes, all fighting ceased in America after Yorktown. However, winning the war in the field seemed to intensify the problems of civil government. Congress was impotent under the new Articles of Confederation to raise money or conduct the affairs of the nation. The individual states consistently refused any plan that would have taxed their own citizens, and there was a growing political struggle between those who favored a loose national confederation and those who insisted on a strong central government. This debate continued for many years and was not resolved—even for the time being—until the adoption of a new Constitution in 1789. Meanwhile, the nation showed ominous signs of falling apart in 1782 and 1783, just as victory was in hand. The spirit of cooperation and patriotism so evident in 1775 when Virginians, for example, rallied to the plight of Bostonians was dormant if not dead. The national treasury was empty, and no statesmen arose to revive Congress as an instrument of national will.

Much of the crisis during 1782 and 1783 focused on the army. In early 1782 Washington withdrew most of the troops to headquarters at Newburgh, N.Y., where both the officers and men began to agitate for back pay and retirement benefits from Congress. Advocates of a strong central government played on the fears of the army, and in March 1783 a near-conspiracy among officers at Newburgh threatened Congress unless payment was settled. Washington quashed the threat by force of his own personality, but he could do nothing to resolve the underlying issue. He furloughed almost all the enlisted men of the Continental Army in May 1783, but in June members of a Pennsylvania regiment marched on Congress, demanding back pay. When the state of Pennsylvania refused to protect them, the delegates fled to Princeton, N.J., and the work of government virtually came to a halt. Meanwhile, the British evacuated their last bases, taking thousands of Loyalists with them for resettlement in Canada or England.

With the final British threat gone, Washington bade farewell to the army and resigned his commission in December 1783. Difficult days and years lay ahead for the new nation, but the Revolution itself was at an end.

★ 1782 ★

January 1782
LONDON. King George III remains unconvinced that he must give up the idea of subduing the Americans. He goes so far as to prepare a statement of abdication, since he would rather vacate the throne than admit defeat. The clamor for peace in Parliament—spurred by the defection of the rural landowners who have so long supported the king's policy and the war—disgusts the king; however, he is persuaded by his ministers that talk of abdication will only bring on a worse crisis.

An example of Continental paper money in use during the Revolution.

7 January 1782
PHILADELPHIA. The new national bank opens for business and temporarily relieves some of the most acute financial problems of Congress, but the national treasury is still bare, with no prospects of replenishment by income from the states.

11 February 1782
LONDON. After weeks of vacillation, the king finally accepts Lord George Germain's resignation. The former secretary of state is created Viscount Sackville in reward for his services during the war. The king still resists the notion that peace must be made, but his governmental majority appears to be eroding rapidly in Parliament.

4 March 1782
LONDON. After several close votes during the preceding weeks, the House of Commons passes a resolution that says anyone who attempts to continue the war in America is an enemy of the country and the king. A further vote enables the king to make a peace.

20 March 1782
LONDON. The final crisis for the government of Lord North arrives. His majorities in the House have declined steadily over the preceding weeks, and if he is to avoid the humiliation of a formal vote of no confidence, he must resign. He sends a letter to the king, who vacillates, but finally accepts the end of the American policy. North announces his decision in the House. The king has no choice but to turn to the opposition to form a new govern-

ment, after he fails to devise a coalition.

22 March 1782

LONDON. The Marquis of Rockingham agrees to form a new government, on the condition that Great Britain recognize the independence of the United States. Lord Shelburne becomes secretary of state in charge of American affairs and will conduct peace negotiations.

1 April 1782

NEWBURGH, N.Y. Washington establishes a new headquarters for the Continental Army at Newburgh. Aside from forces still in the field in the Carolinas and troops watching the upper Hudson, most of the remaining armed soldiers of the United States gather at the new camp. Washington wants to keep the army together until all danger of further British resistance dissipates; however, the straitened conditions of the previous months continue with almost no money available for pay and supplies. Both officers and men begin to grumble loudly as the euphoria of victory wears off.

4 April 1782

LONDON. The new government appoints Sir Guy Carleton commander-in-chief of British forces in North America. The Cabinet instructs Carleton to attempt no offensive action, but to prepare to withdraw from all bases in the United States. He is also to protect any Loyalists who may now want to abandon the former colonies for British territory. If the large number of British troops in New York, Savannah, and Charleston can be quickly evacuated, they can be used elsewhere against the French and Spanish who threaten British bases in the West Indies and the Mediterranean.

12 April 1782

PARIS. Richard Oswald, appointed by the new Rockingham government to negotiate with the American peace commissioners, arrives in Paris. He has only Benjamin Franklin to talk to. John Adams is still in Holland, hoping to negotiate a much-needed loan, and John Jay is in Madrid finishing a difficult and fruitless mission to the Spanish court. Henry Laurens is still in British custody, although he is soon to be released, and Thomas Jefferson has declined to serve on the commission. Franklin is in a challenging position. Officially, Congress has instructed the commission that it is to insist only on a recognition of independence from Great Britain and to follow France's instructions in all other matters. However, as the war is now over, it becomes clear that France has little concern for the United States and is really interested in supporting the claims of Spain in the New World. The Spanish have never recognized American independence and want to stifle any future expansion of American influence. Spain wants American territorial claims limited severely, and itself wants control of the Floridas and the Mississippi Valley. The United States—despite the official policy induced by French blackmail during the last year of the war—wants to secure fishing rights off Newfoundland and free navigation of the Mississippi, but Franklin must play his hand cautiously.

WEST INDIES. Adm. George Rodney deals a crushing blow to the French fleet, capturing Adm. De Grasse and his magnificent flagship and dispersing the rest of the French warships. The victory eases British fears of the French.

19 April 1782

THE HAGUE. The Netherlands formally recognizes the independence of the United States and receives John Adams as its ambassador.

9 May 1782

NEW YORK. Sir Guy Carleton arrives to take command.

22 May 1782

NEWBURGH, N.Y. The states have managed to improve supplies to the army, and the men are now reasonably well fed and clothed, but there is still no money to provide pay. Some officers—especially those who fear impoverishment after discharge—believe the Congress under the Articles of Confederation will never solve its problems. A small group decides that a return to monarchy is the only answer, and they approach Gen. George Washington with a proposal (stated in a letter from Col. Lewis Nicola, a supply officer) that he seize the government and be declared king. Washington, a republican through and through, is horrified. He immediately writes to Nicola in "surprise & astonishment" to reject the idea unequivocally: "Let me conjure you then, if you have any regard for your country—concern for yourself or posterity—or respect for me, to banish these thoughts from your mind, & never communicate, as from yourself or anyone else, a sentiment of like nature." The plot collapses.

4 June 1782

SANDUSKY, OHIO. Col. William Crawford leads an attack on Indian villages in the Upper Sandusky region. His considerable force has marched with no attempt at deception straight to its objectives, and his plans and movements have been known to his enemies from the beginning. His men initially gain the advantage over a small force of Butler's Rangers and Indians, but British reinforcements with artillery arrive, and the Americans panic and retreat in disarray. Crawford and several other officers are captured and tortured to death.

23 June 1782

PARIS. John Jay arrives from Madrid, where his efforts to persuade the Spanish to support American claims have met complete rejection. He now believes Spain to be almost as great an enemy of the American cause as the British.

VIRGINIA. Rochambeau's army begins a march northward to Boston.

1 July 1782

LONDON. Rockingham dies and Lord Shelburne assumes office as prime minister. Shelburne's Cabinet is less contentious than Rockingham's, which eases the task of setting new policies. The new leader still hopes to avoid recognition of American independence as talks between Oswald and Franklin continue in Paris.

11 July 1782

SAVANNAH, GA. The British evacuate the city, taking away on their ships nearly 4,000 Georgia Loyalists and 5,000 black slaves.

20 July 1782

PHILADELPHIA. Congress adopts a Great Seal of the United States. Committees have been working on a de-

The Great Seal of the United States, approved by Congress in 1782.

sign since July 1776. The new seal bears an eagle with arrows and an olive branch on the front with the motto *Annuit Coeptis* (He [God] favors our undertakings). The reverse has a pyramid and the words *Novus Ordo Seclorum* (A new age now begins).

23 July 1782

PARIS. Jay and Franklin confer on strategy for renewed discussions with the British.

19 August 1782

BLUE LICKS, KY. A force of Indians and Loyalists, led by the infamous Simon Girty, has attacked several frontier outposts during the preceding days. A band of American frontiersmen, including Daniel Boone, pursues the raiders to this hilly spot on the Licking River. The Americans blunder into an ambush and seventy are killed or captured within minutes.

27 August 1782

COMBAHEE FERRY, S.C. Gen. Mordecai Gist detaches a small force of light infantry and cavalry from Greene's army in front of Charleston and sets off to attack British foraging parties and shipping on the Combahee River. Americans under Col. John Laurens (Henry Laurens' son) march into an ambush set by the larger British force. Laurens and one other American are killed, and the British escape without losses. This is the final land engagement of the war between organized forces of Britain and the United States.

9 September 1782

PARIS. John Jay learns that Vergennes has sent his secretary, Rayneval, to England to conduct separate talks with the British. Correctly fearing that the French will put Spanish interests ahead of those of the United States, Jay urges Franklin to make a new initiative with Oswald and Shelburne. Franklin proposes that Great Britain authorize Oswald to deal with the "United States" rather than the thirteen colonies. This will amount to a tacit recognition of independence and undercut the French.

19 September 1782

LONDON. The Cabinet changes Oswald's instructions and allows him to negotiate with the "13 United States" as Franklin has asked. The ministers see this as a cheap price to pay for prying apart the American–French alliance.

1 October 1782

PARIS. Franklin and Jay begin formal peace negotiations with Oswald. Until now, the talks have been informal. The American commissioners are resolved to make their own deal with the British, irrespective of the French.

5 October 1782

PARIS. The American commissioners and Oswald reach an agreement on draft terms. They agree on new boundaries for the United States, the evacuation of British troops from American bases, American access to fishing banks off Newfoundland, and free trade and navigation on the Mississippi River.

8 October 1782

THE HAGUE. Adams signs a treaty of commerce and friendship with the Netherlands.

26 October 1782

PARIS. His duties in Holland complete, peace commissioner John Adams arrives in Paris to join his colleagues in the final negotiations with Great Britain.

1 November 1782

PARIS. Adams adds his weight to Jay's arguments that the peace commission should proceed without telling the French. Franklin agrees.

5 November 1782

PARIS. Franklin, Jay, Adams, and Henry Laurens (who has just arrived) reach agreement with the British on a slightly revised set of articles for peace. These become the basis for the final treaty with almost no further modification.

30 November 1782

PARIS. Peace commissioners of the United States and Great Britain sign a provisional treaty. Pending only the formal approval of the governments of both nations, this ends all hostilities and sets the conditions of the postwar settlement. The American commissioners have, in effect, concluded a separate peace with the enemy and ignored the wishes of France and Spain.

14 December 1782

CHARLESTON, S.C. The British garrison evacuates the city.

17 December 1782

PARIS. Franklin tells Vergennes of the provisional treaty. The French minister is outraged at first but can do little to change affairs now. Franklin's deft handling of Vergennes placates the foreign minister, and France grants a new loan of six million livres to the United States.

24 December 1782

BOSTON. The French army withdraws by ship for the West Indies.

★ 1783 ★

6 January 1783

PHILADELPHIA. Gen. Alexander Mc-Dougall, Col. John Brooks, and Col. Matthias Ogden present a petition to Congress on behalf of the army. Although Congress has agreed to officers' half-pay for life as a form of retirement, nothing has been done about the policy and there appears to be little hope of funding the provision. The officers now request full settlement of back pay before discharge and conversion of the promised half-pay to a lump sum, along with a specific method of payment. The officers of the army form one of the nation's largest groups of creditors. Political advocates of a strong central government see the officers as tools in forcing reformation of the Articles of Confederation and begin to seek an alliance with the army—which is, of course, still a potent armed force with the potential to enforce its wishes.

20 January 1783

LONDON. Great Britain signs preliminary articles ending hostilities with France and Spain.

4 February 1783

LONDON. The king formally proclaims the end of hostilities with the United States.

8 March 1783

PHILADELPHIA. Secretary of Finance Robert Morris proposes an ultimatum to the states. He says that the Congress has implied powers under the Articles to devise a way to meet the national debt, and if the states refuse to pay, Congress will levy taxes and import duties directly. He is never able to mount the political support needed to carry out the plan.

10 March 1783

NEWBURGH, N.Y. Unsigned documents known as the Newburgh Addresses pass among the officers of the Continental Army. The first document urges officers to meet in an unauthorized assembly to discuss their grievances with Congress. The second is a fiery pamphlet threatening that the army will not disband until paid and, in the event of further hostilities, the army will not fight. The Address, written by Maj. John Armstrong, Jr., an aide-de-camp to Gen. Horatio Gates, says: "Tell them that, though you were the first, and would wish to be the last to encounter danger: though despair itself can never drive you into dishonor, it may drive you from the field: that the wound often irritated, may at length become incurable; and that the slightest mark of indignity from Congress now, may operate like the grave, and part you forever. . . ." The officers seem on the edge of mass mutiny.

ATLANTIC OCEAN. John Barry, commanding the American ship *Alliance*, is on his way toward Philadelphia with much-needed hard currency for Congress when he and his companion ship, the *Lauzun*, are overtaken by three British warships. A French man-of-war appears and intimidates two of the British ships, but Barry engages the frigate *Sybille* in a three-quarter-hour fight before breaking off. Barry continues toward port.

11 March 1783

NEWBURGH, N.Y. Washington is shocked by the Newburgh Addresses and issues a general order for a meeting of officers. He informs Congress of the unrest.

15 March 1783

NEWBURGH, N.Y. Washington addresses his assembled officers. He tells them that distrust of Congress is unfounded and dishonorable and that the army should remain calm and set an example for posterity. He puts his own personal integrity on the line to dissuade the officers from a rash act that may destroy all they had fought for. He stumbles over his prepared text and pauses to draw forth his glasses, saying: "Gentlemen, you must pardon me. I have grown gray in your service and now find myself growing blind." His performance has the desired effect, and the officers vote to repudiate the Addresses and affirm their loyalty to the nation. Congress subsequently votes to change half-pay to a promise of full pay for five years, to be issued in the form of federal securities.

11 April 1783

PHILADELPHIA. Congress officially proclaims the end of the war.

15 April 1783

PHILADELPHIA. Congress ratifies the provisional treaty of peace already signed by the commissioners in Paris.

26 May 1783

NEWBURGH N.Y. The noncommissioned officers and enlisted men of the Continental Army are furloughed and sent home. They take no money or final pay with them, although they are allowed to keep their muskets for personal use. Congress issues promissory notes for the equivalent of three months' pay but without a specific date or method of redemption. It will be decades before final settlement is made, usually in the form of land grants to veterans. Their discharges will go into effect on signing of the peace treaty. Washington retains command of a small contingent of three-year enlistees until the British evacuate New York City.

13 June 1783

PHILADELPHIA. Congress receives a threatening letter from the sergeants of one of the furloughed Pennsylvania regiments stationed nearby in Lancaster. The men not only state their demands for pay but hint they will march on Philadelphia. Secretary at War Benjamin Lincoln placates the men for the time being.

14 June 1783

PHILADELPHIA. Congress learns that eighty men of the 3rd Pennsylvania are on their way to Philadelphia. Congress asks John Dickinson, president of the Supreme Council of Pennsylvania, for troops to protect the government, but Dickinson refuses. The men arrive and take up residence in an abandoned barracks.

15 June 1783

PHILADELPHIA. While Congress holds an emergency session in the State House, 300 to 400 angry soldiers appear with fixed bayonets and surround the building. Nervous congressmen—left without protection by Dickinson—adjourn at midafternoon and are allowed to pass through the lines without violence.

17 June 1783

PHILADELPHIA. Congress votes to adjourn to Princeton, N.J., to avoid the mutinous Pennsylvania troops and to be closer to Washington's remaining small force, which may provide protection denied by the state of Pennsylvania. The protesting soldiers in Philadelphia disband with no further demonstrations. When the Congress reconvenes in Princeton, it spends most of its time in remonstrations over the humiliating experience in Philadelphia.

July 1783

LONDON. Great Britain establishes a commission to settle claims from American Loyalists damaged by the war. In several states, Loyalist property has been seized and the losses are great. More than 4,000 claims are eventually submitted to the commis-

sion, which awards over 3.3 million pounds in compensation.

August 1783

PRINCETON, N.J. The Congress agrees to move to Annapolis later in the fall. It spurns an invitation to return to Philadelphia.

3 September 1783

PARIS. The formal treaties of Paris and Versailles are signed, ending the war. The terms are nearly identical to those of the provisional and prelimi-

Washington's farewell dinner took place at Fraunces' Tavern at Pearl and Broad Streets.

nary agreements reached months before: Great Britain recognizes the independence of the United States; the boundaries of the new nation exclude Canada but extend westward roughly along the 45th parallel to the Mississippi River and then south to the 31st parallel and east to the Atlantic; Americans have the right to fish off the Newfoundland and Nova Scotia banks; legal debts will be hon-

The Continental Army marching into New York City.

George Washington; this illustration from a painting by Charles Willson Peale was published in Harper's Weekly *in 1889.*

ored by each country; no further penalties will be enacted against citizens for actions during the war; all hostilities cease and all remaining British troops will evacuate; navigation for both nations on the Mississippi River will be free; and all territorial conquests by either nation during the war will be restored.

18 October 1783

NEWBURGH, N.Y. Gen. George Washington issues his final General Order to the army, which begins: "It remains only for the Commander-in-chief to address himself once more, and that for the last time, to the armies of the United States, however widely dispersed the individuals who composed them may be, and to bid them an affectionate, long farewell." Washington reviews the war and the endurance of the army, and celebrates

the winning of independence. He urges conciliation with the national government over debts owed, and he charges his officers to support a strong federal government devoted to "honor, dignity, and justice." One officer writes later: "No language can express the feelings of the army when the foregoing general orders were read. The most hardy soldiers were unable to restrain the copious flow of tears; and to some of us ... the scene was overwhelming."

4 November 1783

PRINCETON, N.J. Congress adjourns. A quorum has been missing during

Benjamin Franklin.

most of its stay in Princeton; at times, only six states are represented. The difficulty will continue for several months after Congress reconvenes in Maryland, with the majority needed to ratify the peace treaties only possible in March of the following year.

25 November 1783

NEW YORK CITY. The final British garrison in America evacuates, taking with it nearly 7,000 Loyalists. In all, close to 100,000 Loyalists have departed since the end of hostilities. Many seek new homes in Canada; others move to England.

26 November 1783

ANNAPOLIS, MD. Congress convenes.

4 December 1783

NEW YORK CITY. A group of officers closest to Washington during the war gathers at Fraunces Tavern to say good-bye to their commander. The meeting is heavy with emotion and strong sentiment. Washington proposes a toast: "With a heart full of love and gratitude, I now take leave of you. I most devoutly wish that your latter days may be as prosperous and happy as your former ones have been glorious and noble." He then tearfully embraces each man and takes his leave for the journey to Annapolis.

23 December 1783

ANNAPOLIS, MD. Washington appears before the assembled Congress, and in an emotion-filled speech which he can hardly manage, he prepares to hand over his commission as com-

Washington resigning his commission as Commander-in-Chief.

mander-in-chief. "I consider it indispensable," he says, "to close this last solemn act of my official life by commending the interests of our dearest country to the protection of Almighty God, and those who have superintendence of them to his holy keeping." His final words are "Having now finished the work assigned me, I retire from the great theatre of action, and bidding an affectionate farewell to this august body under whose orders I have so long acted, I here offer my commission, and take my leave of all the employments of public life." He then withdraws the document from his pocket, hands it to Thomas Mifflin, president of the Congress, and sets out for Mount Vernon.

The American Revolution is over.

THE WAR OF THE REVOLUTION:
★ AN ASSESSMENT ★

Wars are unpredictable, running in directions and taking turns that their makers cannot imagine. The war of the American Revolution, for example, began in 1775 as disorganized, local violence in a dispute over rights and taxes. By 1781 six years of full-scale war had passed and a small corner of Virginia became the central theater of a global conflict. By that time, the independence of the former American colonies was no longer in doubt, even if the British could have avoided military defeat. Between these two points, the course of the war twisted, turned, and changed.

The first and last battles of the conflict symbolize the changes: Lexington and Concord (and the British retreat to Boston) came about almost casually and were a ragged, unplanned affair of outraged armed citizens against slightly bewildered British regulars who thought they were on a simple mission into the rural countryside; Yorktown was a formal siege, conducted by a large, well-trained, well-equipped, multinational army supported by a powerful war fleet. Between the two events in the spring of 1775 and the fall of 1781 the American rebels, despite many failures and shortcomings, built up a serviceable if flawed capacity to wage war and secured the support of a powerful European ally, much to the horror of the British, who until near the end continued to believe that superior tactical organization and control of the sea lanes would ultimately prevail. The British, however, were never quite able to overcome the problems of fighting a difficult enemy a great distance from home. Could the British have dealt the first fumbling American armies a crushing blow at any time before 1777, they might well have won the war outright, although complete reversion to political status quo antebellum would have been unlikely. After the Americans formed a coalition with France in early 1778, it is difficult to imagine any circumstances in which the British could have won a clear-cut victory, although they might well have forced much more favorable terms by more success in arms during the last years of the conflict.

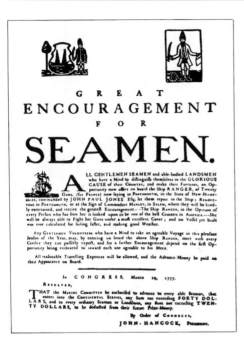

A naval recruiting poster calling for men to serve on John Paul Jones' ship Ranger.

The geography of America played a key role in how the war was fought. Both sides tended during the entire affair to underestimate the difficulties of terrain and distance, although the British suffered most from this blind spot.

The far-northern theater, from the Canadian cities of Montreal and Quebec to the lower Hudson Valley, was mostly wilderness, difficult to maneuver in and nearly impossible to cross with large armies except by following the lakewater routes, which only ran so far. However, both the Americans (who should have known better) and the British (who after all had fought the French in this same region only fifteen years before) were seduced by the prospect of easy gains, if only they could push sufficient forces over and through the forests and rivers. The American expeditions against Canada early in the war are prime examples. Deluding themselves that Canada was ripe for prying away from the bosom of England, American strategists ignored logistics and the realities of geography when they launched ill-supplied armies northward. The disasters ate up men and resources that the nascent American nation could little afford to waste. Carleton's sensible conclusion in 1776 that he could not really cross from the foot of the lakes to reach the retreating Americans was lost on the British planners the following year, and the notion of separating New England by Burgoyne's thrust from the north came to disaster in the woodlands of upper New York, although Burgoyne's ineptitude certainly diminished any chance the scheme might have had. His defeat was pivotal in bringing the French into the conflict. It was a hard-learned truth that eighteenth-century armies could not campaign effectively in the wilderness.

The same was, of course, not true of the more suitable terrain of the Middle Colonies. It was no accident that most of the great stand-up battles of the War of the Revolution were fought in New York and New Jersey. Here there was room to maneuver large forces and, in the beginning at least, ample supply for armies in the field. The topography offered traditional battlefields that resembled those of Europe. The superior organization and training of the British army came to greatest advantage here during the campaigns between 1776 and 1778. Only Washington's tenacity in the face of what others might have conceded as defeat preserved the American cause. The American commander-in-chief somehow kept at least a minimally viable army in being and struck telling blows at Trenton and Monmouth at just the right moments, which eventually forced a stalemate. Had the Americans' willpower not been so strong and their arms even slightly weaker, the British might well have won in the arena best suited to their strengths.

Both the Americans and the British exhibited good understanding of geographic realities in their Southern campaigns of 1779 and 1780. While great stretches of the Carolinas and Georgia were difficult places to maneuver because of the rivers and swamps—a circumstance the Americans used cleverly—the long, accessible coastline provided a major advantage to the British navy's control of transport and expedition by sea. There was very little the Americans could do to prevent the series of British triumphs at Savannah, Charleston, and elsewhere, given the relative facility with which the enemy could move forces up and down the coastline. The best the Americans could manage, which proved to be just good enough, was annoying but minor harassment and forcing a series of Phyrric victories on the British. The few clear-cut American triumphs (as at King's Mountain and the Cowpens) and Nathanael Greene's strategic acumen were barely enough to prevent a British victory on a scale that might have made a decisive difference. The final deciding factor was, of course, the appearance of the French fleet off the Chesapeake in 1781 and its narrow but sufficient repulse of the Royal Navy at a crucial juncture—almost the only time the American cause benefited from the circumstance of seacoast geography so long exploited by the British.

The second major factor conditioning the course of the war was the nature of the opposing forces and the bare success of the Americans in overcoming their initial shortcomings and illusions. The first battles of 1775 imprinted on both American and British minds notions that were hard to throw off. The relative success of the "minutemen" in driving back and nearly destroying the British column on the road from Lexington and Concord illustrated the situation: Ill-organized militia could seriously damage regular troops, even some of the best regular troops in the world, but at the same time and not well understood by the Americans, the military weaknesses of volunteer amateur soldiers made it virtually impossible for them to really defeat a trained army.

Bunker Hill and Breed's Hill only reinforced these conclusions; the American militia almost destroyed the cream of the British army from behind fortifications, but the militia's poor logistics and disgraceful

This engraving of an American soldier was published in Harper's Weekly *in 1876.*

A musket drill, from an 1802 American manual of arms showing the drill exercises of the Continental soldiers.

coordination on the field gave disciplined and well-led troops the ultimate advantage, although at great cost. Many Americans, especially
the politicians in Congress, read into these first battles more than was
warranted. They hoped that basically untrained militia would suffice
to fight and win a war, and so the organization and training of a genuine
army waited until almost too late. The British, on the other hand, were
perhaps overly impressed with the costs of direct assault against well-
positioned marksmen. For a time the Americans became too aggressive
and the British too timid.

The subsequent battles and campaigns in the middle states during
1776, 1777, and 1778 (roughly from the Battle of Long Island to the
Battle of Monmouth) demonstrated the long-term advantages of the
British. It often appeared on the surface that the Continental Army
was a powerful force, equal to the challenge of fighting British and
German regulars, but in fact seldom were the amateurs up to the task.

A very early version of the Stars and Stripes.

In battle after battle—Long Island, White Plains, Fort Washington, Brandywine, and Germantown—either American tactical leadership failed or the inexperienced and basically untrained troops gave way. Washington, for all his great attributes, never won a clear-cut victory in the field against a British army that was ready to fight. His greatest military moment came at Trenton, where his speed and surprise won against torporous and overconfident mercenaries. Granted, Monmouth was a near-run thing for the British, but the Continental Army at that stage was still not an instrument quite up to the task of delivering a final blow in a formal battle, despite the great improvements realized under von Steuben during the winter of 1777.

Sir Henry Clinton was sufficiently impressed, however, with Washington's reasonable facsimile of a European army that he never again really challenged the Americans in New York or New Jersey. In truth, from 1778 on, the American armies had at the core good troops, who could face up to the best the British could offer—finer men than the Maryland and Delaware Continentals, for example, never took the field—but Washington had to stave off other, nearly fatal weaknesses. As the war dragged on, the bloom of revolution wore off for the civil government and the shaky union of the states, and an almost catastrophic financial crisis deepened. During 1780 and early 1781, Washington's force dwindled to a few understrength, mutinous regiments that he could not pay and barely supply with food and clothing. Rochambeau's 6,000 first-line troops in Rhode Island offered the hope that the alliance with France might make the crucial difference, but without an active and cooperative French fleet, nothing decisive could be attempted—and previous experience with admirals like d'Estaing did nothing to inspire confidence.

The combination in the late summer of 1781 of De Grasse's momentary fit of confident activity and Cornwallis' poor judgment tipped the balance just enough, however, when combined with Washington's unquenchably bold instincts. The American commander's decision to concentrate all his forces in a march south to Virginia, gambling that for once the French navy would actually appear at the right time and place, was a larger-scale analogy of Washington's surprise attack at Trenton. It was a roll of the dice with ultimate victory the stakes.

The coalition army that appeared in front of the fortifications at Yorktown and proceeded to invest Cornwallis in the most traditional fashion—secure in the knowledge that for once the Royal Navy would not come to the rescue—was a tribute to Washington's combination of tenacity and daring.

The margin was still paper-thin, however. At several key points during the previous six years, the British might have ended the affair. Had their leadership been only a little more creative and their problems

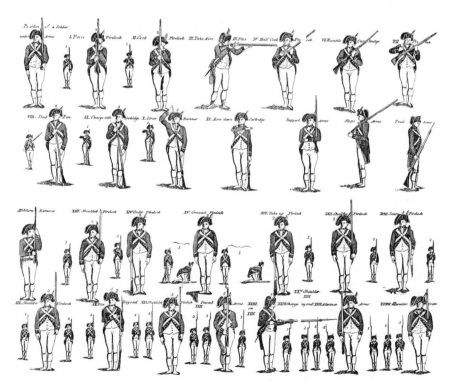

Further musket drills, from an 1802 American manual of arms.

fewer, the war might have concluded on their terms. The subjection of the rebellion could, perhaps, have been accomplished in 1775 or 1776 by a more massive effort by the British, but the difficulties of raising sufficient troops (illustrated by the need to hire from the German principalities) and the immense problems of supply and communications from an island base across a broad ocean were understandably too great.

Likewise, had there really existed a deep and reliable base of Loyalist support, an illusion the British clung to for years, things might have been different. However, as the conflict wore on, the opportunities grew fewer and fewer for an ultimate British victory, despite many local successes. When the war spread to include the revenge-minded French in a significant way and the Spanish and Dutch in at least nuisance roles, the odds grew long indeed, even though a British victory remained possible until the end if the Americans had allowed any of their major weaknesses to prevail.

★ BIOGRAPHIES ★

ADAMS, John
1735–1826
President, statesman, diplomat. One of a handful of American patriots who truly deserve the title of Founding Father, John Adams was at the heart of politics and diplomacy during the American Revolution. He was instrumental in forcing the breach with Britain, and during the later years of the war his duties as a diplomat were vital. Adams was born in Braintree, Massachusetts (now known as Quincy), and taught school in Worcester after graduation from Harvard in 1755. He turned to the study of law and was admitted to the bar in Boston in 1758. In 1764 he married Abigail Smith, forming a happy and fortuitous alliance. In 1765 Adams assumed a prominent role in opposing the British and formed close political ties with other patriot leaders. His writings set forth the ideas that would lead to independence. He was elected to the first Continental Congress in 1774 and drafted a declaration of rights. His ideas moved more and more toward independence and the necessity for the colonies to form their own individual governments. In the second Congress he forged ties with the powerful delegates from the Southern colonies and did much to defuse their suspicions of Massachusetts. He pushed for independence and was appointed to the committee to draft the Declaration in June 1776, and his legislative skills were vital to the document's passage. He left Congress for an interval in late 1776, returned in February 1777, and departed again in November. Adams then entered a long period of service as a diplomat in Europe. He sailed for France with his ten-year-old son John Quincy in February 1778 to take a

place on the American commission to France. Despite French recognition of the independent colonies, the position of the American emissaries was delicate and difficult. He returned to Massachusetts in 1779 and wrote the constitution adopted by the state convention of Massachusetts. He was called away again to France late in the year. Along with Franklin and John Jay, Adams negotiated the 1783 Treaty of Paris that formally ended the War. Two years later, he was appointed minister to Great Britain. In 1789 Adams was chosen as the nation's first vice president and eight years later elected the second president of the United States. His single term of office, however, was fraught with difficulties. He was defeated by Jefferson in the election of 1800 and withdrew to Braintree after more than a quarter-decade at the center of national affairs. His later years were taken up with study, writing, and observation of the rising political fortunes of John Quincy. In a great historical coincidence, Adams died on 4 July 1826 on the fiftieth anniversary of the Declaration of Independence, a few hours after Thomas Jefferson.

ADAMS, Samuel
1722–1803
Revolutionary, delegate to Congress. A master propagandist and political organizer, Adams was the chief figure of resistance in Massachusetts during ten years leading up to the Revolution. He was born in Boston, the son of a prosperous brewer and merchant and educated at Harvard but failed to find a career and was abysmal in business affairs, living in debt most of his life. However, no one in the colonies equaled Adams' ability to organize

and arouse popular and political passion. He galvanized resistance to the Stamp Act and the Townshend Acts in Boston and helped organize the Sons of Liberty. Although he seldom overtly advocated violence, Adams kept the burning issues alive and pounded away at the constitutional questions of the rights of the colonies to be free of unwarranted taxation and abuse from the royal government. Adams led the fight against paying duties on tea that culminated in the Boston Tea Party. In 1774 he represented Massachusetts in the first Continental Congress. Despite his election to the second Congress and signing the Declaration of Independence in 1776, Sam Adams' role diminished after the outbreak of hostilities. He played little important part in Congress after 1775. He held a succession of public offices during the following years, and in 1793 became governor of the state but he served with slight distinction. He died in Boston in 1803.

ALEXANDER, William (Lord Stirling)
1726–1783

Continental major general. Despite his aristocratic background, social ambitions, and dissolute style of living, Alexander served the revolutionary army hard and well throughout all Washington's tough campaigns of the early years of the war. Born in New York, he was the son of a well-to-do merchant family. He lived in Great Britain from 1756 until 1761, where he unsuccessfully claimed the lapsed title of the Earl of Stirling but continued to style himself Lord Stirling the rest of his life. On his return to America, Alexander frittered away his fortune and held himself above the revolutionary fray. However, in 1774

he declared himself a patriot and was appointed to command of the New Jersey militia. In 1776 his troops joined the army at New York and Washington made Alexander a brigadier. During the battle of Long Island, Alexander's brigade fought extremely well, but his force was cut off and he was captured. He was exchanged within a few months and appointed again to brigade command. Alexander's Continentals fought at Trenton and throughout the New Jersey campaign. In February 1777 he was promoted to major general and commanded significant parts of the army under Washington at Brandywine, Germantown, and Monmouth. He was the president of Charles Lee's court-martial and acting commander-in-chief of the Continental Army while Washington was away to confer with Congress. In 1782, his health began to decline, and he died of acute gout in January 1783.

ALLEN, Ethan
1738–1789

Vermont leader, Continental brevet colonel, militia major general. The annals of the American Revolution contain no more colorful and controversial figure than Allen. He was born in Litchfield, Ct., but his life was tied up with the eventual state of Vermont, known then as the New Hampshire Grants and disputed between New Hampshire and New York. Allen formed a vigilante militia called the Green Mountain Boys, and by 1774 he virtually ruled the Grants. During the War of Independence Allen put Vermont's interests first, even to the point of treason. His first act after Lexington and Concord was a strike at Fort Ticonderoga, where on 10 May

1775 Allen and a small company surprised the sleeping British troops. In Allen's own account, he demanded surrender of the king's property "In the name of the Great Jehovah and the Continental Congress." (Others reported that he said "Come out of there you sons of British whores, or I'll smoke you out.") Allen's subsequent wartime career was less successful than at Ticonderoga. After successfully petitioning Congress to absorb the Green Mountain Boys into the new Continental Army, Allen was promptly voted out of command. He attached himself to Gen. Philip Schuyler's army and was captured at Montreal. Transported at first to an English prison, he was exchanged in May 1778 and received a commission as brevet colonel in the Continental Army before returning to Vermont. Over the following two years, Allen re-established his local influence, accepted a commission as major general of militia, and bent all his efforts toward gaining recognition for Vermont. Rebuffed by Congress, Allen schemed to turn the region over to the British, a plot that failed. The remainder of his life was devoted to business and writing, and he died of an apparent stroke in early 1789.

ANDRÉ, John
1751–1780
British officer, spy. André was a romantic and ultimately tragic figure. He arrived in America in 1774 and was captured at St. John's in November 1775, spending the following year in captivity. After his exchange André joined the British force that occupied Philadelphia, where he formed a friendship with Peggy Shippen, who was soon to marry the American hero

Benedict Arnold. After the British withdrawal to New York, André became aide-de-camp to Sir Henry Clinton. In the spring of 1780, André learned of the treasonous correspondence between American Maj. Gen. Benedict Arnold and British headquarters and took over the main responsibility of dealing with Arnold. When Arnold managed to be named commander of the fortress at West Point, a meeting between Arnold and André was arranged. Against orders, André disguised himself for the meeting. He sailed up the Hudson, landed on the American-held side of the river, and parleyed with Arnold. Dawn found André still ashore, unable to return to his ship. At Arnold's urging, André decided to return to the British lines overland with incriminating documents in Arnold's handwriting. He was stopped by three scruffy American militiamen, searched, and turned over to an officer. Arnold escaped, but André's true identity was soon revealed. He had been captured behind American lines in disguise, using an assumed name, with incriminating documents hidden on his person. Sentenced as a spy, André was hanged at Tappan, N.Y., on 2 October 1780.

ARBUTHNOT, Marriot
1711–1794
British admiral. Of unknown parentage, Arbuthnot came slowly to rank in the navy, reaching captain in 1747, and he developed an unimaginative, pompous personality with a prickly regard for his own dignity and position. In 1775 he was appointed commissioner at Halifax, where he served until his recall to Britain and advancement to flag rank in 1778. The follow-

ing spring he was named to replace Gambier as commander of the American station. Effective cooperation between Arbuthnot and Sir Henry Clinton, the commander of land forces, might have led to British success, but Arbuthnot was tactless as well as slow-witted, and the two commanders failed to coordinate. In late 1779 the French admiral d'Estaing threatened the British occupation of Rhode Island, yet Arbuthnot could not decide on a course of action. Combined British operations broke down almost entirely in 1780, when Arbuthnot allowed the French expeditionary force to land at Newport. The nadir came in March 1781, when a powerful French squadron under Destouches forced Arbuthnot to battle off the Virginia capes. Arbuthnot's confusion resulted in considerable French-inflicted damage to the British squadron, and Arbuthnot withdrew to Lynnhaven Roads after the inconclusive fight. Following the battle he was recalled to London. Despite advancement in rank following his American assignment, Arbuthnot was never again employed by the Admiralty.

ARNOLD, Benedict
1741–1801
Continental general, traitor. Both one of America's finest combat generals and its most notable traitor, Arnold was born in Connecticut and was a prosperous merchant before the Revolution. On hearing news of Lexington and Concord, Arnold marched his militia company to Cambridge. During the first months of the war he participated in the capture of Fort Ticonderoga and attacked St. John's. In September 1775 Arnold headed an ex-

pedition against Quebec as part of a two-pronged attack on the British control of Canada. After a legendary wilderness journey, the campaign failed and Arnold was severely wounded. Appointed a brigadier general, he then turned back a British invasion at Valcour Island. Assigned to a post in Rhode Island by Washington, Arnold was sent into a fury in February 1777 when he learned that Congress had promoted five officers junior to him to the rank of major general. In July 1777 he submitted his resignation, but was persuaded by Washington to take a post with the army to the north, which was preparing to face Burgoyne. Arnold played a crucial role in defeating the British force—he was the undisputed hero of the second Battle of Saratoga—before falling with a new wound. In 1778 he was placed in military command of Philadelphia, where he courted and married the eighteen-year-old Margaret Shippen. In May 1779 Arnold took the first fatal steps, offering to divulge military information to the British and even to sell out his command. Working through intermediaries, Arnold carried on the treasonous correspondence for nearly a year and a half before the affair reached a climax. In September 1780, Arnold demanded a meeting with Major André. Following the meeting, the British officer was apprehended with documents that incriminated Arnold. In a series of events worthy of cheap fiction, Arnold escaped just ahead of capture. Arnold's subsequent career was anticlimactic. Commissioned by the British as brigadier, he led a force into Virginia and later a raid against New London, Connecticut. He and Peggy moved to England, but Arnold faced both public and private disdain. He turned to privateering and then to business, locating for a time in Canada, but he was never able to repair his fortunes. He died deeply in debt in London.

ATTUCKS, Crispus
c. 1723–1770

Little in life so became Attucks as his death as a martyr of the Boston Massacre. A very large man for his day and age, topping six feet and heavily built, Attucks was apparently born near Framingham, Mass., likely of mixed African and Indian parentage, and ran away from slavery about 1750 to the life of a free sailor. On 5 March 1770 he was living in Boston under the name Michael Johnson and took leadership of a mob that confronted a small detachment of British soldiers at the Customs House. By contemporary accounts he wielded a cordwood club and stood at the head of the assembly, berating the redcoats. He grabbed a bayonet, turned it aside, and struck at a soldier. The frightened troops opened fire, and Attucks was killed instantly by two musket balls in the chest. Anti-British Bostonians staged an elaborate funeral for Attucks and the three other Bostonians killed in the Massacre. During the trial of the British soldiers, defense lawyer John Adams focused on the role of Attucks in provoking the attack, just as the prosecution made him out as a hero. Attucks' name has since come to be a symbol of courage in the face of oppression, especially among black Americans, and a monument to him stands on Boston Common.

BARRAS, Louis, comte de
d. c. 1800

French admiral. Barras began his naval career in 1734 as a garde. By 1778 he was a squadron leader and was promoted to the rank of naval lieutenant general in 1782. He assumed command of part of the French fleet in American waters under d'Estaing following the death of Adm. Ternay. In 1781 he was in command at Newport when requested by Washington and Rochambeau to cooperate in the rapid movement of troops and supplies south to bottle up Cornwallis in Virginia. Barras was contrary, however, and wanted instead an independent expedition to move on Newfoundland with the troops from Newport. He was persuaded otherwise, and in September sailed to meet the fleet of De Grasse that was to arrive in the Chesapeake with re-enforcements from the West Indies. Barras carried with him part of the vital artillery that formed the siege train at Yorktown. He was reluctant to serve under De Grasse, who was technically his junior, but the two managed to paper over differences. After the conclusion of the Virginia campaign, Barras sailed south with De Grasse to engage the British. In 1782 he captured Montserrat and retired the following year due to ill health.

BARRY, John
1745–1803

Continental navy captain. Barry, known as The Father of the American Navy, was an Irishman who had immigrated to Philadelphia about 1760. In 1776 he was commissioned by Congress captain of the *Lexington*, a sixteen-gun brig. When he took the

British tender *Edward* off Cape Charles, Va., in April, he claimed the honor of making the first capture of a British warship by a regularly commissioned U.S. vessel. In part as reward, he was placed in command of the thirty-two gun *Effingham* in October 1776. Barry spent the winter of 1776–1777 on land as commander of a unit of Pennsylvania militia volunteers. When Howe moved on Philadelphia, Barry was forced to abandon the *Effingham* to British torches, but he successfully harassed British shipping on the Delaware throughout the winter. In September 1778, Barry took command of the frigate *Raleigh*, sailing from Boston. While on patrol, he was surprised by two British ships and forced to run his frigate aground after a long running battle. In his next ship, the *Alliance*, Barry managed to capture several prizes after a storm in mid-Atlantic scattered a British convoy. He then ferried Lafayette back to France, and fought one of the final sea battles of the Revolution in an indecisive engagement against the *Sybille* in January 1783. When Congress raised a new navy in 1794 to resist the pirates of Algiers, Barry was named senior captain and given commission of the *United States*, which he commanded during the naval hostilities with France from 1798 to 1801.

BAUM, Friedrich
d. 1777
German lieutenant colonel. Baum commanded the dragoon regiment of the mercenary forces hired by the British from the Duke of Brunswick to flesh out the armies in North America. Baum's heavy cavalry numbered 336 men on departure from their home in February 1776. They sailed to America without their horses, although they retained their elaborate and cumbersome gear. Baum spoke no English, but was apparently an experienced soldier. Serving under the command of Riedesel, the Brunswickers were assigned as part of Burgoyne's army in 1777 and marched with that force as it attempted an invasion of upstate New York from Canada. On 9 August Burgoyne gave Baum command of an 800-man contingent and directed the mercenary colonel to march toward Bennington, Vt. Baum was to bring back horses and cattle. He was also instructed to recruit among the supposed Loyalists of the region, although without a common language this task would have been difficult. As Baum and his slow-moving troops advanced toward Bennington, a large American force of New Hampshire and Vermont men gathered under the command of prickly Gen. John Stark. Baum suspected he was badly outnumbered, and on 16 August he found himself in a difficult position, defending hilltops but unable to concentrate his disciplined regulars against twice the number of Americans who split forces and launched an enveloping attack. Despite a fierce resistance, the Germans were badly defeated, and Baum himself was struck mortally as he tried to carve his way out after being surrounded. He died two days later.

BOUDINOT, Elias
1740–1821
Statesman. Although born in Philadelphia, Boudinot spent most of his life as a prominent New Jerseyan and was a leading member of the New Jer-

sey bar in the decade before the war. He was also a staunch early patriot and a persistent foe of New Jersey's royal governor, William Franklin. In 1774, Boudinot served on the New Jersey committee of correspondence and supported the New Jersey Assembly in approval of the Continental Congress. He was a delegate to the New Jersey Provincial Congress in 1775. He is credited with sending much-needed gunpowder to Washington's army at Boston in August of that year. He eventually became close to Washington and in 1777 was appointed as commissary of prisoners with the equivalent rank of colonel. He was elected to Congress from New Jersey in late 1777 but took his seat reluctantly. In 1782, he was elected to a one-year term as president of the Congress, which under the Articles of Confederation also made him the chief executive officer of the nation. During his time in office he also served as secretary of foreign affairs and signed the preliminary peace terms with Great Britain. In the midst of his presidential term, dissident soldiers threatened Congress over pay issues and the body precipitously adjourned to Princeton. After presiding over Congress in his home town, Boudinot requested he not be re-elected. He was, however, elected again to Congress after the adoption of the Constitution, and in 1795 he was appointed to a stormy term as superintendent of the national mint.

BRANT, Joseph
1742–1807
Indian leader. A Mohawk chieftain, Brant supported the British effort against the Americans as a raider in the campaigns on the Northern frontier. Born in Ohio and named Thayendanegea, he resided with his parents at Canajoharie Castle in the Mohawk Valley, N.Y. Following his father's death, his mother married an Indian who was called Brant by the white settlers—hence his own anglicized name. At thirteen Brant, whose sister became the wife of Sir William Johnson, British superintendent of Indian affairs, served with Sir William at the Battle of Lake George (1755); subsequently Johnson sent him to school at Lebanon, Connecticut. In 1763 Brant served as a missionary's interpreter and also joined the Iroquois fighting with the British to suppress Pontiac's Rebellion. In 1765 he married the daughter of an Oneida chief. Brant converted to Anglicanism and helped to translate the Book of Common Prayer and other religious texts into his native language. In 1774 he became secretary to Guy Johnson, who succeeded Sir William (his father-in-law) as superintendent. Brant worked hard at persuading members of the Six Nations to support the British, and in 1775 he was commissioned a captain and sent to England, where he was presented at court. Benjamin West depicted him in a double portrait with Guy Johnson. Returned to America, Brant fought at The Cedars and in St. Leger's expedition and led the ambush at Oriskany in 1777 before joining with the Johnsons and Walter Butler in the Border Wars, participating in the Cherry Valley Massacre. He was regarded by his foes, however, as humane, wise, and honorable. The king appointed him Colonel of Indians. As the Revolution neared its end he worked for peace on the frontier and

then became a leader of the Mohawks in Ontario, where he purchased land with funds given him by the crown and helped to establish the Old Mohawk Church.

BURGOYNE, John
1722–1792
British general, politician. Pompous, prolix "Gentleman Johnny" Burgoyne was a moderately competent soldier who suffered the greatest defeat of British arms during the Revolution. In 1740 he entered the army, and after a creditable performance as a field commander he won the favor of the king, who endowed the officer with several lucrative posts and eventually raised him to the rank of major general. He also was a member of Parliament and supported the government throughout most of the period leading up to the eve of the American Revolution. Burgoyne was dispatched to Boston in April 1775, where his main contribution to the defense of the city was to write a pretentious and silly proclamation to the rebels. In 1776 he returned to England and put forward a scheme to split the Northern colonies. He proposed to move by water down the river and lake route, recapture Fort Ticonderoga, and then strike toward Albany through the forests and hills. Departing in June, Burgoyne easily captured Ticonderoga and began the cross-country march. Despite a mild victory at Hubbardstown in July, Burgoyne faced increasing difficulties and came up against a large American force near Saratoga, N.Y. Two fierce battles ensued, the first near Freeman's Farm on 19 September and a second at Bemis Heights on 7 October. Burgoyne was forced to surrender, although he maneuvered American commander Gates into signing terms of a "convention" rather than a capitulation. Burgoyne returned to England and spent the rest of his life in and out of political favor and writing plays.

BYRON, John
1723–1786
British admiral. Sent to America to succeed Adm. Lord Howe in the summer of 1778, Byron opposed the French fleet in the West Indies during most of his tour as naval commander in American waters. He had first sailed in 1740 as a midshipman with Lord Anson on a voyage to the Pacific and was shipwrecked on 14 May of that year off the south coast of Chile. Byron's account of this adventure inspired a scene in *Don Juan*, an epic poem composed by his grandson George Gordon, Lord Byron. In the years 1764–1766 Byron explored the South Seas, earning his nickname "Foul-weather Jack." From 1769 to 1772 he served as governor of Newfoundland. In March 1775 he became a rear admiral and, in January 1778 a vice admiral. On 9 June 1778 he sailed from England to replace Howe and to hunt down Adm. d'Estaing's French fleet, arriving too late off New York to confront his quarry. In December he sailed for the West Indies, where on 6 July 1779 his fleet engaged d'Estaing's and took a beating before the French unexpectedly withdrew, allowing Byron to escape defeat. Pleading ill health, Byron asked to be recalled. He left for England on 10 October 1779. At the time of his death Byron was vice admiral of the White, one of the three operating squadrons —the others being the Red and the Blue—of the British navy.

CAMPBELL, William
1745–1781

Militia officer. A giant frontiersman and leader of the Virginia militia, Campbell helped secure the patriot victory at King's Mountain. His family had migrated from Argyll, Scotland, and settled in the Holston Valley of Virginia. Campbell married Patrick Henry's sister Elizabeth. As a member of the Virginia militia with the rank of captain Campbell fought against the Cherokees and also in Dunmore's War of 1774. In December of that year he became captain in Patrick Henry's 1st Virginia Regiment, helping to expel Dunmore from the colony. Resigning his commission in the fall of 1776, he fought on the frontier, was an honorary commissioner in negotiations with the Cherokees, became a colonel in the militia, and served in the Virginia House of Burgesses. Isaac Shelby, a leader of the Over Mountain Men (frontiersmen from what is now Tennessee), persuaded Campbell to join the Western force organized to combat Tory troops commanded by Patrick Ferguson. Led largely by Campbell with the support of Shelby and John Sevier, the militiamen defeated Ferguson at King's Mountain, S.C., on 7 October 1780. Campbell was promoted to brigadier general. He and some of his riflemen joined Nathanael Greene for the Battle of Guilford Courthouse (N.C.) on 15 March 1781, subsequently helping to reinforce Lafayette in Virginia. Campbell became ill soon after the battle at Green Spring, in which he did not participate, and died on 22 August.

CARLETON, Guy
1724–1808

British general, governor of Canada. An able administrator and military leader, Carleton was born into an Irish Protestant family. He joined the army in 1742 and became a lieutenant three years later. He entered the 1st Foot Guards in 1751 and was made lieutenant-colonel of the regiment in 1757. In July 1758, he served at Louisburg, and at the end of the year, he was made colonel and quartermaster-general for Gen. James Wolfe. He fought with Wolfe at Quebec on 13 September 1759 and was wounded. As an acting brigadier general Carleton participated in the siege of Belle Isle in 1761 and served at Port Andro, where he was again wounded. Promoted to full colonel in 1762, he was wounded once again during the siege of Havana. On 2 April 1766, he became lieutenant governor of Canada and succeeded to the governorship the next year. Returning to England in 1770, he was made colonel of the 47th Foot Regiment and later major general. He supported the Quebec Act in the House of Commons in 1774, returning to Canada at the end of the year. In January 1775, Carleton was appointed governor of Quebec, becoming independent commander of the British forces in Canada later that year. He successfully defended Canada against the American invasion led by Benedict Arnold, pursuing the invaders back into New York. Subsequently he was knighted. He supported Gen. Burgoyne's doomed campaign against the Americans but asked to be recalled to England. In the summer of 1777, still in Canada, he was made lieutenant general, and in 1778 he became governor of Charlemont, Ireland, a position he held for life. In early 1782, the Rockingham ministry made him commander-in-chief in America and governor of New York. In New York City, Carleton assisted the peace process and then evacuated the city on 25 November 1783 to return to England. In April 1786 he once more became governor of Quebec, where he was popular because he favored religious toleration. He served in this post until July 1796, except for a two-year hiatus in 1791–1793. Shipwrecked on his return journey to England, Carleton survived and reached Portsmouth on 19 September 1796. The remainder of his life was spent in retirement.

CLARK, George Rogers
1752–1818
General. As the outstanding military figure in the West during the Revolution, Clark epitomized the frontier soldier. Born near Charlottesville, Va., he worked as a surveyor and emerged as a leader during Lord Dunsmore's War in 1774, when he served as a captain of militia. In 1776, the American outposts in Kentucky were under constant pressure from Indian raids organized by the British at Detroit. Clark was commissioned a major in the Virginia militia, and he organized a force of frontiersmen to march on the British-held settlements in the Illinois country (which were mostly inhabited by French settlers). On 26 June 1777 the small army left the Falls of the Ohio and marched overland the 120 miles to their first objective, the settlement of Kaskaskia. Clark captured the small garrison without a shot and set about charming the local French and Indians into cooperation. Within a few weeks he had also secured the settlements at Prairie de Rocher and Cahokia. In August Clark's men also occupied the larger settlement of Vincennes. The British recaptured Vincennes, but Clark captured it again in turn. Although he then held the West securely, Clark was never able to mount a full offensive against the principal British base at Detroit. Not yet thirty, Clark's best years were over, and he descended into a life of thwarted schemes, debt, and ill health. He died a forgotten man.

CLINTON, George
1739–1812
Governor of New York, Continental general. Clinton had a checkered military and political career. He was born in Little Britain, N.Y. In 1757 he served as a subaltern under John Bradstreet during the British conquest of Fort Frontenac. After brief service as a privateer in 1758, he studied law and began a legal career. He became a member of the New York assembly in 1768, functioning in that body as Philip Schuyler's rival for leadership of the advocates of revolution. Elected to the second Continental Congress in 1775, he missed the signing of the Declaration of Independence because George Washington had ordered him to assume command of the defenses of Hudson Highlands in July 1776. He was appointed brigadier general of the New York militia and in March 1777 assumed the same rank in the Continental Army. His leadership failed to save New York from Sir Henry Clinton's expedition, leading to the loss of forts Clinton and Montgomery and the destruction of Kingston (Esopus). Elected governor of New York in April 1777, he assumed that post by way of acknowledging his inadequacies as a military commander. As governor he was occupied with the Border

Wars and Indian–Tory raids. Popular as a wartime governor, he was re-elected five times. Clinton opposed the federal Constitution and wrote articles arguing against Alexander Hamilton's articles in favor. As an ally of Aaron Burr and the Livingstons he was again elected governor in 1800 after refusing to run in 1795 following six consecutive terms. He became vice president of the United States in 1804 and again in 1808, serving with presidents Jefferson and Madison and dying in office.

CLINTON, Henry
1738–1795
British general. The longest-serving British commander-in-chief during the Revolution, Clinton was raised in New York, where his father, Adm. George Clinton, served as governor in 1741–1751. Returning to England with his father, he became a lieutenant in the Coldstream Guards. He was promoted to lieutenant colonel in the Grenadier Guards in 1758. He served as aide-de-camp to Prince Ferdinand of Brunswick during the Seven Years' War and was wounded at Johannesburg in August 1762. In May 1772 he became major general and also began a career as a member of Parliament, assisted by his cousin the second Duke of Newcastle. His wife's death in August 1772 left him deranged, but on recovering, Clinton sailed in 1775 with generals Howe and Burgoyne to Boston, then under siege. Clinton served gallantly in the Battle of Bunker Hill and was made lieutenant general, second in command to Howe, who succeeded Gage. Howe sent him on the unsuccessful Charleston expedition in 1776. Rejoining Howe, he fought well in the Battle of Long Is-

land in August. Howe, wanting to be rid of him, sent Clinton to capture Newport, R.I. Clinton then returned to England, where he was knighted. He returned to New York City in July 1777, where Howe assigned him to the defense of the city. In October he captured the Hudson Highlands from the Americans. He succeeded Howe as commander-in-chief in May 1778 but was forced back to New York after an indecisive battle against Washington in New Jersey. In 1779, Clinton captured Stony Point and Verplanck's Point and staged raids on the Connecticut coast. Clinton led a successful expedition to take Charleston in 1780 and then returned to New York, where he was succeeded by Carleton in 1782. In 1783 he published his *Narrative of the Campaign of 1781 in North America*. In 1784 he lost his seat in Parliament after quarreling with his cousin, but he was re-elected in 1790. Clinton was promoted to full general in 1793, and in 1794 he was made governor of Gibraltar. He died on 23 December 1795 while serving in that post.

CORBIN, Margaret
1751–1800
Patriot heroine. Known as "Captain Molly" and often confused with Margaret Hays ("Molly Pitcher"), Corbin was born in Pennsylvania and orphaned at age four by Indians. In 1772 she married John Corbin of Virginia, who enlisted in the Pennsylvania artillery. During the battle of Fort Washington in November 1776, her husband was killed while serving his gun, and Margaret stepped forward to take his place. She was severely wounded in the action and captured with the rest of the garrison, but she

was evacuated to Philadelphia, where she recovered. She was awarded half-pay for life by Congress in 1779 for her valor. She died in Westchester County, N.Y., and is now buried at West Point.

CORNWALLIS, Charles
1738–1805

British general. Cornwallis was born in London, the son of the first Earl Cornwallis, and educated at Eton. At eighteen he became an ensign in the Grenadier Guards. While attending a military school in Turin he was called to active duty under Prince Ferdinand of Brunswick in the Seven Years' War. In 1759, he returned to England with a promotion to captain in the 85th Regiment. Cornwallis was elected to Parliament in 1760 and made lieutenant colonel and commander of the 12th Regiment. In 1762, he became Earl Cornwallis following his father's death and entered the House of Lords as a Whig. In succeeding years he served in varied capacities, including as aide-de-camp to George III. He became a major general in 1775 and arrived in New York in 1776 in time to serve in the battles of Long Island, Kip's Bay, Fort Washington, and Fort Lee that year. He lost to Washington at Princeton in January 1777. After a sojourn in England, Cornwallis returned to America in June 1777 and participated in the New Jersey campaign. He played a key role in the Battle of Brandywine and the capture of Philadelphia. Returning to England in January 1778, he was made lieutenant general, becoming second in command to Henry Clinton upon his return to America in the summer. Cornwallis again returned to England in December 1778 because his wife was dying, and he came back to America a year later, joining Clinton in the Charleston expedition of 1780 and thereafter assuming command of British forces in the South. He defeated the Americans at Camden, but in trying to pursue Nathanael Greene he overextended his forces while achieving a string of tactical victories that so depleted his army he was forced to withdraw to Yorktown, Va. He allowed himself to be penned up in the city, and when the French fleet cut his seaward line of communication, the allies laid siege. He surrendered in October 1781. In 1786 Cornwallis became governor-general of India, where he defeated Tippoo Sultan and served well as an administrator. He returned to England in 1793, became governor-general of Ireland in 1797, and in 1805 returned to India, where he died.

DE KALB, Johann
1721–1780

Continental major general. Known to the Americans as Baron de Kalb, a German volunteer who served in the Continental Army, De Kalb was born into a peasant family named simply Kalb in Huttendorf, Bavaria. He left home at age sixteen, and in his early twenties he surfaced as a lieutenant named Jean de Kalb in a French infantry unit. De Kalb served through the War of the Austrian Succession (1740–1748) and rose to the rank of major in 1756 at the beginning of the Seven Years' War, in which he fought with distinction. In 1764 he married an heiress, and in 1765 he retired from the military. During the early months of 1768 De Kalb traveled in the American colonies as a secret agent for Etienne François Choiseul, the French foreign minister. After Louis XVI inherited the throne in 1774, De Kalb returned to military service. He was commissioned a brigadier general in November 1776. Desiring to serve in America, he became one of Silas Deane's recruits in Paris, and in April 1777 he sailed for the United States along with the Marquis de Lafayette, for whom De Kalb acted as a mentor. The pair demanded major general's rank from Congress. Encountering indifference from Congress, De Kalb was preparing to return to France when Congress relented and appointed him major general in September 1777. He joined Gen. Washington in November, spending the winter at Valley Forge. Finally, in April 1780 he was given an assignment matching his rank—the relief of Charleston. He arrived too late to aid the city, however, and took over command of the few remaining American forces in North Carolina until Congress appointed Gen. Horatio Gates to head the Southern Department. Serving under Gates, who ignored his advice, De Kalb fought bravely in the Battle of Camden (S.C.) on 16 August, holding the field while Gates and the fickle militia fled. De Kalb suffered severe wounds and died three days later.

DE GRASSE, François
1722–1788
French admiral. An aristocrat born into one of France's oldest families, De Grasse attended the naval school at Toulon when he was only eleven, and at twelve he became a page to the grand master of the Knights of Saint John at Malta. In 1740 he served in the French navy during the War of Jenkins' Ear. In May 1747 De Grasse was captured during a battle off Finisterre and spent three months as a prisoner in England. Subsequent naval service

took him to India, the West Indies, Morocco, and throughout the Mediterranean. In 1774 De Grasse became commander of the marine brigade stationed at Saint Malo. In 1775 he served as commander of a ship at Haiti. In 1778 he was made a commodore and commanded a force at the battle of Ushant. In the Americas De Grasse commanded a squadron under Adm. d'Estaing in the battles against Adm. Byron's fleet off Grenada and also served at Savannah. For a short time he was in command of the French fleet in the West Indies. In ill health, De Grasse returned home, arriving in Cadiz in October 1780. In March 1781 he was promoted to rear admiral and set sail with a sizable fleet bound for the West Indies. In September and October he and his fleet played a major role in the victory at Yorktown, driving the British fleet off the Chesapeake capes and bottling up Cornwallis. In November he returned to the West Indies, and in February 1782 he captured St. Kitts. But in April he was defeated and taken prisoner by the British. In London he had several conversations with Lord Shelburne, which led to his serving as an intermediary in the preliminary peace negotiations. In May 1784 a tribunal exonerated De Grasse for his losses in the West Indies. Following his death in Paris, the French Revolution exploded, and the revolutionaries destroyed his country estate. His children, however, managed to escape to America.

DEANE, Silas
1737–1789
Diplomat. A member of both the first and second Continental Congress, Deane served as an American representative in Europe during the Revo-

lution. He was born in Groton, Ct., and graduated from Yale in 1758. He opened a law practice in Wethersfield in 1762. Deane supported the patriot cause, leading opposition to the Townshend Acts in the Connecticut General Assembly in 1772 and serving as secretary of the Committee of Correspondence in 1773. He represented Connecticut in the Continental Congresses in 1774–1776. In 1776 the Congress sent Deane to France as a secret agent to negotiate with the French government, making him the United States' first diplomat. He was able to secure eight shiploads of arms and supplies for the patriots, and he commissioned several European officers for the cause. But Deane began to advocate reconciliation with England, raising suspicions in Congress, which sent Franklin and Arthur Lee to negotiate with France. Deane returned home in 1778 following charges of disloyalty and embezzlement. Under attack in Congress, he began to denounce the war in letters to friends, some of which were printed in a Tory newspaper in New York, driving Deane into exile in London. There in 1789 he published a defense of his actions. While on board ship for a return to America in the same year he died and was later buried in Deal, England.

D'ESTAING, Charles Hector Theodat
1729–1794
French admiral. The comte d'Estaing was born in the Auvergne. At sixteen he was colonel of a regiment and at twenty-six a brigadier. He went to the East Indies in 1757, and in 1759 the British captured him at the siege of Madras. He violated his parole by leading naval operations against the

British, who again captured him in 1760 and imprisoned him for a while at Portsmouth. D'Estaing became a lieutenant general in the French navy in 1763 and a vice admiral in 1777. In 1778 he was given command of a fleet to combat the English in America. He failed to help dislodge the British at New York and Newport, abandoned a Franco–American plan to attack Halifax and Newfoundland, and headed for the West Indies. There in 1779 he backed off from a battle he appeared to be winning with Adm. Byron. Returning to North American waters, he participated in the disastrous attempt to retake Savannah, a humiliating defeat for the French and Americans. D'Estaing returned to France in 1780. At Cadiz in 1783 he was involved in organizing a fleet for operations in the West Indies when the war ended. D'Estaing was elected to the Assembly of Notables in 1787. He was made commandant of the National Guard in 1789, and in 1792 the National Assembly appointed him admiral. Though favoring reforms, d'Estaing remained loyal to the king and defended Marie Antoinette. In 1794 he was tried and executed.

DICKINSON, John
1732–1808
Government official, writer. Born in Talbot County, Md., Dickinson studied law in Philadelphia and subsequently at the Middle Temple in London in 1753–1757. He opened a law practice in Philadelphia in 1757. Dickinson became a member of the Assembly of Lower Counties (Delaware) in 1760 and represented Philadelphia in the Pennsylvania legislature in 1762–1764 and 1770–

1776. In 1765, the legislature appointed him to the Stamp Act Congress, where he drafted the declaration requesting repeal of the Stamp Act. Responding to the Townsend Acts in 1768, Dickinson published *Letters from a Farmer in Pennsylvania*, which disputed England's right to tax the colonies and advocated nonimportation of goods from Great Britain. In 1774 he served as chairman of the Committee of Correspondence and became a member of the first Continental Congress. Dickinson represented Delaware in Congress in 1776–1777 and again in 1779–1780. As an advocate of reconciliation and peace he voted against the Declaration of Independence, but with the outbreak of war Dickinson joined the Revolution, serving as a colonel in the 1st Battalion mustered in Philadelphia. He also helped draft the Articles of Confederation. In 1781 he became president of the Supreme Executive Council of Delaware, and from 1782 to 1785 he served as president of the Supreme Council of Pennsylvania. In 1786 he was president of the Annapolis Convention. Delaware sent him as a representative to the Constitutional Convention in 1787. In a series of letters signed *Fabius* he advocated adoption of the Constitution. Dickinson died in Wilmington, Del. Dickinson College, which he helped found in 1783, is named in his honor.

DUPORTAIL, Louis
1743–1802

Continental major general. Known to the Americans simply as General "Duportail" during his service as a volunteer in the Continental Army, Duportail was actually an aristocrat born in Pithiviers, France, the son of a King's councilor with the full surname of Le Begue de Presle Duportail. In 1762 he became a lieutenant and a student at the school of engineering at Mezières, graduating three years later. Duportail was promoted to captain in 1773. When Benjamin Franklin asked the French government to provide trained military engineers to help the American cause, Duportail was one of four the ministry chose. Duportail reported for duty in the Continental Army on 13 February 1777; in July he was made colonel of engineers, backdated to February. In November he became a brigadier general and chief of engineers for the army. Duportail served in the Philadelphia campaign and was in charge of upgrading the forts on the Delaware River. He stayed with Washington through the winter encampment at Valley Forge and the campaign at Monmouth, and in June 1778 he was sent to strengthen the defenses at Philadelphia. In 1779, Duportail served in the Hudson Highlands and received the new title Commandant of the Corps of Engineers and Sappers and Miners. In March 1780 he was put under Benjamin Lincoln's command but reached Charleston too late to be of significant service. Taken prisoner on 12 May 1780, Duportail was exchanged in October in time to join Washington for the Yorktown campaign. He was promoted to major general in November 1781. Resigning from the Continental Army in October 1783, Duportail returned to France and assumed the post of brigadier general of infantry. In November 1790 Duportail became minister and secretary of state for war, a post he held for only a year. In January 1792 he was promoted to lieutenant general and given command of the Moulins region, but being a supporter of Lafayette, then under political suspicion, he was prevented from assuming this post. Charged with political disloyalty, he went into hiding for two years. Escaping to America, he settled on a small farm near Philadelphia. Duportail's name was removed from the proscribed list in June 1797, but he died aboard ship while returning to France in 1802 and was buried at sea.

FRANKLIN, Benjamin
1706–1790
Statesman. One of America's renaissance figures—printer, author, editor, inventor, scientist, politician, diplomat—Franklin was nearly seventy when the Revolution began. Born in Boston, he had little formal schooling before beginning work in his father's tallow shop. He later worked as an apprentice printer with his brother James. In 1723 he ran away to Philadelphia, arriving with only one Dutch dollar and a copper shilling; by 1730 he was sole owner of a printing business and the *Pennsylvania Gazette*. In 1727 Franklin founded a debating society, the Junto, and in 1732 he set up a circulating library and also began to publish *Poor Richard's Almanac*, which he continued to edit until 1757. In 1743 the Junto was transformed into the American Philosophical Society. Franklin also was the primary force in establishing Philadelphia's first fire company, an academy, and the University of Pennsylvania (1747). By 1748 he had amassed a sufficient fortune to turn over the printing business to his partner and devote his energies to scientific pursuits. His *Experiments and Observations on Electricity*, published in 1751, established his reputation in Europe as a scientist. Elected to the Pennsylvania Assembly in 1751, Franklin served in that body through 1763. The British government appointed him deputy postmaster general of the colonies in 1753, a position he held until 1774. At the outset of war with France in 1754 Franklin attended the Albany Convention and submitted a proposal that became a precedent for the eventual American union. The Pennsylvania Assembly sent Franklin to London as its agent during the years 1757–1762 and again for 1764–1775. He also served as agent for Georgia and Massachusetts. Though initially a strong supporter of American ties to the crown, Franklin became an outspoken advocate of American dissent during his second tour in England, asserting that Parliament should have no authority over the colonies and speaking out against the Stamp Act in the House of Commons in 1766. He returned to Philadelphia in 1775 a supporter of revolution and was immediately selected to serve in the Continental Congress. He helped draft the Declaration of Independence. In 1776, Congress sent him to Paris to help negotiate a treaty of alliance, raise loans, and secure supplies. In 1778–1785 in Paris he was American minister plenipotentiary, serving on the commission that negotiated the Treaty of Paris (1783) that ended the Revolutionary War. Returning to Philadelphia in the fall of 1785, Franklin was soon elected president of the Supreme Executive Council of Pennsylvania, holding that post for three years. In 1787, he also became president of the Pennsylvania Society for Promoting the Abolition of Slavery and a member of the Constitutional

Convention representing Pennsylvania. Although none of his major proposals was approved for inclusion in the Constitution, he urged its unanimous adoption. In recognition of his achievements Harvard, Yale, Oxford, William and Mary, and St. Andrews all awarded him honorary degrees. Franklin had begun the writing of his *Autobiography* while in London, but it remained incomplete at the time of his death.

GAGE, Thomas
1721–1787

British general. The last royal governor of Massachusetts and the British commander-in-chief in America for the years 1763–1775, Gage was born in Firle, England, the descendant of a French nobleman who came to England with William the Conqueror. He was educated at Westminster School. In 1740 Gage was commissioned an ensign, and in 1743 he became a captain and aide-de-camp to Lord Albemarle. Gage fought at Fontenoy and Culloden in 1745. He also participated in the Low Countries campaign of 1747–1748. Gage thereafter became a member of the 44th Foot Regiment, and in 1751 he was promoted to lieutenant colonel. When the French and Indian War began Gage's regiment was ordered to America to serve under Gen. Edward Braddock. He served in Braddock's disastrous Pennsylvania campaign of 1755, becoming an acquaintance of George Washington during the expedition. In 1758, Gage was slightly wounded during the unsuccessful attack on Ticonderoga. He also was promoted to brigadier general and married in that year. In 1759 he became commandant of Albany and also

participated in the conquest of Canada. After the French surrender in 1760 Gage became governor of Montreal and a district that encompassed Crown Point and an area reaching to the shores of Lake Ontario. In 1761 he was promoted to major general, and in 1763 he became commander-in-chief in America, assuming his post in New York City. As rebelliousness rose in Boston Gage traveled to that city and enhanced its garrison. In 1773 he and his family returned to England, but he was sent back to America the following year as both commander-in-chief and governor of Massachusetts, serving in this capacity during the events leading to the battles at Lexington, Concord, and Bunker Hill. In late 1775 Gage was recalled to England. Out of favor with the North government he struggled to make ends meet until he was appointed to the staff at Amherst in 1781. In 1782, with Germain out of power, he was made a full general. Over the succeeding years his health steadily deteriorated.

GALVEZ, Bernardo de
1746–1786

Spanish official, soldier. The Spanish governor of Louisiana and Florida, Galvez came from a distinguished family, his father having been viceroy of New Spain and his uncle minister-general of the Indies. Galvez served with the Spanish army in Portugal, Algiers, and New Spain and attended military school at Avila. He was sent to Louisiana with the rank of colonel; in 1777 he became governor. He pursued policies that weakened the British in the region, seizing British privateers and supporting the American agent Oliver Pollock's efforts in

New Orleans to obtain supplies for the rebels. After Spain entered the war on America's side Galvez captured British outposts on the Mississippi River, including Baton Rouge and Natchez. In 1780 he took Mobile, and in 1781 he forced the surrender of Pensacola, securing control over western Florida. These successes resulted in Britain's cession of both East and West Florida to Spain in the Treaty of Paris, giving Spain control over not only the Floridas but also the mouth of the Mississippi. Galvez was in Spain in 1783–1784 as an adviser on policy affecting the future of the Florida and Louisiana territories. He was made major general, awarded Castilian titles of nobility, and appointed captain-general of the Floridas and Louisiana. In 1785, Galvez was appointed viceroy of New Spain. Barely forty years old, he died of a severe fever while in Mexico in 1786.

GAMBIER, James
1723–1789
British admiral. A officer who served in America and in the West Indies and was naval commander-in-chief in America in 1770–1773, Gambier became a lieutenant in the navy in 1743. He participated in operations at Louisburg in 1758 and in the following year in the West Indies. From 1770 till 1773, Gambier was commander-in-chief of naval operations in America. Promoted to rear admiral in January 1778, he became second in command to Adm. Lord Howe and later to Adm. John Byron, filling in as temporary commander-in-chief in America when Howe and Byron left. Gambier returned to England in April 1779. He was promoted to vice admiral in 1780, and in 1783–1784 he served as commander-in-chief in Jamaica, relinquishing this post because of poor health.

GATES, Horatio
1728–1806
Continental major general. Born in England, the son of a housekeeper for the Duke of Leeds, Gates joined the British army while quite young. He served in North America during the French and Indian War and was with Gen. Braddock in the unsuccessful effort to capture Fort Duquesne in 1755. He also fought in Martinique. Gates retired from the army at half-pay in 1765 with the rank of major. In 1772, helped by George Washington, he settled on a farm in Virginia. Siding with the patriots, Gates entered the Continental Army in June 1775 as Washington's adjutant general with the rank of brigadier general. In May 1776 he was promoted to major general and sent to the Northern Department to serve under Gen. Schuyler. By the end of the year he rejoined Washington for the New Jersey campaign. In the spring of 1777 Congress sent Gates to be commander at Ticonderoga, ostensibly in preparation to succeed Schuyler as commander of the Northern Department. But Congress reneged, and Gates traveled to Philadelphia to protest his treatment before the delegates. After Ticonderoga fell to the British, Washington sent Gates in August to replace Schuyler as commander of the Northern Department, and he was in charge of the northern army during the defeat of Gen. Burgoyne's offensive, earning him credit in Congress as the Hero of Saratoga. Following the victory, there was a movement to make Gates commander-in-chief, replacing Washing-

ton, which led Congress to appoint Gates president of the Board of War created in October 1777 and also to the so-called Conway Cabal effort to discredit Washington. After re-establishing his working relationship with Washington Gates resumed command of the Northern Department in April 1778, and later that year he became commander of the Eastern Department in Boston. In July 1780, without consulting Washington, Congress appointed Gates commander of the Southern Department, but his disastrous loss at Camden and subsequent personal flight from the battlefield resulted in his replacement by Gen. Nathanael Greene. Gates retired to his farm and for two years tried to get a congressional inquiry to clear his name, finally succeeding and returning to the army at Newburgh in 1782 for the last year of the war. Gates then retired once again to his farm. His wife died in 1784, and he remarried in 1786. In 1790 Gates freed his slaves and moved to New York City. He served in the New York legislature in 1800–1801.

GEORGE III
1738–1820

King of Great Britain. Grandson of George II and his successor as king of Great Britain and Ireland, George William Frederick ascended to the throne in 1760 when he was twenty-two. He set about diminishing the power of the Whigs, succeeding in terminating the government of William Pitt. He also succeeded in controlling the terms of the Treaty of Paris of 1763 that brought an end to the Seven Years' War. The king's ten-year struggle to gain control over Parliament finally resulted in 1770 in the installation of Lord North, doggedly loyal to George III, as prime minister. But the repressive policies toward the American colonies the king effected through the North ministry backfired. After news of the British defeat at Yorktown reached London, George III finally allowed North to resign in March 1782 and authorized peace negotiations to end the American Revolution. Following conclusion of the Treaty of Paris the king appointed William Pitt the Younger prime minister, in December 1783. In the fall of 1788 the symptoms of congenital illness that had first appeared in 1765 overwhelmed the king, rendering him mad, but he recovered and, with the outbreak of the French Revolution, his popularity among the people revived. In 1811, however, after the death of his favorite daughter, he became permanently ill and the Prince of Wales assumed the role of regent. Before his death George III also became blind and deaf.

GERMAIN, George Sackville, Lord
1716–1785

British minister. The son of the first Duke of Dorset, who served as lord lieutenant of Ireland during the reign of George II, Germain attended the Westminster School and received an M.A. degree from Trinity College, Dublin, in 1734. In 1737 he was made a captain in the 7th Horse Regiment of the Irish Establishment, and in 1740 he became a lieutenant colonel of the 28th Foot Regiment. In 1741, Germain became a member of Parliament. He fought as commander of his regiment in the Low Countries and was wounded at the Battle of Fontenoy in May 1745. The following year he became commander of the

20th Foot Regiment and, in 1749, of the 12th Dragoons. Then in 1750 he became colonel in command of his original regiment. Germain served as his father's personal secretary and secretary of war during his father's second stay in Ireland in 1751–1756. In 1755 Germain was promoted to major general. He served as the Duke of Marlborough's second in command in Hanover under Prince Ferdinand, assuming command when Marlborough died in September 1758. Misconduct at the Battle of Minden in 1759 resulted in Germain's being court-martialed and judged unfit for military service in 1760. It was in 1770 that he took the name Germain upon inheriting property from Lady Betty Germain. In November 1775 Germain became secretary of state for the colonies and also lord commissioner of trade and plantations, so that he was in control of the British forces prosecuting the war against the Americans throughout the Revolution. During the war he had many conflicts with generals Howe, Carleton, and Clinton, whereas he strongly favored generals Burgoyne and Cornwallis. Thus his own policies contributed to the British defeat. Germain resigned in February 1782 and was given a peerage as Viscount Sackville. He retired to his country home in Sussex in poor health in 1783 and died a year and a half later.

GLOVER, John
1732–1797
Continental general. Glover played a key role at several points in the Revolutionary War, usually at the head of his specialized regiment of Marblehead Mariners. He was born in Salem, Mass., but moved at an early age to the seaside village of Marblehead. He was a well-to-do fisherman, shipowner, and merchant, active as an officer of the local militia. In April 1775 Glover was commissioned a colonel by the Provincial Congress, and he raised the 21st Massachusetts Regiment, made up of fishermen and seafarers from Marblehead who were expert in handling small craft in all weathers and conditions. Glover's Mariners first proved their worth in August 1776 when they evacuated George Washington's army from Long Island. Four months later, on Christmas Day, Glover and his men moved to the forefront of history when they rowed the army across the Delaware River in the middle of a bitter winter storm. Glover's men not only pulled their oars through the night but they also formed up and advanced as part of Washington's force, blocking the Hessian escape route from Trenton. After the victory, the Mariners marched back to the river, took to their boats again, and moved the American army and 900 prisoners back to safety. The amphibious regiment broke up with the end of its enlistment in 1776, but Glover accepted a commission as brigadier general in June 1777. He retired on half-pay due to ill health in 1782 and was breveted major general a year later. After the war he served as a member of the Massachusetts convention that ratified the Constitution.

GRANT, James
1720–1806
British general. Grant entered military service as captain in the 1st Battalion of the Royal Scots in the fall of 1744, serving at the battles of Fontenoy and Culloden. In February 1757

he became a major in the 77th High-landers. He led an 800-man unit into severe defeat at Fort Duquesne on 21 September 1758 and was taken to Montreal as a prisoner. Grant was nevertheless promoted to lieutenant colonel in 1760, and in 1761 he led the Cherokee expedition to success. When Britain gained possession of the Floridas in 1763, Grant was made governor, a post he held until 1771, when he returned to England because of ill-ness. The following year he was in command of the 40th Foot Regiment in Ireland. In 1773 Grant became a member of Parliament. In December 1775 he was made a colonel in the 55th Foot Regiment, and he came to America as a brigadier general. He fought at Long Island in August 1776 and then succeeded Cornwallis as commander of British posts in New Jersey, where he was in charge when Washington successfully attacked Trenton and Princeton. Grant served at Brandywine and Germantown. In 1778 he led the unsuccessful effort to trap Lafayette at Barren Hill and also was unsuccessful at protecting the rear of Clinton's army at the Battle of Monmouth. In December of that year he was sent with a detachment of Clinton's troops to the West Indies and captured St. Lucia. Grant served well as commander in the West Indies and returned to England in the late summer of 1779. He was promoted to lieutenant general in 1782 and full general in 1796. Grant served in Parliament in 1787, 1790, 1796, and 1801.

GREENE, Nathanael
1742–1786
Continental major general. Born in Warwick, R.I., Greene was a descendant of English immigrants who ar-rived in Massachusetts in 1635 but moved on to Rhode Island to escape religious persecution as Quakers. He worked in his father's iron foundry in Potowomut until 1770, when he assumed control of his family's iron forge in Coventry. From 1770 until 1772, he served in the colony's general assembly, returning to the assembly again in 1775. In September 1773 he was denied the sanction of the Quaker meetinghouse because he had attended a military parade. In October of the following year Greene helped raise a militia unit called the Kentish Guards but was denied service as an officer because of a game knee. But in the following May, with the onset of the Revolution, he was made a brigadier general when the state raised three militia companies. He led these regiments to Long Island in June and was appointed the youngest brigadier general in the Continental Army. Although incapacitated and unable to serve during the Battle of Long Island in August 1776, he was promoted to major general and placed in command of the army in New Jersey. He suffered a severe defeat at Fort Washington in November but recouped with his performance at Trenton in December, after which he joined Washington in winter quarters. Washington sent Greene to confer with the Continental Congress and thereafter, with Gen. Knox, to reconnoiter the terrain of the Hudson Highlands. In the fall of 1777, Greene served well at both Brandywine and Germantown. In February 1778, with the army again in winter quarters, he reluctantly accepted appointment as quartermaster general. Returning to the field, he led troops at Monmouth in June and again at Newport in August before resuming

his quartermaster duties in October in Rhode Island. His policies of establishing supply depots and improving transportation increased the army's mobility, but in 1780 he encountered criticism from Congress at the behest of his former rival as quartermaster, Thomas Mifflin, and resigned his post in August. Subsequently, Greene served as president of the board that condemned Maj. John André, and he replaced Benedict Arnold as commander in the Hudson Highlands. In October Washington placed Greene in charge of the Southern Department, where he won a decisive strategic campaign over Lord Cornwallis and limited British control in South Carolina to the area of Charleston, despite never winning a single battle. In 1783 Greene returned to a hero's welcome in Rhode Island. His personal finances, however, were in severe straits, and he was obliged to sell his properties in the North. In 1785 he took up residence in Georgia on the former estate of the Loyalist lieutenant governor near Savannah that the state gave to him. Greene died in 1786 of sunstroke.

HALE, Nathan
1755–1776
Patriot spy. Hale was born in Coventry, Ct., one of nine sons of a successful farmer. He graduated from Yale in 1773 and thereafter taught school, first in East Haddam and then in New London, until the Revolution began. In July 1775, Hale was commissioned a lieutenant in the 7th Connecticut Militia. In January of the following year he became a captain in the Continental Army's 19th Regiment and then participated in the siege of Boston. In April he arrived in New York City. He is believed to have been a member of a group of seamen from his company who captured a British supply sloop the next month. Hale served in the Battle of Long Island and was with Washington on the retreat from Brooklyn. Thomas Knowlton chose Hale as commander of a company of his rangers, and when Gen. Washington requested that a captain from the rangers volunteer to gather intelligence before the Battle of Harlem Heights, Hale accepted the duty. Disguised as a Dutch schoolteacher, he left the American encampment at Harlem Heights in September and made his way to Long Island, where he gathered the desired information about the disposition of British forces. But while returning to his own lines on the night of 21 September he was captured. Hale was taken to Gen. William Howe's headquarters, where incriminating documents were found when he was searched. Since he was in disguise instead of uniform, Gen. Howe ordered that he be hanged for spying the very next day. Having written letters to his brother Enoch and to Knowlton (whom he did not know was already dead), Hale went to the gallows with composure. A witness reported that he made a brief speech ending with "I only regret that I have but one life to lose for my country."

HAMILTON, Alexander
1757–1804
Continental officer, statesman. One of the primary architects of the new republic, Hamilton was born to a Scottish merchant and his Huguenot mistress (she was divorced but legally

precluded from remarrying) in Nevis, British West Indies. His mother died in 1768 estranged from his father, thus leaving Hamilton effectively orphaned. He had been tutored by his mother and a Presbyterian minister in St. Croix and knew French fluently. Hamilton went to work as a clerk in St. Croix. In 1772, his aunts provided him funds to travel to New York and enroll in King's College (now Columbia University). Hamilton wrote a series of cogent pamphlets opposing British policies, and in 1775 he formed a volunteer artillery company. In March 1776 Hamilton was commissioned a captain in the Provincial Company of New York Artillery. In this role he served well in the battles of Long Island, Harlem Heights, Trenton, and Princeton. In March 1777, at twenty, Hamilton was appointed secretary and aide-de-camp to Gen. Washington with a promotion to lieutenant colonel. He held this post for nearly four and a half years, regarded by Washington as a trusted adviser with a solid grasp of military and political affairs. In December 1780 Hamilton married Elizabeth Schuyler, a member of one of the most powerful families in New York. Leaving service with Washington in July 1781, Hamilton assumed command of a battalion under Lafayette and fought in the Yorktown campaign; he left military service in December 1783. Hamilton served in the Congress in 1782–1783 and thereafter practiced law in New York. His efforts at the Annapolis Convention in 1786 helped lead to the Constitutional Convention in 1787, at which Hamilton served as a delegate from New York and advocated a strong central government. He worked hard for ratification, joining John Jay and James Madison in writing the *Federalist* papers and helping to secure ratification by the New York Convention. From 1789 to 1795 he served as the nation's first secretary of the treasury. He was a powerful member of Washington's cabinet and a strong advocate of Federalism. Hamilton resigned in January 1795 to return to his law practice in New York but continued to advise Washington and helped write his Farewell Address of 1796. In 1798, with war between the United States and France threatening, Hamilton was commissioned a brigadier general and appointed inspector general of the army. Hamilton's political maneuverings alienated President John Adams and contributed to Adams' defeat in 1800, when Aaron Burr and Thomas Jefferson tied as finalists for the presidency. Though Hamilton opposed Jefferson both politically and personally, he helped secure the presidency for him. In 1804 he also helped to defeat the movement to elect Burr as governor of New York. The resulting enmity between the two men led to their duel at Weehawken Heights, New Jersey, on 11 July 1804. Hamilton died the next day in New York from the wounds he received. He was buried in Trinity churchyard.

HAMILTON, Henry
? –1796

British officer. Hamilton served at the battles of Louisburg and Quebec and in the West Indies, and during the years 1775–1779 was lieutenant governor of Canada and commandant at Detroit. His command included only a few regulars from the 8th Regiment, but Hamilton recruited Indians and renegades, including Simon Girty, to assist in attacks on American frontier settlements. He received orders to undertake the attacks in June 1777, but following an attack on Wheeling in September his Indian forces joined the Burgoyne expedition, so not until early 1778 was Hamilton able to launch a concerted effort against the settlers. The campaign of George Rogers Clark disrupted these efforts, leading to Hamilton's march to retake Vincennes. Clark captured him in February 1779. Detained as a prisoner at Williamsburg, Va., for several months, Hamilton was then paroled and sent to New York. Hamilton was nicknamed The Hair Buyer by the Americans, who believed that he offered payments to the Indians for the scalps of settlers, although no proof exists that he did. Hamilton became lieutenant governor of Quebec in 1784, serving for a year. From 1790 to 1794 he was governor of Bermuda and then served for a year as governor of Dominica.

HANCOCK, John
1737–1793
American statesman. Merchant, governor of Massachusetts, and signer of the Declaration of Independence, Hancock was born in Braintree (Quincy), Mass. Orphaned as a youngster, he was adopted by his uncle Thomas Hancock, Boston's wealthiest merchant. He attended Boston Latin School and graduated from Harvard in 1754. In 1763 he was made a partner in Thomas Hancock and Company; the next year he inherited the firm, at the age of twenty-seven. He favored the patriots' views and circumvented the excises imposed by the Stamp Act (1765) by smuggling. In 1768 the British authorities seized his merchant ship *Liberty* and its cargo of Madeira because he had failed to pay duties. The prominence he gained as a result of this episode led to his election in 1769 to the Massachusetts General Court, in which he served until 1774. In 1770 Hancock became head of the Boston town committee formed to investigate the Boston Massacre. He also gained favor with Sam Adams. Hancock was treasurer of Harvard in 1773 and served as president of the Provincial Congress in 1774–1775. When Gen. Thomas Gage sent troops in 1775 to arrest him and Sam Adams, the two men fled to Lexington. Hancock then went to Philadelphia, where he became a delegate to the Continental Congress, serving as president from May 1775 to October 1777. As president he was the first signer of the Declaration of Independence. After resigning the presidency he returned to Boston. In 1778 he commanded Massachusetts troops as brigadier general during the operations at Newport. On 1 September 1780 Hancock became the first governor of Massachusetts. He resigned in 1785 to serve as president of Congress but never assumed the post because of ill health. He was re-elected governor in 1787 and in every election thereafter until his death. In 1788 Hancock served as president of the Massachusetts Convention that ratified the Constitution.

HANSON, John
1721–1783
American official. By virtue of serving as the president of Congress after official adoption of the Articles of Confederation, Hanson technically became the first "president" of the

United States. Born in Mulberry Grove, Md., Hanson was an early staunch advocate of independence and the patriot cause. He served as a member of the Maryland House of Delegates from 1757 until 1773. He was a member of the committee that drew up the instructions for Maryland's delegates to the Stamp Act Congress in 1765. Hanson signed the nonimportation agreement Maryland adopted as a response to the Townshend Acts in 1769. He also supported the Association of Maryland, which sanctioned armed resistance to the British, in 1774. Hanson served as treasurer of Frederick County in 1775 and established a gun-lock factory in Frederick. He was very active in raising troops and finding armaments for the Continental Army. In June 1780 Hanson began service as a delegate to the Continental Congress, and he worked hard to convince others to ratify the Articles of Confederation, persuading authorities from Virginia and other states to relinquish their claims on Western lands. In November 1781 Hanson was elected the first president of the Confederation Congress, serving a one-year term before retiring from public service.

HAYS, Mary Ludwig (Molly Pitcher)
1754? –1832
Legendary heroine. The name "Molly Pitcher" has been attached to several women who fought side by side with men in the Revolution, but the leading candidate for the honor is Mary Ludwig Hays McCauley, a domestic servant from Carlisle, Pa. Married to John Hays, a barber, Mary went along when he enlisted as gunner in a Pennsylvania regiment in 1775. By 1778 she was apparently an established camp follower, seeing to washing and cooking for and nursing of the troops in the field. On 28 June, during the battle of Monmouth, she was carrying water to the front lines (hence the nickname Molly Pitcher) when her husband fell wounded or exhausted at his gun. According to legend, Mary took his place as cannon-loader for the rest of the fight, helping to keep the gun in action. After the war, Mary and her husband returned to Carlisle, where she worked as a cleaningwoman. Following Hays' death she married John McCauley. In 1822 the Pennsylvania legislature voted her a payment of forty dollars and an annuity "for her services during the revolutionary war." Described by contemporaries as an uncouth, tobacco-chewing, foul-mouthed character—the perfect picture of an old trooper—she was also known for warm-heartedness and generosity.

HEATH, William
1737–1814
Continental general. Soldier, farmer, and politician, Heath was born in Roxbury, Mass., where his ancestors had settled in 1636. He was a delegate to the Massachusetts General Court in 1761 and also in 1771, serving from then until the British dissolved the assembly in 1774. In 1765 Heath joined the Ancient and Honorable Artillery Company of Boston. In 1774–1775 he served as a member of the Massachusetts Provincial Congress, which appointed him brigadier general in February 1775, and also of the Committee of Safety. Following the British retreat from Lexington and Concord, he was the first American general to appear, ordering deployment of troops to begin the siege of Boston. He also

organized American forces at Cambridge before the Battle of Bunker Hill. In June 1775 he was appointed brigadier general in the Continental Army, serving with Washington. In March 1776 he led the first detachment of Continentals to New York, where he served as Gen. Putnam's second in command. In November he was put in charge of the troops defending the Hudson Highlands. After leading an unsuccessful attack against Fort Independence in January 1777 he was censured by Washington, who denied him other field commands for the rest of the war. As successor to Artemas Ward in command of the Eastern Department Heath had brief custody over Burgoyne and the Convention Army. In June 1779 he was placed in command of the troops on the east side of the lower Hudson River and remained at this post till the end of the war except for a three-month sojourn in Providence to manage the arrival of Rochambeau and his troops from France. Heath returned to Roxbury in July 1783. In 1788 he served on the Massachusetts Convention that ratified the Constitution, and he was a member of the state senate in 1791 and 1792. In the latter year he also served as a member of the probate court in Norfolk. Elected lieutenant governor in 1806, Heath declined to serve.

HEISTER, Leopold Phillip von
1707–1777
German mercenary general. As commander-in-chief of the Hessian troops, von Heister led the first contingent of German mercenaries to America. He set sail from Spithead in May 1776 with 7,800 German mercenaries and 1,000 British troops.

Arriving in Halifax, von Heister discovered that Gen. Howe had already sailed for New York, and he joined the British force there on Staten Island in July. Von Heister led the center of the British troops during the Battle of Long Island and personally accepted the surrender of Lord Stirling (Gen. William Alexander). He commanded the German troops at the Battle of White Plains in October 1776. But following the defeat at Trenton in December 1776 and conflicts with Gen. Howe, von Heister was recalled in 1777 and replaced by Baron Wilhelm von Knyphausen. He died in November of the same year, still distraught over his loss at Trenton.

HENRY, Patrick
1736–1799
Orator, politician. Henry was born in the frontier area of Hanover County, Va., the son of an immigrant from Aberdeen, Scotland. When he was fifteen Henry became a store clerk, and at sixteen he opened his own store in partnership with his brother. At eighteen he married and began farming, but a disastrous fire forced him back into storekeeping. Heavily in debt, he obtained a law license in 1760 and began a very successful legal career. In 1763, in the Parson's Cause case he argued that in disallowing a Virginia law the king had violated the compact between the crown and its subjects and thereby forfeited claims to his subjects' obedience. Henry became a member of the Virginia House of Burgesses in 1765 and championed American dissent, advocating seven resolutions that comprised a radical response to the Stamp Act, including a declaration of Virginia's legislative

autonomy. His supporting speech ended with "If this be treason, make the most of it." The resolutions evoked widespread agitation and established his renown throughout the colonies. After Lord Dunmore dissolved the House of Burgesses, Henry led the delegates in meetings at the Raleigh Tavern. In a speech delivered in March 1775 he argued for armed resistance to the crown and declared "Give me liberty or give me death." Henry served in the first and second Continental Congress in 1774–1776, but his opposition to complete independence from Britain cost him a role as a national leader. Although Henry was appointed colonel of the first regiment formed in Virginia, he was precluded from command by his political opponents and therefore resigned. But in May 1776 he helped draft the Virginia constitution, and he became the first governor at the end of June, serving until the summer of 1779. He authorized George Rogers Clark's expedition into the Northwest Territory. In the last months of his tenure as governor Virginia was ravaged by a series of British coastal raids. Henry was succeeded by his friend and ally Thomas Jefferson and retired to Henry County, southwest of Richmond. In 1781 he supported a faction seeking an investigation of Jefferson's conduct as governor, generating hostility between the two men that lasted till the end of his life. Henry served again as governor in 1784–1786. As a delegate to the Virginia Convention in 1788 he opposed ratification of the Constitution on the principle of states rights but was instrumental in the adoption of the Bill of Rights. In 1795, Henry publicly praised Washington after declining the president's offer to the po-

sitions of secretary of state and chief justice. In January 1799 he acceded to Washington's request that he campaign for a seat in the Virginia House of Delegates as a Federalist, thus changing political sides and opposing his former allies. Although he defeated John Randolph for the seat, Henry died before he could be sworn in.

HERKIMER, Nicholas
1728–1777

Militia general. Herkimer was born to German immigrants who settled in the Mohawk Valley near present-day Herkimer, N.Y. As a lieutenant in the militia during the French and Indian War he served as commander of Fort Herkimer in 1758. An active patriot in Tryon County, Herkimer served as head of the county's committee of safety. In 1776 he was made brigadier general of the New York militia and charged with defending the state against attacks by Tories and Indians. In July 1777 Herkimer conferred with Joseph Brant in an unsuccessful effort to obtain the neutrality of the Mohawks. In early August he began a march to relieve Fort Stanwix from attack by St. Leger's Expedition but was ambushed by Tories and Indians at Oriskany on 6 August. The battle ended St. Leger's attempt to join Burgoyne, but Herkimer was severely wounded, and ten days later he bled to death following amputation of his leg by a French surgeon.

HOPKINS, Esek
1718–1802

Continental naval officer. The first commander-in-chief of the Continental Navy, Hopkins was born on a farm near Providence, R.I., now part of Scituate. He went to sea in 1783, succeeding as a captain and later, during the French and Indian War, as a privateer. He retired to the family farm in 1772. As his brother Stephen was the most prominent politician in Rhode Island, so Hopkins was interested in local politics. In October 1775, he became brigadier general and was appointed to command the state militia. A delegate to the Continental Congress and a member of its Marine Committee, Stephen apparently maneuvered Esek's appointment in December as commander-in-chief of the newly created navy, while Esek's son John was made a captain. Hopkins encountered difficulties in equipping and finding crews for the few ships available to him. Given the daunting assignment of clearing the Chesapeake and the Carolina and Rhode Island coasts in February 1776, Hopkins instead sailed to the West Indies and captured Nassau in March. On his return he encountered HMS *Glasgow* but failed to capture it, even though he had superior force. The result was an investigation by Congress, which censured Hopkins for insubordination, suspended him from command in March 1777, and dismissed him in January 1778. Hopkins served as a deputy in the Rhode Island General Assembly from 1779 to 1786. From 1782 till 1802 he was a trustee of Brown University. He also served as collector of imposts in 1783.

HOWE, Richard
1726–1799
British admiral. Popularly known as "Black Dick" because of his swarthy complexion, brother of Gen. William Howe and commander-in-chief of the navy in America during the years 1776–78, Howe was born in London.

He began his naval career at the age of fourteen serving on an around-the-world voyage with Adm. George Anson, but his own ship was forced to return home because of damages after rounding Cape Horn. Howe served in the West Indies in 1742 and was promoted to lieutenant. He served in American waters during the French and Indian War as captain of the *Dunkirk*. When his elder brother died at Ticonderoga in 1758, Howe inherited the Irish title of viscount. In 1762 he represented Dartmouth in Parliament. In 1763 and again in 1765 he served on the Admiralty Board, and from the latter year until 1770 he was treasurer of the navy. Howe was promoted to vice admiral in December 1775, and the following February he was appointed commander of the navy in America, where his brother William was military commander. The two brothers were empowered to negotiate a peace settlement with the colonies—a futile endeavor despite their sympathy for the Americans. Howe provided naval support during the New York campaign. Disgruntled over what he regarded as inadequate support from London and also over the arrival of the Carlisle peace commission in 1778, Howe resigned but stayed on long enough to defend New York and thwart the Franco-America attack on Newport in August 1778. When Admiral Byron arrived Howe returned home, refusing to serve again as long as Lord Sandwich headed the Admiralty. When the Rockingham government came to power in March 1782 and Lord Sandwich retired, Howe accepted command of the navy in the British Channel and succeeded in relieving the British garrison on Gibraltar. Except for several months in

1783, Howe served as First Lord of the Admiralty from January 1783 until August 1788. When war with France broke out in 1793, Howe again took command of the navy in the Channel, performing very effectively in 1794 despite his age. In 1797 he was sent to terminate the naval mutiny at Spithead, his last service. Howe was awarded the United Kingdom title of viscount in 1782 and became baron and Earl Howe in 1788.

HOWE, Robert
1732–1786

Continental major general. Born in Bladen County, N.C., and educated in Europe, Howe amassed a fortune before the Revolution as owner of a rice plantation. He served as justice of the peace for Bladen County in 1756 and in the same capacity for Brunswick County in 1764. From 1764 until 1775 he was a member of the North Carolina Assembly. Howe was militia commander of Fort Johnston in 1766–1767 and again 1769–1773. After his second tour in this post he was made a colonel of artillery and served in Gov. Tryon's expedition against the Regulators. In 1774 he served as delegate to the Colonial Congress that met in New Bern, N.C. Howe was a member of the North Carolina Committee of Correspondence and helped raise and train rebel militiamen. After the Revolution began he was commissioned a colonel in the 2nd North Carolina Regiment. In January 1776 he fought ably in the actions that drove Lord Dunsmore out of Virginia, earning an appointment as a brigadier general in the Continental Army. In the fall of 1777 he was promoted to major general and placed in command of the Southern Department. His ex-

pedition against the British at St. Augustine, Fla., however, was a complete failure. He was replaced as southern commander by Benjamin Lincoln in September 1778 but continued in command in Georgia. With the British capture of Savannah in December he was recalled to the North, exonerated of fault at Savannah by a court-martial, and placed in charge of Benedict Arnold's court-martial for misconduct as commander in Philadelphia. Washington then put him in command of West Point and outposts in the Hudson Highlands in February 1780, to be succeeded by Arnold in August. In September he served with the board of officers that recommended Maj. John André be hanged. In January 1781 Howe commanded the troops that suppressed the mutiny of Pennsylvania and New Jersey soldiers. In 1783 he led his troops in dispersing the furloughed troops that had driven Congress from Philadelphia. Howe returned to his rice plantation that same year, but in 1785 Congress appointed him to help with the boundary negotiations being conducted with the Indians. In 1786 he was elected to the North Carolina legislature but died before he could take his seat.

HOWE, William
1729–1814

British general. Commander-in-chief of British forces, brother of Adm. Richard Howe and an aristocrat by birth (the Howes' grandmother had been the mistress of George I), Howe was educated at Eton. In September 1746 he became a cornet in the Duke of Cumberland's Light Dragoons, and in 1747 he was promoted to lieutenant. Howe joined the 20th Foot Regiment in January 1750 and became a captain in the spring of that year. In January 1756, he became a major in the 58th Foot Regiment, attaining the rank of lieutenant colonel by the end of 1759. Howe commanded his regiment at Louisburg, but he gained greatest fame for leading Gen. Wolfe's troops onto the Plains of Abraham for the victory at Quebec. He also helped to capture Montreal in 1760. The next year he fought at Belle Isle, and in 1762 he assisted in the capture of Havana. In 1758, Howe succeeded his eldest brother George, killed at Ticonderoga that year, as member of Parliament representing Nottingham, holding this post until 1780. In Parliament he strongly opposed the government's repressive policies toward the Americans. Howe was made colonel of the 46th Foot Regiment in Ireland in 1764, and four years later he became lieutenant governor of the Isle of Wight. He was promoted to major general in 1772. In February 1775 he was ordered to America. He arrived in time to participate in the Battle of Bunker Hill, and he assumed command of the army in Boston in October. In April 1776 Howe was named commander-in-chief of British forces in the colonies, replacing Gen. Thomas Gage. Howe evacuated Boston early in 1776 to make his headquarters in New York and subsequently defeated Washington's army in the Battle of Long Island in August, driving the Americans from Manhattan and pursuing them north but turning back at White Plains in October. Washington exacted revenge at Trenton and Princeton in December, however. The campaign was rejoined in the summer and fall of 1777,

with fighting in New Jersey and Pennsylvania and British victories at Brandywine and capture of Philadelphia. But Howe felt inadequately supported by the British administration and submitted his resignation. Replaced by Gen. Henry Clinton, Howe sailed for England in May 1778. In May 1779, following agitation in Parliament, a formal inquiry into the conduct of William and his brother Adm. Richard Howe was begun; it ended inconclusively in June. In 1782 Howe was appointed lieutenant general of the ordnance, and in 1793 he was promoted to full general. In 1799 he succeeded to the Irish title of viscount upon the death of Richard. Howe resigned as general of ordnance in 1803 because of health problems—a long, painful illness that led to his death eleven years later.

JEFFERSON, Thomas
1743–1826
Statesman. Like Franklin one of the renaissance men of his era, Jefferson was a statesman, philosopher, scientist, diplomat, politician, architect, and farmer. Born in Albemarle County, Va., Jefferson was related to the Randolphs, one of the colony's most prominent families, through his mother Jane Randolph. His father was a surveyor who drew up the first accurate map of Virginia, served as a burgess, and left Jefferson 2,750 acres of land at his death in 1757. Jefferson graduated from the College of William and Mary in 1762. He was licensed to practice law in 1767, a career he pursued for only seven years. In 1769 Jefferson was elected to the Virginia House of Burgesses, serving until his election to the Continental Congress in 1775. Publication in 1774 of his

Summary View of the Rights of America, a radical attack on the crown, made him a leading revolutionary figure and a clear choice as drafter of the Declaration of Independence. Following his absence from the Congress from late December 1775 until mid-May 1776, Jefferson was appointed in June to a committee to write the declaration, which turned out to be almost entirely his work. Although reelected to Congress and offered a post as commissioner to represent the United States in Paris, Jefferson chose instead to return to Virginia and pursue reforms there. He became a member of the House of Delegates in October 1776 and was chosen to serve on a five-man board to revise the laws of the state. In June 1778, the board proposed 126 bills, of which 100 were eventually approved, achieving Jefferson's objectives of abolishing primogeniture, entail, and an established church. In June 1779 Jefferson succeeded Patrick Henry as governor of Virginia. But he proved inept as a wartime leader when the British invaded in 1781, forcing the government to flee in May. Jefferson himself barely escaped capture. He subsequently went home to his estate at Monticello, effectively giving up the governorship. The legislators chose Thomas Nelson, Jr., in his place and ordered an investigation of Jefferson's conduct. The investigating committee reported in December that there were no grounds for censuring Jefferson, who nevertheless suffered a severe loss of public esteem. During the years 1781–1783 he worked on his *Notes on the State of Virginia.* Jefferson's wife died in September 1782, and he was appointed a peace commissioner in November but never joined the commission in France. Elected to Congress in June 1783, Jefferson drafted a bill in March 1784 that formed the precedent for the Ordinance of 1787 and called for a ban on slavery in the Western territories after 1800. In August 1784 he was in Paris to assist Benjamin Franklin and John Adams in negotiating treaties of commerce with France. He succeeded Franklin as minister to France the following year, when he also negotiated a treaty of commerce with Prussia. Jefferson returned home in the fall of 1789 and accepted appointment as Washington's secretary of state, beginning his duties in March 1790 and continuing in the post until December 1793. In 1796 he was elected vice-president when John Adams won the presidency and, in 1800, he became president after a tie vote with Aaron Burr threw the selection into the House of Representatives. Jefferson was the first president to be inaugurated in Washington, D.C., which became the seat of government in 1800. His achievements as president included the Louisiana Purchase in 1803 and the subsequent Lewis and Clark Expedition. He was re-elected in 1804. Leaving the presidency in 1809, Jefferson spent the remainder of his life at Monticello. He served as president of the American Philosophical Society from 1797 until 1815. He was responsible for founding the University of Virginia in 1819 and was the architect of the school's original buildings. The Embargo of 1807, Jefferson's own achievement, destroyed his finances, forcing him to sell his 10,000-volume library to the government in 1815. In 1819 he again suffered a severe financial reversal. Jefferson died on the fiftieth anniversary of the signing of the Declaration of Independence, followed in death on the same day by John Adams.

JONES, John Paul
1747–1792

Continental naval officer. Commander in the Continental Navy, Jones was born in Kirkcudbrightshire, Scotland, as John Paul (he added the name Jones in 1773). He became apprenticed to a shipowner in Whitehaven at age twelve. After his employer went bankrupt Jones joined the crew of a slave ship and at nineteen was first mate on the slaver Two Friends in the trade between Jamaica and the coast of Guinea. Leaving this service, he booked passage on a ship to England of which he took command when both the captain and first mate died of fever. As reward the owners gave him 10 percent of the cargo and command of their merchantship John, whose home port was Dumfries. Jones captained the ship on two voyages to the West Indies in 1769–1770; but on the second voyage he flogged the ship's carpenter for neglecting his duty, resulting in the man's death two weeks later, and Jones was arrested for murder upon his return to Scotland. He was cleared of the charge, and in 1773 he became master of the Betsey out of London. In Tobago, West Indies, he killed the leader of a mutiny by his crew, and to avoid a trial he sailed in secret for America, where he assumed the name Jones. Unemployed when the Revolution began, Jones went to Philadelphia, where he was hired to help fit out the Alfred, the first ship purchased by Congress for the Continental Navy. Through the influence of two congressmen he had befriended, Jones was commissioned in December 1775 as first lieutenant on the Alfred. In 1776 he was given command of the Providence. Following his successes with this ship, Jones was made captain and provided with a small fleet with which to pursue the capture of more British shipping. In June 1777 Jones was given command of the Ranger and was sent to France to take command of the Indien, only to discover the ship was being given to France. He sailed in the Ranger from Brest in April 1778 for a series of coastal raids on Scotland. Returning a hero to France, Jones was given command of the French ship Duras, which he renamed Bonhomme Richard in honor of Benjamin Franklin, who had pleaded Jones' cause in France. Jones set sail in August 1779, and in September, he won the famous battle with the Serapis. Jones sailed for America in December 1780. In 1781 Congress made him commander of the navy's largest ship, America, but upon its completion the ship was turned over to the French. After the Continental Navy was decommissioned Jones returned to France as an American agent to claim the prize money for the ships he had captured. Louis XVI made him a chevalier, and during his final visit to the United States in 1787 Congress awarded him a gold medal, the only one awarded to an officer of the Continental Navy. In 1788 Jones accepted Catherine the Great's request that he serve in the Russian navy against the Turks, but his service in May in the Black Sea was unrewarding. He left Russia in September 1789, returning to Paris, where he died two years later.

KNOX, Henry
1750–1806

Continental general, government official. A self-taught soldier, Knox commanded the Continental artillery throughout the War of the Revolution. Born in Boston, he was the proprietor of a local bookstore and a member of the militia when the war broke out in 1775. Even in his youth he was a huge man (by middle age he weighed 300 pounds) but he was energetic and was very good at managing his men. He formed a lasting, close relationship with George Washington almost as soon as they met, and the commander-in-chief appointed Knox colonel of artillery after Bunker Hill, where Knox served as a volunteer. Knox's first great feat of the war was to bring captured artillery from Fort Ticonderoga to Boston during the winter of 1775. Washington's army had the British penned in Boston, but without siege guns there was little hope of dislodging them. Knox went to Ticonderoga, organized the building of sleds, and supervised moving sixty heavy guns across 300 miles of tough countryside. After he arrived at Boston, the placement of the guns forced the British to evacuate. Knox slowly learned the skills of the artilleryman and supported Washington's army with his guns during the battles of Long Island. He performed with distinction at Trenton and was appointed a brigadier general two days later. Knox commanded the Continental artillery during the rest of the New Jersey campaign and at the battles of Brandywine, Germantown, and Monmouth. In the fall of 1781, he was in charge of the American siege artillery at Yorktown. Following Cornwallis'

surrender, Knox moved back north and took command of the American post at West Point. He became a major general in 1782 and commander-in-chief of the army at Washington's resignation in late 1783. After the war, Knox was appointed secretary of war under the Articles of Confederation. At Washington's election as president, Knox became the first secretary of war under the Constitution, serving until 1794. He retired from public life in that year and indulged himself in a luxuriant style of living. He died at the age of fifty-six, when a chicken bone lodged in his intestines.

KNYPHAUSEN, Wilhelm von
1716–1800

German mercenary general. A tough and competent professional soldier, Knyphausen was the senior German military figure in America during much of the war. He had served in the Prussian army since the mid-1730s and held the rank of lieutenant general in 1776, when he sailed for America in command of 4,000 mercenaries from Hesse-Kassel. He arrived too late to take part in the battle of White Plains, but thereafter took important roles in the subsequent British campaigns in New York and New Jersey. When Gen. Leopold von Heister was removed as senior German officer after the debacle at Trenton, Knyphausen took his place. He commanded half of Howe's army at the Battle of Brandywine and escorted the baggage train during the British movement from Philadelphia to New York in 1778. His role increased in 1779 when Sir Henry Clinton went south to conduct the campaign against Charleston. Knyphausen assumed command of the British forces in New York City during Clinton's absence, and he launched several movements into New Jersey against the Americans, although with only moderate success. His health began to fail in 1781, and with Clinton's return Knyphausen took a lesser role. He returned to Europe and retired in 1782. Subsequently he served as military governor of Kassel.

KOŚCIUSZKO, Tadeusz
1746–1817
Continental general, Polish patriot. Born in what is now Lithuania and well trained as a soldier, Kościuszko was one of the more effective European volunteer soldiers to serve the American patriot cause. He was orphaned as a boy but managed to attend both the royal military school in Poland and the French army school of engineering and artillery. He was skilled in several areas needed by the amateur Continental Army. He came to America in 1776 on his own and Congress commissioned him a colonel of engineers. He was assigned to the command of Horatio Gates and planned the entrenchments at Saratoga, which played an important role in Gates' victory over Burgoyne. The Polish engineer became a close friend of Gates and went south to join him in 1780 after planning the defenses of the American fort at West Point on the Hudson. Kościuszko arrived in Carolina after Gates' disaster at Camden, however he remained on the staff of Nathanael Greene and had charge of Greene's transportation during the race for the Dan River crossings ahead of Cornwallis. In 1781 Kościuszko directed engineering at the siege of Ninety-Six, S.C., which failed to take the British post. During the following months he served Greene as a commander of cavalry. In 1783 he was made a brigadier general, and the next year he returned to Europe. The rest of his life was devoted to the cause of Polish independence. He lead a futile campaign against the invading Russians in 1792 and then moved to Paris. He was captured by the Russians in 1794 after another unsuccessful uprising. On his release he came again to the United States, where he received a lump-sum payment and land in Ohio in gratitude for his revolutionary service. He returned to Europe in 1798.

LAFAYETTE, Marquis de (Marie Joseph du Motier)
1757–1834
Continental general, French volunteer. The best-known and most prominent of the Frenchmen who served the American Revolution, Lafayette became a hero to the American public as a result of his glamour and highly visible role in the war. He was born to a wealthy, aristocratic family but orphaned at an early age. He entered military service while a teenager (he married at age sixteen) but was an inexperienced soldier when smitten with the romantic notion of helping to free the Americans from the trammels of Great Britain. He and his mentor, the spurious "Baron" De Kalb, persuaded American envoy Silas Deane to guarantee them commissions as major generals. They sailed for America in 1777, reaching Philadelphia in August. After some grumbling, Congress granted the commissions but awarded no actual command to the nineteen-year-old Frenchman. Fortunately for Lafayette,

Gen. George Washington took an instant liking to the amiable youth and ever after shepherded his career in America. Lafayette fought at Brandywine as a volunteer on Washington's staff and took a wound that provided a sign of his earnestness. In late 1777 Congress appointed him to a division of Virginia light infantry. At the battle of Monmouth Lafayette commanded on the field with reasonable distinction. He then had charge of two brigades in the near-fiasco of the first joint French–American venture at Newport. When it began to appear that France might genuinely support the American Revolution with troops, Lafayette returned to France to lobby for a major French expedition to the New World. He returned in April 1780, just ahead of Rochambeau's expeditionary force. While he wished to play a central role in liaison between Rochambeau and Washington, the French commander kept Lafayette at arm's length. Washington gave the "boy" command of an army in Virginia with orders to stop British depredations, and Lafayette was successful in holding the armies of Arnold, Phillips, and subsequently Cornwallis at bay, although he achieved no major victories. His army pinned Cornwallis at Yorktown while Washington and Rochambeau moved south from New York during the late summer of 1781. He commanded one of the three major American divisions during the siege of Yorktown and defeat of Cornwallis. Lafayette returned to France within two months of the surrender at Yorktown. His subsequent career as a revolutionary in France was mixed. He served in several assemblies and had command of a French army in 1792 when he was condemned by a radical faction and forced to flee. He spent several years as a prisoner of the Austrians and Prussians but was freed by Napoleon. He turned down an offer to become American governor of Louisiana, but he did accept a grant of money and extensive lands from the United States. In 1824 Lafayette returned to America for a year-long triumphal tour, during which he was hailed by Americans as a symbol of French support for the Revolution nearly fifty years earlier.

LAURENS, Henry
1724–1792

Patriot, congressman, diplomat. Born in Charleston, Laurens was one of the principal men of South Carolina and one of its wealthiest merchants before the Revolution. Despite several years of residence in England, Laurens became a staunch patriot during the early and mid-1770s. He served on the Charleston Committee of Safety and wrote extensively in support of the patriot cause. South Carolina selected him as a delegate to the second Continental Congress in 1777. He was elected president of the assembly the following year, but his implacable opposition to Silas Deane put him in the midst of a political rift and he resigned in 1778. Congress nonetheless selected him in 1779 as an emissary to Holland. He sailed for Europe in 1780 to negotiate a treaty with the Netherlands and a mission to secure a large loan. The British captured his ship, however, and Laurens was imprisoned in the Tower of London under the harshest conditions. He suffered miserably and became increasingly ill but declined British offers of pardon in return for cooperation. He was finally released in 1782 and exchanged for Cornwallis. While he was in prison, Congress named him one of the peace commissioners. He joined the commission only days before the treaty was signed. During 1782–1783 Laurens acted as an unofficial ambassador to Great Britain. He returned to the United States, retired from politics, and lived thereafter in South Carolina, where he attempted to repair his lost fortunes.

LEE, Arthur
1740–1792

Diplomat. One of the famous Lee brothers of Virginia, Arthur Lee was a principal American representative in Europe during most of the Revolution. He was born in Virginia and studied medicine in Edinburgh. He practiced in his native state for two years but returned to England in 1766 to study law. He first came to public notice through a series of letters to publications in Virginia and London during the late 1760s. Massachusetts appointed him its representative in London in 1770. He combined with Beaumarchais in 1775 to devise the spurious Hortalez & Cie in order to supply arms to the revolutionaries in America, but Lee soon became suspicious of his fellow patriot agents in Europe. Appointed to join Silas Deane and Benjamin Franklin as one of the American representatives to France in 1776, Lee soon was at extreme odds with Deane. The subsequent controversy put Lee in opposition to the hapless Deane and left bitter relations with Franklin. Lee undertook missions to Spain and Berlin but returned to America in 1780. He then served in the Virginia House of Delegates and was elected to Congress in 1782. Lee

was so cantankerous and cynical that he failed to serve constructively in Congress, and he withdrew in 1784. Despite subsequent service on various commissions and boards, he was never an effective politician.

LEE, Charles
1731–1782

Continental general. Lee was one of the disappointments of the American Revolution. He was an experienced and apparently competent soldier who volunteered for service despite his background, yet he proved a weak commander and a treacherous colleague. Born in Britain to a military family, he joined his father's regiment in 1747 to embark on a career in the British army. His first trip to America was as part of Braddock's expedition in 1755, and he fought during much of the Seven Years' War in North America. He returned to England in 1761 and served under Burgoyne in Portugal before retiring on half-pay as a lieutenant colonel. In 1765 Lee went to Poland, where he served as a soldier of fortune for the Polish crown, off an on, until 1770. He moved to America in 1775 and purchased an estate in what is now West Virginia. Soon thereafter he petitioned Congress for a commission in the new Continental Army and was appointed a major general. After serving with little distinction in the New York campaign, he accepted command of the Southern Department in 1776 and directed the successful defense of Charleston against a British invasion. He was doubtless an ambitious man whose jealousy of Washington (whom Lee regarded as a rank amateur) got him into difficulty. During the New Jersey campaign in 1776, Lee failed to support Washington as requested, and to many it appeared he actually hoped Washington would fail, presumably because Lee was the next in line to become commander-in-chief. Lee was guilty of writing several letters to politicians that betrayed his contempt for Washington. On 13 December 1776 Lee was captured at Basking Ridge by a British raiding party and taken captive to New York City. During his confinement he proposed to Howe a plan to defeat the rebels by splitting the Middle Colonies (evidence of his treason did not come to light until the mid-1800s). Lee was exchanged in time to take command of part of the army at Monmouth, where he failed so miserably to support Washington at a crucial moment and complained so after the battle that he was charged with disobedience and misbehavior. The court-martial found him guilty and suspended him from command for a year. At the end of his suspension, he wrote such an offensive letter to Congress that the body dismissed him from the service of the nation. He retired to his estate in the Shenandoah Valley.

LEE, Henry ("Light-Horse Harry")
1756–1818
Continental lieutenant colonel, state official. Lee has a deserved reputation as one of the best cavalry leaders of the war. He was a scion of a prominent Virginia family and was preparing to go to England to study law when the war began. Appointed a captain of Virginia calvary, he was with Washington's army in the North during the spring of 1777 when he caught the eye of the commander-in-chief. In reward for several adroit but minor actions against the British, Lee was named to

command a special elite force of dragoons and infantry known as Lee's Legion. Under his leadership the Legion became one of the truly outstanding units in all of the American army. Its first important victory was at Paulus Hook, N.Y., in August 1779, an action that won Lee the thanks of Congress and one of the few medals awarded by the national government during the war. Lee was promoted to lieutenant colonel in November of the same year. Washington sent Lee and his Legion south in 1780 to join Greene in the Southern campaign. Throughout the following two years, Lee was everywhere in the Southern theater and took part in nearly every important action. His men acted both as the core of the American army's cavalry and as partisans, raiding British outposts in the Carolinas, often in conjunction with the forces of Francis Marion or Andrew Pickens. Lee (along with William Washington) probably saved Greene's army at the battle of Eutaw Springs in 1781. Following the victory at Yorktown, Lee withdrew from active command, apparently a victim of battle fatigue. While he served in several political offices during the rest of his life, including a term as governor of Virginia, he was a troubled man, beset by bouts of depression and declining personal fortunes. His *Memoirs of the War in the Southern Department of the United States* is one of the best accounts of the war by a participant. He was the father of Robert E. Lee.

LINCOLN, Benjamin
1733–1810
Continental major general. Lincoln experienced both extreme highs and lows during his service to the Revo-

lution. He was a native of Massachusetts and a moderately prosperous farmer who was much involved in militia affairs before the war. When hostilities began he was a brigadier of the Massachusetts militia and given responsibility for militia troops around Boston and subsequently New York City. Although he held no previous commission in the Continental Line, he was appointed full major general in February 1777, an act that outraged many below him on the seniority list (including Benedict Arnold). Lincoln was ordered to New England in August 1777 and managed to prompt the recalcitrant Vermont militia to undertake the attack on Baum's Hessians at Bennington. He then repaired to Saratoga, where he commanded the defenses at Bemis Heights. During the latter stages of the engagement he suffered a bad wound and was invalided for several months. In September 1778 Congress appointed him to command the Southern Department, neglecting to consult Washington first. Lincoln found a difficult situation in the South. He arrived too late to do anything about the British seizure of Savannah, and he allowed himself and most of his army to be bottled up in Charleston. A good campaign by Sir Henry Clinton forced Lincoln to surrender the city in 1780, marking one of the worst American defeats of the war. Lincoln was taken prisoner, although he was paroled before the end of the year. In 1781 Lincoln was given charge of the American army during its march south to invest Yorktown, and he commanded one of the three divisions of the army during the siege. He stepped forward to accept the British gesture of surrender at Yorktown. A few weeks later Lincoln was ap-

pointed by Congress as the nation's first secretary at war, a post he held until the formal end of the war in 1783. He returned to Massachusetts, where he held several government offices in later years, and in 1787 he commanded the troops sent against Shays' Rebellion.

MADISON, James
1751–1836
Statesman. Although Madison's major role in American history came after the Revolution itself, he was active in state affairs during the early years of the conflict and moved into national politics in the later months. He came from an old landed Virginia family and graduated from the College of New Jersey (Princeton) in 1771. He became a member of his local Committee of Safety in 1775 and was elected to the Virginia convention the following year. He helped draft the Virginia state constitution and became a member of the first state assembly, although he was not re-elected for a second term. He served, however, on the governor's council after his assembly term. He was elected a delegate to Congress in 1779. During his three years in Congress he helped to shape the terms of American diplomacy and to work out a compromise between the states over western land claims, one of the major stumbling blocks to national unity after the war. He also negotiated the formula for counting slaves for purposes of political representation. He is most famous, perhaps, for writing many of The Federalist papers in support of ratification of the proposed Constitution, and his arguments and phrases entered the basic vocabulary of the American political system. He later served as sec-

retary of state under Jefferson and became president himself in 1809. His two terms in office were marred by the War of 1812, and he retired to private life at the end of his second term in 1817.

MARION, Francis ("The Swamp Fox")
c. 1732–1795
A brilliant leader of partisan campaigns in the Carolinas during the latter years of the war, Marion has been to some extent mythologized, yet he genuinely deserves a place in the Revolutionary firmament. He was a small, ill-favored man whose unprepossessing appearance often caused both friend and foe to underestimate him. A native South Carolinian, he first came to notice as an Indian fighter with South Carolina militia. At the beginning of the war he was both a delegate to the state provincial congress and a captain in the militia. By 1776 Marion was a major and played an important role in defending Charleston under Moultrie. He then took over command of a full regiment of South Carolina militia and was gradually given more and more responsibility. Because of a freak accident that broke his ankle, he was evacuated from Charleston before the fall of the garrison in 1780. The British victory eliminated all organized American armies in the state, so Marion turned to irregular tactics with his troops of partisans. He and his men inhabited the dense swamps of the state, moving often and avoiding British forces by speed and stealth. They in turn attacked British outposts and isolated units with ferocious effectiveness. Marion worked well in conjunction with Nathanael Green during the campaigns of 1781, and he often teamed with Light Horse Harry Lee or William Washington to field a formidable, mobile striking force. Marion was less successful in working with Thomas Sumter, and several of their joint ventures against the British went awry. Marion's greatest moments may have come at the Battle of Eutaw Springs in September 1781, when his actions helped save the American army from a severe defeat. After the war he served sporadically in state offices.

MARTIN, Josiah
1737–1786
Royal governor of North Carolina. Martin epitomized, perhaps, the position of the royal governors of the colonies and how several failed to truly appreciate the nature of the Revolution. Martin refused to accept that there was not a firm Loyalist majority in North Carolina, and for much of the war he lobbied London to provide the men and arms that he thought would quash a thin layer of resistance and unleash a wellspring of Loyalist sentiment. He was, of course, wrong in his judgment. He came from a military background, having served in the British army for twelve years before selling out his lieutenant colonelcy in 1769. Two years later he was appointed governor of North Carolina. The gathering forces of rebellion confronted him early in his tenure. The collapse of the judicial system forced him to operate the criminal courts by royal prerogative by 1773, and within another year rebels were meeting in an extralegal provincial assembly. Martin believed he could resist the organized patriot militia, but he was forced to flee the state aboard a British ship in July 1775. In New York, Mar-

tin petitioned for an armed return to his state, where he thought certain a British army would be greeted by a Loyalist uprising to support it. He sailed with the expedition to retake Charleston in 1776, but the British were rebuffed. When Scots Loyalists were crushed at Moore's Creek Bridge the same year, Martin's hopes began to fade. He subsequently served as a volunteer officer under Cornwallis when the latter finally captured Charleston and the Carolinas in 1780. Martin left for England in the spring of 1781.

MONROE, James
1758–1831
Continental officer, statesmen. Another of the men from Virginia prominent during the early years of the United States, Monroe was a young student at the College of William and Mary when the war began. He left his books and took up arms with the Virginia Line of the Continental Army. He served as a junior officer in most of the early engagements of the war, and he was wounded on the streets of Trenton during Washington's daring attack on 26 December 1775. The following year Madison was promoted to major and made an aide-de-camp to Lord Stirling. He fought in the battles of Brandywine, Germantown, and Monmouth, after which he resigned his commission. In 1780 he began to study law with Thomas Jefferson. At the end of the war Monroe was elected a delegate to Congress. His stance on the Constitution was Anti-Federalist, but he served as senator from Virginia and as envoy to France in addition to sitting a term as governor of Virginia. In 1811 he was appointed U.S. secretary of state, and he later moved to the office of secretary of war. He was elected president of the United States in 1816 and served two terms. He is perhaps best remembered as the author of the Monroe Doctrine that declared the New World off limits to European aggrandizement.

MONTGOMERY, Richard
1738–1775
Continental general. Montgomery was a well-educated native of Ireland who joined the British army as an ensign and fought in North America from 1757 until 1760. He then served in the West Indies. After ten years in England, Montgomery sold out his commission and moved to New York state, where he became a farmer. Even though he had been in America only three years when the War of the Revolution began, he accepted a commission as a brigadier in the Continental Army and was ordered north as Phillip Schuyler's second in command on the expedition against Quebec in 1775. When Schulyer became ill, Montgomery assumed command of the army. The forces he had at his disposal were ill-equipped, ill-trained, and poorly supplied, but he made the best of the situation and moved resolutely toward Quebec, taking St. John's along the way. The fortress at Quebec was well defended, and Montgomery's strength ebbed daily as the winter weather closed in. He was forced to mount an assault on the last day of the year before the enlistments of most of his men ran out and they returned to their homes. The attack faltered, and Montgomery himself was killed leading the assault.

MORGAN, Daniel
1736–1802
Continental general. Morgan was one

of the most talented, if unorthodox, military leaders of the American Revolution. He was born in New Jersey and left home for the Shenandoah Valley as a teenager. He served as a teamster during Braddock's expedition in 1755. During the following year he ran afoul of a British officer and received five hundred lashes—the scars from which he often referred to during the Revolution. He fought in several of the colonial Indian wars when not farming. He was commissioned to raise a company of Virginia riflemen in June 1775 and became famous as a leader of these unique American marksmen. His rifle company marched to Boston and joined Washington, who ordered Morgan and his men north as part of Benedict Arnold's expedition against Canada in the fall of 1775. They survived the terrible journey, and Morgan was in the van of the assault on Quebec, taking charge when Arnold was wounded. Morgan was captured, however, and held at Quebec until paroled and exchanged during the following year. In late 1776 he was commissioned a colonel and raised a corps of five hundred riflemen. Attached to Gates' army, Morgan and his men played crucial roles in the two pivotal battles at Saratoga that defeated Burgoyne. The heavy woods and rough terrain of the Saratoga campaign well suited the tactics of the riflemen, who were deadly at long range but who were slow to load and vulnerable to open-ground attacks by regulars. After wintering with the Continental Army at Valley Forge, Morgan and his rifle corps served with Washington until the summer of 1779, when Morgan abruptly resigned his commission. He pleaded ill health, but in fact he was

unhappy to have been passed over for higher rank and significant command. He withdrew to his farm in Virginia to nurse his grievances and the arthritis that genuinely afflicted him. Learning of the disastrous American defeat at Camden, N.C., in 1780, Morgan relented and rejoined the fight. Nathanael Greene, the new commander in the South, gave Morgan responsibility for the light infantry and Congress belatedly appointed him to the rank of brigadier general. Morgan's finest moments came in January 1781 at the Battle of the Cowpens, when his innovative use of militia and his personal leadership gave him a stunning victory over Tarleton. Soon thereafter Morgan again pled ill health and retreated to his rural home. He reappeared on the scene briefly in Virginia, but contributed little. Morgan continued to farm and speculate in land after the war. He also commanded troops in putting down the Whiskey Rebellion in 1793 and served in Congress.

MORRIS, Gouverneur
1752–1816
Politician. Born into the aristocratic Morris–Gouverneur families of New York, Morris was one of the staunchest supporters of the Revolution and a skilled writer, politician, and diplomat. He attended King's College (later Columbia) and became a lawyer before age twenty. He held a strongly expressed aversion to democracy all his life, but he embraced the principles of the Revolution early, serving in the New York provincial congress in 1776 and 1777 and helping to draft the constitution of the new state. In 1778 Morris was elected to the Continental Congress, where his interest

in finance and diplomacy and his facile pen were put to good use. He became entangled in New York state politics over the question of claims to Vermont and was defeated for re-election. He then moved to Philadelphia. In early 1780 he published a series of articles on finance that led to his appointment as assistant to the new superintendent of finance, Robert Morris (to whom Gouverneur was not related). During the same year, he fell from his carriage and suffered amputation of a leg as a result of the accident—a handicap that seldom slowed his activities in subsequent years. He aided Robert Morris in the arduous but ultimately unrewarded tasks of national finance until 1785, devising a system of decimal coinage, for example. He supported the Constitution and a strong central government, although railing against the mob. He served with distinction as a diplomat in the 1790s, first in England and then in France during the Reign of Terror. Still a relatively young man, he returned to New York and rebuilt his fortune and family home.

MORRIS, Robert
1734–1806
Financier, government official. Known as "the Financier of the American Revolution," Morris was one of the central figures of civil government during the latter years of the struggle for independence. Had his efforts garnered more support, the first decades of the new nation might have been easier. He was born in Liverpool, England, and moved to Maryland with his father at age thirteen. He subsequently moved to Philadelphia and went to work in a counting house. By the eve of the Revolution he was a partner in Willing, Morris & Co., the leading mercantile firm in the colonies, a business that controlled a large share of colonial trade. Morris was a delegate to the First Continental Congress and took key roles in Pennsylvania revolutionary activities during 1775. He was re-elected to Congress again in 1776 and signed the Declaration of Independence. As a major figure in Congress, he served on the Secret Committee and eventually became entangled in the Silas Deane affair. Morris continued to prosper as a private businessman while at the same time devoting much of his personal fortune and financial acumen to the patriot cause. He often undertook major assignments to manipulate the shaky finances of Congress. He personally provided funds and supplies to Washington's army at crucial moments, and may be said to have kept the war afloat at crucial junctures. He left Congress in 1778, but with the near-total collapse of national finances in 1780 and 1781, he was appointed the first superintendent of the department of finance (and later as secretary of finance). He was faced with an insurmountable set of problems—rampant inflation, worthless Continental currency, and a total lack of income for the national government—but he struggled to put things aright. He pushed through the charter for the first national bank and stretched foreign loans to the limit to establish credit for the government. He finally left his post in 1785, unable to convince the states to support a central governmental financial system. He subsequently turned down the post of secretary of the treasury

during Washington's first administration. In later years his own financial empire collapsed, and he was imprisoned for debt. He died penniless.

MOULTRIE, William
1730–1805

Continental general. Moultrie was one of the heroes of the first years of the war. He was born in Great Britain and came to Charleston, S.C., with his father as a boy. He first came to notice as a leader of militia during Indian fighting in the 1760s. At the outbreak of the Revolution he received a commission as colonel and became one of the principal military leaders of his state. Elected to Congress twice, he declined to serve both times. His fame came from his spirited defense of the palmetto-and-sand Fort Sullivan in Charleston harbor during the British attempt to take the city in 1776. He skillfully prevented the British fleet under Adm. Parker from gaining control of the harbor and thus frustrated the ill-conducted British campaign to take a major American port. The fort was renamed in his honor. Moultrie was advanced in rank to brigadier general, and after the British seizure of Savannah he led troops against the invasion of Prevost. In 1779 Moultrie won another notable victory at Beaufort, S.C. The following year, however, he was captured when Charleston fell to Clinton: the defenses of Fort Moultrie had been allowed to deteriorate and the British this time easily took control of the water approaches and surrounded the American army within the city. He was exchanged in 1782 and promoted to major general but took no further part in the war.

NORTH, Frederick, Lord
1732–1792

British official. As prime minister for George III during the entire American Revolution, North was at the center of British policy and decisionmaking. He was the son of a nobleman and educated at Eton and Oxford. Elected to Parliament at twenty-two, he first held office as a lord of the treasury in 1759 and progressed through a series of increasingly important government posts over the next decade. He became prime minister in March 1770. He and the king formed a close association, with North doing all he could to maintain the king's policies and majorities in Parliament. North also was directly responsible for much of the policy leading up to the war, including the continuation of the import tax on tea and the Boston Port Bill of 1774. While most of the day-to-day direction of the war fell on others, North's major role was to keep the king's party in power. He was convinced by the defeat of Cornwallis in October 1781 that the war was hopeless, but the king insisted that North remain in office and continue to press for renewed efforts. When his majorities dwindled, however, North resigned his office in March 1782. He continued to play a role in politics off and on during the following years, despite going blind in 1789.

PAINE, Thomas
1737–1809

Writer, soldier. Doubtless the greatest phrasemaker and popular writer of the Revolutionary period, Paine's seminal publications helped shape the course of the American cause. Born in England and trained as a corsetmaker,

Paine came to America in 1774 at the urging of Benjamin Franklin. During the winter of 1775–1776 when the issue of independence was still open, Paine wrote an anonymous pamphlet titled *Common Sense*, in which he urged Americans to separate from Great Britain. While his language was often eloquent it was also straightforward and free of the highflown phrases that so often marred the writing of other patriots. *Common Sense* could be read and understood by the common man. Within months the pamphlet sold tens of thousands. In 1776 Paine joined the army and served as an aide to Gen. Nathanael Greene. Following the American defeats in New York, Paine again took up his pen and produced a series of essays called *The Crisis*. The first appeared in December 1776 and began: "These are the times that try men's souls. The summer soldier and the sunshine patriot will, in this crisis, shrink from the service of their country: but he that stands it now, deserves the love and thanks of man and woman. Tyranny, like hell, is not easily conquered." He was appointed by Congress to a post as secretary of the committee dealing with foreign affairs but got entangled in the Silas Deane episode and was forced to resign. After the war, he received a confiscated Loyalist estate from the state of New York and a cash bonus. In 1787 he went to England and began to write *The Rights of Man*. He moved on to Paris four years later and was elected to the revolutionary French assembly but was thrown in prison in 1793 after a change in revolutionary regimes. While a prisoner he wrote *The Age of Reason*. After his release, he returned to the United States, where he lived until his death.

PREVOST, Augustine
1723–1786
British general. A Swiss by birth, Prevost directed the first stages of the British attempt to conquer the Southern states during the last years of the war. He joined the British army in 1756 and served under Wolfe during the Seven Years' War, suffering a serious wound at Quebec. He was in charge of British forces in East Florida with the rank of colonel when the War of the Revolution began. An able commander, seldom defeated by the Americans, he took part in the British capture of Savannah in late 1778 and then assumed command of all British forces in the South. He gained several more important victories, including the repulse of an American effort to retake Savannah, and solidified the British hold on Georgia by the end of 1779, when he returned to England.

PULASKI, Kasimir
1747–1779
Continental general. Like all too many of his fellow European soldiers of fortune, Pulaski was a thorn in the side of the Revolution and ineffective as a military leader. He was born to a noble family in Poland and fought with his father's troops against the Russians. At the First Partition of Poland he fled to Turkey, where he served in the Turkish army. He eventually made his way to Paris, and made friends with Franklin, who advised him to come to the United States and provided a recommendation to Congress. He arrived in 1777 and served as a volunteer aide to

Washington at the battle of Brandywine. At Washington's suggestion, Congress commissioned Pulaski commander of the newly authorized cavalry with the rank of brigadier general. Pulaski fought ineffectively at the Battle of Germantown and then retreated with the Continental Army to winter quarters in Valley Forge. Here he displayed the usual defects of foreign adventurers serving in the American cause: an overly high estimate of their own worth and an inability to get along with American colleagues. Pulaski quarreled with the American officers assigned as his subordinates (no mean trick considering that he spoke no English) and preferred charges against his second in command for having given some slight to the noble Pole. He resigned as commander of the cavalry in 1778 and won permission to raise his own "elite" corps, which he proceeded to recruit from among British deserters and prisoners. The Pulaski Legion proved to be more hazard to friends by its routinely destructive behavior than to the enemy. It enjoyed little success at any of its assigned tasks. Finally stationed in the South, Pulaski led his Legion in a foolish cavalry charge during the American attack on Savannah in late 1779. He was hit in the groin and died two days later aboard an American ship after unsuccessful surgery.

PUTNAM, Israel
1718–1790

Continental major general. One of the colonies' veteran soldiers when the war began, Putnam proved that personal courage and goodwill were no substitute for military competence. Despite his prewar reputation as a fighter and his elevation to major general early in the war, he failed consistently to perform adequately as a field commander. Born in Massachusetts, he lived most of his life in Connecticut as a farmer. He joined Roger's Rangers in 1755 during the Seven Years' War and eventually rose to the rank of lieutenant colonel of militia. His service experience was harrowing, to say the least. In 1758 he was captured by Indians, tied to a stake, and watched as a fire was prepared. Only the intervention of a French officer saved Putnam at the last minute from roasting alive. After he was exchanged, Putnam sailed with an ill-fated mission against Havana. The entire force was shipwrecked off Cuba, and Putnam was one of the few survivors. By the eve of the Revolution he was a relatively prosperous farmer and tavernkeeper with more than a local reputation for his previous exploits. He early joined the Sons of Liberty and supported the growing rebellion in New England. After Lexington and Concord, Putnam hastened to Boston and became colonel of a Connecticut regiment and brigadier of Connecticut militia. He was one of the two commanders at the Battle of Bunker Hill, where his personal courage showed to good advantage. Congress appointed him one of the original major generals of the Continental Army within days of the battle. When Washington moved the army to New York, Putnam was given command at Long Island. His careless disposition of troops, failure to reconnoiter the ground, and lack of tactical skill were largely responsible for the American debacle there. While still nominally a field commander throughout the New Jersey campaign, he was seldom again entrusted with anything vital. When given charge of American defenses in the Hudson Highlands, he promptly allowed Clinton to seize two vital forts. He was reduced to recruiting and a minor command in Connecticut when removed from active service by a paralytic stroke in 1779.

REVERE, Paul
1735–1818
Patriot, silversmith. One of the finest American craftsmen of the late eighteenth century, Revere was immortalized in poetry for his famous "midnight ride" of 1775, and few modern-day Americans can think of him other than spurring down the road to Lexington with a shout of "The British are coming!" on his lips. Revere was born in Boston and learned his trade of silversmithing from his father. He served as an officer in the Seven Years' War and then returned to Boston and set up in trade as a silversmith. He also taught himself copper engraving and soon was well-known locally for his skill in both crafts. He was an early and active patriot as anti-British protest grew in Boston. He was a leader in the Boston Sons of Liberty and played a major role in popularizing resistance to the Stamp Act and the Boston Massacre through his widely circulated engravings, his depiction of the latter event becoming one of his most famous. He helped plan and carry out the Boston Tea Party in 1773. He was a good rider, so he also served as a courier between rebel organizations. His most famous exploit came on 18–19 April 1775, when he set out on horseback from Boston to warn patriot leaders John Hancock and Sam Adams in Lexington that the British were marching to catch them and seize rebel arms. He delivered his warning to Lexington and proceeded toward Concord with fellow messenger William Dawes and Dr. Samuel Prescott. A British patrol stopped the trio, and Revere was captured. He was released without his horse and returned to Lexington on foot. During the war he did valuable service for the American cause as a manufacturer of gunpowder, a commodity in short supply in the states, and as an engraver for Congress and other official bodies. He also served briefly as a lieutenant colonel of militia and had to take responsibility for his role in the disastrous Massachusetts expedition to Maine in 1779. After the war he returned to silversmithing and his other businesses, including the manufacture of copper.

RIEDESEL, Baron Friedrich von
1738–1800
German mercenary officer. Riedesel was one of the more attractive "Hessian" generals employed in North America by the British to command German mercenary troops. He was, in fact, a native of Hesse but was serving the Duke of Brunswick when appointed to head the first contingent of Brunswickers sent to America. A veteran of the Seven Years' War, Riedesel was an experienced European soldier holding the rank of colonel. He arrived in Quebec with nearly 2,300 men in the summer of 1776. His charming and intelligent wife, Frederica, the daughter of one of the duke's generals, joined him in Canada. In 1777, Riedesel was assigned as part of Burgoyne's command and led the German contingent. Burgoyne would have benefited from closer attention to Rie-

desel's advice during the march across the wilderness. The German counseled, for example, against sending Baum on the expedition toward Bennington. During the two battles at Saratoga, Riedesel distinguished himself both by vigor on the field and by his skillful direction of his troops. He was held by the Americans after Burgoyne's surrender until 1780, when he was exchanged. Riedesel then held command at Long Island. In 1781 he returned to Canada as an adviser. He and his family returned to Europe in 1783. His wife's memoirs of the experience in America provide charming insight into Riedesel's character and activities.

ROCHAMBEAU, Jean Baptiste Donatien de Vimeur, comte de
1725–1807
French general. Rochambeau was an experienced, skillful, and, most important, a diplomatic soldier sent to command French troops in America in 1780. He worked closely and well with Washington, forming a team that succeeded in dealing the British the final defeat at Yorktown. As required of all officers of the French army, Rochambeau was of aristocratic birth. He joined the army during the War of the Austrian Succession, and by 1747 he was a colonel and aide-de-camp to the Duke of Orleans. He performed with great distinction during the Seven Years' War and was promoted to brigadier after recovering from wounds suffered in 1760. During the decade before the American Revolution, Rochambeau was inspector of cavalry. In 1780, when the French government finally resolved to send troops to fight in America, Rochambeau was promoted to lieutenant general and made commander of the

expeditionary force. He arrived with about 6,000 troops in Newport in July (several thousand more soldiers were left behind for lack of transport). He and his retinue were greeted with near-empty streets, and he had to roust out local officials and identify himself. This was, unfortunately, something of a portent for the first year of the French presence in America. Washington's Continental Army was so depleted by previous campaigns, expired enlistments, and lack of funds that the American commander-in-chief could not organize a new campaign that might use the French. Rochambeau was the soul of patience and diplomacy, however, and not only placed himself at Washington's command, but also worked effectively at Washington's side during the remainder of the war. Finally, in 1781, Rochambeau and Washington devised a plan to attack British bases in upper Manhattan, hoping to draw Sir Henry Clinton out of New York City. Before the plan was launched, however, news came of the French fleet sailing to the Chesapeake. Washington and Rochambeau set their men on the march south to Yorktown. Rochambeau and his army formed the bulk of the trained troops who laid siege to Cornwallis. Following the British surrender, Rochambeau remained in Virginia. He returned to France early in 1783. He subsequently took command of armies in France but was arrested during the Reign of Terror and narrowly escaped execution.

SCHUYLER, Philip
1733–1804
Continental major general. A complex figure with many attributes as well as some disabling traits, Schuyler

was a member of the powerful New York Dutch Schuyler–Van Renssalaer–Van Cortland clans. He was born to great wealth and reared as a gentleman, but he had a consuming interest in military affairs. He served in the Seven Years' War as a captain, showing most promise as an organizer of supplies and as an administrator. He resigned his commission in 1757 but continued to supply the British army as a private commissary. He rejoined as a major the following year and fought in several engagements, retaining his role as a supplier. Schuyler went to England in 1761 to settle claims with the government. At the end of the Seven Years' War he inherited huge tracts of land in northern New York state and settled in to life there as a lord of the manor. While a patriot from the beginning of the agitation against Great Britain, he disliked the more radical elements among the Sons of Liberty. Schuyler served as a commissioner in the disputes over Vermont, and he alienated many New Englanders with his decisions in favor of New York and what they considered to be his high-handed manner. For political reasons, Schuyler was one of the first major generals appointed by Congress in 1775, representing New York state. He was put in charge of the invasion of Canada, but the combination of his slow preparations and irritation of the New England troops caused major problems. He was hit with an attack of chronic gout before the expedition set off, and Richard Montgomery marched north in his place. Schuyler then found himself embroiled in a dispute with Congress that further diminished his standing. He commanded the Northern Department in the face of Bur-

goyne's invasion, but when the British easily took Fort Ticonderoga, Congress replaced Schuyler with Gates. He resigned his generalship in 1779 but continued to work with Washington as an adviser and administrator. He was also a delegate to Congress, involving himself in financial affairs. In later life he was U.S. senator from New York.

SHERMAN, Roger
1721–1793
Statesman. Sherman was the only man to sign all four great documents of the Revolution: the Articles of Association, the Declaration of Independence, The Articles of Confederation, and the Constitution. A self-made man, Sherman was born on a farm in Massachusetts and moved to New Milford, Ct., where he amassed large land holdings and a considerable fortune. When elected to the Continental Congress in 1774, he was an experienced, hard-working, and widely respected veteran of public affairs. He served in Congress from 1774 until 1781 and again in 1783–1784. Sherman's most prominent task in the early days was on the committee that drafted the Declaration of Independence, but he also served on the committee of ways and means, the board of war and ordnance, the treasury board, and the committee on Indian affairs as well as the committee that drafted the Articles of Confederation. In the estimation of several of his colleagues, he was the most influential member of the Congress by the end of his service. In 1784 he returned to Connecticut as judge of the superior court and mayor of New Haven. Called back to national service with the Constitutional Convention

in 1787, one of his greatest achievements was to introduce the idea of dual representation in the new federal government (the Connecticut Compromise). He was subsequently elected to the House of Representatives and helped draft the Judiciary Act of 1789, which established the federal court system. He was later appointed senator from Connecticut, the office he held at his death.

STARK, John
1728–1822

Continental and militia general. Stark was almost as much trouble to his commanding officers as he was to the British, but his battlefield skill and valor redeemed his prickly independence. He was born in New Hampshire and grew up in the frontier region of that colony. As a child, he was kidnapped by Indians and ransomed back to his parents. During the Seven Years' War he served as a captain in Roger's Rangers. When the conflict began with the British, Stark immediately recruited a regiment and marched to join the gathering militia army around Boston. He and his men were stationed at the far left of the American battle line at Bunker Hill, crouched behind a flimsy, grass-stuffed fence. Under his leadership, his men poured a deadly fire into the first assaults by the British regulars and did much to establish the legend of the battle. In 1776 Stark received a commission as colonel in the Continental Army, and he served nobly at Trenton and Princeton. He was not, however, rewarded with elevation to general's rank after the New Jersey campaign, so he resigned in pique and returned to New Hampshire. He assumed command of the state militia,

with the condition he not be responsible to the orders of Congress or Continental Army officers. When Burgoyne marched down from Canada in 1777, Stark was ordered by Benjamin Lincoln to join the American army across the Hudson but flatly refused. He had his own ideas of how and where to fight. When Burgoyne detached Baum and his Germans to foray toward Bennington, Stark saw his opportunity. The subsequent battle was a debacle for the Germans. Stark skillfully enveloped the mercenaries and nearly annihilated them. Only the indiscipline of his militia prevented Stark from achieving an even greater victory. Congress did reward him this time, and he received a brigadier's commission after Burgoyne's surrender. He retired at war's end and took no further part in public life.

STEUBEN, Baron Friedrich Wilhelm von
1730–1794

General. Arriving at a crucial moment, von Steuben organized and trained the Continental Army during the winter of Valley Forge. In his earlier days von Steuben had been a genuine Prussian staff officer in the service of Frederick the Great, but by the time of the Revolution he was a down-at-the-heels, half-pay captain, not the lieutenant general his dossier claimed. Moreover, he spoke no English and scarcely any French. Nonetheless, Congress accepted his volunteer services, and Washington appointed him acting inspector general of the Continental Army. Communicating through several French-speaking aides, he began to organize and train the army. During the winter, he not only wrote the first American army manual of drill and regulations, but he also put on a diverting show for the cold, half-starved troops, parading up and down in his full Prussian gear and swearing at their ineptness in an incomprehensible mixture of languages. Von Steuben continued as a one-man general staff for Washington during the following months, devising a system to curb waste, acting as liaison with Congress, and helping to reorganize the structure of the army. In the fall of 1780 he moved south to take command of American forces in Virginia under Lafayette but played only a relatively small part in the final campaign of the war. Discharged from the army in 1784, he became an American citizen and retired to New York.

SULLIVAN, John
1740–1795
Continental major general. More a politician than a military man, Sullivan nevertheless was involved in most of the war in the North from 1775 until 1779. A native of New Hampshire, he figured prominently in the state's politics. A practicing lawyer, Sullivan was an early and avid patriot and even helped lead a raid to capture gunpowder before Lexington and Concord. He served in the First Continental Congress in 1774 and received a commission as a brigadier general at the formation of the army in 1775. Sullivan led an ineffective relief column toward Canada in 1776. He returned to take temporary command of the army at Long Island under Washington, assuming the rank of major general. He was captured during the British victory but exchanged within a few weeks. He again joined

Washington's command and served well at Trenton and throughout the New Jersey campaign and at the battles of Brandywine and Germantown. He embroiled himself in conflict with Congress, however, and was usually on the political defensive thereafter. He may have been involved in the Conway affair, although evidence is not clear. Sullivan remained high in Washington's opinion nevertheless. One of his worst showings was as American commander of the disastrous joint assault with the French on Newport, R.I., in 1778 when he lost most of his command. A similar aborted attack on Staten Island earned an inquiry from Congress, which may have been inspired mostly by politics. In 1779, he was dispatched with a large force to ravage the Iroquois nation, a task he accomplished during the late summer by destroying most of the Indian villages in upper New York. He resigned his commission after returning from this final campaign. Sullivan returned to Congress in 1780 and thereafter held a procession of offices in New Hampshire. In 1789, Washington appointed him judge of the U.S. district of New Hampshire.

TARLETON, Banastre
1754–1833
British officer. As the most dashing, successful, and ruthless British commander during the Southern campaigns, Tarleton's name usually struck fear into patriots. He was the son of a rich and prominent Liverpool merchant and a graduate of Oxford when he joined the army as a coronet in 1775. He was posted to America and served with the unsuccessful 1776 expedition against Charleston.

His subsequent activities in New York brought him little distinction except advancement in rank. By 1778 he was named lieutenant colonel and formed the British Legion—a composite force of green-clad dragoons and light infantry, mostly made up of Loyalists. Tarleton and his Legion were dispatched as part of Sir Henry Clinton's expedition to South Carolina in late 1779. All of Tarleton's horses expired during the difficult voyage south, but he soon set about finding new mounts by defeating American cavalry and taking their horses. He made his first mark by smashing victories at Monck's Corner and Lenud's Ferry. His reputation for ruthlessness came mostly from the aftermath of his triumph at Waxhaws on 29 May 1789. Not only did his men devastate the last remaining American force outside Charleston, they also massacred many prisoners after surrender, meting out what soon came to be known ironically as "Tarleton's Quarter." None of the American forces left in the Carolinas could match Tarleton's speed of movement or efficiency in battle during the ensuing months, and he won engagement after engagement, becoming Cornwallis' main mobile striking force. At the Battle of Cowpens, however, Tarleton met his match in Daniel Morgan and suffered a nearly total defeat, barely escaping with his life. His reputation tarnished, especially among his fellow British officers (who regarded him as too cocky), Tarleton regrouped his command and was again successful in battles against Greene's army and in raiding in Virginia. At Yorktown he commanded the troops holding the landings at Gloucester. After the surrender he

was paroled and returned to England. He entered Parliament in 1790, the same year he returned to active duty in the army. He was promoted to major general in 1794 and served in several posts until 1812, when he became a full general. He was created a baronet in 1815 and knighted in 1820.

WARD, Artemus
1727–1800

Continental major general. Ward was the highest-ranking colonial officer during the first weeks of the Revolutionary War, but was quickly eclipsed by George Washington. Ward was born in Shrewsbury, Mass., and graduated from Harvard. He was active in politics and government, serving the colonial legislature. He was a lieutenant colonel of state militia during the Seven Years' War. When the storm-clouds of war began to gather in Massachusetts in 1774, Ward was appointed brigadier and commander-in-chief of the Massachusetts militia. He was sick in bed during the outbreak of hostilities at Lexington and Concord, but he hastened to Boston and assumed command of the state militia that gathered there to form a spontaneous army laying siege to the British in the city. He contributed little, however, remaining at his headquarters during the battle of Bunker Hill, for example. When Congress adopted the army and named Washington as commander-in-chief, Ward resented being passed over, even though he was granted major general's rank and appointed second in command to Washington. With the British evacuation of Boston in 1776, Ward resigned his commission. He served as president of the Massachusetts executive council from 1777 to 1779 and was a delegate to Congress from 1780 until 1782. He later was elected to the U.S. House of Representatives as a Federalist.

WASHINGTON, George
1732–1799
Commander-in-chief, first president. His persona is so encrusted with myth, legend, and hagiographic biography that it is hard now to remember that beneath it all was a very great man whose special qualities were exactly those needed during and after the Revolution. While no plaster saint, Washington truly deserves the title "Father of His Country." He was born the second son of a prosperous Virginia planter and grew up with education in little beyond the duties and pleasures of the Southern squirearchy. Washington's father died when the boy was eleven, and for most of his early years the future leader lived in the shadow of his elder brother, Lawrence, who had inherited Mount Vernon and most of the family's wealth. Washington lived most of the time at another estate near Fredericksburg, Va. At sixteen he became a surveyor. When Lawrence died in 1752 Washington was the next in line and eventually inherited a fortune in land and slaves. He was closely involved in local military affairs, and in 1753 was dispatched by the royal governor of Virginia on a mission to the French in the Ohio Valley. He was appointed lieutenant colonel of militia the following year and took an expedition back to the northwest, fighting in the opening skirmishes of the Seven Years' War and losing at Fort Necessity. In 1755 he became Braddock's aide-de-camp and then commander of the Virginia militia. He was successful in several subsequent campaigns.

He resigned his commission in 1759 and married a rich widow, Martha Custis, making him one of the wealthiest men in the colonies. The couple moved to Mount Vernon and Washington settled into the life of an influential planter. He was a member of the Burgesses and supported the rights of the colonies against the crown from very early in the revolutionary struggle. He was selected to represent Virginia in the first Continental Congress and returned on adjournment to urge military preparations in his home state. He served again in the second Congress, and in June 1775 was voted to the post of commander-in-chief of the new Continental Army. A man of immense dignity and impressive bearing (remarked on by all his contemporaries), Washington proved a tenacious commander, agile politician, and able administrator. He combined a streak of daring with a long-term doggedness that would not admit defeat. Washington was, however, no military genius, and he seldom won a clear-cut victory on the battlefield. He lost disastrously to the British during the campaign in New York, and his army was saved only by his ability to get it to move rapidly under difficult circumstances. His greatest triumph was his surprise raid on the Germans at Trenton in 1776—a crucial victory after a string of defeats. He subsequently was unable truly to beat the British, but at Monmouth he came close. His most important service, perhaps, was to keep a small, ragged, and ill-supported army in being as the civil government first nearly squabbled itself to death and then went flat broke. At the crucial moment in 1781 he gambled that the French fleet would arrive in time to cut off Cornwallis, and Washington launched his army (along with Rochambeau's larger French force) south to grab the final victory. During the long two years of anticlimax after the surrender of the British at Yorktown, Washington performed magnificently in managing the disgruntled and unpaid army until the final British troops departed. He then resigned his commission and returned to Virginia. His repose was short-lived, however, and he returned to the political service of his country in 1787 as presiding officer of the convention to revise the Articles of Confederation, where he threw his immense prestige onto the side of a strong new central government. When the new nation was established by the Constitution, he was the unanimous choice as the first president of the United States, and he was re-elected for a second term in 1792. He declined a third term (setting a precedent for future presidents), and after a farewell address in September 1796 he retired again to Mount Vernon.

WAYNE, Anthony
1745–1796
Continental general. One of the most successful American generals of the Revolutionary War, "Mad" Anthony Wayne combined the ability to plan well with a ferocious impetuosity on the battlefield. He was born in Pennsylvania and worked as a tanner before the war. He served in the Pennsylva-

nia legislature during 1774–1775 and was appointed colonel of the 4th Pennsylvania Battalion in January 1776. He led his troops northward to fight at Trois Rivières. He then had command at Ticonderoga. Wayne was promoted to brigadier in February 1777, and he had field commands during the battles of Brandywine and Germantown. He was taken by surprise by the British at Paoli, however, and many of his men were killed. One of Wayne's great triumphs was the carefully planned and executed night attack that retook Stony Point, N.Y., on 16 July 1779. He continued to serve in New York throughout 1779 and 1780. In January 1781 he helped settle the mutiny of the Pennsylvania Line and subsequently moved his troops south to join Lafayette in Virginia. At the Battle of Green Spring on 6 July 1781, Wayne's small force was isolated on the battlefield and faced Cornwallis' entire army head-on. Wayne ordered a startling charge, which allowed most of his troops to escape. At the end of the war he was breveted major general. Following several years as an unprosperous farmer, he was elected to Congress in 1791 but denied his seat. The following year Wayne was named a major general and commander of an army assigned to fight the Indians in the Old Northwest. His skillful campaign resulted in the decisive victory at the Battle of Fallen Timbers in August 1794.

★ INDEX ★

Washington, George (*cont.*)
187, 188, 204, 215, 226, 232, 261, 262,
273, 292, 315; assassination plot, 88; at
Boston siege, 52, 55, 57–58, 59, 63, 68,
72, 76, 79; at Brandywine, 138–39; at
Monmouth Court House, 177–79; at
Morristown, 195, 226–27, 230–31, 232,
242–43; at Newburgh, 298, 299; at
Valley Forge, 154, 155, 157, 159, 162,
165–66, 168, 169, 176; at White Plains,
183; Conway Cabal response, 149, 158,
161, 162–63; dictatorial powers, 109–
10, 114; farewells, 305–306, 307; final
orders, 304–305; in Connecticut, 276,
277; in New Jersey, 108, 109, 112–14,
117, 118–20, 131, 191; in New York,
50–51, 67, 80, 92, 95–98, 100–101,
103, 107, 211, 270, 278, 279, 280, 281,
296; in Pennsylvania, 118, 133, 135,
137, 140–42, 143; Life Guard, 87, 227;
praises Paine, 73; problems with
troops, 122, 181, 261, 262, 263, 267;
relations with Congress, 197, 198–99,
232, 233, 255; response to Newburgh
Addresses, 304; treason of Arnold, 250
–51, 255; Yorktown siege, 282, 283–
84, 286–91
Washington, Martha, 93, 168, 198
Washington, William, 113–14, 234, 237,
238, 258, 259, 275; at Cowpens, 265; at
Eutaw Springs, 284–85; at Guilford
Courthouse, 271–72
Wasp, 74, 226
Watt, 241
Wayne, Anthony, 85, 86, 187; at
Brandywine, 138; in New Jersey, 127,
164, 177; in Pennsylvania, 140, 143,
145; negotiates with mutineers, 262,
263; Stony Point battle, 195, 211, 212–
14; Virginia campaign, 276, 277–78,
279, 280–81; Yorktown siege, 283, 286
Webster, James, 246

Wedderburn, Alexander, 23
Wemyss, James, 256
Wentworth family, 2
Wentworth, Paul, 155
Wereat, John, 184
West Indies, 107, 157, 165, 191–92, 210,
222, 249, 261, 298, 301; naval
engagements, 186, 210, 237, 241, 268,
275, 278; trade, 7, 33, 189
West Point, N.Y., 207, 230, 248
White, John, 190
White Plains, N.Y., 181, 183; Battle of,
67, 105, 112
Wickes, Lambert, 109, 127–28, 140, 144,
223
Wilkinson, James, 148–49, 162
Willett, Marinus, 45, 123, 134
Williamson, Andrew, 63, 93, 202
Williams, Otho, 246, 247, 257, 269,
270–71
Wilmington, Del., 82
Wilson, James, 43, 72, 73
Winn, Richard, 121
Wirt, William, 35
Witherspoon, John, 88, 89, 201
Wolfe, James, 63
Woodford, William, 60, 62, 64, 177, 227
Woolsey, Melancton, 254
Wooster, David, 41, 60; commands in
Canada, 68, 72, 79, 80–81; in
Connecticut, 124; in New York, 120
Wright, James, 76
Wyoming Valley (Pa.) Massacre, 179, 186,
190

Yankee Hero, 85
Yarmouth, 163
York, Pa., 117, 118
Yorktown, Va., 25, 281; siege, 77, 249,
261, 283–84, 286–91, 308, 315
Young, Joseph, 233